The Unknown City

The MIT Press | Cambridge, Massachusetts | London, England

The Unknown City

Contesting Architecture and Social Space

edited by

Iain Borden, Joe Kerr, Jane Rendell, with Alicia Pivaro

a Strangely Familiar project

This book was set in Garamond and Geometric by Graphic Composition, Inc. and was printed and bound in the United States of America.

Library of Congress Cataloging-in-Publication Data

The unknown city : contesting architecture and social space : a Strangely Familiar project / edited by Iain Borden . . . [et al.].

    p. cm.

  Includes bibliographical references and index.

  ISBN 0-262-02471-3 (hc. : alk. paper)

    1. Architecture and society. 2. Architecture—Human factors. I. Borden, Iain.

NA2543.S6 U55 2000

720´.1´03—dc21

                      00-020375

to London

Here, in the new town,
boredom is pregnant with desires,
frustrated frenzies, unrealized possibilities.
A magnificent life is waiting
just around the corner, and far, far away.

Henri Lefebvre

Contents

Preface

The "Strangely Familiar" program began in 1994, springing from an invitation from the Royal Institute of British Architects (RIBA) Architecture Centre in London to mount an exhibition around the general subject of architectural history. The group that founded the program—the four editors of this book—were a loose affiliation, brought together by the desire to promote communication among different disciplines and a pressing need to interest the public in debates about architecture and the city.

The first Strangely Familiar manifestations—an exhibition and publication—consisted of a collection of narratives and stories produced by an invited group of teachers, writers, and thinkers from a number of disciplines, including architectural history, art history, urban history and planning, feminist theory, geography, sociology, and cultural theory. The loose groupings of the stories into three themes—experience and identity, memory and remembering, resistance and appropriation—offered one strategy of navigating through the collection; but this was by no means the only one, as the contributions overlapped considerably in both content and resonance.

Strangely Familiar: Narratives of Architecture and the City (Routledge, 1996) resulted from a collaboration between the editors and graphic designers Studio Myerscough, in which text and visual identity were integrated on the basis of parity. The aim of this synthetic process was to produce a document both visually stimulating and accessible, particularly in comparison with more conventional academic publications.

0.1 | Strangely Familiar exhibition, RIBA Architecture Centre, London, December 1995–March 1996.

0.2 | Strangely Familiar exhibition, RIBA Architecture Centre, London, December 1995–March 1996.

The design of the exhibition was a collaboration between the group, architects Allford Hall Monaghan Morris, and Studio Myerscough; it was made possible by a grant from the Architecture Unit at the Arts Council of England. Unlike most architectural exhibitions, which tend to be predominantly image-led through drawings and models, the Strangely Familiar exhibition took on the challenge of communicating text, images, and ideas together. A conscious desire to get away from the "boards on walls" approach meant creating an installed environment to which the visitor could relate both physically and intellectually. Each story had its own plinth, color-coded to place it in relation to other stories that investigated the same theme. The plinth held the complete text, a larger phrase or sentence, and an object cased in a Perspex vitrine. These assemblages, of different size, color, and shape, made a cityscape around and through which the viewer navigated, at each turn encountering a myriad of intriguing and unexpected views, words, and ideas—and so partially replicating the syncopated movement and focus of the city dweller. Video, sound, and multimedia elements provided further layers to the installation.

From the RIBA in London, the exhibition toured onward to the Cornerhouse, Manchester; the Angle Gallery, Birmingham; and the Matthew Gallery, Edinburgh. In each space and location the exhibition was arranged in a slightly different format, offering a new configuration of overlaid views, ideas, and objects.

0.3 | Strangely Familiar exhibition, Cornerhouse, Manchester, 1996.

0.4 | Strangely Familiar exhibition. CD-ROM element, produced by Artec.

The symposium, for its part, took the typical format for academic debate. Despite some rather frenzied and pressured attempts to fit seventeen speakers into one day, we learned much. In particular, the symposium highlighted certain key areas that had not been addressed, and that we have consequently specifically tried to include in *The Unknown City*. One response to issues raised at this symposium has been the inclusion here of a number of practitioners in different, urban-related cultural fields.

0.5

As well as these exhibition venues and the symposium, the program stimulated new connections with a number of diverse organizations—including the Institute of Contemporary Arts (ICA), the Photographers' Gallery, and the Urban Research Group—and a number of individuals who have each in different ways contributed to the ongoing life of the program. Through such reexaminations, whatever is thought to be understood, whatever is taken for granted, comes under scrutiny and must, by such intense attention, be rethought once again.

Strangely Familiar is still a loose affiliation. It was generated through interests that still remain intense and still make the group cohere, while the individual relationships have changed significantly. This is the flux, the rubbing against the grain, that moves things forward. Whether it provokes an intellectual tussle or merely a new alliance, the success or impact of such a project is almost impossible to state or quantify: sometimes it seems as if it has taken on a life of its own. The only thing to do is to hold on and to make the most of this unfolding scenario.

The Unknown City is, then, the next manifestation of the program that began in 1994. We always intended to continue the first Strangely Familiar project by publishing a book—but it was initially conceived as a summation. Instead, *The Unknown City* has become more of a transition, presented with the understanding that our grasp of the city can never be complete and knowing. With this book, Strangely Familiar has become an un-knowing of the city. This does not mean that we know nothing, but that there are more things to consider, more complexities to encounter. Furthermore, being addicted to the uncertainty of cultural engagement means keeping on doing something, whatever that something might be. Central to that engagement remains the desire not only to place architecture in a wide cultural context but also, in so doing, to rethink and reenact its very substance and being.

Strangely Familiar
London
March 1999

Acknowledgments

The Unknown City is part of an ongoing program of activities organized under the rubric of the "Strangely Familiar" group. We are indebted to a large number of people who generously offered up not only their ideas and criticisms but also much time and effort. For the exhibition and symposium program that formed the catalyst for Strangely Familiar, we wish to thank the Royal Institute of British Architects (RIBA) Architecture Centre in London. For the other venues around the United Kingdom, we also wish to thank the Cornerhouse in Manchester, the Angle Gallery in Birmingham, and the Matthew Gallery in Edinburgh for their kind invitations and enthusiasm for the project.

For the design and creation of the exhibition, and for the accompanying *Strangely Familiar* publication (Routledge, 1996), we are deeply indebted to Ceri Davies and Paul Monaghan of Allford Hall Monaghan Morris Architects; Kate Last, Vladimir Mandic, Pom Martin, Ralph Sagar, and Jane Placca of ARTEC; Gary Monaghan; and Elizabeth Ismail and Jesse Swash of St. Martin's School of Art. Naomi House provided invaluable help with the database. Above all, Belinda Moore and Morag Myerscough of Studio Myerscough did more than could ever possibly be expected of anyone.

Funding and support for the exhibition and symposium was generously provided by the Arts Council of England, the British Academy, the Institute of Contemporary Arts, Marlin Lighting, RIBA Architecture Centre, University College London Graduate School, and the School of Architecture, and Interior Design at the University of North London.

The Arts Council of England additionally provided financial support for the production of the current volume. And we also are grateful to The MIT Press, Roger Conover, and anonymous reviewers for their suggestions and encouragement.

A large number of other people and groups have helped along the way. We wish to record our gratitude here to Clive Alberts, John Allan, Anderson Fraser, the *Architects' Journal*, Enrico Ariis, Christopher Ash, Ceri Barnes, Roz Barr, Larry Barth, Inge de Beer, Rafe Bertram, Chris Bird, *Blueprint*, Anthony Borden, *Building Design*, Bob Colmac, Colourpath, Steven Connor, Peter Cook, Nicole Crockett, Peter Culley, Nick Delo, James Donald, Tom Duncan, Marion Duursema, Tom Dyckhoff, Miles English, Sue Evans, Hamish Fallside, Daniel Faust, Paul Finch, Mike Fordham, Adrian Forty, Nick Franchini, Fraser, Anna Frisch, Kate Gaylor, Amelia Gibson, Paul Goodwin, Jennifer Graham, Phil Grey, Peter Hall, Lee Harris, Elizabeth Hess, Ian Hill, Holdens Computer Services, Julian Holder, Andy Horsley, Richard Ings, Steve Johnson, Ruben Kenig, Lily Kerr Scott, Nicola Kirkham, Nelson Kon, Richard Learoyd, Katharina von Ledersteger, Alec Leggart, *Living Marxism*, Mark Logue, Sasha Lubetkin, Eleanna Makridou,

Acknowledgments

Lee Mallett, Helen Mallinson, Marx Memorial Library, Jack Massey, Nancy Massey, Demetrios Matheou, Maurice, Clare Melhuish, Jeremy Millar, Sam Montague, Jonathan Morrish, Nadine Nackasha, Lynda Nead, Natasha Nicholson, Nick and Co-ordination, Gerard Nolan and Lloyds Bank, Graham O'Brien, Yael Padan, Paschalinea Panou, Barbara Penner, *Perspectives on Architecture*, the Photographer's Gallery (London), Mark Pivaro, Ellen Praag, Lisa Raynes, Alan Read, Beth Rendell, Vicky Richardson, Routledge, Katerina Rüedi, Barbara Russell, Javier Sánchez Merina, Chris Saunders, *Scan*, Louise Scriven, Richard Sennett, *Sidewalk Surfer*, Gordon Smith, James Soane, Stephen Spier, Bradley Starkey, Yen Yen Teh, *Third Text*, Helen Thomas, Victoria Thornton, Julia Thrift, Jeremy Till, Kate Trant, Helen Tsoi, Marjorie Turton, Audio-Visual at University College London, Media Services at University of North London, Video-Log, Sarah Wigglesworth, Raymond Winkler, and World Backgrounds. We would also like to acknowledge the substantive contribution of Tristan Palmer, who has unfailingly supported the project throughout. And, of course, our deepest thanks to all at The MIT Press for their encouragement and professional expertise in the preparation of this volume.

For us as editors, the central intellectual formations for this book first arose and have been continually developed through discussions held over the past decade at The Bartlett, University College London. We are grateful to faculty and students at the various institutions where we have been tutors, particularly The Bartlett, University of North London, Middlesex University, University of Nottingham, Royal College of Art, Winchester School of Art, and Chelsea College of Art and Design.

Most important, we wish to express our gratitude to all of the contributors—both to this book and to previous Strangely Familiar manifestations. Their patience, efforts, and engagement lie at the core of the project.

Contributors

Iain Borden

Iain Borden is Director of Architectural History and Theory at The Bartlett, University College London where he is Reader in Architecture and Urban Culture. A founding member of Strangely Familiar, he is co-editor of a number of books, including *Architecture and the Sites of History: Interpretations of Buildings and Cities* (1995), *Strangely Familiar: Narratives of Architecture in the City* (1996), *Gender Space Architecture: An Interdisciplinary Introduction* (2000), *The City Cultures Reader* (2000), and *InterSections: Architectural Histories and Critical Theories* (2000). He is currently writing a theorized history of skateboarding as a critical urban practice.

M. Christine Boyer

M. Christine Boyer is a native of Manhattan, and now resides in the West Village. She is Professor of Urbanism at the School of Architecture, Princeton University, and has also taught at Harvard Graduate School, Columbia University, Cooper Union Chanin School, and the Pratt Institute. She is the author of *Cybercities: Visual Perception in the Age of Electronic Communication* (1996), *The City of Collective Memory* (1994), *Dreaming the Rational City* (1983), and *Manhattan Manners: Architecture and Style, 1850–1890* (1985). Her forthcoming book is *The City Plans of Modernism*.

Iain Chambers

Iain Chambers teaches at the Istituto Universitario Orientale, Naples, and has worked on metropolitan cultures, in particular on urban cultural practices and the centrality of popular music as a palimpsest of memories and identities. His studies draw on interdisciplinary critical approaches, and his recent work has been pursued within the context of the increasing globalization of economic and cultural relations and emerging cultures of hybridity. He is author of *Migrancy, Culture, Identity* (1994), *Border Dialogues: Journeys in Postmodernity* (1990), and *Popular Culture. The Metropolitan Experience* (1986), and is co-editor, with Lidia Curti, of *The Post-Colonial Question: Commons Skies, Divided Horizons* (1996).

Jonathan Charley

Jonathan Charley lives in Glasgow, teaches architecture at the University of Strathclyde, and writes.

Nigel Coates

Nigel Coates formed Branson Coates Architecture with Doug Branson in 1985; their projects include the National Centre for Popular Music, Sheffield; the Geffrye Museum, London; the British exhibition for the Lisbon 1998; and Hanover 2000 World Expositions; and the Oyster House at the Ideal Home Exhibition, 1998. Having taught at the Architectural Association, he is currently Professor of Architectural Design at the Royal College of Art. A monograph of his work by Rick Poynor was published in 1989.

Cornford & Cross

Matthew Cornford and David Cross are London-based artists who began collaborating in 1987 while studying at St. Martin's School of Art and afterward at the Royal College of Art. Their practice since then has led to a number of solo and group exhibitions, including *East International* at the Sainsbury Centre for Visual Arts, University of East Anglia; *Power to the People* at the Bluecoat Gallery, Liverpool; *Backpacker* in Chiang Mai, Thailand; *Digital Dreams 4* in Newcastle-upon-Tyne; *City Limits* in Stoke-on-Trent; *Bitter Twist* at UKS, Oslo; and *Something Else* at the Camden Arts Centre, London.

Barry Curtis

Barry Curtis is Director of Research and Postgraduate Studies in the School of Art, Design, and Performing Arts at Middlesex University. He is an editor of *Block* and of *Parallax*. Recent publications include essays on the 1960s and Archigram.

Fashion Architecture Taste (Fat)

Fat is a collaborative, creative, and cross-disciplinary practice that straddles architecture, interior design, fine art, and urban art events. The practice includes architects, artists, graphic designers, and musicians (among others), and is involved in curating large-scale urban art events, designing and constructing architectural projects, research into art and architecture, the making of art, and designing and organizing exhibitions and events. Its work operates at the boundaries between architecture and fine art practice.

Adrian Forty

Adrian Forty is Professor of Architectural History at The Bartlett, University College London, where, with Iain Borden, he runs the master's course in architectural history. His book *Objects of Desire: Design and Society Since 1750* was published in 1986; and a new book, on the history of the critical vocabulary used in architecture, is to be published shortly.

Tom Gretton

Tom Gretton teaches in the History of Art Department of University College London. Among colleagues who work to explain and reinvent the value of expensive pictures, he works primarily on cheap ones. He is completing a book on Posada's place in Mexican "popular" culture, and has contributed to an exhibition on printed representations of the 1848 Revolution, which opened in Paris in February 1998.

Dolores Hayden

Dolores Hayden is Professor of Architecture, Urbanism, and American Studies at Yale University, and the author of several books on the politics of design, including *The Grand Domestic Revolution: A History of Feminist Designs for American Homes, Neighborhoods, and Cities* (1981) and *The Power of Place: Urban Landscapes as Public History* (1995).

bell hooks

bell hooks is Distinguished Professor of English at City College, New York, writer, cultural critic, feminist theorist, and author of fifteen books, among the most recent being two memoirs, *Bone Black: Memories of Girlhood* (1996) and *Wounds of Passion: A Writing Life* (1997) and a collection of essays, *Reel to Real: Race, Sex, and Class at the Movies* (1996).

Patrick Keiller

Patrick Keiller became an architect and practiced in the 1970s. His first audiovisual installations were exhibited at the Tate Gallery, London, in 1982. During the 1980s he made several short films and taught in art and architecture schools. *London* was released in 1994 and *Robinson in Space* in 1997.

Contributors

Joe Kerr

Joe Kerr is Senior Tutor in Humanities at the Royal College of Art, London. A native of London, his love of that city is not diminished by an enthusiasm for the ambitions and artifacts of modernism. A founding member of Strangely Familiar, he is co-editor of *Strangely Familiar: Narratives of Architecture in the City* (1996). He is currently writing, with Murray Fraser, a book titled *The Special Relationship: The Influence of America on British Architecture since 1945*.

Sandy McCreery

Sandy McCreery lectures in the history and theory of architecture at the University of East London and Middlesex University. His current doctoral research is concerned with the relationships between the experience of speed, culture, and architecture. He lives in Hackney, London.

Doreen Massey

Doreen Massey is Professor of Geography at the Open University. She is the author of *Space, Place, and Gender* (1994), *Spatial Divisions of Labour* (2d ed. 1995), and of many articles on spatiality, globalization, and identity. She has co-authored and co-edited a range of other books, including *High-Tech Fantasies* (1992), *A Place in the World?* (1995), *Geographical Worlds* (1995) and *Re-Thinking the Region* (1997). She is also co-founder and co-editor of *Soundings: A Journal of Politics and Culture*.

William Menking

William Menking is Professor of Architecture and City Planning at Pratt Institute in New York City. He has worked as a community organizer for Cesar Chavez, owned a tour business in New York, and been an art director for *Miami Vice*. His critical writings have appeared in various journals, magazines, and newspapers in the United States, Britain, and Europe. He is currently a member of REPOHistory (a working collaborative of artists, writers and performers) and is also curating architecture exhibitions at various venues in the United States. He is on the Board of Directors of the Storefront for Art and Architecture.

Sally Munt

Sally Munt is Reader in Media and Communication Studies at the University of Brighton. She is the author of *Heroic Desire: Lesbian Identity and Cultural Space* (1998), the editor of *Butch/Femme: Inside Lesbian Gender* (1997), and co-editor with Andy Medhurst of *Lesbian and Gay Studies: A Critical Introduction* (1997).

Steve Pile

Steve Pile is a lecturer in the Faculty of Social Sciences at the Open University. He has published work relating to identity, politics, and geography. He is the author of *The Body and the City: Psychoanalysis, Space, and Subjectivity* (1996), and co-editor with Michael Keith of *Geographies of Resistance* (1997) and with Heidi J. Nast of *Places through the Body* (1998).

Alicia Pivaro

A founding member of Strangely Familiar, Alicia Pivaro is co-editor of *Strangely Familiar: Narratives of Architecture in the City* (1996). After training as an architect, with a master's in the History of Modern Architecture, she worked as a creative producer, writer, and tutor in the fields of architecture and design. Her projects include "Tasty—Good Enough to Eat," "Home—Architects' Designs for Living," "Project 2045," and "Y2K+, Cultural Questions for the 21st Century." Former Head of Architecture at the Arts Council of England, where she initiated Architecture Week, she is now Director of the RIBA Architecture Gallery.

Jane Rendell

Jane Rendell is Lecturer in Architecture at the University of Nottingham, and author of *The Pursuit of Pleasure* (2000). A founding member of Strangely Familiar, she is co-editor of *Strangely Familiar: Narratives of Architecture in the City* (1995), *Gender Space Architecture: An Interdisciplinary Introduction* (2000) and *InterSections: Architectural Histories and Critical Theories* (2000).

Edward W. Soja

Edward W. Soja, formerly Associate Dean of the Graduate School of Architecture and Urban Planning at UCLA, is currently a Professor in the Department of Urban Planning. From his early research on problems of

regional development in Africa to his current work on the postmoderniza-
tion of Los Angeles, Soja has been concerned with how we theorize space and
the politically charged spatiality of social life. He is the author of *Postmodern Geographies: The Reassertion of Space in Critical Social Theory* (1989), *Thirdspace: Journeys to Los Angeles and Other Real-and-Imagined Places* (1996), and
co-editor (with Allen Scott) of *The City: Los Angeles and Urban Theory at the
End of the Twentieth Century* (1996). He is currently completing *Postmetropo-
lis*, a comprehensive look at how the new urbanization is restructuring the
contemporary megacity.

Philip Tabor

Professor Philip Tabor runs a graduate design studio and teaches architectural theory at The Bartlett, University College London. He is interested in
the effect of telematic media on the idea of architecture.

Helen Thomas

Helen Thomas trained as an architect at Liverpool University and graduated
as an architectural historian from The Bartlett, University College London.
She has worked as an architect in London and Seville and has taught architectural history, theory, and design at The Bartlett and the University of
North London. She has published various articles on spatial theory and Latin
American architecture, and is currently researching her doctorate on postcolonial imaginations at the University of Essex.

Bernard Tschumi

Bernard Tschumi is principal of Bernard Tschumi Architects and chief architect of the Parc de la Villette, Paris. Having taught at the Architectural
Association in London, the Institute for Architecture and Urban Studies in
New York, Princeton University, and Cooper Union, he is currently Dean
of the Graduate School of Architecture, Planning, and Preservation at Columbia University in New York. He is editor of *D* (*Columbia Documents of
Architecture and Theory*), Member of the Collège International de Philoso-
phie, and recipient of France's Grand Prix National d'Architecture (1996).

Lynne Walker

Lynne Walker was formerly Senior Lecturer in the History of Architecture
and Design at the University of Northumbria and is currently a visiting lec-

turer at the University of East Anglia. Her most recent publication on gender and space is *Drawing on Diversity: Women, Architecture, and Practice* (1997).

Richard Wentworth

Richard Wentworth is an artist, born in Samoa and trained at Hornsey College of Art and the Royal College of Art, London. After periods of travel and work in America, he has lived in London for the last twenty years. His work has been exhibited across Europe, and in America, Australia, and Japan. He has taught at both art and architecture schools in London.

Shirley Wong

Shirley Wong practices as an architect in an interior and furniture design company in Chelsea, London. She was trained at The Bartlett, University College London, where she also received a M.Sc. in Building Design for Developing Countries. Apart from London, she has lived and worked in Hong Kong and Australia. She completed her Ph.D. at University College London on colonialism and architecture in Hong Kong. Her previous publications include "Public Housing and Commercial Buildings in Hong Kong: An Analysis of Post-war Changes in Built Forms," *Architecture + Design* (January–February 1993).

Patrick Wright

Patrick Wright is a writer, broadcaster, and social allegorist. He writes and presents various radio and television programs. His books include *On Living in an Old Country* (1985), *A Journey through Ruins: The Last Days of London* (1990), and *The Village That Died for England* (1995). His forthcoming book deals with tanks and the military imagination.

The Unknown City

{T}he Unknown, the giant city,
to be perceived or guessed at.

Henri Lefebvre
"The View from the Window"
(trans. Eleonore Kofman and Elizabeth Lebas)

Iain Borden, Jane Rendell, Joe Kerr, and Alicia Pivaro

1 Things, Flows, Filters, Tactics

The Unknown City is a book about both the existence and the possibilities of architecture and the city. It is at once a history, geography, and sociology of the urban as it presents itself today and a proposition, a move toward confronting the problems of how we might know of, and engage with, the urban. We offer here an approximation of this problematic, suggesting a move from things to flows, from filters to tactics. In the process, essays shift from objects to actions, stasis to change, between external and internal, city and self, past and present, and so to future—and back again.

      This introductory essay is divided into two parts. The first, Things to Flows, sets out a framework for thinking about architecture and the city based on the tripartite concerns of space, time, and the human subject. The second, Filters to Tactics, sets out the ways in which we negotiate the distance between city and self.

THINGS TO FLOWS

Architecture offers itself to us as an object, and the city as the ultimate technical object: the fantastical concentration of wealth, power, blood, and tears crystallized in office towers, roads, houses, blocks, and open spaces. The appearance of the urban is then seemingly as a thing, as a finite set of spaces—it is alternatively the machine, the artifact, the body, the experiment, the artwork, the reflective mirror, the clothing, the labyrinth, and all the other metaphorical understandings by which people have sought to comprehend its objectival character.

      But architecture is no object. At an interdisciplinary nexus, as an intrinsic element of everyday life, architecture is not composed of isolated and monumental objects. Architecture is ambient and atmospheric, and architecture allows us to tell stories—it is both backdrop to and inspiration for theoretical and poetic musings of all kinds, from love to philosophy, theology to Marxism.

      The work of Walter Benjamin provides an interesting approach to architecture, one that is both thematic and methodological. Architecture is Benjamin's means of "spatialising the world," part of a larger project of developing a theory of modernity wherein it is a mythologized image of the effects of capitalism.[1] Benjamin treats architecture not as a series of isolated things to be viewed objectively but rather as an integral part of the urban fabric experienced subjectively. His subject matter is not a selection of specific buildings and his method is not to analyze these as formal pieces of architecture. His work is not empirical: it does not describe buildings aesthetically or functionally, or categorize them as things in terms of style, form, or production.

Spatialized images, for Benjamin, are representations of philosophical and historical ideas, and consequently architecture is also a dialectical image in Benjamin's work. It exists between antiquity and modernity as an image of modernity in prehistory, and between technology and art as an expression of the tension between the process of modernization and traditional aesthetic values. The point at which the dialectical image is blasted out of history is one where history, the brought-about event, coincides with nature, the never-changing background. As Walter Benjamin notes, "The destructive or critical impetus in materialist historiography comes into place in that blasting apart of historical continuity which allows the object to constitute itself. Materialist historiography does not choose its objects causally but blasts them out of it."[2] Benjamin's dialectic is an instantaneous image, that which occurs at the intersections of nature, myth, and history. Dialectic images recur as different fragments: as fossil (trace), fetish (phantasmagoria), wish image (symbol), and ruin (allegory). This is Benjamin's "microscopic gaze."[3] Such fragments include figures (the collector, flâneur, ragpicker, prostitute), objects (dust), and concepts (fetish): all are interconnected; each is an archaeological fragment capable of telling a spatial story. Such fragments acted in this way for the Strangely Familiar program—and hence also for the images and texts in this book—as metonymic and metaphoric catalysts to thought and action. Ultimately, then, architecture is less the constitution of space than a way of watching and comprehending the spatiality of the city.

Space

There are three important points to note about the spatiality of the city. First, we must consider scale. The city is not confined to the spatial scale of the building, or indeed even that of the city itself, but encompasses the whole, multiscalar landscape produced by human activity: from the corporeal to the global, the worldly to the intimate. Second, the city cannot be reduced to either *form* or *representation*: it is neither a collection of object-buildings nor the equivalent of models, schemas, drawings, and projections of all kinds. Third, the city is not the product of planners and architects. While urban professionals such as planners and architects might believe themselves to be in turn democratic negotiators, community advocates, neutral social scientists, exponents of the beautiful, and masterful shapers of space, they act only as part of much broader, much deeper systems of power, economics, and signification. Too often, architecture is designed (and consequently comprehended) as a purely aesthetic or intellectual activity, ignoring social relations and rendering people passive.⁴ Architecture may thus, as monuments, express significance in the city, but it will simultaneously mask the structures of power that underlie it.

How, then, to further explore these considerations of space, the city, and architecture? Central to the concepts of the Strangely Familiar program (see the preface to this book) as a whole have been the ideas of Henri Lefebvre, and in particular his ideas on the production of space. Although there are many grounds for criticizing Lefebvre's theories— including the relative lack of attention given to global space, cyberspace, and the postcolonial world—these theorizations are, by now, both relatively well known and highly influential, and therefore deserve to be recalled here. Space, Lefebvre postulates, is a historical production, at once the medium and outcome of social being. It is not a theater or setting but a social production, a concrete abstraction—simultaneously mental and material, work and product—such that social relations have no real existence except in and through space.⁵ This relationship between the social and the spatial—in Edward Soja's term, the "socio-spatial dialectic"⁶—is an interactive one, in which people make places and places make people.

Such ideas have, of course, precursors and analogues in the fields of geography and anthropology. Urban geographers such as David Harvey have long been concerned with the social production of space, while anthropologists have argued that space is culturally produced—as an integral part of material culture, space is intimately bound up in daily life, social activities, and personal rituals. Taken together, work in anthropology and geography encompasses all aspects of the built environment rather than treating works of architecture as autonomous "one-off" pieces of fine art or sculpture; thus it includes building users as well as designers and builders as producers of space. Such work has influenced those architectural historians who have critiqued the privileged status of architecture and the role of the architect, suggesting instead that architecture is continually reproduced through use and everyday life.⁷

Feminist geographers and anthropologists in particular have contributed to this kind of work.⁸ Liz Bondi, Doreen Massey, Linda McDowell, and Gillian Rose, among others, have argued that since social relations are gendered, and space is socially produced, then space is patterned by gender.⁹ Gendered space may be produced through its occupation—the different inhabitation of space by men or women—as well as through representations. For descriptions of spatial characteristics may be gendered, both by drawing similarities to the biological body and by prescribing the kinds of spaces and spatial languages considered appropriate for men and women.

Making connections between space and gender relations resonates with the earlier research of anthropologists on "public" and "private" realms, kinship networks, and social relations of exchange, which argues that the relation between gender and space is defined through power—that is, the social status of women defines the spaces they occupy.[10] Shirley Ardener's work, for example, has been particularly important in developing studies that examine both the differing spaces men and women are allocated culturally and the particular role space has in symbolizing, maintaining, and reinforcing gender relations.[11]

Space, then, is a social (re)production. Lefebvre therefore postulates that each mode of production, each epoch, produces its own understanding of space and experiences it accordingly. Thus natural or physical space (a preexistent natural phenomenon over which activities range—the space of prehistory) gives way first to absolute space (fragments of natural space rendered sacred, the space of rites and ceremonies, death, and the underworld—the space of slavery), then historical space (the early towns of the West—the space of feudalism), and finally abstract space (space as commodity, at once concrete and abstract, homogenized and fragmented—the space of capitalism). Each space contains within it both traces of its predecessors and the seeds of the next, creating a complex historical geography of different social spaces.[12]

As a political project, however, this is more than just a history, and so Lefebvre also introduces the notion of a space yet to come. He somewhat ambiguously intimates it to be a more mixed, interpenetrative space that will—or perhaps should—eventually supersede the more rigid fragmentations of abstract space; in it differences would be respected rather than buried under a homogeneity. This is "differential space," which restores the human body, the social body, with its knowledge, desires, and needs. Differential space is thus the spatial concomitant of the total revolution, the path toward the restoration of the total human; it is not a singular, universal entity but the socialist "space of differences."[13] And so this volume is not a pure intellectual reflection but is, we hope, shot through at different moments with intimations, openings, potentialities, and even prescriptions for a different future. The purpose of history, after all, is not just to know the past but to engage with the present and the years to come.

Lefebvre's main underlying formulation for the production of space is, however, not historical or utopian but analytical: the triad of spatial practices, representations of space, and spaces of representation. First, spatial practice (*la pratique spatiale*) concerns the production and reproduction of material life. Encompassing both everyday life and urban activities, it results in the various functional spaces—ranging from single rooms and buildings to large urban sites—that form part of the material production of space. Spatial practice is thus roughly equivalent to the economic or material base. Producing the spatial forms and practices appropriate to, and necessary for, different productive and reproductive activities, it thereby defines places, actions, and signs, the trivialized spaces of the everyday and, conversely, places made special by symbolic means. It is both a space of objects and things and a space of movements and activities. This is space, in Lefebvre's terms, as it is "perceived"—in the sense of being the apparent and often functional form of space that we perceive before considering concepts and experiences. This is space as empirically observed.[14]

The second kind of space, representations of space (*les représentations de l'espace*), relates to the conscious codifications of space typified by abstract understandings such as those advanced by the disciplines of planning, science, and mathematics and by artists of a "scientific bent." Representations of space are a form of knowledge that provide the various understandings of space necessary for spatial practices to take place. They thus display a tendency toward intellectually constructed systems of verbal signs. This is space as conceived, as "the concept without life."[15]

The third and last kind of space, spaces of representation (*les espaces de représentation*),[16] concerns those experienced as symbols and images. In part then, the spaces of representation function similarly to conceptions of reality in conditioning possibilities for action. But they are also liberatory, for at this level resistance to, and criticism of, dominant social orders can take place. In spaces of representation, space can be invented and imagined. They are thus both the space of the experienced and the space of the imagination, as *lived*. Spaces of representation tend toward systems of nonverbal symbols and signs; they are "life without concepts."[17]

This sophisticated conceptualization of the various possible arenas for space not only allows for ideas of space (verbal and visual, conscious and unconscious, real and imagined) but also situates those ideas in an overall notion of spatiality without reducing them to either aberrant misconception or irrelevant abstraction. Taken together, representations of space and spaces of representation provide the conceptions and images necessary for spatial practice to operate.

Furthermore, these kinds of space are not exclusive zones, but only analytic categories. Spatial practices, representations of space, and spaces of representation therefore necessarily incorporate each other in their concrete historical-geographical combinations; the history of space must account not only for each separately but, above all, for their interrelation and linkages with social practice.[18] Real space and spatiality are always constructed in and through some spatially and historically specific configuration of the three.

In *The Unknown City*, "spatiality" then, thus refers both to the production of spatial practices, representations, and lived experiences and simultaneously to the dialectical configuration of those activities that produce it. Such a formulation is necessary if we are to avoid the extremes of pure physiological and biological determinism, where the social is a physical world to which we apply ourselves, and of pure idealism, where social being is an immaterialized abstraction. Both necessarily restrict our conception of the social, either to the empirical horizon of the physical or to the metaphysical floating of the inconcrete idea. For social existence to enable self-production and self-determination—so that people make lives for themselves, not simply surviving and adapting to the natural circumstance to which they are born or projecting life from idealized sources—consciousness and experience must form concrete elements. And as social being must inevitably involve space, so it follows that it must also involve consciousness and experience of space.

Time

As a historical production, space is not independent of time; we must consider how the city comes into being, how buildings are constructed, and also how the whole edifice of the urban is continually reproduced. Clearly, time makes a difference. Social relations in the city are dynamic ones, and although we argue for the importance of space, time is increasingly entering into discussions of the social production of spaces—not solely the time of historical materialism, but also personal and irregular times: bodily rhythms, unconscious and conscious memories, the flux of complexity and chaos.

8
1
9

> She didn't see that first bullet, but it must have hit a wire or something, coming through, because the lights came on. She did see the second one, or anyway the hole it blew in the leather-grain plastic. Something inside her stopped, learning this about bullets: that one second there isn't any hole, the next second there is. Nothing in between. You see it happen, but you can't watch it happening.[19]

Like Chevette Washington in William Gibson's cyberpunk fiction *Virtual Light*, we can sense the process of architecture being built, the process of formation and construction; and we can see the results, the buildings—

holes, but not the "happening." We cannot see the city come into being because no singular space or time reveals it to us; the city is not comprehensible to the single glance or view. This is further complicated in that the process continually recurs, at different locations, scales, and times and with a myriad of different meanings and power relations. To "watch" architecture, then, is not so much simply to slow down the passage of the bullet with a high-speed camera, with an ever more attentive historical lens, but to explode the whole notion of time and space; it requires comprehending with multiple ideas and intellects, with the whole body, with the heart and the hand, with political beliefs as well as with the eye. "Watching the happening" of architecture and the urban means far more than "seeing it happen."

As the periodization of the production of space suggests, this formulation incorporates a production of time. Time is also part of the revolutionary or utopian nature of any political project, seeking a forward projection of the periodization into the future. Knowing the city is ultimately a project of becoming, of unfolding events and struggles in time as well as in space. Thus time and space are not independent constructions but interproductions, processes at once separate but necessarily interrelated.

However, this is not an easy formulation—the relation between space and time remains problematic. There are, nonetheless, a few possible ways of approaching this formulation, which we would like to introduce here.

First we must consider the spatial context of temporal productions. The abstract space of capitalism reduces time to constraints on the usages of space and to a general dominance of time by economic space, thereby rendering time a matter of clocks and labor, something uncelebrated as lived experience. However, time can also resist such reductions, reemerging as a form of wealth, as locus and medium of use and pleasure.[20] How then might this resistance occur?

We might begin by periodizing time, seeking to chart its different conceptions and enactments in different epochs. Such a knowledge would free us from seeing abstract time as the natural or universal time of humanity; we would become aware of the social constructedness of time and, therefore, the potential for different constructions. But here we have not taken this path, which we leave to more past-oriented historians and "geographers of time."

Instead, we look to the different kinds of time that are implicated in social and spatial production. Architecture, in particular, has a special role in representing sanctioned relationships of space and time;

it is commonly perceived in relation to memory, that indefinable human hold on the past which is so necessary to the personal negotiation of change and to the public elaboration of narratives of time. In its most self-conscious expression of time and permanence—that is, the monumental—architecture apparently manages to concretize public, collective memory; yet the unconscious assumption that in memorializing the past architecture can somehow anchor memory is, of course, largely illusory. As Iain Sinclair observes, "Memorials are a way of forgetting, reducing generational guilt to a grid of albino chess pieces, bloodless stalagmites. Shapes that are easy to ignore stand in for the trauma of remembrance. Names are edited out. Time attacks the noble profile with a syphilitic bite."[21]

Memory, however, is but one operation of social time. We must also consider that kind of time which, following Lefebvre again, is diversified, at once social and natural, at once linear (the time of progress and regress) and cyclical (the time of nature, of repetitions, death and life):

> Time in the city and by the city will be independent of natural cycles but not submitted to the linear divisions of rationalized duration; it will be the time of unexpectedness, not a time without place but a time that dominates the place in which it occurs and through which it emerges. This will be the place and time of desire, above and beyond need.[22]

We offer a social or analytical conception of time: time as at once represented consciously, experienced passively, reimagined actively, and embedded into all the myriad of social practices that constitute social being.

Where then could this reassertion of time take place? For Lefebvre, the restoration of time has to start within society itself, with the spaces of representation (the most immediately active and hence the most temporal of Lefebvre's three kinds of space), followed by a reunion with representations of space. It is by facing the constraints of time imposed within contemporary society that people master their own times, and so maximize the production of art, knowledge, and the lived.[23]

Furthermore, it is in the modern city that one must consider the different uses, productions, and inscriptions of time. Rethinking the city necessarily involves the temporal.[24] Thus it is important to consider that architecture is not just the space-time of the permanent, of the great canonic works that stand seemingly immutable over the centuries while all around them decays and is destroyed. It is also the everyday architecture of the city—that which is embedded in all the routines, activities, patterns, and emotions of quotidian life; that which ranges, spatially, from the body to the globe and, temporally, from the ephemeral and the briefest moment to the longer time of the generation, cycles of life and death, and beyond. Architecture is part of the flow of space and time, part of the interproduction of space, time, and social being.

The Human Subject

What, then, of social being? It is also in the human subject—in the body, in the psychoanalytic and in the social and cultural constructions of age, class, gender, ethnicity, and sexuality—that the production of time and space (and hence of architecture and the city) must be sought.

Lefebvre sees different forms of social construction as central to the production of space—principally in terms of class, but also of gender, ethnicity, sexuality, family relations, and age. It is precisely these characteristics that abstract space tends to erase; therefore, the revolutionary project must be directed toward restoring them. These are the social constructions that differential space preserves and emphasizes, ensuring that the right to the city is not the right to buildings or even public space but rather the right to be different, the right not to be classified forcibly into categories determined by homogenizing powers. Against Gilles Deleuze, Lefebvre formulates difference not as something based on originality, individualism, and particularity but as that which emerges from struggle, the conceptual, and the lived.[25]

Central to Lefebvre's thinking on this matter is the human body, as site not just of cultural endeavor but also of self-appropriation and adaptation. The body is particularly useful for thinking about the triad of the perceived, conceived, and lived: spatial practices (perceived) presuppose the use of body, hands, sensory organs, and gestures—the practical bases of the perception of the outside world; representations of space (conceived) include representations of the body, derived from scientific and anatomical knowledge, and relations with nature; and spaces of representation (lived experience) include bodies imbued with culture and symbolism. It is thus the body that helps render the triad concrete, not purely abstract. It is the body that unites cyclical and linear time, need and desire, gestures and manipulations of tools; it is the body that preserves difference within repetition and is, therefore, the source of innovation out of repetition. This is a recovery of the body abandoned within Western philosophy, a living body that is at once subject and object.[26]

This body is practical and fleshy. Contemplating space with the whole body and all senses, not just with the eyes and intellect, allows more awareness of conflicts and so of a space that is Other. This is a body of tastes and smells, of left-right and front-back orientations, of hearing and touch. It resists the tendency of abstract space and its attendant domination of the visual to replace sex with the representation of sex, to pulverize the body into images, to erase history, to reduce volume to surface, and to flatten and fragment the experience of space.[27]

It is also a body that is ideational and mental. Although there is an undercurrent of psychoanalytic thought in Lefebvre's work,[28] it is feminists—specifically Hélène Cixous, Luce Irigaray, and Julia Kristeva—who have most prominently used psychoanalytic as well as semiotic models to discuss the sexual construction of the subject. They have critiqued the phallocentric constructions of the subject developed by Sigmund Freud and Jacques Lacan, which prioritize the male subject and the visual, insisting instead that the female subject is constructed from a position of difference, based metaphorically on the morphology of the female body.[29] Here the female subject position is defined not by the visual but by a spatiality that relates differently to concepts of surface, depth, and fluidity. Critiquing the dominance of the visual allows us to understand the city and the female as more than objects of the male gaze,[30] opening up possibilities both of self-representation for women and of new ways to comprehend the experiential qualities of the city.

Once the human subject and its body have been introduced, we see immediately that this is at once a physical and conceptual entity, being and becoming, acting and thinking. It is to ways of urban knowing—the various filters and tactics—that we now turn.

FILTERS TO TACTICS

Critical work is made to fare on interstitial ground. Every realization of such work is a renewal and a different contextualization of its cutting edge. One cannot come back to it as to an object; for it always bursts forth on frontiers. . . . Instead, critical strategies must be developed within a range of diversely occupied territories where the temptation to grant any single territory transcendent status is continually resisted.

—Trinh T. Minh-Ha, When the Moon Waxes Red: Representation, Gender, and Cultural Politics

Filters and *tactics* refer to the ways in which we negotiate the distance between city and self. In the Strangely Familiar program we initially thematized various relations to architecture and the city in terms of appropriation, domination, resistance, memory, experience, and identity, and we adopted a narrative form to highlight the differences in each kind of social-spatial relation. Here we extend the attempt to create a framework, or generalized schema, through which we can relate and critique a complex series of interactions, arguing that memory, experience, and identity are filters and that appropriation, domination, and resistance are tactics.

Filters are epistemological mediations of existing urban conditions. We attempt to understand the city as subject and context through a series of filters or ideologies—not as pure descriptions, proscriptive beliefs, or false consciousness but as means of thinking and enacting the relation of the self to the external world.[31] Filters may stand in for the city as our only relation to a city from which we are physically distant, but they are also part of the cities we occupy. They are metaphoric and metonymic. Filters represent an aspect of the city to us: they may be visual and/or scripted, static and/or dynamic. The relationship between such representations (stories, histories, films, images of the city) and the "real" city describes an interplay of reality, ideas, and representation.

Tactics are a more proactive response to the city: they are practices, or what Michel Foucault refers to as discourses that produce objects.[32] These tactics may be words, images, or things; they may be theoretically and/or empirically based; and they may be romantically and/or pragmatically driven. They may be attempts to solve urban problems with housing programs, planning policies, and political agendas; and they may also be attempts to reconceptualize the relation between the city and the self. Whatever their form, they differ from filters in their intentionality. Tactics aim to make a difference.

But both filters and tactics are necessary parts of urban living, working dialectically as ways of knowing, thinking, and acting. Tactics tend to the concrete and filters to the abstract, but each contains the other in different relations. In *The Unknown City* we take further the problem of organizing writing on the city by considering tactics and filters not only on their own terms but also as "filtering tactics" and "tactical filters"—a quadripartite structure that is explained in more detail below.

Filters

Separations between city and self are not so crude as a thinking subject of flesh and bone set against a passive collection of bricks and mortar. Nonetheless, there are distances. The self takes positions, adopts strategies of engagement, and responds to the environment in active ways, creating buildings and making places. The possibilities for engaging with the city and its architecture are spatial and temporal, determined by internal desires, boundaries, and thresholds that define possibilities for the self, as well as through the politics of external spaces, events, and moments. Although the self is in part constituted through an occupation of space and an understanding of the city, and the city too is created by the actions of its inhabitants, neither can be completely collapsed into the other.

As an artifact, part of material culture, the city is a socially produced entity, negotiated through systems of representation (both image and script) and experienced in ways that depend on individual and social positioning. If we are to know the city, we must first know ourselves; we must attempt to deal with our underlying motivations and use them to generate an analysis of the city. By such engagement we equip ourselves with some of the theoretical tools and practical processes required to understand the city in the abstract and in the concrete.

The city creates problems that we must understand; different kinds of knowing may then illuminate further areas of study, which in turn transform the city. This is a dialectical process. The places in cities explored in the following chapters provide both the problems and solutions from which diverse forms of urban knowledge emerge, as attempts at or ways of understanding the complex series of relations that constitute a city. In this way, the objects of study are not only cities but also ourselves.

Cities are complex systems of representations, in which space and time are understood and experienced in the form of a representation. All systems of representation are composed of signs: written words, speech, painting, photographic images, maps and signals, filmic narratives, choreographic movements, installations and events, buildings and places. Signs combine a signifier and signified, a material and a conceptual component. Material objects are capable of signifying or meaning something, though representations may be of different orders of materiality. Signs exist within a larger system and are always related to and contrasted with other signs or relations of value.

Once the city is understood as a series of representations, we henceforth take its meanings to be socially constructed rather than pregiven and self-evident. Furthermore as various French intellectuals have argued, systems of representation do not communicate meaning transparently. For example, Jean-François Lyotard's work has addressed the death of the all-knowing subjects, the end of history, and the suspension of belief in the metanarrative. Foucault, by rethinking the historical project, has concluded that history is not about recovering truth or origin but about constructing discourses of knowledge. And

Jacques Derrida has deconstructed the binary systems of meaning that were purport to reflect reality unproblematically. These ways of thinking dispute the truth of history, argue for the death of the human subject, and question how meaning is communicated.

The issue of representation is a particularly problematic one for feminists, since representations constructed through patriarchy contain assumptions about sex and gender. Such assumptions have obscured the lives of real women and an understanding of female subjectivity and identity. Influenced by postmodern theory, feminists have shifted from searching for the origin of women's oppression to interpreting the ways in which oppression is represented, focusing on the decoding of systems of representation in textual and other signifying practices. To consider gendered representations as constructed rather than natural takes a feminist critique further than looking at the asymmetries inherent in the categories of women and men to deal with the construction of identity and the ways in which class, race, and sexuality, as well as gender difference, are organized within representational forms.

In theorizing subjectivity, identity, and experience, feminists suggest that position is integral to knowing.[33] Their discussions of difference are described in spatial language, such as "standpoint," "locality," and "margins."[34] Such spatial metaphors highlight the epistemological importance of the occupation of space in the construction of identity—conceptually and materially, in the abstract and the concrete. Spatial metaphors are also important for feminist philosophers in exploring new conceptions of gendered space and time.[35] These metaphors are places where conceptual work can illuminate our knowledge of the city, and vice versa. The interaction of real and metaphoric space is a site of collision of city and self: representations of the self and representations of the city touch momentarily, providing potential starting points for tactical work.

Tactics

In a world, then, in which spatiality and sexuality are fundamental experiences, and in which sexuality, race, class and gender have been constructed as significant axes of difference, it should come as no surprise that struggles organised around these differences feature prominently in a process like urbanisation.

—Lawrence Knopp, "Sexuality and Urban Space: A Framework for Analysis"

We need to envisage a new cultural project that encompasses democracy, sociability, adaptations of time and space and the body, life beyond the commodity, and the slow transformation of everyday life. Human activity must therefore be directed at new forms of content, seeking not just to symbolize but also to transform life as a kind of generalized artistic practice. "Let everyday life become a work of art!"[36]

How such a critical sensibility might actually be achieved has been the point of departure for a succession of twentieth-century artistic and political movements—none more influential than the Situationist International, whose desire for "the revolution of everyday life" led to activities intended to illuminate the enfeebling mediocrity of normal life. According to Sadie Plant, the Situationists believed that "Only an awareness of the influences of the existing environment can encourage the critique of the present conditions of daily life, and yet it is precisely this concern with the environment in which we live which is ignored."[37] In particular the techniques of psychogeography, a very specific use of urban "knowing," suggested new ways to expose the soporific complacency that seemed to characterize everyday experience under late capitalism. This emphasis on the subjective sense of place has contributed greatly to establishing that spatial formation and usage are critical determinants of urban understanding.

Many of the chapters in *The Unknown City* acknowledge the debt of contemporary thought to the Situationist movement; of particular importance both to this book and to the Situationists themselves was the radical tactical program they developed for cultural agitation. They devised ways in which artists, architects, writers, and others might actively politicize their practices in the services of urban thought and action. In response to a similar impulse, *The Unknown City* project has sought to embrace practitioners from a broad array of cultural disciplines, who themselves have attempted to elaborate tactics for engaging with the urban. Individual authors of course adopt a variety of approaches, from describing a theoretically informed understanding of cities to prescribing a critical practice. Some might wonder with Cixous: "What am I going to do with my theories, all so pretty, so agile, and so theoretical. . . . All my more and more perfect, beautiful theories, my shuttles and my rockets, my machines rivaling in precision, wit, and temerity the toughest research brains, all the champion theories I have so carefully shaped, with such satisfaction, all of them."[38]

In such formulations, the city and its architecture become not just aesthetic objects but dynamic, practical realizations of art, unique and irreplaceable "works" and not reproducible products—polyrhythmic compositions of linear and cyclical times and different social spaces, born from many labors. This is art not as the prettifying of urban spaces but as making time-spaces into works of art.[39]

Above all, the interproduction of time, space, and social being should be about use values and not exchange values in the city. Lefebvre reminds us, "Use value, subordinated for centuries to exchange value, can now come first again. How? By and in urban society, from this reality which still resists and preserves for us use value, the city."[40] The aim is appropriation, not ownership: production as creativity in the widest sense. Such interproduction means representing and thinking, but also doing, acting, and transforming everything—thought, politics, work, the self—in the process.[41]

This is why, having stressed throughout *The Production of Space* the importance of the interrelation of representations of space and spaces of representation, Lefebvre returns at the end of his book to the necessity of spatial practices—the things people do, and the patterns and physicality they create—for disrupting abstract space. The "potential energies" of groups act to transform and create new social spaces; as he points out elsewhere, "The city is not only a language, but also a practice."[42] Experience and representation are here returned to action, to new activities in which they are embedded. And in political terms, this marks the move from critical thought to contesting practice, from writing to more active speech, at which point the subjective becomes an objective intervention. Activity concretizes the life-world (as Benno Werlen notes in his reading of Lefebvre), both as the negative critique that undermines the illusory rationality of the political state and social hierarchy, and as that which keeps different social space-times together.[43] Lefebvre insists, "Only an *act* can hold—and hold together—such fragments in a homogeneous totality. Only action can prevent dispersion, like a fist clenched around sand."[44] In this way we become true subjects in time and space, not simply users or experiencers of but produced by, and productive of, the architecture around us.

Such a claim reconceptualizes the human subject. Lefebvre rejects the terms "users" and "inhabitants" because they imply marginality and underprivilege.[45] "Subjects," however, suggests a body of social construction, a subject-body that does something. This final attribute of Lefebvre's thought that we discuss has been largely unrecognized by Lefebvrian critics and commentators: the idea of activity. "It is not a question of *localizing* in pre-existing space a need or a function, but on the contrary, of *spatializing* a social activity, linked to the whole by *producing* an appropriate space."[46] For the historian, geographer, and sociologist and for urban thinkers and interventionists in general, a simple yet profound lesson now emerges. Activities as particular rhythms of time and space are not universal constructs: they are constructed in specific conditions. To attempt to understand human history, to attempt to understand the unknown-ness of the city—as we consider the conceived and the lived, representations and experience—we therefore must be explicit about what particular activity or activities are being undertaken: what are the energies deployed, what patterns do they create, what objects do they produce? In short, what productive work is being studied?

Planners, architects, and builders produce objects out of things and divide spaces with objects. But, as we argued at the start of this chapter, our consideration of the city should not be solely limited to such architectural objects, nor to architecture qua object. Instead we must also consider objects such as the visual images created by artists and filmmakers, through which we view certain parts of the city. Similarly, we should consider the words deployed by writers to communicate ideas. These words have a specific relation to space—they describe or prescribe space—and they too produce the city.

In relating to the urban realm, practices cannot engage with only one kind of object—words, images, or things. Each has a different relation to space and to the communication of meaning; thus the interrelation between them, which enables one to inform the other, is vital. But ultimately such interpenetration can happen only if the areas themselves are redefined and transposed: words as things, words as matter, images as objects, objects as ideas, and so on.

However elusive the notion of knowing a place might be, it is nonetheless at a particular location that particular actions, words, images, and things come together. "Knowing a place," a useful and necessary process, ranges from the tourist's simple claim of familiarity with a visited location to the intricate understandings of the permanent inhabitant. In all cases, of course, what is being referred to is a personal and unique ordering of applicable knowledge, a mental structuring of spatial, cultural, and temporal data to create an internalized encapsulation of that place—wholly individual, largely incommunicable, but utterly essential for any degree of engagement with a given urban locale.

Anyone who seriously contemplates the political possibilities inherent in knowing a place, in being not merely a resident but an active citizen, sees the necessity of developing the critical tools to expose and to critique how meanings and values are produced and manipulated in the realm of urban space. To do so requires an elaborate weaving of theoretical knowledge with the comprehension of the material realities of any single place.

We must therefore realize, with Michel de Certeau, that subjective self-knowledge and collective understanding of the community are the necessary stores from which the particularities of real cities can be revealed to resist the totalizing concept of the "city."[47] Turning to personal and subjective categories of knowledge does more than directly oppose the objective, functionalist, and technocratic discourses of modernism; it also suggests an order of understanding wholly at variance with the scientifically based urbanistic view that such discourses produce. In many of the essays that follow, readers will discern a tradition of thought and practice led by French theorists, one that permits the reimagination of the city, and of cities, in order to resist the elimination of the unique and the irrational that the abstracted vision of the "concept city" implies.

A particular mode of constructing "pictorial" narratives of the everyday world, rooted deeply in the insights of surrealist practices and depending on the defiant privileging of the detail over the whole, or the arbitrary juxtaposition of the mundane with the significant, evokes not merely the urban landscape but simultaneously the existence of the narrator in that place. Such a narrator can capture just something of the subjective sensation, the sheer vividness, of urban experience and movement and perhaps hint at the "secret history" of the city, as Iain Sinclair demonstrates:

> Walking is the best way to explore and exploit the city; the changes, shifts, breaks in the cloud helmet, movement of light on water. Drifting purposefully is the recommended mode, trampling asphalted earth in alert reverie, allowing the fiction of an underlying pattern to reveal itself. To the no-bullshit materialist this sounds suspiciously like *fin-de-siècle* decadence, a poetic of entropy—but the born-again *flâneur* is a stubborn creature, less interested in texture and fabric, eavesdropping on philosophical conversation pieces, than in noticing *everything*. Alignments of telephone kiosks, maps made from moss on the slopes of Victorian sepulchres, collections of prostitutes' cards, torn and defaced promotional bills for cancelled events at York Hall, visits to the homes of dead writers, bronze casts on war memorials, plaster dogs, beer mats, concentrations of used condoms, the crystalline patterns of glass shards surrounding an imploded BMW quarter-light window. . . . Walking, moving across a retreating townscape, stitches it all together: the illicit cocktail of bodily exhaustion and a raging carbon monoxide high.[48]

From the rhythms of walking, seeing, and other bodily constructions, to the everyday routines of urban life, to the deeper and more structured rhythms of economics, nation-states, and politics as they influence
and are reproduced by the subject: through such processes, buildings
cease to be objects and become places of epistemological and social negotiation conducted through the figure of the subject. Nonetheless, it is still
from the ground of the city, from its wealth of different spaces, times, and
peoples, that change and new life must emerge; there is no point in envis-
aging a utopia as an entirely new creation formed in a distant land and
future time from unsullied minds. Instead, the utopian impulse must be
applied to the situation in which we find ourselves today. We must treat the
city and its architectures as a "possibilities machine," as what Lefebvre
refers to as an oeuvre—a place of artistic production in its widest sense,
where the "texture" of the city is its creation of time-spaces through the
appropriative activities of its inhabitants; a place of nonlabor, joy, and
the fulfillment of desires rather than toil; a place of qualities, difference,
relations in time and space, contradictory uses and encounters.

The city should bring together the micro architectural and
macro planning scales, the everyday realm and the urban, inside and outside, work and nonwork, the durable and ephemeral, and so forth; it must
be situated between the perceived and the lived.[49] Architecture then
emerges not as an object, not as a thing, but as a flow—or, more properly,
as a flow within other flows—the merely apparent pattern of a much more
complex set of forces, dynamics, and interrelations within the space of
the city.

THE UNKNOWN CITY

As one of the anonymous reviewers for this volume pointed out, there is an
emergent "new movement in urban studies," one that offers an "anti-
formalist, post-structuralist, even Situationist perspective for understanding the city"; this volume represents "the first instance of the
diversity of postmodern theories applied to the field." Apart from offering
this diversity of theoretical discourse, The Unknown City also, we feel,
makes a significant contribution in at least two other ways. First, the book
utilizes both images and texts in a manner highly unusual—outside of architecture and art history, at least—for this kind of academic subject. Second, and perhaps more important, the various contributors go beyond
simply describing or interpreting and attempt to mobilize ideas within the

20

1

21

domain of practice(s) ranging from poetic writing to public art, from architectural design to the elucidation of "archaeological" data.

Before we explain the structuring of this book, a few caveats. Many of the essays, although by no means all, refer to places in the "Western world." This does not mean, however, that the insights gleaned are only applicable to the cities on which they are based, for in this age of globalism, all cities are to some extent open to similar processes and conditions. Nor does this selection mean that there is nothing to be learned from other cities not included here. Far from it. Indeed, we would hope that any geographic or urban omissions that the reader might identify would act as stimulation for new interpretations, new texts, new works of all kinds.

The Unknown City is divided into four parts: "Filters," "Filtering Tactics," "Tactics," and "Tactical Filters." Each section, and each essay contained within, deals simultaneously with Lefebvre's spatial practices, representations of space and spaces of representations. Each deals with ideas and action. Each deals with spaces, times, and subjects.

The first stage in understanding the contemporary metropolis is to comprehend—that is, to filter—preexistent urban conditions. Part I, "Filters," focuses primarily on this process, paying particular attention to those conditions which threaten and challenge more liberatory practices. Chapters 2 through 4 consider different ways in which memory, architecture, and the city may be tied to dominant modes of urbanism. For M. Christine Boyer (chapter 2), this means examining the attempt to alternatively erase and remember New York's Times Square, such that the city itself becomes a simulation of its own history. Barry Curtis (chapter 3) undertakes a similar investigation, this time showing how Venice occupies the interstitial ground between past, present, and future, and thus between heritage, modernity, and progress. Joe Kerr (chapter 4) looks at the ways in which memorialization has been used to represent, remember, and reremember aspects of war in London.

Chapters 5 through 9 examine forces and processes of urban domination. William Menking (chapter 5) unearths the burgeoning process of suburbanization—not, however, in the suburbs themselves but in the most urban of all locations: Manhattan. Philip Tabor (chapter 7) looks at another insidious form of capitalism, that of surveillance and the videocam, simultaneously capturing its controlling and seductive qualities. In a rather different approach to the notion of seduction, Jane Rendell (chapter 6) considers how urban rambling in Regency London represents the city as a place of male pleasure. Urban and architectural representations are critiqued as ideological instruments of colonialism in the Maidan area of Calcutta (Helen Thomas, chapter 8) and in the nineteenth-century headquarters of the Hongkong and Shanghai Bank (Shirley Wong, chapter 9).

Part II, "Filtering Tactics," turns to particular urban conditions that might be recognized for their resistive, celebratory, and liberatory practices: that is, for their tactical qualities. Iain Borden (chapter 10) proposes skateboarding as a model for performing a critical remapping of the spaces and architecture of the city. In other essays that similarly address forms of movement and remapping, Sally Munt (chapter 14) gives an account of the flâneur from the perspective of lesbian women enjoying anonymity and the city, while Steve Pile's essay (chapter 15) reflects on the possibilities of psychoanalytic theory for rethinking the hidden and subterranean worlds "buried below the surface."

Sandy McCreery (chapter 13) and Edward W. Soja (chapter 16) both provide instances of particular spatial practices, respectively in west London and Amsterdam, where residents have fought to maintain distinctive modes of living and to creatively disrupt forces of urban renewal whether in the form of roads or of gentrification. Lynne Walker (chapter 17) describes how women in the nineteenth-century city transformed domestic space, fashioning an arena of feminist politics. The occupation of space is also the premise of Adrian Forty's essay (chapter 11), which shows how the Royal Festival Hall operated as a place of democracy. Tom Gretton (chapter 12) identifies a rather different space of democracy, this time in the populist newspaper imagery of José Guadalupe Posada in revolutionary Mexico.

Part III, "Tactics," brings together some of most overtly interventionist modes of practice, tactics that think about as well as engage with the city. Bernard Tschumi (chapter 22) is the architect who has most consistently addressed the importance of theory for radical practice, and the experience of space for imaginative design. Nigel Coates (chapter 18) similarly reinterprets architecture in the city in terms of tension and juxtaposition, considering thematics such as theater and gardens, discord and movement, reference and change. Recent projects from Fashion Architecture Taste, a.k.a. Fat (chapter 20), also address the transitory nature of architecture, employing multiple programs, everyday imagery, and challenging, politicized agendas.

The projects of Cornford & Cross (chapter 19) and of Dolores Hayden and The Power of Place (chapter 21) provide alternative modes of art practice in the public realm of the city. While the former describe their own work as a "twisted critique" of specific sites and urban conditions, the latter is more concerned with the purposeful celebration and re-claiming of forgotten histories and erased lives. While these two inter-vene in the city through product and process, it is the city as backdrop, the mundane and the everyday, which appears as Richard Wentworth's art practice (chapter 23)—his photographs and words document the street as a place of the aleatory and the out-of-control.

The final element—Part IV, Section 4, "Tactical Filters"—once more includes examples of transformative practice, this time specifically relying on the medium of the written word. Using critical theory, Iain Chambers (chapter 24) postulates a notion of "weak architecture" as the place between stability and instability, between dwelling and decay. In her essay, bell hooks (chapter 26) evokes a different mode of theorized prose, this time from more personal reflections on love, home, and the city. Draw-ing on both family history and political critique, Doreen Massey (chapter 28) reflects on social relations and aging in the spaces of the garden city. The personal appears again in Jonathan Charley's account of Moscow (chapter 25), here as a semifictionalized, semirealist diary.

If the intersection of the personal with the political, the concrete with the abstract, helps academic analysis to resonate with everyday life, so, conversely, should the physicality and groundedness of the city provide a datum from which to speculate, imagine, and purposefully critique. Therefore, the apparent documentary and factual nature of Patrick Keiller's essay (chapter 27) should be situated in the context of his films, enabling his words to assume a more evocative role and creat-ing a heightened awareness of the (post) industrial landscape. Patrick Wright (chapter 29) also starts off from particular factual conditions of Thatcherite Britain, where political concerns rapidly engender a pas-sionate attack on decay, mismanagement, and false ideology as he jour-neys through the streets of London.

The Point Is to Change It

A central ambition of *The Unknown City* is to suggest and explore possi-bilities for radical interventions both in the articulation of new under-standings of the city and, equally, in forms of practice that seek to influence the production and reproduction of urban form and space. A characteristic statement of the earlier Strangely Familiar project was that "architecture and cities are far more than architects and planners of-ten consider them to be."[50] In elaborating that proposition we sought to ex-pose other forms of activity, conscious and unconscious, that shape the objects and meanings from which the city is constructed. The process is continued here by expanding the interdisciplinary collaborations so critical to this intellectual project, in order to embrace forms of cultural practice that seek new ways to engage with, and influence, the city itself.

Our course of action exposes a potential contradiction in the aims of the project. On the one hand, the body of work contained here, taken as a whole, merely serves to confirm that the city of late capitalism is too complex, and too fragmented in its physical and ideological formations, to ever permit a unitary comprehension. And yet, on the other hand, what we desire is that new understandings can lead to new tactics for restorative and redemptive action in the city. Without necessarily advocating a prescriptive path, our comprehension of the city must nonetheless be enacted.

Notes

1   See Walter Benjamin, *One-Way Street and Other Writings,* trans. Edmund Jephcott and Kingsley Shorter (London: Verso, 1992), and Walter Benjamin, *Charles Baudelaire: A Lyric Poet in the Era of High Capitalism,* trans. Harry Zohn (London: Verso, 1997); quotation from *One-Way Street*, p. 13.

2   Benjamin is quoted in David Frisby, *Fragments of Modernity: Theories of Modernity in the Work of Simmel, Kracauer, and Benjamin* (Cambridge, Mass.: MIT Press, 1986), p. 114.

3   Benjamin, *One-Way Street*, p. 19.

4   Henri Lefebvre, *The Production of Space,* trans. Donald Nicholson-Smith (Oxford: Blackwell, 1991), pp. 95, 200–201, 361–362.

5   Ibid., pp. 101–102, 129, 306–308, 402–404, 411.

6   Edward W. Soja, *Postmodern Geographies: The Reassertion of Space in Critical Social Theory* (London: Verso, 1989), pp. 76–93.

7   See Anthony D. King, ed., *Buildings and Society* (London: Routledge and Kegan Paul, 1980); Anthony King, *The Bungalow* (Oxford: Oxford University Press, 1995); Amos Rapoport, *House Form and Culture* (Englewood Cliffs, N. J.: Prentice-Hall, 1969); and Amos Rapoport, *Human Aspects of Urban Form* (Oxford: Pergamon Press, 1977).

8   See Rosalyn Deutsche, "Men in Space," *Strategies*, no. 3 (1990): 130–137; Rosalyn Deutsche, "Boys Town," *Environment and Planning D: Space and Society* 9 (1991): 5–30; Doreen Massey, "Flexible Sexism," *Environment and Planning D: Society and Space* 9 (1991): 31–57; Gillian Rose, review of *Postmodern Geographies*, by Edward Soja, and *The Condition of Postmodernity*, by David Harvey, *Journal of Historical Geography* 17, no. 1 (1991): 118–121.

9   Liz Bondi, "Feminism, Postmodernism, and Geography: A Space for Women?" *Antipode* 22, no. 2 (1990): 156–167; Liz Bondi, "Gender Symbols and Urban Landscapes," *Progress in Human Geography* 16 (1992): 157–170; Liz Bondi, "Gender and Geography: Crossing Boundaries," *Progress in Human Geography* 17 (1993): 241–246; Doreen Massey, *Space, Place, and Gender* (Cambridge: Polity Press, 1994); Linda McDow-

ell, "Space, Place, and Gender Relations, Parts 1 and 2," *Progress in Human Geography* 17 (1993); Gillian Rose, "Progress in Geography and Gender: Or Something Else," *Progress in Human Geography* 17 (1993): 531–537; and Gillian Rose, *Feminism and Geography: the Limits of Geographical Knowledge* (Cambridge: Polity Press, 1993).

10   See Shirley Ardener, ed., *Defining Females: The Nature of Women in Society* (London: Croom Helm, 1978); Eva Gamarnikow et al., eds., *The Public and the Private* (London: Heinemann, 1983); Rayna R. Reiter, ed., *Toward an Anthropology of Women* (New York: Monthly Review, 1975); and Michelle Zimbalist Rosaldo and Louise Lamphere, eds., *Woman, Culture, and Society* (Stanford: Stanford University Press, 1974).

11   Shirley Ardener, "Ground Rules and Social Maps for Women," in *Women and Space: Ground Rules and Social Maps*, ed. Ardener, rev. ed. (Oxford: Berg, 1993), pp. 1–30.

12   Lefebvre, *Production of Space*, pp. 11–14, 31, 34, 46–53, 86, 234–254, 285–292, 306–321, 352–367; and Henri Lefebvre, introduction to *Espace et politique* (Paris: Anthropos, 1973), translated in Lefebvre, *Writings on Cities*, ed. and trans. Eleonore Kofman and Elizabeth Lebas (Oxford: Blackwell, 1996), pp. 188–194.

13   Lefebvre, *Production of Space*, pp. 48–50, 52, 60, 409; Henri Lefebvre, "Space: Social Product and Use Value," in *Critical Sociology: European Perspective*, ed. J. Freiberg (New York: Irvington, 1979), p. 292, quoted in Mark Gottdiener, *The Social Production of Urban Space* (Austin: University of Texas Press, 1985) p. 128; and Derek Gregory, *Geographical Imaginations* (Oxford: Blackwell, 1994), p. 360.

14   Lefebvre, *Production of Space*, pp. 33, 38, 288, 413–414; and Henri Lefebvre, *La production de l'espace* (Paris: Anthropos, 1974), pp. 42, 48.

15   Lefebvre, *Production of Space*, pp. 33, 38–39, 371–372; and Lefebvre, *La production de l'espace*, pp. 43, 48.

16   The term appears in *La production de l'espace* as "les espaces de représentations" (pp. 43, 49), which Donald Nicholson-Smith translates in *Production of Space* as "representational spaces." We have used the more direct "spaces of representation," as translated by Frank Bryant in Henri Lefebvre, *The Survival of Capitalism: Repro-*

duction of the Relations of Production (New York: St. Martin's, 1976).

17 Lefebvre, *Production of Space*, pp. 33, 39, 371–372; and Lefebvre, *La production de l'espace*, pp. 43, 49.

18 Lefebvre, *Production of Space*, pp. 17–18, 40, 116, 230, 288.

19 William Gibson, *Virtual Light* (Harmondsworth: Viking/Penguin, 1993), p. 240.

20 Lefebvre, *Production of Space*, pp. 95–96, 370–371, 393; and Henri Lefebvre, *Introduction to Modernity: Twelve Preludes, September 1959–May 1961*, trans. John Moore (London: Verso, 1995), p. 185.

21 Iain Sinclair, *Lights Out for the Territory: Nine Excursions in the Secret History of London* (London: Granta, 1997), p. 9.

22 Henri Lefebvre, *Everyday Life in the Modern World*, trans. Sacha Rabinovitch (London: Transaction, 1984), p. 190; see also pp. 3–6, and Lefebvre, *Production of Space*, p. 268.

23 Lefebvre, *Production of Space*, pp. 42, 96, 175; and Lefebvre, *Writings on Cities*, pp. 214–215.

24 Lefebvre, *Writings on Cities*, pp. 16–17, 115.

25 Lefebvre, *Production of Space*, pp. 49–50, 55, 247–248; Henri Lefebvre, *Critique of Everyday Life*, vol. 1; *Introduction*, trans. John Moore (London: Verso, 1991), pp. 37–38, 193; Lefebvre, *Everyday Life in the Modern World*, pp. 148–149, 183, and passim; Lefebvre, *Introduction to Modernity*, pp. 152–161, 187, 195, 384–386; Lefebvre, *Survival of Capitalism*, pp. 23, 35, 106–107, 115–116, 162–163; Henri Lefebvre, *The Explosion: Marxism and the French Revolution*, trans. Alfred Ehrenfeld (New York: Monthly Review, 1969), p. 26; Lefebvre, *Writings on Cities*, pp. 140, 157; and Henri Lefebvre, *Le manifeste différentialiste* (Paris: Gallimard, 1970), summarized in Eleonore Kofman and Elizabeth Lebas, "Lost in Transposition," in *Writings on Cities*, by Lefebvre, pp. 26–27.

26 Lefebvre, *Production of Space*, pp. 39–40, 203, 372–373, 407.

27 Lefebvre, *Production of Space*, pp. 61, 174, 183, 197–200, 309–313, 391; and Lefebvre, *Everyday Life in the Modern World*, pp. 112–113.

28 See Derek Gregory, "Lacan and Geography: The Production of Space Revisited," in *Space and Social Theory: Interpreting Modernity and Postmodernity*, ed. Georges Benko and Ulf Strohmeyer (Oxford: Blackwell, 1997), pp. 203–231; Steve Pile, *The Body and the City: Psychoanalysis, Space, and Subjectivity* (London: Routledge, 1996), pp. 145–169, 211–217; and Virginia Blum and Heidi Nast, "Where's the Difference? The Heterosexualization of Alterity in Henri Lefebvre and Jacques Lacan," *Environment and Planning D: Society and Space* 14 (1996): 559–580.

29 Hélène Cixous, "The Laugh of the Medusa," trans. Keith Cohen and Paula Cohen in *New French Feminisms: An Anthology*, ed. Elaine Marks and Isabelle de Courtivron (London: Harvester, 1981), pp. 245–264; and Luce Irigaray, "When Our Lips Speak Together," in *This Sex Which Is Not One*, trans. Catherine Porter (Ithaca: Cornell University Press, 1985), pp. 205–218.

30 On the dominance of the visual, and sexuality, see Jacqueline Rose, *Sexuality in the Field of Vision* (London: Verso, 1986).

31 Raymond Geuss, *The Idea of a Critical Theory: Habermas and the Frankfurt School* (Cambridge: Cambridge University Press, 1981), pp. 4–44.

32 Michel Foucault, *The Order of Things: An Archaeology of the Human Sciences* (London: Routledge, 1989).

33 Liz Bondi and Mona Domosh, "Other Figures in the Other Places: On Feminism, Postmodernism, and Geography," *Environment and Planning D: Space and Society* 10 (1992): 199–213.

34 Jane Flax, *Thinking Fragments: Psychoanalysis, Feminism and Postmodernism in the Contemporary West* (Berkeley: University of California Press, 1991); Elspeth Probyn, "Travels in the Postmodern: Making Sense of the Local," in *Feminism/Postmodernism*, ed. Linda Nicholson (London: Routledge, 1990), pp. 176–189; and bell hooks, *Yearnings: Race, Gender, and Cultural Politics* (London: Turnaround Press, 1989).

35   See Rose, "Progress in Geography and Gender," pp. 531–537; Elizabeth Grosz, "Women, Chora, Dwelling," *ANY*, no. 4 (January/February 1994): 22–27.

36   Lefebvre, *Everyday Life in the Modern World*, p. 204.

37   Sadie Plant, *The Most Radical Gesture: The Situationist International in a Postmodern Age* (London: Routledge, 1992), p. 58.

38   Hélène Cixous, *The Book of Promethea*, trans. Betsy Wing (Lincoln: University of Nebraska Press, 1991), p. 6.

39   Lefebvre, *Production of Space*, p. 70; Henri Lefebvre, "Toward a Leftist Cultural Politics: Remarks Occasioned by the Centenary of Marx's Death," in *Marxism and the Interpretation of Culture*, ed. Cary Nelson and Lawrence Grossberg (London: Macmillan, 1988), p. 83; Lefebvre, *Writings on Cities*, pp. 173, 222–223; and Lefebvre, *Introduction to Modernity*, pp. 175, 279.

40   Lefebvre, *Writings on Cities*, p. 167.

41   Lefebvre, *Production of Space*, pp. 341, 356; Lefebvre, *Explosion*, p. 120; Lefebvre, *Everyday Life in the Modern World*, p. 204; Lefebvre, *Introduction to Modernity*, p. 93; and Lefebvre, *Writings on Cities*, pp. 66, 167–168.

42   Lefebvre, *Writings on Cities*, p. 143.

43   Lefebvre, *Production of Space*, pp. 138–139, 365, 391; Lefebvre, *Everyday Life in the Modern World*, pp. 177, 182–183; Lefebvre, *Explosion*, pp. 68, 110; Lefebvre, *Critique of Everyday Life*, p. 72; and Benno Werlen, *Society, Action and Space: An Alternative Human Geography*, trans. Gayna Walls, ed. Teresa Brennan and Benno Werlen (London: Routledge, 1993), p. 4.

44   Lefebvre, *Production of Space*, p. 320.

45   Ibid., pp. 362, 381.

46   Lefebvre, *Writings on Cities*, p. 188.

47   Michel de Certeau, *The Practice of Everyday Life*, trans. Steven F. Rendall (Berkeley: University of California Press, 1984), p. 94.

48   Sinclair, *Lights Out for the Territory*, p. 4.

49   Lefebvre, *Production of Space*, pp. 64–65, 222, 235; Henri Lefebvre, "Reflections on the Politics of Space," *Antipode* 8 no. 2 (1976): 34; Lefebvre, *Survival of Capitalism*, p. 16; and Lefebvre, *Writings on Cities*, pp. 75, 101, 131, 193–194.

50   Iain Borden, Joe Kerr, Alicia Pivaro, and Jane Rendell, introduction to *Strangely Familiar: Narratives of Architecture in the City*, ed. Borden, Kerr, Pivaro, and Rendell (London: Routledge, 1996), p. 9.

Part I

Filters

*Things must be twice-told
in order to be safely redeemed
from time and decay.*

Guido Fink
"From Showing to Telling: Off-Screen
Narration in the American Cinema"

M. Christine Boyer

2

Twice-Told Stories: The Double Erasure
of Times Square

2.1 | "Clean as a whistle." The BID cleans up New Times Square.

2.2 | (detail, next page)

In the late 1990s, Manhattan shows signs of suffering from a series of "Disneyfications" and theme park simulations. Times Square/42nd Street, for example, the meeting of two triangles that form an **X** at 42nd Street, was once the popular entertainment district of vaudeville and the Broadway theater. This rowdy playground has been the central public place where New Yorkers have celebrated New Year's Eve since the early twentieth century. Frequented by thousands of daily commuters who arrive via its labyrinthian subway system, Times Square/42nd Street has been rendered by Disney and turned into a wax museum with the likes of Madame Tussaud's. It is regulated by guidelines that call for a requisite number of *Lutses* (light units in Times Square) and controlled by urban designers who have planned its spontaneous unplannedness. Times Square/42nd Street has become Disney's "New York Land." Patrolled by private policemen, its garbage picked up by private collectors, and its signage refurbished by private allocations—under the general guidelines set down by its Business Investment District (BID)—it is as clean and pure as a whistle.

How has this happened to such an iconic place of popular culture? Will Times Square/42nd Street survive, its competitive chaos and tough-guy allure holding out against the latest onslaught of improvement

schemes? Or has a grand mistake been made, and has this dysfunction junction been mauled by disimprovement policies amending its authentic nature instead of addressing its corruption? Has Times Square/42nd Street become another "non-place" instantly recognizable from the images that circulate on television and cinema screens, but a space that is never experienced directly?[1] Is it in danger of extinction or disappearance, reduced to "any-space-whatever"? Gilles Deleuze claims that "any-space-whatever is not an abstract universal, in all times, in all places. It is a perfectly singular space, which has merely lost its homogeneity, that is, the principle of its metric relations or the connections of its own parts, so that the linkages can be made in an infinite number of ways. It is a space of virtual conjunction, grasped as pure locus of the possible."[2] Certainly, Times Square/42nd Street appears to be a postmodern any-space-whatever—a heterotopic space juxtaposing in a single real place several types of spaces. This open-ended disjunctive set of sites coexists simultaneously as a retro-theater district, a media center, a Disneyland, a suburban-style shopping mall, an advertising zone, a corporate office park, a movie but also a song, a novel, a play, a street, and a way of life—a place where prostitutes, pimps, hucksters, or teenagers rub shoulders with out-of-town conventioneers, theater audiences, corporate executive secretaries, tourists, and families. Can it also be a center for the visual arts, a place of emerging electronic industries, a truly plugged-in space connected to the rest of the world?

Even the "Great White Way," the razzle-dazzle electronic wizardry of great neon signs that have turned the night lights of Time Square into a midtown Coney Island since the mid-1920s, has been tampered with by requiring that neon signage now adorn every new structure. Lutses have been turned loose in the square—a 1987 ordinance mandates the amount of illuminated signage and the degree of brilliance that new buildings *must* carry. The first luts appeared on the giant juke box exterior of the Holiday Inn Crowned Plaza Hotel at Broadway and 48th street in 1989. The city wants these new signs to be as flashy as possible, and advertising is clearly allowed, hoping to cover over the fact that Times Square has become a dull and dark canyon of overlarge skyscraper office towers, the unintended result of zoning bonuses that operated in the territory around the square between 1982 and 1987.

Artkraft Strauss Sign Corporation has kept the competitive glow of Times Square alive since the first animated ball dropped in 1908. It has been responsible for the famous Camel ad that belched rings of smoke into the square, the moving-headline "zipper" around the Times Square Tower created in 1928, and even the Fuji Film panel on 43rd Street. Artkraft has put up about 99 percent of the signage in the square—more than 200 miles of neon. It has designed the new fast-paced triple zipper on the Morgan Stanley building on Broadway between 47th and 48th Streets, which tells the spectator the latest financial data and stock quotes.[3] There is plenty of new signage to be seen in the square: Eight O' Clock's steaming coffee mug, Calvin Klein's computer-colored vinyl billboard, 55 tons of fiber optics on the scrolling ticker of the Coca-Cola sign. In fact, Times Square is now so bright at night that not only can you see its glow from lower Manhattan, but a new ball was required for New Year's Eve in 1995 because the old one no longer stood out in the blaze of lights.[4] But a cry has been heard on the Internet that this traditional media center is losing its vitality and will never survive the electronic media revolution.[5] It is feared that Times Square/42nd Street, register of the cultural pulse, is doomed to become a ghetto of quaint neon signage and saccharine musicals like *Cats* or *Beauty and the Beast*, for the operative word on the square is nostalgia—or staged chaos—not reconceptualizing the future. Instead of retro signage, Times Square needs a dozen fast-paced flex-face billboards that change every thirty seconds. And it should become a space incubating the new electronic arts rather than providing yet more shopping and fun as proposed.

All of these so-called improvements took place in the early 1990s under the watchful eyes of the self-proclaimed "three witches" who kept an eye on "the gestalt of Times Square": that brew of the "electric, vital, colorful and sort of in your face, a certain aesthetic chaos." Cora Cahan was president of the New 42nd Street, a nonprofit organization responsible for

2.3 | *Luts* time: the Triple Zipper, Morgan Stanley building.

restoring the eight outmoded theaters on the block between Seventh and Eighth Avenues; Rebecca Robertson headed the 42nd Street Development Project, the state agency in charge of redevelopment along 42nd Street; and Gretchen Dykstrat was president of the Times Square BID established in 1992, which has $6 million in annual assessments to spend.[6] But will all this improvement activity salvage the trashy, glitzy, raffish quality of the underbelly of life that once defined Times Square? Or is that desire only blatant nostalgia, what Gretchen Dykstra calls "romanticizing the gutter"?[7]

As the 1933 movie musical proclaimed, *42nd Street* was a "naughty, bawdy, gaudy, sporty" place already well in decline when it lent its iconic title to the film that opened at the Strand Theater, five blocks away.[8] Even so, 42nd Street was still the most intensely imagined yet glamorous street in the world—it was the hub of the entire theater world for thousands who dreamed of becoming an actor or dancer. "That little thoroughfare," in "the heart of old New York," invites the spectator to "come and meet those dancing feet"; and as the heroine begins her tap routine, the chorus line—in one of Busby Berkeley's great production numbers—turns its back and mounts the stairs, enabling the spectators to see the animated image of the New York skyline. While the buildings sway, the chorus line begins to exit along the prone body of the Empire State Building. The movie had the lean, hungry, underlit look of gangster films of the same era—a "hardboiled Musical," as Hollywood called it[9]—for it had a social message that spoke to the times. The spectacle of *42nd Street*, the act of putting on a play, or a show within a show, is largely about securing a job in the theater. In fact, the movie was called the "Times Square of the assembly line."[10] The narrative on which the movie was based emphasizes that "the machine could not pause to brook over the destinies of the human beings that are caught up in its motion. Machines are impersonal things not given to introspect and retrospect. All that driving force was pounding relentless toward one goal—a successful premier on Forty-Second Street."[11] The film parodies Siegfried Kracauer's 1927 comments on the Tiller Girls:

> Not only were they American products; at the same time they demonstrated the greatness of American production. . . . When they formed an undulating snake, they radiantly illustrated the virtues of the conveyor belt; when they tapped their feet in fast tempo, it sounded like *business, business*; when they kicked their legs high with mathematical precision, they joyously affirmed the progress of rationalization; and when they kept repeating the same movements without ever interrupting their routine, one envisioned an uninterrupted chain of autos gliding from the factories of the world, and believed that the blessings of prosperity had no end.[12]

The movie captured the ethos of the Depression years. Its opening coincided with the inauguration of Franklin D. Roosevelt as president; opportunistically, Warner Brothers advertised the film with the slogan "Inaugurating a New Deal in Entertainment."[13] Upon taking office Roosevelt said, "If I have read the temper of our people correctly, we now realize as we have never realized before our interdependence. . . . If we are to go forward, we must move as a trained and loyal army willing to sacrifice for the good of a common discipline."[14] Cooperation was the new deal, and Peggy Sawyer, the heroine of the movie, embodies this new sense: she works hard, resists temptation, and gets her break, but she does so as a cog in a vast machine, cooperatively following orders.

Commenting on Americanism and Fordism in the 1920s and 1930s, Gramsci noted that

> American industrialists are concerned to maintain the continuity of the physical and muscular-nervous efficiency of the worker. It is in their interests to have a stable skilled labor force, a permanently well-adjusted complex, because the human complex (the collective worker) of an enterprise is also a machine which cannot, without considerable loss, be taken to pieces too often and renewed with single new parts.[15]

The New Deal in Entertainment was a lullaby on Broadway, a dreamworld of escape from the repetitions and fragmentations of the conveyor belt and the assembly line. Sergei Eisenstein noted the same mechanism of escape in the animated cartoons of Disney in the 1930s, labeling them compensation for the suffering and the unfortunate whose lives were graphed by the cent and the dollar and divided up into squares:

> Grey squares of city blocks. Grey prison cells of city streets. Grey faces of endless street crowds. The grey, empty eyes of those who are forever at the mercy of a pitiless procession of laws, not of their own making, laws that divide up the soul, feelings, thoughts, just as the carcasses of pigs are dismembered by the conveyor belts of Chicago slaughter houses, and the separate pieces of cars are assembled into mechanical organisms by Ford's conveyor belts.[16]

But now, as the global economy shifts and turns, information or data processing has replaced the production of goods; the computer stands in for the machine; and leisure time, not work time, is on the rise. Thus Americanism has turned into consumerism, transforming the landscape of cities into new *imagescapes* for the display of commodities, while leisure time has been utilized to stitch the worker into a commodified network of pleasurable and innocent entertainments. Long ago, Walter Benjamin noted that architecture was always consumed by the collectivity in a state of distraction; all acts of forgetting take the form of distractions, never allowing the essence of a thing to penetrate perception. Thus it should be no surprise that Times Square/42nd Street is the latest urban territory to be shaped by global capitalism, or that it substitutes signs of the real for the real.[17] Distracted, we forget what role architecture in the city once might have held.

Since the decline of legitimate theater along 42nd Street—or "the Deuce," as the block of 42nd Street braced by Times Square and Eighth Avenue is called—Times Square/42nd Street has watched pornography and a sordid undercurrent of crime and prostitution take over its terrain. The last legitimate stage production on 42nd Street closed in 1937, and most of that street's theaters became movie houses shortly after the Brandt Organization bought them in 1933. Of the thirteen fabled theaters that once adorned 42nd Street—all built between 1899 and 1920—only five survive. After 1982, when John Portman's fifty-story Marriott Marquis Hotel was built, the city has waged a war to "clean up" the area. But Times Square has always had its burlesque shows and its fleapit paradises; and it has also had other improvement crusaders, vice squads, and prohibitions. So why do its improvers continue to tell tall tales of the decline, danger, and sordidness of Times Square and its need for redevelopment? Why erase this popular goodtime place from the city's collective memory?

No other American place stands more prominent than Times Square as a monument to raucous commercial enterprise. After two decades of debate, this famous space has been placed in a state of suspension; only time will tell whether it has been weakened beyond repair or been given a new lease on life. Will the city be strong enough to override these disimprovements and invade the square's sanitized domain? Even though the city promised the developers of the four major towers known as Times Square Center—designed several times by Philip Johnson and John Burgee in the early 1980s—unbelievably large tax abatements in return for their land costs (abatements that may have extended as long as fifty years),[18] in 1992 the controversial project was postponed until the twenty-first century, when the real estate market was expected to have regained its full strength. Meantime, the public and architects have been given time to rethink the importance of Times Square, as the crossroads where consumers and producers of popular culture inevitably meet.

Of course, it is still an open debate whether 42nd Street—or the Deuce—was either as seamy, honkytonk, and full of sleazy characters or as grim and eerie a reminder of its old vaudeville glitter and theatrical bustle as some accounts insist. Rebecca Robertson believes "that 42nd Street is a

2.4 | The cancer of recovery: Times Square vice.

street that means New York to a lot of people, but for many years what 42nd Street has meant is six to seven crimes a day. . . . It's meant child prostitution. It sometimes seems to me the people who sentimentalize it are up in their houses in northern Connecticut."[19] Even many of the legitimate businesses, the development corporation claimed, were no better than stash houses for drug dealers or manufacturers of false identification cards. The street was seen as a cancer preventing Times Square's recovery; and as long as dozens of private owners controlled the street, Robertson contended, there was no chance for revitalization.[20] The *New York Times* architectural critic Herbert Muschamp pointed out that

> the goal of the $20 million plan [of "42nd Street Now!" was] . . . not so much to overhaul the street physically as to reconstruct people's perception of it. . . . A lot of time, money and public relations have gone into constructing the image of 42nd Street as a squalid corridor of horrors that can only be redeemed by ripping it apart. The image is not unconnected to reality. The decay, crime, drugs, pornography and prostitution are real, and no one thinks that these are civic assets. Still, even in its most blighted state the street continued to draw people who came to enjoy the bright lights, crowds and budget movie tickets. And it has never been clear that real estate development is the ideal deterrent to squalor or crime.[21]

We could claim that New York City real estate values, and the midtown zoning district that operated between 1982 and 1987 and allowed taller and bulkier skyscrapers from Time Square to Columbus Circle along the Broadway spine, killed Times Square and turned it into a corporate office park. Or we could stress that in competing with the Wall Street area in lower Manhattan, Times Square was favored as a new office park because it lies near the city's most densely populated mass transit hub, close to commuter rail lines at Grand Central Station and Penn Station. And of course the city's economic development policies have pushed family-style entertainment for the masses as a tourist incentive and have demanded that the gutter sordidness and notorious vice of Times Square be erased by relocating sex to safety zones on the periphery of the city. Since this rezoning went into effect in November 1996, Times Square together with its architecture of ludic pleasures has been considerably diminished. It will keep, for the sake of nostalgia, six to ten of its original porn shops—but more than ten evidently would tip the scales and produce repugnant secondary effects such as crime, drugs, and declining real estate values.

NARRATING THE STORY OF DISAPPEARANCE

Real estate values alone do not explain why a void exists in Times Square that allows its improvers to tell tall tales about crime, prostitution, drugs, and illicit businesses. Perhaps, instead, the role this public space has held in the popular memory of the city needs to be examined, for we will find that two gaps have occurred—one in the late 1940s and another in contemporary times—facilitating the telling of twice-told tales. These ruptures enable a distinction to be made between realistic representation and simulated effects. And this distinction, in turn, engenders a twice-told story that lingers nostalgically over the memory of Times Square, attended by those who would keep it from change and destruction.

Deleuze argues that "any-space-whatevers" began to proliferate after World War II—they were demolished or reconstructed towns, places of undifferentiated tissue, or underutilized and fallow lands such as docklands, warehouses, or dumps.[22] Represented in film, these any-space-whatevers became spiritual spaces: an amorphous set that eliminated what had happened and acted in it, a nontotalizable space full of shadows and deep black holes.[23] They were pessimistic sites, offering no promise of comfort or retreat. Times Square as a vortex of negation and indeterminacy was a quintessential any-space-whatever.

In postwar America, when the first memory gap occurred and the first story was told, central places such as Times Square were beginning to be threatened with disappearance. Seldom experienced directly, these places were retreating into abstraction. As a result, Times Square and other important places of the city were reduced to representational images that could stand in for places no longer explored by pedestrians or remembered from the details of direct encounters. This was a way of memorializing their loss without relying on nostalgic reenactments. A certain degree of command and control over these unknown terrains could be effected, however, by narrating a series of technical facts and enumerating their characteristics. The detective story and the police narrative are two such devices that can be used to focus on, underline, point out, and re-member parts of the city that have been covered over by mysterious events.

Edward Dimendberg argues in "Film Noir and Urban Space" that the dominant visual trope of the genre of detective films known as film noir is the material deformation and visual dematerialization of a city that once held a physical center or series of experienced urban spaces. These had been known to the pedestrian through numerous strolls and routines, or through representational stereotypes such as gridded street patterns, skyscraper skylines, public parks, and landmarks. Abandoned for the suburbs, fragmented by urban renewal, and tormented by the automobile, the postwar American city was a place of discomfort and disorientation, a space that was increasingly unknown to the spectator. The dark city of film noir not only played on this experience of loss and anxiety but also offered a set of mapping procedures, synoptic views, and other communicating devices that presented an imaginary centered and legible city, thereby enabling the spectator to "cognitively map" or gain control over a place that was no longer experienced directly.[24]

Kevin Lynch uses the term "cognitive map" in *The Image of the City* to explore how mental images not only affect a spectator's sense of identity, well-being, and belonging to a particular city but also make the city memorable or imageable.[25] A good city form would have readable or identifiable nodes, paths, edges, districts, and landmarks. Such readable symbols form a cognitive map orienting spectators in space and time. Fredric Jameson argues that this cognitive framework enables a spectator to project an imaginary image of the total city, even when its image may appear broken in bits. The spectator is able subsequently to gain a sense of place and to construct a composed ensemble that, retained in memory, can be used to map and remap the city along flexible and changing trajectories.[26] In postwar cities, however, the relationship between the spectator's perception of the physical structure of the city had been shattered and a cognitive map could no longer be based on direct experience. Some other mediating device had to render the city readable. A cognitive map could be produced, for example, by the realistic images of cities depicted in films and photographs.

The semidocumentary film *The Naked City* (1947), directed by Jules Dassein, provides an excellent example of such an instrument to cognitively map the city. Not only is this the first crime film to use location shooting but it created remarkable verisimilitude by presenting the 107 streets, places, and landmarks of Manhattan as its feature attraction. Evidently the cameraman, Bebe Daniels, learned from Erich von Stroheim that "reality lays itself bare like a suspect confessing under the relentless examination of the commissioner of police."[27] And so this narrated story attempts to represent the city in the raw, with naked and objective images and facts: a city of steel and stone, of buildings and pavements, of thousands of stories and everyday events. Through enumeration of such places and incidents, the film tried to save at least the memory of the city from disappearing.[28]

In addition, the film's use of voice-over is unusual. By borrowing the authority that documentaries try to assume, the voice-over both enhances the story's factual base and elevates its realistic narration of the methodology of crime detection.[29] The voice-over annotates the development of the police case and ties together the 107 different locations filmed in the streets and buildings of New York City.[30] It maps out a city that once might have been well known by the audience—or that used to mean something to the everyday life of the viewer—but now required a guide to link together its landmarks and places.[31] The *American Cinematographer* noted that "several buildings of the city were photographed for the last time, having since been demolished to make room for the United Nations Buildings."[32] Interiors were shot in the Roxy Theater, offices of the Mirror newspapers, Stillman's Gym—none of which survived beyond 1947. In addition, the Third Avenue El at 59th Street was gone, as was Livingston's Dress Shop on 57th Street.[33] From the movie's beginning, viewers are presented with a bird's-eye view of the city, stretched out below in the hazy distance, waiting for inspection—not unlike "a patient etherised on a table."[34] This is a truthful story, the Naked City whose facts will be exposed, whose crimes will be revealed. And it is voice-over narration, a streetwise voice, that takes this information—raw data, overheard conversations, telephone messages—and composes it into an invisible labyrinth that must be penetrated by the detective. "[Voice-over] is the oral map-making of [the detective's] journey through the labyrinth," an analyst of film noir points out.[35]

There are several layers to the voice-over narration of *The Naked City* that help establish a cognitive map for the spectator and remind the audience that there are "eight million stories in the Naked City and this is just one of them."[36] The narrator, Mark Hellinger, is above all a storyteller who maps out the space of New York while simultaneously directing the flow of narration. His voice-over remarks on the next move, the next action, in syn-

2.5 | *The Naked City* (1947; director Jules Dassein).

chronicity with the visual narrative. At bottom, the voice-over informs the viewer of police routines and offers background information on the characters. It enables the spectator to dip in and out of "representative" New Yorkers' minds as they go about their daily routines. For example, during the opening series of early morning shots we are told that "a city has many faces—it's one o'clock in the morning now—and this is the face of New York City—when it's asleep on a hot summer night,"[37] while the shots themselves, such as a deserted Wall Street, a cat digging into a garbage pan, a tugboat on the Hudson towing two barges, are reminiscent of the exploratory techniques of the Lumière brothers' *Actualities* of the 1890s.[38] Then the narrator withdraws omnisciently to a higher contemplative level—gazing back on the city—from which he weaves together the montage of images and story lines as the camera constantly shifts its visual and narrative focus.[39] Hellinger speaks as the young detective Halloran is staring out a large window that looks out over the city: "There's the layout, Jim. The man who killed Jean Dexter is somewhere down there. Can't blame him for hiding can you?"[40] It is up to this detective to make the connections that solve the mystery, just as he slowly blocks out one street after another street on his sectional map of lower Manhattan, searching step by patient step for the killer's address. The framing of the city as a closed system and the solving of a crime, as the spectator visually progresses alongside the detective through the streets of the city, become important elements of the mise-en-scène.

Voice-over narration functions much as do the film's many images of telephone exchanges and communication devices. The telephone is one of the many invisible networks that tie the city together, that move the story line along. Police telephone switchboards, police radio operators, the detective's office phone, the young detective's home phone, the phone in the subway booth, the older detective's bedroom phone, and the drugstore phone booth are all represented in the film. As the chase closes in, the police headquarters radio operator speaks into the microphone:

> Emergency. . . . All squad cars on the East Side of 14th Street to the Williamsburg Bridge, from 1st Street to 5th Avenue, proceed immediately to Rivington Street between Essex and Delancey. Block off and surround both sides of the street. Institute immediate house-to-house search for . . . two men—Detective James Halloran and William Garza. Halloran is twenty-eight years old.[41]

The film thus actually maps out sections of the city for the spectator, sections that were threatened with urban renewal and blocks that would never survive the bulldozer's rout. The closing shots on the Williamsburg Bridge are among the best in the film. As the murderer finds himself trapped at the top of the structure, the camera moves out from this dangerous and precarious site to provide a sweeping panoramic view of the city below—revealing a city indifferent to the life-and-death concerns of its many inhabitants.[42]

In 1960, Parker Tyler assessed *The Naked City*:

> It is Manhattan Island and its streets and landmarks that are starred. The social body is thus, through architectural symbol, laid bare ("naked") as a neutral fact neither, so to speak, good nor bad, but something which, like the human organism itself, may catch a disease—the criminal—and this disease may elude its detectors. . . . The fact is that the vastly complex structure of a great city, in one sense, is a supreme obstacle to the police detectives at the same time that it provides tiny clues as important as certain obscure physical symptoms are to the trained eye of a doctor.[43]

It was the scriptwriter Malvin Wald's task to break down the essential information of how crooks operate and how police detectives track them down in order to make these procedures intelligible to the spectator, just as it was the cameraman's work to establish shots that follow the detective as he walks through the city, that capture him mapping out block after block on his map. These shots and the skyline panoramas and views out over the city, in addition to the invisible lines of telecommunication, cognitively map the city for the viewer, offering a synoptic view that spatial fragmentation—both the reality of the postwar American city and the filmic process of montage—increasingly rendered impossible.

It should be noted that the title for Hellinger's movie was taken from a 1945 book of photographs titled *Naked City*, by Weegee, the sensational crime photographer.[44] He turned the prying eye of his camera on the bizarre and disorderly life of New York. He recorded the spectacle of its streets: the cruelty and violence of murders, fires, and accidents and the compelling scenes of loneliness, homelessness, and poverty. His sensational snapshot of a car accident captures a policeman's futile gesture toward a paper-covered corpse while a movie marquee just above ironically announces the *Joy of Living*. This street photography sets up a virtual monument to the death of the city—the withdrawal of life, money, and people from communities that were being "killed" by the bulldozer or being wracked by a demeaning capitalist society. The dark photographs of *Naked City* map this death, this twilight of the life of a great city and the blackness that smothers it and cannot be erased.

By the summer of 1957, the Mouvement Internationale pour un Bauhaus Imaginiste (MIBI), one of the precursors of the Situationist International, had reappropriated the title *Naked City* for a map of Paris created by Guy Debord.[45] This map, like its predecessors, underscored a developing crisis in both the construction and perception of contemporary urban form. It consisted of nineteen cutouts from a pocket guide to Paris printed in black ink and linked together with red directional arrows. Each section of the city depicted what Guy Debord called a "unity of atmosphere"—a special place such as the Luxembourg Gardens, Les Halles, the Ledoux Rotunda, or the Gare de Lyon—often a wasteland or an old district, left behind in the wake of modernization, that contained unusual attractions for strollers and encouraged unforeseen encounters. The arrows symbolized the random turns of direction a stroller might take through different "atmospheres," disregarding the normal connections that ordinarily governed his or her conduct. This experimental map represented a system of playful spontaneity, enabling sensitive participants to experience the city's many marvels, to recode and repossess its terrain for themselves.[46]

Thus the map of *The Naked City* becomes a heterotopic narrative of open possibilities, where each follower must choose different paths through the city and overcome the obstacles the city presents. As the film titled *The Naked City* strips Manhattan bare, making its streets and landmarks the stars of the film in the process, so the sectional cutouts are the stars of Paris. If the city of New York offered only tiny clues to the solution of unsolved crimes, then Paris too yielded only tiny indications of a future of new possibilities. And if the film inverted the synoptic view of mapping the city, adding only to its fragmented reality and heightening the threat of dismemberment, then so too Debord's map fragments the experience and perception of the pedestrian who drifts from one selected "unity of atmosphere" to another without knowing either how these juxtaposed sites are connected or how they might present an illusion of the city as a totality. With this self-reflective map, Debord intended to actualize—and thus to make the spectator aware of—the artifice of spatial construction, stressing the city planners' arbitrary creation of spatial districts and their imposition of a false unity on the face of the city. By foregrounding the experience of pedestrians and their attempts to recode the city through random promenades through the city, Debord's map outlines the spatial contradictions that capitalism produces, its false appearances and creations, its erasures and disappearances.[47]

Yet another attempt to provide the spectator with a cognitive map of the troubled terrain of the postwar American city can be found in Stanley Kubrick's film *Killer's Kiss* (1955). Dimendberg points out that Kubrick's cinematic settings such as Times Square and Penn Station are nostalgic landmarks; they remind the spectator of an earlier time, before the automobile came to dominate pedestrian spaces such as Times Square and made the railway station redundant as the major gateway to the city. Unknown to the film director, however, Penn Station, which frames the narrative in opening and closing shots, would be destroyed eight years later. Thus it not only stands as a reminder of the industrial city, but it forecasts the ruination that the modernist city will spread. Throughout the film, Times Square represents a landscape of centrality where events emerge either in memory of its being a site of traditional rituals or in expectation of the deserted center it would soon become. It is a landscape that has the power to reconcile the characters and the spectators to the alienating experience of the metropolis.[48] "In an age of suburbanisation," Dimendberg argues, "the experience of the urban center cannot escape an ambivalent oscillation between attraction and repulsion. And as the physical face of the city slowly loses its traditional landmarks, the psychophysical correspondence we experience in cinema allow us to redeem the urban environment from a non-existence that is increasingly real, rather than virtual."[49]

NARRATING A TWICE-TOLD STORY ABOUT TIMES SQUARE

The first-told story relied on a taste for realistic representation that grew out of a failure of memory caused when the city began to disappear from everyday experience. But now a distinction must be drawn between these 1940s and 1950s realistic representations of urban space and our contemporary representations that display a taste for simulation. We now delight in wax museums, theme parks, retro-architectural splendors, and the suspension of disbelief that allows "planning [to] create the appearance of the unplanned" in the redevelopment of Times Square.[50] In other words, in the contemporary production of spaces such as Times Square, we are given a twice-told story that depends on a second memory gap and creates a different effect. We are no longer searching for photographic realism, for mapping techniques, for documentary rendering of a city that is beginning to disappear from our lived experience and collective memory. Now the technical apparatus that can produce the illusionary reappearance of Times Square or the Great White Way is foregrounded, and the masterful display of this artistry, with all of its theatricality, pretenses, and tricks, itself becomes the show. This reenchanted world depends on the power to simulate, and it distorts the proclaimed purity and objectivity of representative realism.

In order to explore further this twice-told story, I will turn to the late nineteenth century, when simulation as a means of popular entertainment achieved its height. My example is Paris's famous wax museum, the

Musée Grévin. Founded by journalist Arthur Meyer and newspaper carica-turist Alfred Grévin in 1882, the museum was designed to mimic the news-paper, offering a random juxtaposition of tableaux much as newspaper columns presented their readers with a series of unconnected stories.[51] It offered the spectator the novelty of visualizing in precise detail familiar newspaper stories, famous people, and well-known events, at a time when photographs were not easily reproducible and had yet to accompany newspaper reports. These three-dimensional tableaux vivants, along with panoramas, dioramas, magic lantern shows, photographs, and stereoscopic views, offered the nineteenth-century spectator a new kind of visual realism by utilizing the most advanced technical means.[52] Not only did they faith-fully represent all the details, texture, and look of actual events or things, but they were "mirror[s] with a memory" that reflected events and objects from the past and projected them onto the present.[53] They relied, further-more, on technical means or an apparatus of vision to organize, manage, and produce their effects. As Don Slater argues, it was not representational real-ism but mechanical or instrumental realism that enthralled spectators in the late nineteenth century. They flocked to theatrical spectacles that were pro-duced by mechanical means and thrilled as scenographic appearances were magically transformed by machines and devices. This was one way that Vic-torian society could become accustomed to living with machines and me-chanical processes. Technical accomplishments became the spectacle itself, for at that time "to represent, to know, to transform become not only mu-tually reinforcing but united activities, three forms of appropriation of the material world which both produce and assimilate the modern experience of command and control."[54]

Paradoxically, however, once instruments of realistic vision had de-prived the world of wonder, once too much understanding had destroyed oc-cult and supernatural effects, the nineteenth century then reenchanted this view in theatrical events, visual spectacles, and quasi-magical shows. It sim-ulated the aura of magical effects and the spell of inexplicable processes, simultaneously hiding the apparatus of display and highlighting the technical artifice of re-creation. No matter how great the factual details of realism were, there was always a pressure to move from mere representation and factual understanding to simulation and the demonstration, not expli-cation, of how effective illusions and wonders were produced. On the other side of rational and instrumental control over material reality lay the will-ing suspension of disbelief and the pleasurable immersion in fantastically simulated worlds. Pleasure resided not just in seeing the world duplicated in realistic exactitude—an act demonstrating that one could appropriate that world, could master, map, project, or reconstruct it—but also in being able to simulate that world. Such simulation required an apparatus or technician to create such special effects and to demonstrate the extent of human control over physical reality. Wonder had been transformed from acknowledging the perfection of draughtsmanship or a particular scenographer's theatrical skills, as was admitted in front of a spectacular panorama, to the instrumental ability of mechanical techniques to produce an appearance of reality. Immersed in illusory effects, the spectator lost the sense of being in a constructed world.[55]

The same dynamic seems to be at work in contemporary Times Square, whose simulated arrangements have produced an ontological confusion in which the original story has been forgotten and no longer needs to be told. Simulation, which plays on this shifting of ground, is enhanced when an unstable relation exists between representation and experience. Times Square, by now, is known only through its representations, its sign systems, its iconic cinematic presence; and pleasure is derived from experiencing the illusion of the Great White Way, by marveling at its Lutses, by planning its unplannedness, by foregrounding the apparatus that produces these manipulated representations. Since the need for realistic representation that provides a cognitive map of unknown terrain has declined, the pressure to offer simulation as a twice-told story increases. Now the narra-

2.6 | "42nd Street Now!" Robert A. M. Stern's Theme Park Vision.

tion of stories resides in the combinatorial replay embedded in the codes of a computer memory, in the technical apparatus of simulation, in the regulatory controls of urban design. These devices have become this era's mirrors with a memory.

Consequently, Times Square as a quintessential public space of an American city has been transformed into a simulated theme park for commercial entertainment. Once Robert A. M. Stern was put in charge of the interim plan for "42nd Street Now!" (giving the project a decidedly razzle-dazzle orientation), many hoped that architects would remember that the real star of the show was Times Square—"our most democratic good-time place."[56] Calling for just the right kind of alchemy, the architectural critic of the *New York Times* reminds us that "this Crossroads of the World has long been a symbolic intersection between art and communication. Here, advertising attains the dimension of a cultural monument, while theater sustains intermittent hope that art should aspire to broad popular appeal."[57] It appears, however, that the guiding light behind the 42nd Street revitalization plan is Robert Venturi's 1966 proclamation that "Main Street is almost alright." New Yorkers will be given an opportunity to "learn from 42nd Street" as they once learned from Las Vegas, for the double coding of the new plan—paradoxically based on a principle of unplanning—is a set of design guidelines that extrapolates from the realism of the street's popular and commercial features and returns it to privileged spectators who then can relish the commercial illusion in a sanitized and theatricalized zone. Each of the thirty-four refurbished structures that line the street between Broadway and Eighth Avenue must now be wrapped and layered with spectacular signage—some animated and some lighted, but all legible from a distance, and all with outstanding visual impact. A chart of coordinated colors has been developed; diversity in styles, scales, and materials encouraged; and a melange of restaurant and retail types expected.[58] The *New York Times* architectural critic reports:

> In short the plan is devised to reinforce the street's existing characteristics. The layered accretion of forms over the past century. The mix of styles and scales. The lack of visual coordination. . . . Above all, the street will be unified by the prominence given to signs: video screens, painted billboards, theater marquees, faded murals from the past, LED strips, holograms—an uninterrupted commercial interruption.[59]

This play with popular forms, drawn from America's image-saturated commercial landscape, helps destabilize the position that architecture once held in the city. Architecture no longer determines a city's

2.7 | "Disneyfied" Times Square/42nd St.

unique visual identity but is reduced to nostalgic stereotypes. Borrowing from a ubiquitous series of already determined and ordinary advertisements, signs, and billboards, and even relying on the potential drawing card of Mickey Mouse and Donald Duck, Times Square has been incorporated into a larger sense of assembled space, where all of its simultaneity and immediacy can evaporate into astonishing imagescapes. Here, as the earlier commercial entertainments of the diorama, panorama, and lantern slide shows demonstrated, spectators thrill at the re-creation of the real, wondering at the technical procedures that convincingly transport them into an experience that in fact may never have existed. But now, in contemporary times, designers bring all of their information-processing abilities into play in order to demonstrate the technical and organizational power of planning regulations and design controls that can turn the material form of the city into such an effective illusion. The result is similar to any successful magic show: spectators are doubly thrilled when the illusion is produced by invisible means, when the prosaic world can be reenchanted and disbelief suspended—albeit for a moment.

Notes

1   Marc Augé, *Non-Places: Introduction to an Anthropology of Supermodernity*, trans. John Howe (London: Verso Press, 1995).

2   Gilles Deleuze, *Cinema 1, The Movement-Image*, trans. Hugh Tomlinson and Barbara Habberjam (Minneapolis: University of Minnesota Press, 1986), p. 109. He credits Paul Augé with the term *any-space-whatever*.

3   Thomas J. Lueck "Brighter Lights and Brighter Promises Light Times Square," *New York Times* (hereafter abbreviated *NYT*), 31 December 1995, sec. 13, p. 7.

4   A new Times Square subway entrance at the southeast corner of 42nd Street and Seventh Avenue was planned to have "a glitzy exterior of glass and bright lights and colored discs and strips" (Bruce Lambert, "Times Square Subway Station: Putting a There There," *NYT*, 10 December 1995, sec. 13, p. 6). And the high-tech flashing-neon visual frenzy that is Times Square was used as a model for a new fence, a 164-foot-long artwork displaying thirty-five bright orange faces, forged in coiled steel, from 48th to 46th Streets, the work of Monica Banks (Douglas Martin, "Public Art: A Fence with Faces to Grace Times Sq.," *NYT*, 27 December 1995, B3).

5   Dale Hrabi, "Will the 'New' Times Square Be New Enough?" (dhrabi@aol.com). Downloaded from the Web and faxed to the author on 17 September 1996.

6   Bruce Weber, "In Times Square, Keepers of the Glitz," *NYT*, 25 June 1996, B1, B6.

7   Dykstrat is quoted in ibid.

8   J. Hoberman, *42nd Street* (London: British Film Institute, 1993), p. 9.

9   Quoted in ibid., p. 19.

10   Hoberman, *42nd Street*, p. 9.

11   Rocco Fumento, *42nd Street* (Madison: University of Wisconsin Press, 1980), p. 12.

12   Siegfried Kracauer, "The Mass Ornament" (1927), quoted in Hoberman, *42nd Street*, p. 34.

13   Fumento, *42nd Street*, p. 21.

14   Roosevelt is quoted in Hoberman, *42nd Street*, p. 69.

15   Gramsci is quoted in Jonathan L. Beller, "City of Television," *Polograph* 8 (1996): 133.

16   Sergei Eisenstein, *Eisenstein on Disney*, ed. Jay Leyda, trans. Alan Upchurch (London: Methuen Paperback, 1988), p. 3.

17   As the president of New York City Economic Development Commission put it, "good glitz" or "showboating" has never hurt Times Square; he heralded the 1996 opening in Times Square of a Virgin megastore, the largest record, movie, book and multimedia store on earth (located on Broadway between 45th and 46th Streets). Thomas J. Lueck, "Times Square Heralds Megastore," *NYT*, 24 April 1996, B2.

18   Thomas J. Lueck, "Financing for Times Square Leads to Harsher Criticism," *NYT*, 28 July 1994, B3.

19   Robertson is quoted in James Bennet, "Taking the Deuce," *NYT*, 9 August 1992, p. 44.

20   David Dunlop, "Times Square Plan Is on Hold, But Meter Is Still Running," *NYT*, 9 August 1992, p. 44.

21   Herbert Muschamp, "42nd Street Plan: Be Bold or Begone!" *NYT*, 19 September 1993, sec. 2, p. 33.

22   Gilles Deleuze, *Cinema 2, The Time-Image*, trans. Hugh Tomlinson and Robert Galeta (Minneapolis: University of Minnesota Press, 1989), p. xi.

23   Deleuze, *Cinema 1*, p. 111.

24   Edward Dimendberg, "Film Noir and Urban Space" (Ph.D. diss., University of California, Santa Cruz, 1992).

25   Kevin Lynch, *The Image of the City* (Cambridge, Mass.: MIT Press, 1960).

26   Fredric Jameson, *Postmodernism, or, The Cultural Logic of Late Capitalism* (Durham: Duke University Press, 1991), pp. 51–52, 415–417.

27   Carl Richardson, *Autopsy: An Element of Realism in Film Noir* (Metuchen, N.J.: Scarecrow Press, 1992), p. 94.

28   Ibid., p. 108.

29 Voice-over enables the audience to hear someone, although never seen on the screen, narrating a story. The voice comes from another time and space than that of the film; as an overlay, it can comment and draw together parts of the story. Sarah Kozloff, *Invisible Storytellers: Voice-Over Narration in American Fiction Film* (Berkeley: University of California Press, 1988), pp. 2–3, 82.

30 Added during postproduction, voice-over allows the filmmaker to include important exteriors or scenes shot in the noisy streets of New York without the background interference. See Kozloff, *Invisible Storytellers*, p. 22.

31 For comments on location shooting, see Malvin Wald, "Afterword: The Anatomy of a Hit," in *The Naked City: A Screenplay by Malvin Wald and Albert Maltz*, ed. Matthew J. Bruccoli (Carbondale: Southern Illinois University Press, 1949), pp. 137, 144.

32 Quoted in Richardson, *Autopsy*, p. 90.

33 Ibid., pp. 89–91.

34 Ibid., p. 88.

35 Nicholas Christopher, *Somewhere in the Night: Film Noir and the American City* (New York: Free Press, 1997), p. 9.

36 Wald, "Afterword," p. 140.

37 Wald and Maltz, *The Naked City*, p. 3.

38 Richardson, *Autopsy*, pp. 4–5.

39 Sarah Kozloff observes, "by the film's end, we have a very clear sense of the narrator's personality—his self-aggrandizement, his cynicism, his sentimentality, his devotion to The City and its inhabitants. This narrator combines both authority and the voice of one man, part lecturer, part tour-guide, part barside raconteur." See *Invisible Storytellers*, pp. 86–96; quotation, p. 96.

40 Wald and Maltz, *The Naked City*, p. 31.

41 Ibid., pp. 126–127.

42 Richardson, *Autopsy*, p. 93.

43 Parker Tyler, *The Three Faces of the Film* (1960), quoted by Wald, "Afterword," p. 148.

44 Hellinger bought the rights to the title for a thousand dollars. See Wald, "Afterword," p. 144.

45 Thomas McDonough, "Situationist Space," *October* 67 (winter 1994): 61, and Simon Sadler, *The Situationist City* (Cambridge, Mass.: MIT Press, 1998), p. 60.

46 McDonough, "Situationist Space," pp. 62–66.

47 Ibid., p. 75.

48 Dimendberg, "Film Noir and Urban Space," pp. 143, 154, 160.

49 Ibid., p. 162.

50 This latter is the intention specified in the planning report for Times Square, produced by Robert A. M. Stern and M & Co., "42nd Street Now! A Plan for the Interim Development of 42nd Street," in *Executive Summary* (New York: 42nd Street Development Project, New York State Urban Development Corporation, New York City Economic Development Corporation, 1993).

51 Vanessa R. Schwartz, "Cinematic Spectatorship before the Apparatus," in *Viewing Positions: Ways of Seeing Film*, ed. Linda Williams (New Brunswick, N.J.: Rutgers University Press, 1994), pp. 94–105.

52 The following account draws a distinction between representation and simulation. It closely follows the work of Don Slater, "Photography and Modern Vision: The Spectacle of 'Natural Magic,'" in *Visual Culture*, ed. Chris Jenks (London: Routledge, 1995), pp. 218–237.

53 This phrase was used by Oliver Wendall Holmes to describe the daguerreotype in 1859. Quoted by Slater, "Photography and Modern Vision," p. 218.

54 Ibid., p. 222.

55 Ibid., pp. 218–237.

56 Stern and M & Co., "42nd Street Now!" p. 2.

57 Herbert Muschamp, "The Alchemy Needed to Rethink Times Square," *NYT*, 30 August 1992, sec. 2, p. 24.

58 Stern and M & Co., "42nd Street Now!"

59 Muschamp, "42nd Street Plan," p. 33.

Barry Curtis

3

That Place Where: Some Thoughts on
Memory and the City

3.1 | Joseph Heinz il Giovane, *Capriccio.*

Place is the product of a relationship—part subjective projection, part internalization of an external reality. It is also distinct from a spatial continuum. Among the evaluative mechanisms that discriminate place from space is memory; correspondingly, amnesia is an operation which reverses that process and dissolves place back into the indifference of space. In this chapter I explore some of the determinations of place.

Any architectural act seeks to establish a place through a process of enclosure and metaphoric association, but the role of the consumer has been progressively advanced in constituting significance. Certainly since the 1960s, the idiosyncrasy of place has become firmly established in writings on urbanism. The imposition of meaning has been allowed to be idiomatic and subjective; at the same time, meanings have increasingly been acknowledged as belonging to different interest groups.

As a result, processes of planning that seek to create meaningful conjunctions and memorable epiphanies for an undifferentiated public have been exposed as fragile and perspectival. The modernist projects, which proposed making urban forms ephemeral and responsive to change while implying that technology could be definitively represented in timeless and Purist styles, have been put in doubt. Interest has been renewed in the past, the provisional, the symbolic, the deferred—and in various local and ecological solutions.

The article I contributed to the *Strangely Familiar* catalogue was about Venice and a recent proposal to modernize it by building a metro system.[1] I was interested in the perpetual plight of that city, because for me it clearly exemplifies how meanings can both persist and be subject to the relativism of constant historical rearticulation. Venice, as well as being a potent memory theater, also engaged me in the pleasurable experience of tourism—surrender, visiting and belonging, and participation in the "Venetian" game of masking and revealing. Georg Simmel's observation that "Venice presents dualities that cannot be resolved into a synthesis"[2] gestures toward the more general undecidability of urban experience.

The paradoxical nature of Venice has been firmly established by innumerable admirers and detractors. It has been acknowledged as a universal city—the sort of paradigmatic text deployed by Italo Calvino—but it is also a bizarrely retarded supplement to the development of cities up to the industrial age. It can be refigured as everlasting and perpetually "in peril," as a pedestrian precinct par excellence, as a city of aged inhabitants, as an ecological conundrum, as a heritage city, as an international cultural center, as a city of carnival and hedonism, and even as an attraction for a modern telecommunications infrastructure.[3] It is both a freak and an archetype. What interests me most here is that it is a paradigmatic "place."

That Venice is primarily conceived as a paradox spurs us to further considerations on the nature of cities, the relationship between past and present, nature and culture, the ceremonial and the everyday, the appearance and the reality. The exceptional status of Venice is that of a city supposedly arrested and preserved in time. This "timelessness" has enabled memory to work on it in a number of ways as a memory of the "first home" and as a memory preserved by the nature of the changes enacted on the memorial city. The various mythic understandings of the city have come to constitute its meaning in ways that are more fundamental than those deployed to reconstruct cities that have been adaptive to change. Venice is not layered; it cannot be analogized like Pompeii, as corresponding to the levels of consciousness; it is built on artificial foundations. Something of its unique nature is captured in Simmel's cryptic description of it as "a perfect mask that hides being, or rather reveals the loss or absence of being."[4]

Venice as a densely produced "place" generates a kind of ideal in its intensity and condensation, not just as an urban form but as a labyrinth, maze, or trap: "a ritual circulation" in which confrontations with others and self are produced. As Jean Baudrillard has also said, "there is no side exit in Venice."[5] The city in addition represents the inexhaustibility of place. As early as 1494, Canon Pietro Casola expressed a perception that has been repeated down the centuries and is echoed in every current guide book: "So much has been said, there appears to be nothing more to be said."[6] But the very fixity of Venice has enabled it to be perpetually recast as a world city, a meeting place between East and West, a city of surveillance, an inspirational megastructure, and a model for cities of ritual and democratic participation. Adrian Stokes, in his linking of the peculiar architecture of Venice and the ways in which dream and memory are capable of reconfiguring significance, finds a profound paradox: "So deeply laid are the imaginative foundations of Venice, to such an extent has stone abrogated the meaning of soil in our minds, that decay, as we have seen, takes the form of metamorphosis and even of renewal."[7] It is a model of the unknown and unknowable city, endlessly put into classifications yet still capable of entering into new relationships and meanings.

It is not surprising that Venice and other urban fragments that were not heavily marked by the requirements of industrialization and modernism should now be appropriable as models of place sharing what David Harvey has defined as the dominant concerns of the postindustrial city. He conceives that city as beyond the paradigms of function and organism, as a lost plenitude and operatic scene—"the projection of a definite image of place blessed with certain qualities, the organisation of spectacle and theatricality, achieved through an eclectic mixture of styles, historical quotation, ornamentation and diversification of surfaces."[8]

3.2 | Sites of bombs dropped by Austrian aircraft during the Great War.

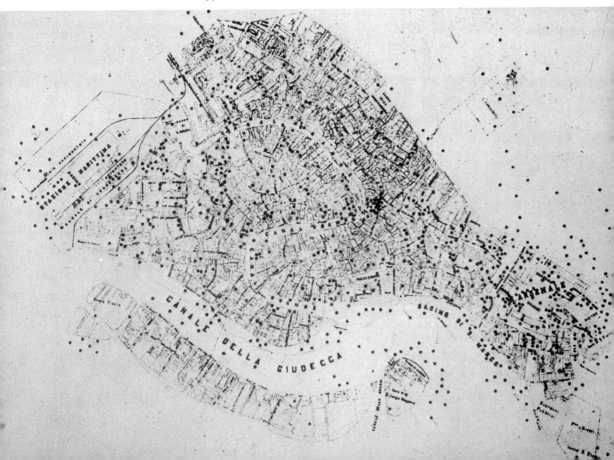

3.3 | Proposed rail route into the center of Venice.

As most guidebooks point out, experiencing Venice involves a process of aimless circulating, surrendering to complexity, and experiencing sudden encounters. On at least two occasions it has been the site of formal *dérives* (conducted by Ralph Rumney and Sophie Calle), but most visitors enjoy a self-conscious experience of pragmatic reverie, which numerous writings about walking in the city have explored. Venice is an exceptional city, which provides an understanding of the general rules of urban conduct. Patrizia Lombardo believes that "Venice, small and ancient as it is, with no cars, apparently so ideal as a refuge from the hustle and bustle of today's world allows a powerful intuition of modernity."[9]

The literature of cities has explored the relationship between memory and movement. The moving point of view is what makes possible the relation of place to self by way of narrative and parallax. Since the late nineteenth century, records of experiencing the city have tended to deploy a moving or montaged point of view. The city has also been seen as destabilizing static perceptions. Richard Sennett has written persuasively on a decisive shift away from the conceiving of streets as ceremonial approaches to viewing them as fixed objects in a system of circulation that emphasizes the journey and the potential for travel and connection. He links this metaphor of circulation to the emergence of free trade and the literal mobility of people in pursuing it, describing the construction of flexible economic space in cities as "a conjuction of functional use of space and opportunistic use of time."[10]

In considering the claims of place, we must account for the relationship between modes of fixity, with all that these imply for community and residential meaning, and the transitions and connections provided by modernity. Is place more plausibly conceived as habituation, or is it produced from a dialectic of travel and return? Speed of transit and passage have traditionally been considered as inimical to the integrity of place. The argument between conservers and modernizers in the case of Venice has often centered on the issue of transport—the rail link, the road link to Piazzale Roma, the plans for tunnels, bridges, and subways—all conceived as ending forever the distinctive claims of the city as an integrated "place."

Provision for transit has been widely conceived as an enemy of ritual reflection. This is vividly demonstrated by the poignant trope, represented on television news, of marking the sites of urban tragedies at bus stops, curbs, and walls with flowers or childrens' toys: attempts to furnish non-places with meanings appropriate to remembrance. Place has been intimately associated with dwelling, as part of the problem of devising satisfactory urban architecture that can intensify and commodify meaning. The forms of electronic communication being developed at the turn of the millennium constitute the latest mode of transit and association; it remains to be seen if their impact will reinforce "placelessness" or stimulate a recognition of place's importance.

Modernism, in seeking an aesthetic and ethical transformation of ways of living, neglected in its polemics the historical claims relating to the importance of place. Modernist architecture and planning maintained a dialectic between eliminating place in favor of continuum while at the same time seeking to understand spatial organization from "primitive" and exotic sources. As Adrian Forty has suggested, the possibility that building could be conceived in terms of other things can be seen as evidence of discontent with modernism.[11] The space between an ahistorical past and a transhistoric future is one that various revisions of the modernist grand narrative have sought to fill. As part of the rediscovery of "place" in the late twentieth century, space has been conceptualized as practice and event. This represents the continuation of an anthropological sensibility that was part of the modernist project; but it has been progressively nourished by existential and poststructuralist notions of subjectivity and identity. The literature of travel and tourism has attained a priority in the fusion of those concerns with particular relevance to transcultural traveling and cultural negotiation.

The period immediately after the 1939–1945 war was marked by a distinct turning away from functionalism to explore the mysterious aspects of urban monuments and cores. The revised concerns of the Congres Internationaux de l'Architecture Moderne (CIAM) betray this interest in rediscovery—especially as it related to the "living" quality of cities. Such interest involved inquiries into the constituents of significance and pleasure, as well as determined attempts to understand the "everyday" aspects of habitation. Venice, and particularly St. Mark's Square, became a model for constructing social and democratic space,[12] historically linked to the highly validated notion of the agora and, at the same time, suggesting a model for post-authoritarian and post-laissez-faire urban life. The problems of leisure, learning, and self-determination, traditionally key concerns of the tourist, became tropes of postwar planning theory. The versions of authority that the new planning was intended to circumvent—commercialism, communism, traffic, advertising, and mass media—were also conceived as the enemies of "place." The claim that Mediterranean cities and their culture provided defenses against the encroachment of those enemies suggested urban models that presented both classical and picturesque solutions based on a mixed economy of constraint and freedom.

The recovery of "place" has been theoretically informed by anthropological and perspectival understanding. It has taken place in relation to reconceiving the city as system that relates to larger systems, both natural and cultural. Concerns about reconceiving place have come at a time of danger—when various anxieties have emerged regarding the loss of place in the general decay of narratives, in the face of globalization, simulation, and indifference. In particular, the triumph of the market in its related drives both to make generic and to differentiate has put the notion of "public space" into crisis. Anthropologists, cultural geographers, and theorists of racial and gendered space have provided alternative readings of authorized urban texts that demonstrate that place, like memory, is a work in progress.

As in Venice, where every adjustment threatens the densely coded past, every urban solution now self-consciously walks the line between conservation and development. Elizabeth Wilson builds on this abstract dichotomy in her suggestion that most of us would like to inhabit a city balanced between the two now-dominant urban models—one dangerous, vital, and chaotic; the other prettified, intimate, and themed.[13]

The economies of space are displayed in every real estate agent's window. "Real estate" is subject to a complex system of values, personal and collective, that puts a premium on "centrality," "exclusion," and "proximity." The complex needs that these promises address are indicated in Doreen Massey's phrase "the spatiality of life."[14] Desirable place is often a paradoxical blend of closeness and distance. The formula "secluded, yet minutes from" recurs as a compelling spatiotemporal device mediating "backwater" and "mainstream"; it measures movement between the past and the present, the interior and the exterior, as much as mere distance. One experiences the conflation of time and space in the city where the passage of time is imag-

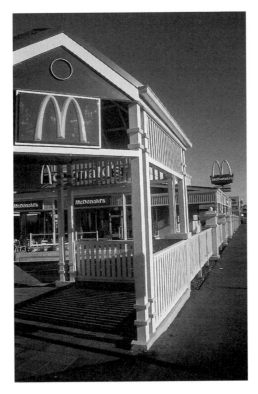

3.4 | McDonald's.

ined to vary between locales—densely concentrated and stored in the "historic centers" and present only as redundancy and decay elsewhere.

Evaluation is inherent in all planning procedures, particularly when the object is to integrate or separate place from non-place. In recent years the supposedly anomic experiences provided by modernization have been discredited in favor of modes of village and street life. However, the neutral spaces that are committed to contract and consumption have considerable appeal as antidotes to the complexity and contradiction of postmodern life. One customer in a Harlem McDonald's has observed, "Ain't no hip-hop here, ain't no profanity. The pictures, the plants, the way people keep things neat here, it makes you feel like you're in civilization."[15] Marc Augé, writing on the characteristics of "non-place," has described the experience as "contractual," involving elements of identity loss and role-playing.[16] These spaces provide not just symbolic reference to history and context, but also a refuge from a palimpsest of references that can be seen as an obstacle to a neutral present; they win back the mood of modernism at the expense of intertextuality.

Many writings on the urban culture of the present converge in their accounts of the increasingly immaterial, eccentric, and communicative na-

ture of late-twentieth-century cities. Although modernism as a universal-
izing and progressive project attempted to unite aesthetics and social function, it did so at the cost of defining function narrowly. The fantasy of a
definitive solution, what Jean-François Lyotard has called a "final rebuilding," failed to account for the complex relationship of new architecture to
the past, as an embodiment and a commentary on the passage of time.

Architecture obliterates and constitutes the past. It establishes itself in relation to a time and place of origin, and it also endures and is
marked by the passage of time and interpretation. Architecture is always
suspended between inventory and memory, so that its significance articulates meanings at once in syntagmatic and paradigmatic dimensions. It provides containers for memories in a culture where they are superabundant.
Marc Augé has suggested that the term "super modern" is a more effective
way of describing the present than "post modern" in order to account for
"this time overloaded with events that encumber the present along with the
recent past."[17]

Cities as a matrix of routes, junctions, and structures function as a
compelling metaphor for memory. Elements acknowledged to be "historic"
are surrounded by superimpositions that in some cases replace other build-

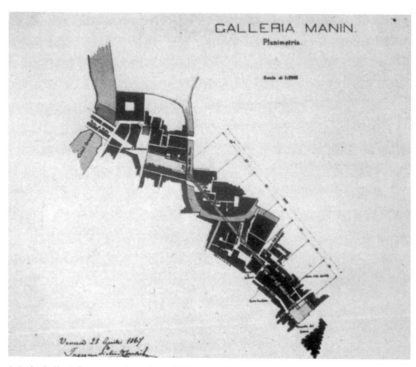

3.5 | Galleried street project, from S. Marco to the Rialto.

ings of note, or significant sites, but usually stand on the foundations of "lost" structures. As buildings and space configure forcefields of memory, significance spills over into locales and districts, or fails to find attachment. Extensions, changes of use, transformations of status, growth, decay, and gentrification—the variously prioritized geometry of main roads, back-streets, culs-de-sac, and shortcuts—all resonate with ways of memorializing existence.

It is inevitable that cities provoke psychic analogies and meditations on the reciprocity of urban experience and the realms of consciousness. Lewis Mumford used the geological metaphor of "strata" to describe the layering of cities. As a modernist, he tended to favor the newer, more flexible and renewable "deposits" and assumed that overbuilding was inevitable. Sigmund Freud, employing a more purely architectonic metaphor, was careful to distinguish between "authentic" remains and the superstructures built upon them by the subject. Georg Simmel identified the ramified city as characteristic of modernism by virtue of its temporal complexity, its proliferation of historical styles, and its general density of reference, all of which played a part in the intensification of stimuli he regarded as symptomatic of the urban experience.

Memory is one of the key ingredients in the creation of place, although it is important to acknowledge that memory is subject to political as well as psychic operations. Although it can be regarded as an antidote to selective and tendentious histories, memory can also be structured and guided. A number of the essays in the 1996 *Strangely Familiar* collection focus on how power is exercised over memory to construct various regimes of access and control. Dolores Hayden suggests ways in which memory can be comoposed to supplement and realign existing histories, Iain Chambers indicates how memory and habituation constitute indwelling resistances to "progress," and Christine Boyer considers the role of memory in the transition from realism to simulation.[18]

Although memory is involuntary and transient, it can also be stimulated and preserved. James Young, writing on Holocaust memorials, asserts the importance of memory as a disruptive practice:

> By returning to the memorial some memory of its own genesis, we remind ourselves of the memorial's essential fragility, its dependence on others for its life, that it was made by human hands in human times and places, that it is no more a natural piece of the landscape than we are. For, unlike words on a page, memorial icons seem literally to embody ideas, to invite viewers to mistake material presence and weight for immutable permanence. If, in its

glazed exteriority we never really see the monument, I shall attempt to crack its eidetic veneer, to loosen meaning, to make visible the activity of memory in monuments. It is my hope that such a critique may save our icons of remembrance from hardening into idols of remembrance.[19]

Worried about the capacity of memorials to absorb and negate memory, Young suggests that it is necessary to remember the process of memorialization, to recast memory in ways that recognize its need to change, and to acknowledge our different motives for remembering.

Memorials as outcrops of the past have been seen as particularly intrusive at times when the future is conceived as unproblematically "progressive." As Christine Boyer has pointed out, such a view of the future is increasingly untenable at the end of the twentieth century. When utopian desires are primarily focused on restoring lost totalities and certainties, there is a danger of repressing that aspect of the past which Aldo Rossi has referred to as "a museum of pain."[20]

The process of uncovering the past is dialectically related to bringing the present into question. Even the most nostalgic and factually remote versions of lost "golden ages"—classical Greece, medieval England, Victorian values—have been potent generators of radical politics. The metaphoric relationship between archaeology and psychoanalysis is rooted in a dynamic of building on the foundations of the past, where "memory traces" lie dormant until cathected in the present.

Memory is rarely without contradictions, and it must be compromised in order to function. It can be attached to place in ways that are transactional and unpredictable. In *Invisible Cities*, Italo Calvino contemplates a sampling of five ways in which memory can play a part in the experience of urbanity.[21] In one city, the visitor perceives the same components that he has witnessed previously in other cities; but as in all generic texts, there is a significant difference. In a second city, everything that is desirable is referred to his memory of having visited before as a younger man, so that the desire itself is a memory. In the third, the city is a palimpsest of the past, heavily marked with the signs of the passage of time. In the fourth, the city functions as an armature for memory, structured in such a way that it aids recollection. In the last, the inhabitants are preoccupied with representations of the city as it was years before, and pleasurably regret the loss of its grace and distinctiveness.

Like memory, the city is a play of perspectives and constellations created by points of view adopted in time and space. Walter Benjamin has commented that memory "is the medium of past experience, as the ground is the medium in which dead cities are buried."[22] As the modern city supplied the compressions and dislocations of meaning that served as an inspiration and model to the modernist avant-garde, it also generated the traumatic collisions that provoke particular kinds of memory. Benjamin, recollecting the Berlin of his childhood, commented on the irrational intensity of some memories and the imprinting of memories by shock.[23] Modernist urbanism sought to eradicate these theatrical and fractal qualities. One sign of the eclipse of rational modernism is the restoration of detail and mnemonics to the urban landscape.

There is a well-established relationship between memory and narrative. Cities are a densely coded context for narratives of discovery and the recovery of experience. They have a capacity to act as social condensors and to integrate complex aspirations and assimilations of people, styles, and ideas. Among the defining characteristics of cities is their ability to relay information and enable meanings to be "built" on historical and spatial axes. With the coming of modernity, and forms of capitalism that could successfully interpellate citizens as consumers, new relationships were established between mobile subjects and a city of signs, enclaves, and clues. In the writings of Dickens, Baudelaire, Doyle, Aragon, and Benjamin there is a preoccupation with detachment and investment—a fascination with the uneven development of cities. These writers dwell on resistances to change, discrepancies between facade and "indwelling," and the significance of telltale displacements. Heroes emerge who are capable of decoding the mysteries of "mean streets" without themselves becoming mean—men who retain their integrity in the face of disintegration.

My own essay for *Strangely Familiar* took a customary route, associating the experience of Venice with urban dreams and *dérives* and considering the city as a kind of model for contemplating the relationship between past, present, and future. Venice is fascinating because it is at once unique and paradigmatic. It offers in literal and pedestrian forms frequent encounters between two fundamental architectural tropes, the "bridge" and the "door." Georg Simmel conceived those as metaphors for connecting and separating, respectively. Venice is remarkable in the way that it provides an intense urban experience of extremes of public and private space.

Cities have always functioned in these spatially metaphoric ways, creating opportunities for the coming together of disparate meanings. Meaning is concentrated and dispersed by processes that can be analogized to the operation of memory. Certeau's conceptualization of "spatial practices" involves an interpretation of the work of J.-F. Augoyard in which he uses the terms "synechdoche" and "asyndetonal" to describe the ways in which experiencing urban space can involve taking parts for a whole or

3.6 | Photographic *capriccio*. The Campanile reconstructed on the north flank of the Duomo.

eliminating the transitional space between significant objects to create partial or denser experiences.[24] In ideal tourist spaces there is a surreal clarity of meaning produced by these effects.

Tourists are increasingly the interpellated inhabitants of cities. The ideal tourist embodies the detachment of the flâneur and the engagement of the ideal consumer. Although the practices of tourism are increasingly stratified and specialized, they normally promise a totalizing experience that engages memory in the encounter with novelty. Certeau paraphrases Claude Lévi-Strauss's *Tristes Tropiques*: "we travel abroad to discover in distant lands something whose presence at home has become unrecognisable."[25]

Urban cultures of the late twentieth century have responded to the privileged relationship implied by tourism. The tourist experience proposes an overview that allows priority to the plenitude of the imaginary over the symbolic. In that respect it operates in the realm of art, film, and dreams. Set against the organized itinerary between sites of discovery and memory, the tourist is offered a representative urban experience in a place that can be endlessly explored but only provisionally known.

Notes

1   Barry Curtis, "Venice Metro," in *Strangely Familiar: Narratives of Architecture in the City*, ed. Iain Borden, Joe Kerr, Alicia Pivaro, and Jane Rendell (London: Routledge, 1996), pp. 42–46.

2   Georg Simmel, *Roma, Firenze e Venezia*; quoted in Patrizia Lombardo, "Introduction: The Philosophy of the City," in *Architecture and Nihilism: On the Philosophy of Modern Architecture*, by Massimo Cacciari, trans. Stephen Sartarelli (New Haven: Yale University Press, 1993), p. lvii.

3   See William J. Mitchell, *e-topia—Urban Life, Jim—But Not as We Know It* (Cambridge, Mass.: MIT Press, 1999) pp. 76–77.

4   Cacciari, *Architecture and Nihilism*, p. 95.

5   Jean Baudrillard, "Please Follow Me," *Art and Text*, March–May 1987, p. 108.

6   Casola is quoted in *Venice, an Illustrated Anthology*, comp. Michael Marqusee (London: Conran Octopus, 1988), p. 7.

7   Adrian Stokes, *Venice: An Aspect of Art* (London: Faber and Faber, 1945), p. 7.

8   David Harvey, *The Condition of Postmodernity: An Enquiry into the Origins of Cultural Change* (Oxford: Blackwell, 1989), pp. 92–93.

9   Lombardo, "Introduction," p. xx.

10   Richard Sennett, *Flesh and Stone: The Body and the City in Western Civilization* (London: Faber and Faber, 1994), p. 188.

11   Adrian Forty, "Masculine, Feminine, or Neuter?" in *Desiring Practices: Architecture, Gender, and the Interdisciplinary*, ed. Katerina Ruedi, Sarah Wigglesworth, and Duncan McCorquodale (London: Black Dog, 1996), p. 148.

12   See the endplates and references throughout in J. Tyrwhitt, J. L. Sert, and E. N. Rogers, eds., *CIAM 8: The Heart of the City* (London: Lund Humphries, 1952).

13   Elizabeth Wilson, "Looking Backward: Nostalgia and the City," in *Imagining Cities: Scripts, Signs, Memory*, ed. Sallie Westwood and John Williams (London: Routledge, 1997), p. 132.

14   Doreen Massey, "My Mother Lives Now in a Nursing Home," in Borden et al., *Strangely Familiar*, p. 75.

15   Quoted by Martin Woollacott in "Coke and Big Macs Aren't the Real Thing," review of Mark Predergast's history of the Coca Cola Company, Guardian, 4 January 1997, p. 14.

16   Marc Augé *Non-Places: Introduction to an Anthropology of Supermodernity* (London: Verso, 1995), p. 101.

17   Ibid., p. 29.

18   Dolores Hayden, "The Power of Place: Urban Landscapes as Public History" (pp. 47–51); Iain Chambers, "Naples, the Emergent Archaic" (pp. 52–56); and M. Christine Boyer, "Twice Told Stories: The Double Erasure of Times Square" (pp. 77–81); all in Borden et al., *Strangely Familiar*.

19   James E. Young, *The Texture of Memory: Holocaust Memorials and Meaning* (New Haven: Yale University Press, 1993), p. 14.

20   Aldo Rossi, "What Is to Be Done with the Old Cities?" in *Architectural Design no. 55, 5/6, The School of Venice*, ed. Luciano Semerani (London: AD Editions, 1985), p. 19.

21   Italo Calvino, *Invisible Cities*, trans. William Weaver (London: Secker and Warburg, 1974).

22   Walter Benjamin, "A Berlin Chronicle," in *One-Way Street and Other Writings*, trans. Edmund Jephcott and Kingsley Shorter (London: New Left Books, 1979), p. 314.

23   Ibid., p. 345.

24   Michel de Certeau, *The Practice of Everyday Life*, trans. Steven F. Rendall (Berkeley: University of California Press, 1988), pp. 91–114.

25   Ibid., p. 50.

The Power of Place—the power of ordinary urban landscapes to nurture citizens' public memory, to encompass shared time in the form of shared territory—remains untapped for most working people's neighborhoods in most cities, and for most ethnic history and women's history. The sense of civic identity that shared history can convey is missing. And even bitter experiences and fights communities have lost need to be remembered—so as not to diminish their importance.

Dolores Hayden
The Power of Place

Engulfed and enframed by a set of new constraints forged in contemporary times, these fragments from the past appear denigrated by nostalgic sentiments that fuel their preservation or reconstruction, while our collective memory of public places seems undermined by historicist reconstructions. When juxtaposed against the contemporary city of disruption and disarray, the detached appearance of these historically detailed compositions becomes even more exaggerated and attenuated.

Christine Boyer
The City of Collective Memory

Joe Kerr

4

The Uncompleted Monument: London, War, and the Architecture of Remembrance

Little more than fifty years ago, London was fought over for the first time in its modern history, and in the process suffered terrible destruction. The consequences of that bitter conflict have shaped the lives of every subsequent citizen of London. But as the distance from those events lengthens and the real memories of that war become merely secondhand, new generations are coming to consciousness for whom the war must seem very remote to their lives and experiences. The war will soon be represented only by the abstracted remembrance of the museum and the memorial, or will be forgotten. It is thus a critical time to examine the processes by which immaterial memory is transformed into concrete monument; as the sanctioned histories of that period become solid and permanent, these received meanings must be contested now, or else the right to question them be permanently relinquished. This chapter considers the metamorphosis of experience into memorial, and how this flow contributes to "knowing" the city.

My inquiry builds upon a contemporary debate about the memorialization of the urban landscape, and the problematic relationship between the act of memory and its institutionalization in built form. The paradigms of this highly polarized argument are articulated in the recent writings of two contributors to *The Unknown City*: on the one hand is the view of urban history as an instrument of revelation, embodied in Dolores Hayden's "Power of Place" project with its clarion call to "nurture citizens' public memory";[1] on the other hand, in cautionary opposition to this instrumentalist use of collective memories, are M. Christine Boyer's warnings of the dangers inherent in "merchandising history" and in "nostalgic sentiments that fuel . . . preservation or reconstruction."[2]

These arguments over what David Lowenthal has dubbed "the spoils of history"[3] are perhaps more visible and implacable in London than in any other city or culture. There the opposing camps of history and of heritage struggle to impose their conflicting interpretations on every place, piece, and archive of the past, with the hope of substantially shaping the values and forms of the future.

MEMORY

In focusing on this debate about the conflicting uses of historical knowledge in interpreting the city, I wish to explore how one particular system of public memory—monuments—helps to reveal or conceal the complexities of urban history. Specifically I consider the changing role, the transformations in form, and last the transmutation of what was commemorated in London's modern war memorials. This raises a number of issues about memorial culture and its relationship to public memory and knowledge of the city, including the question of how economic, political, and especially cultural change has been manifested in the production and reproduction of the memory of war. However, beyond simply accounting for this process of change, I wish to question the commonly held assumption that the city merely serves passively as the locus or the reservoir of public memory; instead I suggest ways in which London has been actively constituted as a memorial itself—in memory of itself—and in so doing has been "written" as an irrefutable text of official history. While many have argued that historic European cities increasingly function as little more than active museums of themselves, I claim here that not just is the fabric of those places reconstituted as "heritage" but also the significant memories that attach to those places are conserved, their meanings becoming fixed and permanent, creating what Boyer calls the "imaginary historical museum."[4]

It is necessary to consider exactly how this constituting of the city's fabric and its attached memories has actually occurred, how these particular constructions of the past are creating the future meanings of cities as they are reconfigured as pure environments of consumption. Conversely we must examine how, in opposition to this commodifying role for history, particular forms of historical knowledge—memory and experience—might be deployed in the struggle to empower citizens' command of the past, and thus to maintain their democratic knowledge of the city.

MONUMENTS

In the history of all cities are momentous events that are irrevocably associated with the popular imagination of that place. A psychohistorical evocation of London would probably contain as its most vivid moments of cataclysmic change two devastating fires, in 1666 and 1940, both necessitating the wholesale economic, social, and physical reordering of the city. The remembrance of these events has been sustained through popular stories, pictures, and testimonies and through the presentation of officially sanctioned histories. But the memories people hold of significant events are intimately connected with a specific sense of space and place; and for an event-memory to be adequately invested with visible, public meaning it is necessary for some tangible connection to be suggested and enforced between circumstance and site. While the fabric of the city itself represents a visible aide-mémoire, it is the act of abstracting through the erection of monuments that permanently inscribes the image of that event. The Great Fire of London destroyed most of the comparatively small city in just a few days. It is publicly remembered by the Monument, the identification between the event and Wren's column being so complete that no more precise name is needed. Monuments can be seen as the tangible trace of collective memory, or perhaps as the mnemonic device that can reactivate accumulated memories.[5]

WAR

The simple process of abstraction and commemoration in the premodern London of the late seventeenth century could not conceivably be compared to the infinitely more complex sequences of event and ideology that have given shape to the monuments of the modern city. Yet the desire to invest urban space with public meaning, to render readable the text of the city, has remained a constant ambition of urban societies, and it is certainly a highly visible impulse of postmodernity. To one attempting to unravel the imperceptible mechanisms by which the immaterial constructions of memory are metamorphosed into the tangible architectures of commemoration, no instance is more revealing than the wartime history of London and the process of remembrance that developed during and after the Second World War.

For much of this century the experience of both world wars has been a visible fact of everyday life in London. My own childhood recollections are shared by countless others: the elderly men sunning themselves in wheelchairs, their uneven distribution of arms and legs bearing eloquent testimony to the brutal fashions of field surgery on the Western Front; the khaki tunic, three stripes on the arm, found in the dark recess of the wardrobe; the gaping holes of cleared bomb sites and the roofless churches still remaining from the Blitz. Above all else it was this last, the deliberate and catastrophic destruction inflicted from September 1940 to May 1941, that has irrevocably transformed the physical and social fabric of London.

COMMEMORATION

The complexity of this matrix of events, memories, and places renders the process of memorialization highly problematic, for to develop a memorial culture requires that a restricted set of meanings be abstracted, a process that necessarily implies that other meanings be forgotten. Interpreting how this has happened, and indeed is continuing to happen, is essential if we are to contemplate real resistance against received interpretations of the recent past.

These general lines of inquiry have emerged from a concern with the Lenin Memorial,[6] a monument created in 1942 as a manifestation of Anglo-Soviet relations and destroyed in 1948 as a direct result of obvious transformations in that relationship. This extraordinary object, designed by the celebrated modernist architect Berthold Lubetkin, is in effect a war memo-

4.1 | The erasure of memory: the destruction of the Lenin Memorial, 1948.

rial: for it was created during the war, for the war, and it served as the focus of collective emotions generated by that conflict.

Of particular historical significance was its unplanned role as the site for a local enactment of the global conflict against fascism, and what that suggests to us about the reality of London's wartime experiences. For instance, that this monument was continually attacked by fascist gangs is a telling insight into what Angus Calder has labeled "the myth of the Blitz,"[7] that popular conception of a time when ordinary citizens heroically pulled together in a communitarian effort against the fascist enemy. This carefully orchestrated construction of history, as we shall see, has remained central to the telling and retelling of London's wartime experience, and to the monumentalization of that experience.

But in terms of theorizing the public meanings of monuments, it is paradoxically the arbitrary destruction of the Lenin Memorial that raises the most intriguing questions about the process of memorialization. For in a country that has no particular tradition of continually creating or destroying official iconography—unlike, for instance, that which Laura Mulvey has shown exists in Russia[8]—this story illuminates important questions about the commemoration of the Second World War. The erasure of this curious artifact of total war was not the necessary precursor to a new, sanctioned system of monuments to reflect the concerns of a different era, and a different kind of war; instead, for half a century the war of 1939 to 1945 has remained without its own dedicated memorial culture, at least of the kind habitually associated with the commemoration of military conflict.

This startling lack of commemoration for such a significant and tragic episode in London's history must be considered in the light of Doreen Massey's statement elsewhere in this book that the purpose of monuments "is to gather together in the consensus of a common belonging, a shared identity, all those who walk by." The absence of monuments thus suggests a fracturing of this sense of a shared identity—what Boyer labels a "memory crisis"—that necessarily carries profound implications for the cohesion of urban society.

THE GLORIOUS DEAD

While critics have recognized that London has historically lacked the kinds of national monuments that have formed such an integral part of the meanings of some other European capitals,[9] the city is nevertheless fully immersed in the culture of war. London abounds in representations of national victories, and monuments to their glorious but dead victors.

Most famous and numerous are the monuments of the Great War of 1914 to 1918 that also pervade every corner of empire and foreign field

4.2 | The glorious dead: the Cenotaph, London. Designed by Edwin Lutyens.

of battle, a thread of commemoration that is wholly stitched into the greater fabric of national identity. Indeed the Cenotaph, the Lutyens-designed memorial in Whitehall in commemoration of the Great War, has been argued to be the nearest thing Britain has to a national monument. That war provided a memory system so powerful and pervasive that the remembrance services on Armistice Day conducted at memorials throughout the United Kingdom remain perhaps the last widely accepted and observed ritual of national unity. Moreover, the monuments of that one war subsequently came, through the merest addition of a couple of dates, to stand for all later conflicts, obviating the need for more public memorials.[10]

This does not mean that events and memories of the Second World War as it was experienced in London weren't memorialized, but instead that memorialization has happened in a unique way—one that highlights the problems associated with the control and propagation of public, collective memory. So the central question becomes, Why no significant or general memorials of World War II? My answer to this deals with two distinct issues; first, why conventional forms of representation were not employed, and second, what the new and changing ways were in which the war, but especially the Battle for London, has been commemorated over the ensuing half century.

PEACE

One answer to the first of these questions is that there was clearly a collapse in accepted symbolic codes of representation in the aftermath of war. For although Britain underwent no absolute political revolution after 1945, the experience of wartime governance had led both major political parties to a broad consensus on the necessity for radical programs of social reconstruction. Thus the politicians acknowledged that victory could not be too easily interpreted as a vindication of this nation's institutions—unlike, for instance, the Soviet Union, which constructed a profusion of monuments to the "Great Patriotic War." Postwar Britain was only too aware of the pyrrhic nature of its victory, and in the general mood of reconstruction and reconciliation there was little place for crowing triumphalism. The Western victors were already plunging without pause into a new conflict, as the untimely destruction of the Lenin Memorial vividly demonstrated, and one that rapidly turned the taste of victory sour. The intent and title of Labour's famous 1945 manifesto was to "let us face the future" and not dwell on the inheritance of the past, as Britain is wont to do. Doubts about the continued relevance of previous value systems surely contributed to the wholesale collapse and eventual supersession of the traditional typologies and iconographies of war memorial intimately connected to those systems.

TOTAL WAR

For the civilian populations of London and other British cities, the very fact that from 1940 on they had become active participants in the war—that in the new bizarre topographies of aerial warfare, the battlefield was now over and above not only the homeland but even the sanctified space of the home itself—suggests that traditional, abstracted representations of victory, or of noble, disinterested sacrifice in distant and foreign fields (as had appeared on innumerable monuments after 1918), were no longer appropriate or even tolerable. In fact, as Gavin Stamp points out, already a great deal of unease about the suitability of these monuments had surfaced as they had been unveiled from the early 1920s onward; one was contemptuously labeled by the war poet Siegfried Sassoon "a pile of peace-complacent stone."[11]

Moreover, a generation had been slaughtered en masse in the trenches only twenty years earlier, supposedly to bring a permanent end to such conflicts. This firmly held but necessarily transient belief in the efficacy of the Great War is evoked in the words of George V on a pilgrimage to the memorials of the Somme in 1922: "I have many times asked myself whether there can be more potent advocates of peace upon earth through the years to come than this massed multitude of silent witnesses to the desolation of war."[12]

THE DEATH OF MEANING

But even the new inappropriateness of the old representations of remembrance doesn't account for the disappearance of the tangible typology of the monument itself—unless, that is, we consider more general debates about the decreasing ability of certain forms of high cultural expression to convey ideas about the real world. For just as Walter Benjamin famously argued that the literal imagery of mechanical reproduction had robbed painting of its authority to express a commonly recognized reality,[13] so other forms of cultural production had been divested of their power to capture universal meanings.

The experience and trauma of the Great War had convinced the modernist avant-garde of the need to reject the failed ancien régime. They aggressively denied architecture and painting the authority to carry symbolic or figurative codes of meaning, turning instead to abstraction to convey more universal themes of spirit or intellect. The new wish to celebrate technocracy and mass organization in preference to the humanist cult of the individual spelled the demise of historicism and the classical tradition, the very systems of representation that had sustained memorial culture up to and including the First World War. Thus the conventions of the monumental were increasingly redundant, with no desire to articulate an alternative. As Alan Borg notes, "so far as sculptors were concerned, the 1940s and '50s were a period of almost complete abstraction and their work did not conform to the public perception of a memorial style."[14]

In modern war, itself one of the most developed applications of mass production, the universal depiction of everything from the intimate details to the great events of warmaking by the *Picture Post* and *Pathé News* ensured that abstracted images of the wingèd angel or the petrified wreath were no longer adequate to sustain their old meanings of victory, death, and remembrance. On the rare occasions when a suitable means of expression was attempted for memorials to the Second World War, the results were as a rule highly unsatisfactory. Borg describes one notable failure, the Overlord Embroidery, created to commemorate the Normandy landings:

> The intention was to create a 20th century equivalent of the Bayeux Tapestry, but the format, which was itself ancient 900 years ago, is difficult to apply in the context of a contemporary and historically accurate narrative. The result is that the embroidery, though a marvel of workmanship, seems to have no clear purpose. No one who wishes to know the story or see the action of the battle of Normandy would use this as a source; they would rather read books and look at films and photographs.[15]

However, the idea that in the age of mechanical reproduction older conventions of commemoration had become redundant implies the possibility of a reproducible and hence universal memorial culture; and this is precisely what was born out of the 1939–1945 war, the first large-scale conflict to be fought wholly in the glare of the flashbulb. Thus the Battle for London is "remembered" above all else through its photographs, those lasting images that showed "London can take it." Indeed recent research has demonstrated how one image in particular has come to represent the abstracted meanings generated by that battle and by enduring it, to stand as the universally acknowledged symbol of the city at war.[16]

Herbert Mason's famous photograph, which showed the apparently undamaged St. Paul's Cathedral rising stoically above the flames of incendiary bombs, was described as "the greatest photograph of the war"—not by later apologists or historians, but by the *Daily Mail* on the day of its publication, 30 December 1940. The idea that this was more than just an extra-

4.3 | "The greatest photograph of the war": St. Paul's Cathedral, London, 29 December 1940.

ordinary piece of photojournalism was promoted from the very first, and it is in fact a highly doctored, propagandist image. What it represents is an abstraction of officially endorsed sentiment, wholly in the manner of a traditional memorial: no people, no suffering, no death. What remains is simply the image of the city, posed in defiance against an unprecedented offensive.

Through the ephemeral medium of the photograph the city itself is memorialized, but from this a wholly new monument is created from the city. Now it is the very real—and readable—remains of the devastated architecture that form a new language of remembrance. The shattered fabric of buildings have become the testimony to the battle, paradoxically through the calculated conservation of the traces of destruction. This new and highly literal form of urban memorial can be witnessed universally—in Coventry, Dresden, and Hiroshima as well as in London—as the mute testimony to the unspeakable horror of aerial warfare.

Thus in London—first through carefully edited films and photographs, and later through the selective retention of its ruins—the realities of death and destruction were translated into universalized images of national worth and superiority, which have remained powerful and largely uncontested for much of the period since.

NEW ENEMIES

However, these images of the city at war are also testimony to a new problematic of memorial culture: the experience of total war and its political consequences raised unprecedented questions of exactly what it was that should be memorialized and remembered. Two posters from the same wartime campaign—one of an idealized pastoral past, one of a utopian urban future—are symptomatic of a complex confusion of ideologies that lie at the heart of this argument. For during the course of the war it became increasingly less simple to encapsulate what was being fought for, and why. Wartime propaganda widened the definitions of the battlefield to identify new enemies and new causes unique to this conflict. The "Home Front" had become a theater of war not only in the physical sense of bombing and rocket attacks, and enormous concentrations of troops and equipment, but also in a social sense; the very fabric of society emerged as the ideological terrain of the conflict.

At home there lurked other enemies of civilization besides just the Axis powers—especially those christened by Beveridge the "five giants on the road to reconstruction,"[17] as in some monstrous modern fairy tale. Building Tomorrow as opposed to merely Preserving Yesterday became the ultimate purpose of war, with the prospect of social justice in the near future

4.4 | "Fight for it now"—the past. The South Downs, poster by artist Frank Newbould.

4.5 | "Fight for it now"—the future. Finsbury Health Centre, poster by artist Abram Games.

emerging as the necessary price for fighting total war. As the contemporary phrase had it, this had become "the people's war."

"AND NOW—WIN THE PEACE"

As the 1945 Labour election slogan quoted in the heading succinctly phrased it, the end of war was merely the prelude to a new struggle, set in a hypothetical peacetime future. But how does one monumentalize the future? Certainly not with crowing triumphalism. Beneficial memorials, ones that served more purpose than did inert sculpture, had been widely proposed after 1919, and they now increasingly seemed the correct expression of the emergent Welfare State. For instance, one project launched as a national war memorial in 1946 was the National Land Fund. But the idealism that at least temporarily inspired the reconstruction drive was better symbolized by something more substantial and monumental: anticipated victory against the new social enemies became memorialized in the great building programs of the Welfare State.

In a very real sense, the houses, hospitals, and schools that came to dominate the landscape of London were monuments to a yet unrealized, hypothetical, and utopian future, comprising the expeditionary force for a great new campaign. Aneurin Bevan, opening a new London housing estate in 1948 spoke of such buildings as if they were the anticipatory fragments of an equitable society of the future: "I felicitate the new tenants of these charming new flats. I hope they will have a long and happy life, produce many bouncing babies, and find full employment. I hope that in the years that lie ahead they will find a sense of pride in being associated with such a great municipal activity."[18] Rather than trumpeting military victory over external enemies, the city and its architecture became the peaceful monument for peacetime battles.

THERE ARE ONLY INDIVIDUALS

The traditional public monument lost its power to represent a public consensus about national events at the very time of a genuine national consensus about the political and social shape of the future.[19] As long as this consensus held, so then the architecture that represented it could continue to serve as the visible testimony to the sacrifice of war, and the triumph of peace. However, by the late 1970s the politics of Keynesian economics and welfarism, and the modernist cultural creed with which they were so intimately linked, were under sustained attack from a resurgent conservatism, whose triumph came with the election of the Thatcher government in 1979.

With the rapid dismantling of key areas of welfare provision, most visibly the termination of municipal housing programs, such architecture increasingly failed to hold its intended meanings, representing instead discredited symbols of nationhood. In Patrick Wright's memorable phrase, the municipal housing block was demonized as the "tombstone [. . .] of the entire Welfare State."[20]

Yet though the original intended meanings of these concrete monuments have now been largely destroyed, the power of the Second World War to generate pervasive cultural meanings has not been diminished. On the contrary, established values and myths attached to the war remain potent, and new historical interpretations have specifically questioned them. In the mid-1980s Correlli Barnett's *Audit of War* sought to blame postwar British decline in its entirety on exactly the wartime political leadership that later led to the establishment of the Welfare State.[21]

This change has been accompanied by new forms of memorial culture that invest the war and victory in it with a wholly different vision for contemporary London. The old understanding that the experience of war had provided the foundation for a new social justice, based on state-sponsored policies of societal reform and progress, has been superseded by a new polemic. Now the characteristic free-market cult of individual endeavor, untrammeled by the "nanny state," is celebrated.

THE NEW HERO

What has visibly emerged as the new memorial culture has involved reconfiguring particular fragments of the city into museums: the reconstruction of spaces that are genuinely endowed with historical remembrance, but are now filled with new visions and interpretations. Boyer has christened such places the "new public theaters of late capitalism." Simultaneously these spaces have served to turn the memories and images of conflict into a bland and fictive commodity, for passive consumption by an unknowing and uncritical audience.

In 1984, on the instructions of Prime Minister Margaret Thatcher, the Cabinet War Rooms deep under Whitehall were unsealed and thrown open to the public, to provide (according to the director general of the Imperial War Museum) "a permanent reminder of how our embattled government survived and operated in the Second World War."[22] Echoing contemporary debates about the correct empirical content of school history, this statement explicitly celebrates the leaders in this conflict, and not its common participants. However, we are told that this site was ultimately dedicated to the remembrance of just one hero: "Above all else they are Winston Churchill's War Rooms, the place where, had the expected invasion ever happened, the final defence of Britain would have been mounted."[23]

Thus Britain's great war leader, the personification of the defiant nation mounting its last desperate defense, was once more invoked, just as he had been a short while earlier during the Falklands conflict. This new spatial link with Britain's wartime experience did not evoke the familiar Blitz imagery of different classes thrown together in the public shelters, of ordinary people conjoined in a common endeavor, but directly revealed the commander's lair. It leapfrogged the more recent, problematic past to tap into the rich vein of nostalgia represented by Britain in its last moments of world power.

THE PLACE FOR WAR

The Cabinet War Rooms are spaces that genuinely resonate with the memory of their historical import. It is still impressive to enter the site of such significant action, half a century later, a point emphatically made by the director general of the Imperial War Museum:

> Some historic sites are redolent of their history, the air charged with the spirit of the past. The Cabinet War Rooms are in this category, and I know of few places which convey a period so immediately and so effectively. It sometimes seems as if the wartime workers have just left and the Rooms are waiting for the next shift to come on duty.[24]

So it must seem to its expected audience, who are unattuned to the subtle, instrumental manipulations of historical fact and place that have reinvested London's wartime history with such powerful contemporary meanings. But as Lowenthal christened it, this is the age of "heritage ascendant," which he dates from 1980, and the rise of "Thatcher's Britain."[25] For him, history and heritage differ in that the former is an interpretation of the past, while the latter aspires to be a replica of the past, a copy of what has happened. In the case of the Cabinet War Rooms, visitors might not realize that what they see is as much simulation as reality, and the attendant literature certainly does not try too hard to explain this.

To the critical eye, even the excitement of penetrating a space so embedded in personal and collective cultural identity is already diminished by the ersatz sandbags framing the entrance—one of many artificial embellishments intended presumably to meet public anticipation, as if the real space would not be enough on its own, or people's imaginations could no longer connect with events of fifty years previously. A further diminishing of experience occurs inside, when the realization dawns that much on view

4.6

4.7 | The Cabinet War Rooms:
air-conditioned history.

is actually a careful reconstruction, or even enhancement. Waxwork marines, cardboard evacuees, reproduction newspapers, and the taped noise of bombs and sirens—which could never have been heard in this underground bunker in 1940—are required to orient people, to jog the necessary set of historical references. It is this denial of imagination and interpretation, the predigestion of the past to allow uncritical consumption in the present, that is most worrying about these new urban tableaux. Their meanings are fixed and unassailable, at least in their own space.

The ultimate accomplishment of such fragmentary pantheons is their ability to distance the reality of remembered experiences by presenting simulated participation in dramatized historical events, to be enjoyed as if they really were near-perfect re-creations of what actually happened. In the process, all sense of the problematic nature of this wartime experience, of suffering and of conflict, has been censored—a continuation of the careful process that had ensured the destruction of the Lenin Memorial forty years previously.

THE "EXPERIENCE" OF WAR

London is increasingly represented in spectacles that have no discernible connection with authentic sites or events at all—the total simulation of a nonexistent past. Under railway arches in Waterloo and next to the "Jack the Ripper Experience" can be found the grandiosely titled "Winston Churchill's Britain at War Theme Museum," containing the "Blitz Experi-

4.8

4.9 | "Theming the war: the new battleground."

ence." Here a pathetic collection of objects—"actual relics, from toilet rolls and soap to a complete Anderson Shelter, that you can sit in and hear air raids"[26]—are placed in crude tableaux of wartime pubs and shops, as well as the simulated aftermath of a bombing raid, so crudely rendered that they recall fairground attractions rather more than museum displays.

Being allowed the role of witness, indeed of active participant in this new reconstituted experience of warfare, leads one to question not just the possibility but the very need for any permanent memorial. The danger is that this degree of immediacy, this apparent engagement with the past, may in fact prove to be the most effective block to memory and thus to useful knowledge of the recent past. Raphael Samuel has argued that "heritage culture" is not necessarily the enemy of history, which itself stands accused of being an elitist activity devoted to esoteric knowledge. He claims that simulated museum displays such as the one described above are an authentic part of the modern "art of memory."[27] But to deliberately confuse popular memory and knowledge with these considered constructions of populist sentiment surely runs the risk of diminishing the real significance of common experience and memory in the city.

The historical episodes that can be visited here—Jack the Ripper and the Blitz—are not even remotely connected with this actual place. But reconstituted together in the warm nostalgic glow that increasingly colors all of the past, they offer the tourist an uncritical and easily consumed version of London's heritage. As with so much else of our own city's history, the past has become a seamless text no longer ordered by chronology, in which real and simulated memory cannot easily be differentiated, but which can be "experienced" and consumed equally by all. This devaluing of collective memory, and the reconstruction of London's fabric as essentially a theme park of itself, threatens to render our own recent past as the ultimate seductive spectacle for a passive and depoliticized citizenry.

As a recent book has suggested, historians and politicians are still "re-fighting World War II," and as yet there is nothing resembling a definitive account of that conflict.[28] At the risk of preaching another kind of instrumental history, we cannot allow the memory of war to become a passive act. "Lest we forget" must remain an imperative, both because the fight against fascism is a permanent one and because this truly is our history. The ease with which memory has been appropriated by the forces of capital, and reproduced in its commodified form of nostalgia, not only serves as a barrier to the past but does equal harm in obscuring the possibilities of the future.

THE FUTURE OF THE PAST

Distance in time, and the diminishing of firsthand experience, does not seem to be making the problem of creating an appropriate memorial culture for the Second World War any simpler. Indeed, in many European cities the difficulties of publicly rendering this particular period of history in a form that also satisfies contemporary ideological priorities are currently proving challenging to solve. For instance, in Dresden the bombed ruins of the Frauenkirche, which for nearly fifty years were conserved as a memorial to the city's destruction, are now undergoing a controversial reconstruction. Despite the obvious questions that this act raises about remembrance, as well as considerable reservations among some citizens, its promoters claim that "re-erecting this great church does not mean a failure to confront our history."[29] In Berlin, meanwhile, attempts to construct a vast holocaust memorial are currently beset by controversy on an international scale.

Rather more optimistically, in the East End of London a campaign has been gathering force to erect a monument to the 2,193 local civilian casualties of the Blitz, in what was the most heavily bombed area of any British city.[30] The Civilians Remembered Campaign is particularly interesting because despite having attracted widespread support from political leaders and royalty, it does appear to have started as a genuinely local, popular agitation. Furthermore, the battle to claim a particular site overlooking the River Thames has brought the campaigners into direct confrontation with the London Docklands Development Corporation (LDDC), an unelected body created by the Thatcher government to oversee the commercial redevelopment of London's vast area of redundant docklands, which is vastly unpopular with the local community. Thus this campaign to commemorate a community's experiences of war has simultaneously become a struggle by those citizens to reassert some control over their physical and social environment; they are resisting the construction of still more luxury apartments in favor of reclaiming their own version of the urban cultural landscape. Thus London's wartime past may yet develop its own memorial culture, and this recurrent, troublesome issue of commemoration may prove to be a catalyst for resisting the appropriation of the places of popular history and of public memory.

> Ordered this year:
> A billion tons of broken glass and rubble,
> Blockade of chaos, the other requisites
> For the reduction of Europe to a rabble.[31]

Joe Kerr

Notes

1   Dolores Hayden, *The Power of Place: Urban Landscapes and Public History* (Cambridge, Mass.: MIT Press, 1995), p. 9.

2   M. Christine Boyer, *The City of Collective Memory: Its Historical Imagery and Architectural Entertainments* (Cambridge, Mass.: MIT Press, 1994), p. 1.

3   David Lowenthal, *The Heritage Crusade and the Spoils of History* (London: Viking, 1996).

4   M. Christine Boyer, "Cities for Sale: Merchandising History at South Street Seaport," in *Variations on a Theme Park: The New American City and the End of Public Space*, ed. Michael Sorkin (New York: Hill and Wang, 1992), p. 182.

5   For the idea of architecture as "mnemotechnique," see Anselm Haverkamp, "Ghost Machine or Embedded Intelligence? Architexture and Mnemotechnique," *ANY*, no 15 (1996): 10–14.

6   See Joe Kerr, "Lenin's Bust: Unlikely Allies in Wartime London," in *Strangely Familiar: Narratives of Architecture in the City*, ed. Iain Borden, Joe Kerr, Alicia Pivaro, and Jane Rendell (London: Routledge, 1996), pp. 16–21.

7   Angus Calder, *The Myth of the Blitz* (London: Pimlico, 1992). For a full discussion of this contentious subject, see Philip Ziegler, "Is There a Myth of the Blitz?" chapter 10 of *London at War, 1939–1945* (London: Sinclair-Stevenson, 1995), pp. 163–178.

8   *Disgraced Monuments*, 1992, video, produced by Channel 4. Directed by Laura Mulvey with Mark Lewis. See David Cirtis, ed., *Directory of British Film & Video Artists* (Luton: Arts Council of England, 1996), p. 223.

9   Gavin Stamp, *Silent Cities* (London: Royal Institute of British Architects, 1977), p. 7.

10   The exceptions are those isolated monuments to specific battles built by the Imperial War Graves Commission—in Normandy and in North Africa, for instance. See Stamp, *Silent Cities*, p. 18.

11   Sassoon is quoted in ibid., p. 4.

12   George V is quoted in ibid., p. 19.

13   Walter Benjamin, "The Work of Art in the Age of Mechanical Reproduction," in *Illuminations*, ed. Hannah Arendt, trans. Harry Zohn (London: Cape, 1970), pp. 217–251.

14   Alan Borg, *War Memorials* (London: Leo Cooper, 1991), p. 83.

15   Ibid., p. 119.

16   Brian Stater, "'War's Greatest Picture': St Paul's Cathedral, the London Blitz, and British National Identity" (M.Sc. thesis, University College London, 1996).

17   The 1942 Beveridge Report cited want, squalor, illness, ignorance, and disease as the "five giants."

18   Bevan is quoted in *St. Pancras Gazette*, 1 November 1948.

19   As part of the wholesale revisions of postwar history, the very notion of consensus has been called into question. Some historians, however, still defend it as a useful concept. For this debate, see Paul Addison, *The Road to 1945: British Politics and the Second World War* (London: Pimlico, 1994), esp. "Epilogue: The Road to 1945 Revisited" (pp. 279–292).

20   Patrick Wright, *A Journey through Ruins: The Last Days of London* (London: Radius, 1991), p. 92.

21   Correlli Barnett, *The Audit of War: The Illusion and Reality of Britain as a Great Nation* (London: Macmillan, 1986).

22   Alan Borg, director general, Imperial War Museum, foreword to *The Cabinet War Rooms* (London: Imperial War Museum, 1994), n.p.

23   Ibid.

24   Ibid.

25   Lowenthal, *Heritage Crusade*, pp. 1–31.

26   Lord Charles Spencer Churchill, introduction to *Winston Churchill's Britain at War Museum* (London: Churchill Publishing, 1993), n.p.

27   Raphael Samuel, *Theatres of Memory* (London: Verso, 1994).

28 John Keegan, *The Battle for History: Re-fighting World War II* (London: Pimlico, 1995).

29 Stiftung Frauenkirche Dresden e.V. and Gesellschaft zur Förderung des Wiederaufbaus der Frauenkirche Dresden e.V., *The Re-erection of the Frauenkirche in Dresden* (Dresden: 1995), n.p.

30 This brief account is based on various issues of the *East London Advertiser*, May 1995–July 1997.

31 Roy Fuller, "Soliloquy in an Air-Raid," in *I Burn for England: An Anthology of the Poetry of World War Two*, ed. Charles Hamblett (London: Leslie Frewin, 1966), p. 131.

The suburb . . . has served as an experimental field for the urban development of a new type of open plan and a new distribution of urban functions. . . . Some of the lessons that modern planners first mastered in the suburb must be incorporated into the new concept of the city.

Lewis Mumford
The City in History

William Menking

5 From Tribeca to Triburbia: A New Concept of the City

In 1978 I moved to Tribeca, an intensely urban district of industrial and residential buildings in New York City. I still live on the same lower Manhattan street, but my neighborhood has been transformed into *Triburbia*, a district increasingly as suburban as any in the 100-mile wide metropolitan ring around New York City. The *New York Times* portrays it as a model of successful urban regeneration. The newspaper, which supports gentrification as it does local sports teams, claims that Triburbia is now one of the most popular districts in the region for affluent middle-class families who previously would have wanted to live only in the leafy outer edges of the city, perhaps in Connecticut or New Jersey: "Father's a broker, mother's a lawyer—who would have been looking for a $600,000 house in Short Hills [to] raise their family. But their work is in the city, [and] they have their schools nailed down . . . in the city."[1] However, in its transformation to an affluent residential suburb, much of the dynamic urban life of the area has been lost. It was a neighborhood where artists' studios, working-class tenements, small family-owned business, and busy garment factories coexisted. The edges of the district easily gave way to the surrounding Lower East Side working-class neighborhoods of Chinatown and Little Italy, an abandoned waterfront, and similar blocks of nineteenth-century factory buildings.

How and why my central-city neighborhood transformed itself is a classic case of gentrification, but one with a particularly contemporary twist. To walk its streets is to realize that it has learned and absorbed the "lessons that modern planners first mastered in the suburbs" and morphed into a "new concept of the city"[2]—a suburb in the city center. Lewis Mumford had hoped that low-density "garden cities" would lead to better living conditions for the majority of Americans. Further, he believed these suburbs would even influence the form of city. However, the development of American suburbs has produced a quite different residential condition and influence on cities. Benefiting from the opportunities of the city, yet simultaneously repelled by its cacophonous life, the space and form of the traditional American suburb have almost always been isolated, fortified, and affluent domestic communities focusing on a limited social condition—the nuclear family. More specifically, they represent a balance of private and public, defined by what and who they include and exclude.

But how did the American city get to the point where it began to mimic the suburb? When American cities began experiencing explosive growth in the nineteenth century through immigration, the city was not able to provide adequate services for this largely poor population. The middle classes quickly tired of aiding the poor, except through occasional philanthropic charities (sometimes making a profit), and began moving outside the city's taxing boundary.[3] Since at least 1815, the American middle class has continued to work in the city and use its services but largely live and pay taxes elsewhere. "Between 1815 and 1875," Kenneth Jackson points out, "America's largest cities under went a dramatic spatial change . . . the steam ferry, omnibus, the commuter railroad . . . gave additional impetus to an exodus that would turn cities 'inside out' and inaugurate a new pattern of suburban affluence and center despair."[4] In fact, so many prosperous residents were leaving the tumultuous city by 1850 that New York newspapers complained the city was being "desert[ed] by its men of wealth"; one New York City politician argued against "the improvement of ferry service," hoping thereby to slow the middle-class exodus.[5]

With a declining upper and middle class to help provide for services, the city faced the problem of providing for a population that required but could not pay for social services. Unfortunately, American cities are legally prohibited from trying to plan and regionally tax the escaping suburban middle classes. Unlike in Europe, where cities have historically been self-governing, in America cities derive their power to govern entirely from their state: they have no political power that is not granted to them by the state legislature. If New York City, for example, wants to levy a tax on its commuting suburbanites to help with the city's finances, it must first ask permission of the state legislature. The state of New York, always careful to guard against the power of Gotham and representing conflicting rural, regional, and suburban interests, typically denies the city any such authority.

Contemporary gentrification or urban regeneration is also the result of a thirty-year campaign by government, real estate interests, the media, city planners, and architects to reverse the perceived "urban crises" of the American city in the 1960s and 1970s.[6] These crises began after the Second World War, when the American middle class in ever greater numbers abandoned entire neighborhoods of the country's central cities—with their aging infrastructure and declining government assistance—for subsidized houses, roads, parks, and schools in former farmlands surrounding the old commercial cores. These old inner-city neighborhoods became the home to poor immigrants and racial groups locked out of the new suburbs by segregation.[7] Many buildings, even blocks, of the old city were abandoned and left to deteriorate.

The accelerated deterioration of the city's housing stock, now no longer owner-occupied but controlled by large real estate groups, led to a reduction in the buildings' economic value, causing a simultaneous reduction in the city's tax base. A gap between public needs and the city's ability to meet them led to the much-debated urban crises of the American city. A 1968 survey of homeowners in Boston makes this point:

The Conventional Urban problems—housing, transportation, pollution, urban renewal and the like—were a major concern of only 18% of those questioned and these were expressed disproportionately by the wealthier, better educated respondents. . . . The issue which concerned more respondents than any other was variously stated—crime, violence, rebellious youth, racial tension, public immorality, delinquency. However stated, the common theme seemed to be a concern for improper behavior in public places.[8]

For many, the solution seemed obvious: bring back the middle class, with their higher incomes, at all costs. The middle classes, this theory argued, could be attracted back to the city by the now degraded but still high quality of blocks of nineteenth-century row houses. After they purchased and then upgraded the properties, the value of the city's property would rise. In addition, this theory held that the middle class expected (as if the poor did not) and knew how to demand better social services: schools, sanitation, and parks.[9] The city would be transformed back to its pre-1950s ideal of middle-class rectitude and order.

When I was an architecture student at the University of California in the early 1970s, nearly every studio design project was a variation on this theme of "bringing the middle-income families back to the city." The sites for our projects were usually in old, degraded working-class neighborhoods in San Francisco or Oakland. Developers would visit our design reviews to tell us what the middle class wanted and students would spend time designing parking lots, swimming pools, and surrounding green spaces. Although these use schemes meant to displace the present occupants, this point was rarely discussed in studio. These projects mirrored what our design professors were creating in San Francisco, one of the first cities in America to feel the effects of gentrification. In the 1950s New York City began to redevelop the Upper West Side, the largest area of abandoned and dilapidated blocks in Manhattan. In order to accomplish this rebuilding it "presented a plan of park-like open spaces": tearing down scores of old buildings would create a checkerboard of parks and gardens around once-elegant brownstone row houses. This "West Side Story" hoped to bring the middle-class suburbanites back from the leafy suburbs to a green city.[10] It would also have had the effect of quietly clearing the potentially high-priced land of the undesirable poor. Fortunately, this plan was defeated by local opposition.

Just as the post–Second World War suburbs were created and supported by government legislation like the Veterans Home Loan Guarantee program of 1944 (known as the "G.I. Bill") and the Interstate Highway Act of 1956,[11] so too was New York suburbanized through government intervention. In 1981 the mayor of the city, Edward Koch, began an unprecedented spatial restructuring of the city based not on the historic row house or apartment building patterns of New York, but on the suburbs. His ideas about the future of the city seemed to be grounded not in the needs of the current population of the five boroughs, but in his childhood memories of the city before the Second World War, when it had a large, white middle class. Koch wanted these middle-class residents back in the city and he was not shy about promoting his vision. In 1984 he declared, "We're not catering to the poor anymore . . . there are four other boroughs they can live in. They don't have to live in Manhattan."[12]

Koch would have the poor move to once-thriving but now largely abandoned districts, such as the South Bronx and Brownsville. These decrepit areas would be rebuilt once again, along the lines of suburban communities of single-family houses with yards. In order to accomplish this Koch proposed his "Ten-Year Plan" to rebuild or renovate 252,000 units of affordable housing.[13] The mayor planned to use federal housing programs, initially intended for lower-scale suburbs, for the first time in a high-density urban setting. For example, he utilized a federal "affordable housing program" to build blocks of suburban-like single-family homes on Coney Island. He also encouraged a series of six different housing programs in New York City's poor neighborhoods, including Charlotte Gardens. This project created low-density ranch-style single-family houses in the South Bronx in the shadow of abandoned tenement buildings, many of which had decals affixed to their bricked-up windows to make them look like pleasant apartments. And thousands of low-cost houses, part of the government-supported, private, for-profit Nehemiah Housing Movement, began sprouting all over Brooklyn and the Bronx. The architectural iconography of Nehemiah's medieval half-timbered houses in this largely Hispanic and African American community could not be clearer. Despite an enviable record of creating truly affordable houses for people making between $20,000 and $53,000 a year, the movement promotes a social agenda that asks the poor to believe they are actually middle class.[14] It forces them to buy into a privatized world of home repair, gardening, and bank credit. One must also question the extremely cheap, flimsy quality of these houses, which may have only a twenty-year life expectancy (though they probably were bought with a thirty-year mortgage). Finally, their low density ensures that the thousands of people who need housing in New York will never receive it in these neighborhoods.

But let us return to Triburbia in lower Manhattan, the privileged half of this new urban/suburban model. Those used to identifying suburbs simply as places of freestanding houses and green grass will find at first that

Triburbia doesn't fit the popular image. The district, of course, is sited within the dense urban fabric of a city, not adjacent to it, as is the traditional American suburb. However, on closer inspection it is apparent that it has undergone subtle and unique physical and spatial changes that are as suburban as fences and gates.

I should also point out that suburbs within New York City are not new. Many New York City neighborhoods now considered quintessentially urban were first built as suburbs of the rapidly examining metropolis: Greenwich Village, Harlem, and Brooklyn Heights were once privileged domains outside the swirl of social and economic forces engulfing the great city. Moreover, suburban design has long influenced development in the city: Grammercy Park's gated park established a precedent for Triburbia's own walled Washington Market Park. In 1913 Forest Hills Gardens was built as a suburban residential enclave, now subsumed by the borough of Queens. It reportedly had the "first deliberately photogenic residential development in the United States." Buildings were "aged" from the start to give the appearance of traditional stability[15]—perhaps setting a precedent for themed city districts like South Street Seaport, which Christine Boyer has written about.[16] Even the paradigmatic urban housing type, the apartment building, has since 1912 had more units constructed in the suburbs than in the central city, and many innovations created out of the conditions of the suburb have later been adapted to the city.[17] In the 1950s, for example, New York City architect Philip Birnbaum brought "'Queens to Manhattan' by applying his 'outer borough style' to the island. This style included small balconies, underground garages, circular driveways, canopied entrances, and flashy lobbies."[18]

But Triburbia and gentrified center city districts like it (Soho, Chelsea, etc.) represent a different suburban spatial and physical order than we have so far witnessed. They are not former suburban districts later subsumed by the city or simply urban areas filled with suburban appliqués like canopied entrances in apartment buildings. Built as part of the teeming nineteenth-century city, Triburbia has metamorphosed into a zone of seemingly urban blocks contiguous with the surrounding city; yet they are subtly guarded and controlled spaces that employ design elements first tried in the American suburbs to achieve separation from the city. In other words, suburban spatial elements have been overlaid on the historic fabric of New York.

In *Cybercities* Christine Boyer succinctly notes the "spatial restructuring of American cities, which sets up the dystopian city center as the mirror image of the spreading sprawling suburbs, or which tries to insert a random series of suburban amenities into the heart of the city." She points to the suburban-like landscape of "serpentine promenades, recreational and sports areas, pavilions and ponds that make up the Battery Park City land-scape in lower Manhattan" as a sign of this spatial restructuring.[19] However, from my Triburban window this suburbanization of the city has gone far be-yond just the packaged malling of the city's commercial corridors and the creation of a new suburban community like Battery Park City (Triburbia's immediate neighborhood). In fact, the restructuring is affecting, sometimes overwhelming, every quarter of the old central city.

It is the kind of neighborhood that American cities fantasized about in the 1960s at the height of the urban crises. But it represents a new phase in suburban development—one that is not built on open countryside, but layered over the existing city. The district and its suburban form cannot be understood without describing the "loft phenomenon."[20] Lofts are large, open-floored spaces originally built to accept a variety of different industrial processes in the late nineteenth century, and Triburbia is composed primar-ily of these structures. Their large size (3,000 to 4,000 square feet is com-mon) allows families to stay in the city and live in a family-centered suburb. In a culture that increasingly demands that the family, particularly the nu-clear one, be the basic societal unit, this is as perfect a neighborhood as any suburb. The *New York Times* trumpets Triburbia as the "kind of neighbor-hood where art collectors, bankers, designers, stock brokers and hip upper middle class parents might consider living in enormous sheet rocked spaces" even though a "few years ago the building might have been labeled an eyesore."[21] Like Sigmund Freud, who, strolling through a small Italian village, found himself subconsciously looping back through its red light district, these new Triburbanites seem pleased to find that they live in a sub-urb and not a city.

In *City of Quartz*, Mike Davis describes Los Angeles' heavy-handed response to its contemporary urban crises as "an unprecedented tendency to merge urban design, architecture and the police apparatus into a single, comprehensive security effort." This "epochal coalescence" comes together around private gated communities set amid the gridded landscape of the city. In "defense of luxury lifestyles," L.A. communities are "gathering be-hind walls guarded by gun toting police."[22] It has to be said that Triburbia is far more advanced in its urban restructuring. Without being literal, its walls are just as potent in keeping people out. To enter Triburbia today one passes historic preservation signposts that for New Yorkers, ever keen to the distinctions between areas of affluence and poverty, are as clear as walls. Once in Triburbia one is officially in a landmarked district of unusually (for New York City) clean streets, carefully tended flower boxes, and high-quality stores and services.

Lately, Triburbian real estate interests have been promoting the creation of a local Business Improvement District (usually depicted in the media as an expression of Jeffersonian democracy on the part of like-minded property owners). A BID is a state-chartered entity that allows commercial property owners to assess a surtax (which is most likely then passed on to consumers) on their property and then use the money for their own social service delivery system: trash collection, street cleaning, and even welfare assistance for the homeless. The current city government supports BIDs at the same time it is contracting out social services and firing municipal workers in neighborhoods all over the city. In Triburbia almost everything the middle class would want or need is provided: a new elementary school was built by the city in 1988 and a middle school is planned, while in poor neighborhoods schools are literally falling down.

Landmark district status was granted to the area in order to safeguard real estate investments as much as the buildings. Friedrich Engels claimed that "the bourgeoisie, from which the jury is selected, always finds some backdoor through which to escape the frightful verdict."[23] Triburbanites will make sure that its middle-class domain of high property values and services will not collapse while the poorer parts of the city continue to erode. Ironically, New York City property taxes are now very low when compared with suburban communities, and this disparity is working to the city dweller's advantage. Because the city feels at a disadvantage with the suburbs in providing a high level of services it cannot raise taxes to their level or the remaining middle-class residents will flee. With great schools in the privileged neighborhoods, the middle class is enjoying the best of both worlds—high services and low taxes. In fact, middle-class residents moving into Triburbia now expect a high standard of services, and the city seems willing to provide them even as similar services are contracted out in poor neighborhoods. The result is that the typical American suburban pattern has become the typical urban pattern—new, privileged, self-contained pockets for the wealthy and underserved areas for the poor.

In many respects this new, privileged Triburban city form, like the outer-city suburbs that it emulates, comes together around parks and green open space. In 1967 Paley Park was created on the site of the old Stork Club on 53rd Street in midtown Manhattan. Built at the time when many large corporations were fleeing Manhattan for the suburbs, this park was promoted as a model of a green restructuring that could enable the city to compete with the suburbs. Likewise, in 1983 the city created Washington Market Park: a walled, gated, and privately patrolled space designed in an Olmstedian eclectic and naturalistic style. A walk around its child- and nanny-filled lawns speaks of the suburban world of family-centered leisure,

5.1

5.2

5.1–5.4
Triburbia: Washington Market Park,
New York, 1997.

5.3

5.4

ordered propriety, picturesque repose, and union with nature—all based on the principle of exclusion. This suburban picturesque fits perfectly into the new private realm being created in Triburbia. A second park, North River in Battery Park City, immediately adjacent to Washington Market Park, is similarly gated and privately patrolled and extends a "greenbelt" parkland around Triburbia. This greenbelt, originally designed by Robert Venturi and Denise Scott Brown, will extend a grass- and tree-lined highway along Triburbia's western edge.

Triburbanization is dismantling what remains of the modern "reformist" Olmstedian vision of an open city, in favor of a return to the earlier mercantile tradition of the city. In the nineteenth century the city government, controlled by commercial interests, tried to protect those interests by pushing the working class off the streets and sidewalks. However, during this period the poor depended on the sidewalks for their living, relying on everything from peddling to prostitution.[24] This fight and the social unrest it provoked led to the beginning of a progressive reform tradition in the city. This movement, in turn, led to the creation of Frederick Law Olmsted's New York City parks, including Central Park, which was explicitly intended to be the living room for all the citizens of the metropolis. The fight over public space continues in the 1990s in New York City, and defines and determines in part the city's current notion of "public interest."[25] While the Triburbanization of the city works to defeat all hope for urban reform and social integration, the city, even with its ethnically and racially defined neighborhoods, also aspires to be a place of open, nonsegregated streets and parks.

In detailing this contemporary tale I hope I have made clear that I am appalled at how the new Triburbia is discreetly sealed off for those so privileged to live behind real but invisible walls. I have not mentioned my own role in this suburbanization process. The physical form of Triburbia is that of low-scale factory buildings, many of them landmark cast-iron structures; and their charm and Manhattan location attracted a young class of urban professional artists, writers, and even architectural historians to want to live in the area. Even the abandoned old dockland that formerly lined the district's western edge, before it was torn down for the Venturian "green highway," was so picturesque that it became the neighborhood playground. I and my neighbors used to wander through the rotting and deteriorating piers and docks as we might walk through the Roman Forum. While I was initially drawn to the area in part because I could move into a nearly abandoned building without displacing a family or operating business, I was quite obviously gentrifying the district. It never occurred to me while I and other young professionals were helping to make a desirable urban settlement that we would no longer be able to afford the Triburbia we helped gentrify. We early gentrifiers underestimated the voracious and cunning nature of financial capital as it moves from one site of "underdevelopment" to another. But more important, it reminds us that although people immigrate to the city because it is seemingly a space of social, economic, and cultural fluidity, increasingly this space, like our contemporary political system, is more about segregation and lack of access.

William Menking

Notes

1 "Lofts Designed for Families," *New York Times*, 15 December 1996.

2 Lewis, Mumford, *The City in History: Its Origins, Its Transformations, and Its Prospects* (New York: Harcourt, Brace, and World, 1961), p. 481.

3 Elliot Willensky and Norval White, *AIA Guide to New York City*, 3d ed. (New York: Harcourt Brace Jovanovich, 1988), p. 578. The authors recount the story of Alfred Treadway White, a Brooklyn builder of the famous Tower and Home buildings. His motto "Philanthropy plus 5 percent" has been much quoted.

4 Kenneth Jackson, *The Crabgrass Frontier: The Suburbanization of the United States* (New York: Columbia University Press, 1987), p. 20.

5 Ibid., p. 29.

6 Manuel Castells, *The Urban Question: A Marxist Approach* (Cambridge, Mass.: MIT Press, 1980), p. 402.

7 Ibid., chapter 17.

8 Ibid., p. 382.

9 Henry J. Schmandt and Warner Bloomberg, Jr., eds., *The Quality of Urban Life*, Urban Affairs Annual Reviews (New York: Sage Publications, 1969), p. 155.

10 Robert A. M. Stern, Thomas Mellins, and David Fishman, *New York 1960: Architecture and Urbanism between the Second World War and the Bicentennial* (New York: Monacelli Press, 1995), pp. 728–729.

11 On the G.I. Bill, see Richard Plunz, *The History of Housing in New York City: Dwelling Type and Social Change in the American Metropolis* (New York: Columbia University Press 1990), p. 261.

12 Koch is quoted in ibid., p. 371.

13 Eric Berman, "New York's 10 Year Plan for Housing," *Street News*, 20 May 1990, p. 9.

14 "Housing Pact Is Reached in Brooklyn," *New York Times*, 6 October 1992, p. 61.

15 John R. Stilgoe, *Borderland: The Origins of the American Suburb, 1820–1939* (New Haven: Yale University Press, 1988), p. 225.

16 M. Christine Boyer, "Cities for Sale: Merchandising History at South Street Seaport," in *Variations on a Theme Park: The New American City and the End of Public Space*, ed. Michael Sorkin (New York: Noonday Press, 1992).

17 Larry R. Ford, *Cities and Buildings: Skyscrapers, Skid Rows, and Suburbs* (Baltimore: Johns Hopkins University Press, 1994), pp. 216–217.

18 Tom Shachtman, *Skyscraper Dreams: The Great Real Estate Dynasties of New York* (New York: Little, Brown, 1991), p. 239.

19 M. Christine Boyer, *Cybercities: Visual Perception in the Age of Electronic Communication* (Princeton: Princeton Architectural Press, 1996), p. 163.

20 Sharon Zukin, *Loft Living: Culture and Capital in Urban Change* (Baltimore: Johns Hopkins University Press, 1982).

21 *New York Times*, 14 July 1996.

22 Mike Davis, *City of Quartz: Excavating the Future in Los Angeles* (London: Verso, 1990), p. 224.

23 Karl Marx and Frederick Engels, *Articles on Britain* (New York: Progress Publishers, 1971), p. 65.

24 Elizabeth Blackmar, *Manhattan for Rent: 1785–1850* (Ithaca: Cornell University Press, 1989), p. 151.

25 Ibid., p. 157.

Pleasure and novelty were his constant pur-
suits by day or by night.[1]

The circulation of women among men is what
establishes the operations of society, at least of
patriarchal society.[2]

Jane Rendell

6

"Bazaar Beauties" or "Pleasure Is Our
Pursuit": A Spatial Story of Exchange

I am a feminist, a feminist who wishes to tell you a story, a spatial story,[3] a (hi)story of bazaars in early-nineteenth-century London. The two quotes above summarize why and how I attempt to "know" these architectural places. Contradictory, disorienting, strange even—these twin phenomena, pursuit and exchange, are at the heart of my storytelling.

> To admit that writing is precisely working (in) the in-between, in-specting the process of the same and of the other without which nothing can live, undoing the work of death—to admit this is first to want the two, as well as both, the ensemble of the one and the other . . . a multiple and inexhaustible course with millions of en-counters and transformations of the same into the other and into the in-between, from which woman takes her forms.[4]

In contemporary urban and architectural discourse, we are increas-ingly obsessed by figures that traverse space: the flâneur, the spy, the detec-tive, the prostitute, the rambler, the cyprian. These all represent urban explorations, passages of revelation, journeys of discovery—they are "spatial stories."[5] We all are spatial story–tellers, explorers, navigators, and discov-erers, exchanging narratives of, and in, the city. Through the personal, the political, the theoretical, the historical we believe we are revealing cities in "strangely familiar" ways, but we are also creating cities as we desire them to be. Our desires frame our fragile understanding of architectural space. All we ever offer is a partial glimpse. This chapter offers one such glimpse. "De-sire prevents us from understanding reality with well-known and habitual criteria. The most distinctive feature of such a situation is that it is always new, unfamiliar."[6]

KNOWING THE CITY

In wide arcs of wandering through the city
I saw to either side of what is seen,
and noticed treasures where it was thought
there were none.

I passed through a more fluid city.
I broke up the imprint of all familiar places,
shutting my eyes to the boredom of modern contours.[7]

The Strangely Familiar project set itself a pursuit, an itinerary—to question the understanding of architecture in the city framed through one specific and self-contained discipline: architectural history. The contributors to that project, and now to this extended investigation, bring stories from inside and outside architectural history. This intricate web of narratives shreds urban epistemology and positions partial knowledge at multiple sites, at the interfaces of particular practices that are themselves shifting in their mutual interchange. The exchange of ideas about the city among geographers, sociologists, filmmakers, artists, cultural theorists, literary critics, and architects has located new kinds of spaces and new ways of interpreting, examining, and even living within them. In this more fluid state, our ability to know the city is always contingent, forever in flux.

> Critical work is made to fare on interstitial ground. Every realization of such work is a renewal and a different contextualization of its cutting edge. One cannot come back to it as to an object; for it always bursts forth on frontiers. . . . Instead, critical strategies must be developed within a range of diversely occupied territories where the temptation to grant any single territory transcendent status is continually resisted.[8]

As a historian, I tell spatial stories somewhat differently than do other storytellers; my stories are inspired by a desire to "know" the past, to "tell it as it was" (and, if possible, to explain it). These "attempts at disclosure," as described by Steve Pile elsewhere in this book, are not as revealing as they might seem; indeed, as Pile suggests, "the unknown is not so easily known." But "knowing" history is easy. Who can dispute our reconstruction of places, dwelt in before we were born, today transformed beyond recognition, and left as traces in obscure documents that only we will ever read? Is this the historical imagination running wild? But why not believe these stories—aren't we always encouraged to believe in fairy tales? "[W]hy not then continue to look at it all as a child would, as if you were looking at something unfamiliar, out of the depths of your own world, from the vastness of your solitude, which is itself work and status and vocation?"[9]

KNOWING THE SELF

Believe me, I do not demand the reader to be a disbeliever, but rather request that writers look more closely at the self in their work. Historical knowledge is formed within the person, founded on our own subjectivity. The (hi)stories we tell of cities are also (hi)stories of ourselves. I shape my interest in architecture and history and I can be many things. I am a woman and my fascination with feminism makes a difference to the way in which I know. Questions of methodology embedded in feminist debates have ramifications for understanding space and time, architecture and history. (For example, early-nineteenth-century London holds interest for me because, arguably, it seems to precede the establishment of the dominant paradigm of gender and space, the ideology of separate spheres. In terms of traditional historical periodization, it lies still largely obscured between the so-called long eighteenth century and the Victorian period.)

There are millions of women, a myriad of feminisms, no single way of knowing the city; but for many feminists the personal is an important epistemological site. Negotiating a meaningful relation between the personal and the critical is central to much feminist work. We are all different. Our differences are different. Our sex can make a difference to who we are and how we know, whose work we read and how we write. "Some differences are playful: some are poles of world historical systems of domination. Epistemology is about knowing the difference."[10]

KNOWING THE DIFFERENCE

"Knowing" the city invites, and invokes, a need to know the self, the one who seeks knowledge. This female subject places herself in complex relation to her subject matter. She is desirous of knowledge, but also fears her need to know. For her, clear and certain knowledge, "knowing" without doubt, is a masculinist pursuit that assumes knowing oneself. To make purposeful decisions about historical lines of inquiry and interpretive strategies, one must first know one's own mind. "For the master's tools will never dismantle the master's house. They may allow us to temporarily to beat him at his own game, but they will never enable us to bring about genuine change."[11]

I do not know my own mind. I do not know what is on my mind. I hardly know myself. How then can I be trusted to know the past? How can I make a difference, bring about "genuine change," if I do not know myself? Outward, backward, our ephemeral links to the past lead us ever inward, toward uncertain futures. What we have instead of an afterimage of what has gone before is a view into the murky interior. The urban past, the cities we seek to know, is made in our own self-image. "[T]he city which looked most deeply like the womb with its Arabian Nights gentleness, tranquillity and mystery. Myself, woman, womb, with grilled windows, veiled eyes. Tortuous streets, secret cells, labyrinths and more labyrinths."[12] What we call objective historical knowledge cannot be separated from a fluid network of cross-linking, feedbacking, constantly shifting and reciprocal relations between outer and inner worlds, between the city and the self. "Cities new to us are full of promise. Unlike promises we make to each other, the promise of the city can never be broken. But like the promise we hold for each other, neither can it be fulfilled."[13]

In my pursuit of historical knowledge, in my search to understand architecture and gender, I desired the city. In my attempts to know, to reunite, with nineteenth-century London, I entered poignant forms of exchange—through reading (and rereading). Two pieces of writing seduced me, one theoretical and poetic, the other a bawdy urban narrative. These were sites of methodological struggle—places where difficult questions of spatial and historical knowledge were raised but also where I was offered tantalizing and "knowing" glimpses of the relation between my desirous self and the city, the object of my desire. "When desire takes over, the body gets the upper hand. In our intense contemplation of the beloved—as if to discover the secret of that which binds and confuses—we are looking for our past. We reunite with something that seemed lost but now appears in a new and even more attractive light."[14]

THE EXCHANGE OF WOMEN: WOMEN ON THE MARKET

The "exchange of women" is a powerful
and seductive concept. It is attractive in
that it places the oppression of women
within social systems, rather than in biology.
Moreover, it suggests that we look for the
ultimate locus of women's oppression within
the traffic in women, rather than within
the traffic in merchandise.[15]

As I read Luce Irigaray's "Women on the Market" for the first time, I was overawed. This woman was able to express, critically and poetically, the political anger I felt about women's oppression.[16] Her writing fired me; it served as a political manifesto, and as a source of creative inspiration. I read it in the park, on the bus, in bed. The more I read Irigaray, the more I felt I knew about the way in which space was gendered in nineteenth-century London. Yet I had not looked at a single piece of primary evidence. I had not entered the British Library nor even contemplated visiting archives. I was uttering profanities in the sacred space of historical knowledge.

> She may go anywhere and everywhere, gaining entrance wherever she chooses; she sails through walls as easily as through tree-trunks or the piers of bridges. No material is an obstacle for her, neither stones, nor iron, nor wood, nor steel can impede her progress or hold back her step. For her, all matter has the fluidity of water.[17]

Irigaray uses the Marxist critique of commodity capitalism to show the ways in which women are the commodities in patriarchal exchange. As a commodity, woman's value resides not in her own being but in some transcendental standard of equivalence, whether money or the phallus. For Irigaray, commerce is an exchange played out through the bodies of women, as matter or as sign. Men make commerce of women but not with them: "The economy—in both the narrow and the broad sense—that is in place in our societies thus requires that women lend themselves to alienation in consumption, and to exchanges in which they do not participate, and that men be exempt from being used and circulated like commodities" (p. 172). Like the Marxist commodity, the female body as commodity in patriarchy is divided into two irreconcilable "bodies." Women represent a natural value and a social value—use value and exchange value. Female commodities—prostitute, virgin, mother—are associated with different kinds of use and exchange values, which depend on the spaces they occupy in patriarchy. In patriarchy, men and women are distinguished, through their relationship to property: men own property, women are property. Men own and occupy spaces and women, while women occupy space.

On the market, in the public realm of commerce, the space of public patriarchy, woman as commodity is visible; she represents use for potential buyers, exchange for her owner. As virgin, woman is on the market; her female body has pure exchange value. "She is nothing but the possibility, the place, the sign of relations among men. . . . Once deflowered, woman is relegated to the status of use value, to her entrapment in private property: she is removed from exchange among men" (p. 186). As mother, woman has a natural use value, and she is taken off the market: "As both natural value and use value, mothers cannot circulate in the form of commodities without threatening the very existence of the social order" (p. 185). Within the realm of the private patriarch, virgin and mother are contained as natural values.

The prostitute, in contrast, is defined through her social use and exchange value in relation to her occupation of public space. As woman, her body is "useful" in the public realm; it also has an exchange value. "However, these qualities have 'value' . . . because they serve as the locus of relations—hidden ones—between men. Prostitution amounts to *usage that is exchanged*. . . . The woman's body is valuable because it has already been used. In the extreme case, the more it has served, the more it is worth" (p. 186).

Irigaray's work is suggestive of a way of thinking about the gendering of space that is dynamic. Rather than the static binary of the separate spheres, space is gendered through a series of shifting relations. As men and women traverse space, their positions and pathways vary according to personal, social, and cultural desires, and to relations of power, of class, race, and nationality as well as sex, gender, and sexuality. The spatial patterns composed between them, both materially and metaphorically, are choreographies of connection and separation, screening and displaying, moving and containing. These are relations of exchange, consumption, display, and desire in which women move, or are moved, between men: as objects of exchange and signs of exchange, as commodities, and as values. Reading "Women on the Market" made a difference to the way in which I conceived of the gendering of architectural space in early-nineteenth-century London.

> And all my theories skillfully and gracefully took up position in my own starry night. There was an order. They obeyed my wishes so well that even though they came from me, they surprised and taught me, and even though they were no more than hypothesis and illusion, they always took me to a safe harbor as easily as any real boat. In the end, going from illusion to illusion, one also comes to understand the world.[18]

I had discovered Irigaray through passion, through eros; but now, out of the labyrinth of my personal desire, theory emerged. Theory told back to me what I already knew, but in a different language—one of objectivity not subjectivity, one that I considered could reasonably influence the way I knew and understood events in the past, the way I did history. Before I had looked at any primary documents, I knew why and how space was gendered in early-nineteenth-century London. In theory. My desire to know was mediated through logos. I pursued the ramble in abstraction.[19] But theorizing the personal is one thing, historical textual analysis is another; the two are in constant negotiation. Each document I chose to examine offered me a different form of knowledge, held influence over what I could know.

RAMBLING: THE PURSUIT OF PLEASURE

The verb *to ramble* describes incoherent movement, "to wander in discourse (spoken or written): to write or talk incoherently or without natural sequence of ideas" Rambling is "a walk without any definite route,"[20] an unrestrained, random, and distracted mode of movement. In the early nineteenth century, *rambling* described the exploration of urban space; only later is the word used to refer to a planned rural outing. Despite its random form, rambling is an activity with a focus, physical and conceptual: the pursuit of pleasure, specifically sexual pleasure—"to go about in search of sex."[21]

Our motto is be gay and free
Make Love and Joy your choicest treasures
Look on our book of glee
And Ramble over scenes of Pleasure.[22]

Rambles had been published from the seventeenth century onward,[23] but the years following the Napoleonic Wars saw the publication a large number of best-selling books and prints featuring the rambler, or fashionable and sporting man about town. These semifictional urban narratives told of the initiation of various country gentlemen to the adventures of city life in London under the guidance of a streetwise urban relative.[24] Monthly periodicals, with "rambler" in the title, drew on earlier literature offering lists, locations, and descriptions of prostitutes,[25] in order to cater for male readers in pursuit of sex pleasure.[26]

The rambler represented a new kind of urban masculinity—male, young, heterosexual, and upper-class. Also described as a *corinthian, bruiser,* or *dandy*, the rambler was a man of fashion and sport, of leisure and pleasure, who spent his income on gambling, drinking, and whoring: "A young unmarried Englishman, with a large fortune, spends but a small share of it on his common expenses; the greatest part is destined to his pleasures, that is to say, to the ladies."[27]

The rambler traverses the city, looking in its open and its interior spaces for adventure and entertainment; in so doing, he creates a kind of conceptual and physical map of what the city is. In constant motion, in pursuit of pleasure, leisure, and consumption, the rambler is a specific form of urban representation—he represents the city as multiple sites of desire. "We have already taken a promiscuous ramble from the West towards the East, and it has afforded some amusement; but our stock is abundant, and many objects of curiosity are still in view."[28]

BAZAARS: PLEASURE HOUSES OF COMMODITY CONSUMPTION

The rambler's relation to the city, one of curiosity and desire, also describes the attitude toward the new luxury shopping venues built during the same period. These include exchanges, bazaars, and arcades in the area west of Regent Street.[29] The new bazaars were like both Walter Benjamin's arcades, "a city, indeed a world in miniature," and the world exhibitions, "places of pilgrimage to the fetish Commodity."[30] Physically, the English bazaar was a building of more than one story, which contained shopping stalls rented out to retailers of different trades, as well as picture galleries, indoor gardens, and menageries. The "bazaar" also evoked otherworldliness through the signifying qualities of the name itself—the exoticism of the "unknown" East. Bazaars represented magical spaces of enchantment, sites of intoxication and desire, inspired by the enticing display of luxurious commodities—dresses, accessories, millinery—with satiation promised through their consumption.

"A new kind of establishment for the shew and sale of goods in London has begun, and which by the Indians are called Bazaars, or collections of small shops in one space."[31] The first London bazaar was the Soho Bazaar, a conversion of a warehouse by John Trotter in 1816. It occupied several houses on the northwest corner of Soho Square with counters on two floors. The Western Exchange was built in the same year at 10 Old Bond Street, adjoining the Burlington Arcade. In 1834 the Pantheon, an assembly room on Oxford Street, was converted to a bazaar and picture gallery; it sold drapery, outfitting, accessories, children's clothes, books, sheet music, fancy goods, and toys, with an aviary and conservatory for the sale of birds and plants. Other bazaars followed rapidly in Leicester Square, Newman Street, Bond Street, James Street, and the Strand.[32] By the 1830s they included the Royal London bazaar, the Baker Street bazaar, the Horse bazaar, and the coach bazaar or Pantechnicon at Moycombe Street in Belgravia.

WOMEN AT THE MARKET

"It consists of two large floors, in which upwards of 200 female dealers are daily occupied in the sale of almost every article of human consumption."[33] The Soho Bazaar, as described here, was set up with the express purpose of providing work for women; it was a place where widows and orphans of army officers could sell items that they had made.[34] Women were intended to be the main employees of the bazaars—"the officiating priestesses of this great vanity-fair." Of the two hundred people working there, only two were men.[35] Women were also intended to be the consumers in these new palaces of commodity consumption: "The articles sold are almost exclusively pertaining to the dress and personal decoration of ladies and children; such as millinery, lace, gloves, jewellery etc."[36]

In these nascent spaces of commodity capitalism, it was essential to entrepreneurs, like Trotter, that profits be made. As new consumers, middle- and working-class women had to be present for the bazaar to succeed. Bazaars were promoted as places of charity, where upper-class women sold wares to raise funds for orphans and other destitutes. Contemporary novels aimed at women readers depicted shopping venues as respectable female zones.[37] In a period of rising evangelism, images of femininity and the female body were used to represent middle-class values of virtue and morality. In this developing value system, the women working in the bazaar operated as signs of exchange, representing, through their dress and demeanor, capitalist enterprises as pure: "A plain and modest style of dress, on the part of the young females who serve at the stalls, is invariably insisted on, a matron being hand to superintend the whole."[38]

Ideas of purity were also conjured up through architectural references. Bazaars were safe environments, well-protected, usually under the management of one proprietor. They were physically secure, with safety features such as guards and lockable gates that promoted order and control. For example, the premises of the Pantheon were described as "large, dry, commodious, well lighted, warmed, ventilated, and *properly watched*."[39] These buildings were monofunctional, designed along strict and rational grids. With no hidden spaces or secret activities, the bazaar kept everything on display and in its place. In contrast to the surrounding unruly city, associated with danger and threat, here emphasis was placed on order, both in the layout of the space itself and in the strict rules governing behavior on the premises:

> every stall must have its wares displayed by a particular hour in the morning, under penalty of a fine from the renter; the rent is paid day by day, and if the renter be ill, she has to pay for the services of a substitute, the substitute being such a one as is approved by the principals of the establishment.[40]

"BAZAAR BEAUTIES"

Although the buying and selling of commodities was considered a respectable urban activity, shopping venues were also connected with male sexual pursuit and female display. The oriental connotation of the term *bazaar* suggests sensuality and eroticism, and the rambling texts represented these markets as places of intrigue.[41] For George Cruikshank, bazaars functioned solely as a place for arranging sexual exchanges and transactions; two decades later, another writer described them as "fashionable lounging places for the great and titled ones, and the places of assignation for supposed casual encounters."[42]

The Rambler's Magazine ran a series of monthly features titled "Bazaar Beauties," which undermined the moral aspirations of these venues and exposed their real purpose—as places for men to look at women. "Lord P-t-h-m . . . accosted the lovely and amiable Mistress Hughes, whose table was surrounded by fashionables, laying out their money for the attractions of her blue eyes and smiles, more than real principles of charity."[43] Representations served to reinforce the role of female employees as the site of desire in the bazaar. Rambling texts speculated on the improbable chastity of these demure matrons, representing them not as female subjects but as objects for the projection of male lust, their bodies on display to men, in parts. Lady Agar Ellis was "said to have the finest neck and shoulders of all the ladies who go to court, her lips are thick and pouting"; the Widow of Castlereagh had "a noble Grecian face, and a remarkably small foot"; and Lady Francis F——e was "greatly admired—but particularly her beautifully shaped arm which she displays naked, nearly up to the shoulder."[44]

The importance of visual consumption—the delight in the gaze and the exchange of looks—played a critical role in constructing the social space of these pleasure houses of commodity consumption. Not all observes approved: "All the worth-less elegance of dress and decoration are here displayed on the counters in gaudy profusion. . . . The Bazaar, in a word, is a fashionable lounge for all those who have nothing to do except see and be seen."[45] In visual representations of bazaars, the objectifying function of the male gaze was reinforced by positioning women as the focus of the look within the space of the image. Within the material place of the bazaar, women were located as the main attraction, at booths organized into easily traversed aisles, behind tables full of merchandise on display.

In places of commodity consumption, as in other public spaces, the visibility of women implied their sexual availability, whether through intrigue or through prostitution. The active display by prostitutes of their own bodies—in windows, on streets, and by adopting indecent attitudes, signs, and invitations to attract the attention of passengers—suggested to the male viewer that any woman on display in the public realm was also available for visual, if not sexual, consumption.[46] In Fanny Burney's *The Wanderer*, the heroine, a working woman, notes the careful and exploitative positioning of women in retail spaces such as millinery shops, creating "images of advertisement in a manner that savours of genteel prostitution; the prettier girls are placed at the window to attract male customers and dalliers. The labour is treated as a frivolity, and the girls are being taught to sell themselves."[47]

Removed from the everyday world of the city, and constructed as liminal zones where desires were played out, the bazaar conveyed sexual excitement to the rambler by emphasizing the "feminine" as screen for projecting fantasy. Bazaars were used as pickup zones or for setting up sexual liaisons of a clandestine if not economic nature, and the women who occupied these places were both chaste and lewd, prostitutes and nonprostitutes. It was the rambler's inability to decipher the "true" sexual identity of a woman from her appearance that titillated him. The frivolity and decorative function of many of the items for sale only served to heighten the sexual excitement, striking an analogy with the spatial tension of surface to depth. Ramblers enjoyed imagining how a demure exterior might indicate a suppressed wantonness: "In a Bazaar good and evil are mingled together, there are hundreds of women of rank and fashion, who are known to be daughters of the game."[48]

WOMEN ON THE MARKET

Commodities cannot themselves go to market
and perform exchanges in their own right.
We must, therefore, have recourse to their
guardians, who are the possessors of commodities.
Commodities are things, and therefore lack
the power to resist man. If they are unwilling,
he can use force; in other words, he can take
possession of them.[49]

Of the many sites of desire mapped through the ramble, such as the assembly rooms, the theater, opera house, and street, the public spaces of commodity consumption in early-nineteenth-century London form a particularly interesting locus for discussing the gendering of space through the exchange of women as commodities. Karl Marx has pointed out the impossibility of a commodity performing an act of exchange. But if we follow Irigaray's suggestion that women, in a patriarchal society, are often treated as commodities by men, then we must surmise that women cannot be active subjects in the exchange of commodities: they can only be the commodities exchanged. Such a premise is supported by a close examination of the semiotics of the rambling texts. Women in the bazaar were engaged in the selling of commodities to male customers, but a subject-to-subject, seller-to-buyer relation was not represented. Instead, these women were described using the same language as the goods they sold. When bazaars are discussed, the word "piece" or "article" represents the female body:

> "The Price of a Female Article in a bazaar": A young buck at Liverpool went into a bazaar, and leaning on the table stared a handsome young lady full in the face for some minutes. The lady, at last, holding up a fancy piece of goods, said "Sir, if you are admiring *that* the price is ten shillings." The reply was, "No my dear, I am admiring you as the prettiest *piece* to be seen." "That alters the case, sir, the

price of the *piece* you admire is one guinea." A purchase was made to their mutual satisfaction.[50]

During the early nineteenth century, the word *commodity* was commonly used to describe a woman's genitals—a modest woman was a "private commodity" and a prostitute was a "public commodity."[51] But particular kinds of commodities had stronger connections with sexual licentiousness than others. By spatial analogy, the "snuff box" or "reticule" served to represent female genitalia, often embellished as an "embroidered snuff box," or a "fine fancy gold worked reticule."[52] Reduced to articles or pieces, conflated with the commodities they were selling, bazaar women are also represented in the rambling tales as self-determining in their eagerness to display themselves for sale on the commodity market, in place of, or as well as, the commodities they were selling. They were active agents in the commodification of their own bodies: "Mr. Dick asked her rather impertinently, as she leant over the table—'Do you mean, my lady, to offer yourself or the article for sale?'—'Both,' she answered. 'Some of my friends here can testify, that me and my *article* always go together.'"[53]

Given the low wages and narrow scope of employment available to women, many female workers did gain extra income from prostitution, and some commentators recognized these material reasons for female prostitution: "It is disgraceful the manner in which the poor girls are kept at work at these places: it is no wonder, indeed, so many of them die in decline, and others go on the town."[54] But in the rambling tales, discussions of prostitution were more speculative; they served to arouse and entertain. Reading about women in public spaces, a position indicative of their subversive sexuality or role as prostitutes, was transgressive. The placing of women outside the home, the protected territory of the private patriarch—husband, father, or brother—posed an exciting threat to the constrictions placed on young men by patriarchal order. In public space, the patriarch's female property—mothers, wives, and daughters—is visually and sexually available to other men, including those of different classes. In bazaars, where women were exposed, unprotected, and often in close physical relation to strange men, their sexual reputations were open to lurid speculation. Women working in public spaces of commodity consumption were considered to be prostitutes and described as cyprians.

RAMBLERS AND CYPRIANS

The word *cyprian* is defined as "belonging to Cyprus, an island in the eastern Mediterranean, famous in ancient times for the worship of Aphrodite or Venus," goddess of love, and as "licentious, lewd"; and, in the eighteenth and nineteenth centuries, it was "applied to prostitutes."[55] In the rambling tales, the term was used to describe upper-class courtesans, ladies of fashion or "lady-birds," as well as prostitutes of a lower class: "nymphs of the pavé," mollishers, mots, or doxies. But what defines the cyprian is not her class, for many cyprians mixing in aristocratic circles came originally from lower- or middle-class families, but her spatial position. The cyprian's occupation of public space defines her sexual identity—she is a public woman, a woman of the town, a prostitute.

Together with the prostitute (the only female among the social characters—including the collector, ragpicker, detective, flâneur, and gambler—that Walter Benjamin named as allegories of modern urban life), the cyprian is the only female who figures in the ramble. Texts about London in the early decades of the nineteenth century are populated by many males—ramblers, corinthians, bruisers, dandies—but the cyprian is the only female to move through the streets and public spaces of London. Since walking is an integral part of the definition of the cyprian, she could be described as a female rambler. The cyprian is an urban peripatetic, but her body is also the site of the ramblers' desire and gaze, and these contain her. While the rambler is celebrated as an urban explorer, actively engaged in the constant pursuit of pleasure, the figure of the mobile cyprian is a cause of concern. Her movement represents the blurring of public and private boundaries, the uncontrollability of women in the city. Her mobility, her link to the street, to the public places of the city, is represented as the cause of her eventual destruction.[56]

The ramble serves to confine, both spatially and temporally, women's use and experience of the urban realm. Females who strolled through the streets, parks, and shopping arcades at the time of the ramble were considered to be of loose morals and so were discouraged from occupying urban space. To represent women as cyprians, as sexual and exchangeable commodities in the rambling narratives, articulates male fear concerning female sexuality and works morally and ideologically to control women's movement in the city.

KNOWING THE CITY/SELF

In this spatial story, I have told you of the exchange of women, of the ramble, of men's pursuit of pleasure and their fear of women's mobility in the city. In telling you this story, in representing the gendering of space through the activities of the rambler, my story may work against me; it may serve to define and confine our conception of the urban movement of women. But this is not the whole story. I have also told you of my own pursuit of knowledge through the exchange of ideas—of the fluid relation between the theoretical and the historical, the city and the self. I should also tell you that in writing we are creating new cities, we are also creating new selves. "There is no such thing as a completed definition of woman. A woman is weaving, woven, unravelling, moving female energy and experience."[57]

Notes

1   Pierce Egan, *Life in London* (London: Sherwood, Neely, and Jones, 1821).

2   Luce Irigaray, *This Sex Which Is Not One*, trans. Catherine Porter with Carolyn Burke (Ithaca: Cornell University Press, 1985), p. 184.

3   This spatial story is for Deborah Miller, whose insights in our late-night storytelling sessions always bring me out of, and back to, myself.

4   Hélène Cixous, "The Laugh of the Medusa," trans. Keith Cohen and Paula Cohen in *New French Feminisms: An Anthology*, ed. Elaine Marks and Isabelle de Courtivron Marks (London: Harvester, 1981), p. 254.

5   See Michel de Certeau, "Spatial Stories," in *The Practice of Everyday Life*, trans. Steven F. Rendall (Berkeley: University of California Press, 1984), pp. 115–122.

6   Aldo Carotenuto, *Eros and Pathos: Shades of Love and Suffering*, trans. Charles Nopar (Toronto: Inner City Books, 1989), p. 27.

7   Aidan Andrew Dunn, *Vale Royal* (Uppingham: Goldmark, 1995), p. 9.

8   Triun T. Minh-Ha, *When the Moon Waxes Red: Representation, Gender, and Cultural Politics* (London: Routledge, 1991), p. 229.

9   Rainer Maria Rilke, *Letters to a Young Poet*, trans. Stephen Mitchell (New York: Vintage, 1986), p. 55.

10   Donna Haraway, "A Manifesto for Cyborgs: Science, Technology, and Socialist Feminism in the 1980s" (1985), in *Feminism/Postmodernism*, ed. Linda Nicholson (London: Routledge, 1990), pp. 202–203.

11   Audre Lorde, "The Master's Tools Will Never Dismantle the Master's House" (1979), in *The Audre Lorde Compendium: Essays, Speeches, and Journals* (London: Pandora, 1996), p. 160.

12   In her second diary, Anais Nin wrote of Fez that the image of the interior of the city was an image of her inner self, quoted in Barbara Black Koltuv, *Weaving Woman: Essays in Feminine Psychology from the Notebooks of a Jungian Analyst* (York Beach, Me.: Nicolas-Hays, 1990), p. 7.

13   Victor Burgin, *Some Cities* (London: Reaktion Books, 1996), p. 7.

14   Carotenuto, *Eros and Pathos*, p. 17.

15   Gayle Rubin, "The Traffic in Women: Notes on the 'Political Economy' of Sex" (1975), in *Feminism and History*, ed. Joan W. Scott (Oxford: Oxford University Press, 1996), p. 118.

16   Luce Irigaray, "Women on the Market," in *This Sex Which Is Not One*, pp. 170–191; this essay is hereafter cited parenthetically in the text.

17   Sylvie Germain, *The Weeping Woman on the Streets of Prague*, trans. Judith Landry (Sawtree, Cambs.: Dedalus, 1993), p. 27.

18   Hélène Cixous, *The Book of Promethea*, trans. Betsy Wing (Lincoln: University of Nebraska Press, 1991), p. 7.

19   I am grateful to Lynda Nead, who pointed me in the direction of the ramble.

20   *Oxford English Dictionary*, 2d ed., s.vv. "ramble," "rambling."

21   Eric Partridge, *Dictionary of Slang and Unconventional English* (London: Routledge and Kegan Paul, 1984), s.v. "ramble."

22   "Rambler in London," *The Rambler* 1, no. 1 (1824).

23   See, for example, *A Ramble through London* (1738); *The Country Spy or a Ramble through London* (1750); *The Modern Complete London Spy* (1760); and *A Sunday Ramble* (1774).

24   These texts, originally published monthly and then in book form, include Pierce Egan, *Life in London* (London: Sherwood, Neely, and Jones, 1821); Jonathan Badcock, *Real Life in London* (London: Jones, 1822); William Heath, *Fashion and Folly: The Bucks Pilgrimage* (London: William Sams, 1822); and B. Blackmantle, *The English Spy*, (London: Sherwood, Jones, 1825).

25   See for example, *Covent Garden Magazine* (London: G. Allen, 1773); *Harris's List of Covent Garden Ladies* (London: H. Ranger, 1788); and *Harris's List of Covent Garden Ladies* (London: H. Ranger, 1793).

26   The monthly periodicals include *The Rambler's Magazine* (London: R. Randall, 1783–1789); *Ranger's Magazine* (London: J. Sudbury,

1795); *The Rambler's Magazine* (London: Benbow, 1822); *The Rambler* (London: T. Holt, 1824); and *The Rambler's Magazine* (London: J. Mitford, 1828).

27 M. D. Archenholz, *Picture of England* (Dublin: P. Byrne, 1791), p. 197.

28 Amateur, *Real Life in London* (London: Jones, 1821–1822), pp. 198–199.

29 For other places of commodity consumption, see my "'Industrious Females' and 'Professional Beauties,' or, 'Fine Articles for Sale in the Burlington Arcade,'" in *Strangely Familiar: Narratives of Architecture in the City*, ed. Iain Borden, Joe Kerr, Alicia Pivaro, and Jane Rendell (London: Routledge, 1996), pp. 32–35; "Subjective Space: A Feminist Architectural History of the Burlington Arcade," in *Desiring Practices: Architecture, Gender, and the Interdisciplinary*, ed. Katerina Ruedi, Sarah Wigglesworth and Duncan McCorquodale (London: Blackdog Publishing, 1996), pp. 216–233; "Ramblers and Cyprians," *Scroope*, no. 8 (1996): 85–91; "Encountering Anthropology, Architecture and Gender in the Burlington Arcade," *Architectural Design*, October 1996, pp. 60–63; and "Displaying Sexuality: Gendered Identities in the Early Nineteenth Century Street," in *Images of the Street: Representation, Experience, and Control in Public Space*, ed. Nick Fyfe (London: Routledge, 1997), pp. 75–91.

30 Walter Benjamin, "Paris—Capital of the Nineteenth Century," in *Charles Baudelaire: A Lyric Poet in the Era of High Capitalism*, trans. Harry Zohn (London: Verso, 1997), pp. 158, 165.

31 John Feltham, *The Picture of London* (London: Longman, Hurst, Rees, Orme, and Brown, 1821), pp. 264–265.

32 See *La Belle Assemblée*, no. 13 (April 1816): 191.

33 Feltham, *Picture of London*, pp. 264–265.

34 Gary Dyer, "The 'Vanity Fair' of Nineteenth Century England: Commerce, Women, and the East in the Ladies Bazaar," *Nineteenth Century Literature* 46 (1991): 196–222.

35 N. S. Wheaton, *A Journal of a Residence During Several Months in London* (Hartford: H. and F. J. Huntington, 1830), pp. 189–190.

36 Knight's *London* (1851), quoted in Alison Adburgham, *Shops and Shopping, 1800–1914: Where, and in What Manner the Well-Dressed Englishwoman Bought Her Clothes* (London: George Allen and Unwin, [1964]), p. 22.

37 See especially Frances Burney, *Evelina* (London: Jones, 1822).

38 Knight's *London* (1851), p. 22.

39 *The Gentleman's Magazine*, p. 272; emphasis in original.

40 Knight's *London* (1851), p. 22.

41 See, e.g., "Bazaar Beauties," *The Rambler's Magazine* 2 (1828): 27.

42 Nathaniel Whittick's *Complete Book of Trades* (1837), quoted in Alison Adburgham, *Shopping in Style: London from the Restoration to Edwardian Elegance* (London: Thames and Hudson, 1979). See George Cruikshank, *A Bazaar* (London: J. Johnston, 1816).

43 "Bazaar Beauties," p. 27.

44 Ibid., 26, and "Bazaar Beauties," *The Rambler's Magazine* 2 (1828): 101.

45 Wheaton, *Journal of a Residence*, pp. 189–190.

46 Michael Ryan, *Prostitution in London* (London, H. Balliere, 1839), p. 87.

47 Fanny Burney, *The Wanderer* (1816; reprint, Oxford: Oxford University Press, 1991), p. 452.

48 "Bazaar Beauties," p. 100.

49 Karl Marx, *Capital: The Process of the Production of Capital* (Harmondsworth: Penguin, 1976), p. 178.

50 *The Rambler's Magazine* 1 (1828): 251; emphasis in original.

51 See Francis Grose, *A Classical Dictionary* (London: S. Hooper, 1788); Francis Grose, *Lexicon Balatronicum: A Dictionary of Buckish Slang, University Wit, and Pickpocket Elegance* (London: C. Chappel, 1811); and Pierce Egan, *Grose's Classical Dictionary of the Vulgar Tongue* (London: Sherwood, Neely, and Jones, 1823).

52 "Bazaar Beauties," pp. 27, 28.

53   Ibid., p. 28; emphasis in original.

54   George Smeeton, *Doings in London; or Day and Night Scenes of the Frauds, Frolics, Manners, and Depravities of the Metropolis* (London: Smeeton, 1828), p. 94.

55   *Oxford English Dictionary*, 2d ed., s.v. "cyprian."

56   *Characters of the Present Most Celebrated Courtezans* (London: M. James, 1780), p. 80.

57   Koltuv, *Weaving Woman*, p. 114.

Philip Tabor

7

I Am a Videocam

Architecture is dead. I have read its obituaries. One cultural analyst writes, "After the age of architecture-sculpture we are now in the time of cinematographic factitiousness[;] . . . from now on *architecture is only a movie*."[1] Others call architecture the "subelectronic visual marker of the spectacle," too place-bound and inert to survive the ethereal, ubiquitous lightning flashes of the telematic storm.[2]

And architecture deserved to die. It had committed technolatry: the worship of means at the expense of divine or human ends—ethical miosis. Always complicit with establishment and capital, they say, its aim was domination. To control internal climate it sought power over nature; to control behavior, architecture's other purpose, it sought power over people.

ARCHITECTURE AND THE EVIL EYE

For power over people, architecture had wielded the evil technologies of the eye: spectacle and surveillance. From the cathedral and palace to the housing development and shopping mall—to start with spectacle—architecture has been characterized by grandiloquent display and forceful geometry. Its symmetries, hierarchies, and taxonomies fabricated the intoxicating dreamworlds of authority, commodity, and consumption. As for contemporary surveillance, architecture was at first blamed for *not* providing it. Legcocking underdogs in the early 1970s claimed city territory with threatening Day-Glo squirts; their spray cans seemed almost as threatening as their guns. An influential book blamed modern architecture for not providing, in the words of its title, "defensible space."[3] By this was meant the premodern surveillance of the twitching curtain and the bobby on the beat. Instead came the videocam and armed response.

Architects were blamed for that too, at least partly, because to their misfortune the 1960s and 1970s (first in America, later more famously in France[4]) saw a building type displace Orwell's *Nineteen Eighty-Four* as the dominant metaphor for Western society seen as a surveillance-driven dystopia. The building type was, of course, Jeremy Bentham's Panopticon prison. (The first "real-time" transmission of a photographic image, incidentally, was by telegraph, in 1927. The image, as it happens, was of a federal penitentiary.)[5]

The word *surveillance* derives from the Latin *vigilia*, meaning "wakefulness" or "sleeplessness." So in the thousand eyes of surveillance-night we see reflected the light never switched off in the prison cell, the dazzling antidungeon of the Panopticon, the insomniac horror of Poe's "Tell-Tale Heart." The political Right wishes to shield the private sphere from social intrusion; the Left fears an oligarchy immovably embedded in

7.1

an informatic bunker. Both wings have compelling reasons for fearing the "surveillance society," if it has not yet arrived, and resisting it if it has.

Yet resistance is low, for reasons that are clear. The Right sees that watched workers, watched consumers, stay in line. For the Left, after decades of fighting closed social systems (the patriarchal family, privatization, cocooning, and so on), it feels perverse to argue against transparency, electronic or otherwise. Besides, surveillance protects the vulnerable: rape is statistically less frequent in glass-sided elevators than in opaque ones.[6]

But there are less reasoned motives for not wholeheartedly resisting surveillance. The algebra of surveillance structures the reveries of voyeurism, exhibitionism, and narcissism. To make love in a glass-walled elevator, for instance—moving and open to public gaze—is, I am told, a common fantasy. The disembodied eye of surveillance thrills our dreams.

THE EYE

The video camera is that eye. The single-eyed giants, the Cyclopes (in Greek, literally "the circle-eyed"), were the first technologists, master smiths. They invented the technologies of force and antisurveillance to help Zeus crush the first rebellion, that of the Titans. For Zeus they forged the thunderbolt, for Poseidon the trident, and for Hades the helmet of darkness and invisibility. Later Polyphemus and the others used their single eyes to oversee and control sheep.[7]

THE CARWASH

The videocam is also a carwash. Augustinian Christianity saw the insomniac gaze of God as a flood of light in which believers were drowned—but emerged cleansed and secure, having submitted themselves to fatherly authority.[8]

The unbelieving Bentham used biblical texts ironically to present his Panopticon as the secular equivalent of divine surveillance—omniscient, ubiquitous, and invisible.[9] The inmates, flooded in light, cannot see the overseers, who are masked in the dark center of their universe. It is a confessional with one-way glass. Fearing punishment but never knowing when they are overseen, if at all, the inmates internalize their surveillance, repent, and become virtuous. They are cleansed by light: seen is clean.

The panoptic mechanism echoes that whereby, it is supposed, each child internalizes the prohibitions of his elders by developing a superego or conscience. Behavior originally avoided for fear of an angry parent later in life arouses a different emotion, shame.[10] Who, smuggling nothing through customs past those one-way mirrors, has not felt guilty? Surveillance, then,

7.2

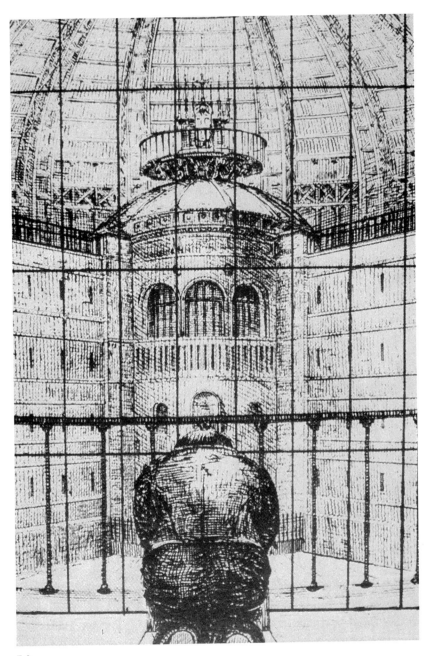

7.3

manufactures conscience—which, as the word implies, completes self-consciousness. It fortifies the individual's identity, and his or her place in the external world.

THE X-RAY MACHINE

The videocam is an X-ray machine. In 1925 Lázló Moholy-Nagy extended the seen-is-clean equation thus: "Television . . . has been invented[;] . . . to-morrow we shall be able to look into the heart of our fellow-man. . . . *The hygiene of the optical, the health of the visible is slowly filtering through.*"[11]

X rays were discovered in 1895. The notion of surveillance clearly arouses the imagination: within a year, advertisements appeared in which a detective agency offered divorce-related X-ray stakeouts, and a corset maker offered lead underwear to thwart X-ray–equipped Peeping Toms.[12] X ray's centenary deserved celebration because the discovery preceded a rage for transparency (reciprocal surveillance) that, especially in architecture, characterizes modernism. This is a vivid instance of how, without apparent causal link, innovations in technology and sensibility coincide. Plate glass had come a little earlier; cellophane, Plexiglas, and nylon arrived rather later.[13] Do we love our technologies because we invent them, or invent them because we love them?

Exposure of dust traps in buildings to the eye and of the body to the sun (and therefore the eye), in nudism and the relative nudism of post-1918 dress, followed medical science. The drive for self-disclosure also responded (with hazy symbolism) to the psychoanalytic concept of a concealed and un-sanitary unconscious. Buckminster Fuller's Dymaxion House of 1927 was the first simultaneously to celebrate advanced technology, transparency, and self-exposure; a model of the house, exhibited at Chicago's Marshall Field's department store, had glass walls behind which naked dolls lay on sheetless pneumatic beds.[14]

Self-exposure was politically correct. "We recognise nothing pri-vate," Lenin had said. "Our morality is entirely subordinate to the interests of the class struggle of the proletariat."[15] Surveillance defends the revolution; reaction must have nowhere to hide. The open plan and picture window, like the sandals and open shirt, were to do their bit to expose pretension, de-molish interpersonal barriers, and maintain social health. The hygiene of the optical: witness is fitness.

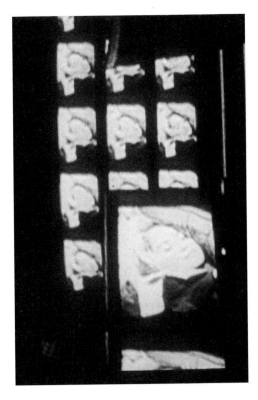

7.4

THE MIRROR

The videocam is a mirror. Grainy surveillance images of ourselves flicker on the subway platform, in the window of electronic goods stores, sometimes on taxi dashboards. Electronic narcissism: we are indeed all famous now, but not just for fifteen minutes. (Vanity can kill. Some of the Communards of 1871, who posed to be photographed on the barricades, were later identified by their images and shot.[16] Encouraged, the French government started using photography for police purposes soon after.[17])

The infant rejoices at its reflected image, which releases it from the subjective prison of its retina and places it in the social and symbolic world: I am seen, therefore I am.[18] So mirrors make me whole. But they also disunite me: reflections create doubles. I am thereafter split between a self seen from within and a self seen from without. I spy on myself.

In 1993 a poll by the U.S. *MacWorld* magazine found 22 percent of "business leaders" admitting to searching their employees' voice mail, e-mail, and computer files.[19] Software applications with names like "Peak & Spy" [*sic*], "Supervision," and even "Surveillance" are available—to monitor continually, for instance, the average number of copies an employee distributes of each e-mail: too many indicates a hostile atmosphere or disaffection, so management is alerted.[20]

So-called dataveillance compounds our fragmentation and, with it, ontological doubt. Each form filled, card swiped, key stroked, and bar code scanned replicates us in dataspace—as multiple shadows or shattered reflections. Sometimes our electronic shadows, like a polished CV or a PR image, are sharper, more seductive than ourselves. More often, what are chillingly called our "data-images" caricature and diminish us, but are seen as more substantial than our selves.[21] Our complaint should logically be that surveillance sees not too much of us but too little. Biotechnical surveillance answers that protest with DNA analysis, voiceprints, retinal scans, and inquisitive toilets.[22]

THE SARDINE CAN

The videocam is a sardine can. Jacques Lacan tells of seeing at sea a floating sardine can, shining in the sun. In what was for him a philosophical epiphany, he realized that while his vision radiated from his eye to encompass the scene, light radiated from the can to encompass *him*. The can "was looking at me," he notes, "at the point at which everything that looks at me is situated—and I am not speaking metaphorically."[23] He was simultaneously observing the can and caught, to use David Jay's happy gloss, "in an impersonal field of pure monstrance."[24]

7.5

7.6

Architects have long known that the window in the tower, the balcony in a facade, and the throne on its dais are to part of our mind occupied even when they are not—and continue to survey us, even when we know there is no one there. And it is not simply that our imagination is conjuring up for these things notional human occupants. By a kind of metonymy the window, balcony, and throne, though inanimate, continue to look at us. The videocam, too, puts us "in an impersonal field of pure monstrance."

THE MOON

The videocam is the moon. Daedalus, which means literally both "the bright" and "the cunningly wrought," is by his very name associated with sight and technology. Daedalus made the first automata. He also engineered the first erotic encounter between flesh and machine, devising for Pasiphaë a wheeled and upholstered wooden cow in whose rear she could hide to seduce Poseidon's bull. The product of this coupling was the Minotaur, half-animal, half-human: nature and culture fused.[25]

Daedalus constructed the Minotaur's labyrinth and the wings with which he escaped it. Soaring with him was his son Icarus—whose name associates him with the moon-goddess, who looks down coldly from above.[26] The Icarian scene was replicated as, in birdlike planes, aviators gazed panoptically down on their colleagues, myopic and mud-bound in the labyrinthine trenches of Flanders. When peace came, architects like Le Corbusier and Hugh Ferriss sought an urbanism of the lunar, Icarian view—

Philip Tabor

serene, objective, and distanced from our fellows.[27] With what pleasure we ride elevators to gaze down on the city and exclaim how inhuman, like ants, seem the pedestrians and cars in the canyons beneath.

The banks of monitors showing arterial flows and congestions in the TV traffic flash, the bird's-eye glide above a desert war, afford us the same glimpse of godlike, invulnerable serenity. Above the fray, the philosophical spy in the sky.

THE KEYHOLE

From spy in the sky to fly on the wall. The videocam is a keyhole, projecting us into intimacy with a world from which we are otherwise excluded, a surrogate life more vivid and immediate than our own. Supposedly nonfictional TV documentaries that eavesdrop at length on a family, firm, or public service proved more gripping than fictional soaps. This fascination was sometimes attributable to a dramatic narrative, but more often it was just the thrill of banal witness: to find we are all the same under the skin.

Fictional dramas, like *NYPD Blue*, learned to mimic the technical artifacts of espionage: overlapping inconsequential dialogue, handheld wobble, spectral lens dazzle, close focus, artless camera angles. "We are witnessing the end of perspective and panoptic space . . . and hence the *very abolition of the spectacular*," writes a celebrated commentator, "the dissolution of TV into life, the dissolution of life into TV."[28]

THE GUN

The videocam is, God knows, a gun—handheld and stealth-black like a pistol, shoulder-mounted like a bazooka, or turreted. Mike Davis, sketching the "scanscape" of central Los Angeles, catches this isomorphism: "The occasional appearance of a destitute street nomad . . . in front of the Museum of Contemporary Art sets off a quiet panic; video cameras turn on their mounts and security guards adjust their belts."[29] The residents of major cities fear that urban space is being increasingly militarized by both sides of the law. But fear is mixed with perverse relish for that warlike tension that supposedly sharpens cities' "creative edge." What the patrol car's siren does for New York, the swiveling lens does for Los Angeles. We feel alert, excited: our designer glasses develop crosshair sights.

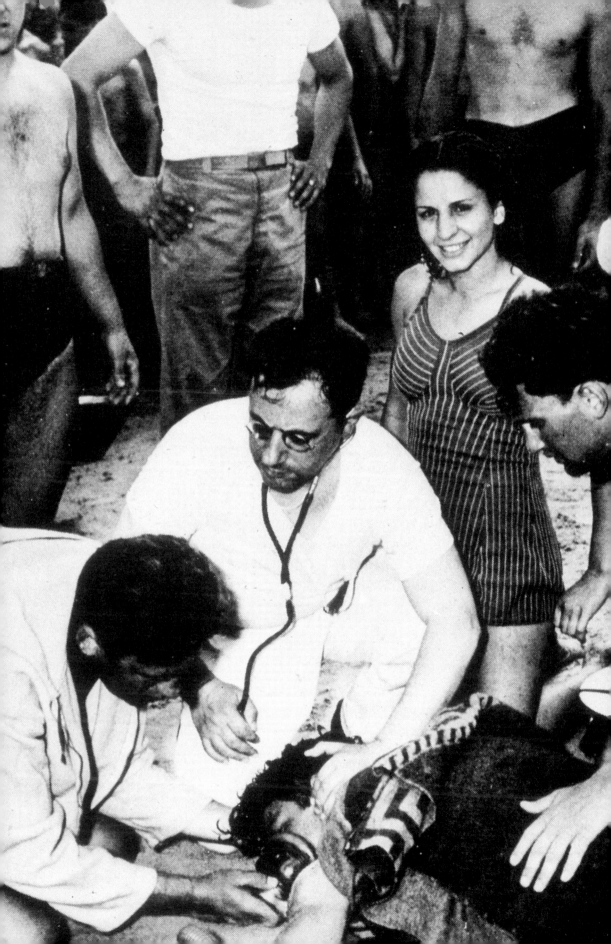

In *Voyeur*, an interactive video, the viewer plays the part of a snooping private eye.[30] Any young boy, peeping through a window at the half-dressed girl next door, is preparing to confront the enemy, maybe years from now, and acquit himself well. So is she, if she knows or imagines she is surveyed. The surveillance camera scans time as well as space for trace of future trouble. Foreseen is forearmed.

We are gun/cameras. Our heads swivel on our shoulders and from our eyes dart—familiarly aggressive tropes—piercing and penetrating looks. Photographers say the camera loves some people but not others. We need no cyborgian robo-erotic fantasy to feel flattered and stimulated when the camera lovingly tracks us. A famous newspaper photograph shows an unconscious man lying on the ground, attended by doctors. He has been pulled from the sea and may die. Kneeling by his side is his fiancée. In the photograph she's just noticed the camera, so she smiles brilliantly at it and adjusts her swimsuit.[31]

THE SHIELD

The videocam is a shield. The eyes of Medusa turn to stone those who look directly at them: her gaze objectifies its target. The three Graeae (literally, "the gray ones") are her old sisters, with just one eye and tooth between them. Age, that is, holds in fragile monopoly the instruments of aggression and surveillance. To augment his strength, Perseus forces them to reveal where the technologies of speed and concealment may be found: Mercury's winged sandals and Hades' helmet of invisibility. Thus equipped he counters Medusa's gaze with indirect surveillance of his own, taking care to track Medusa only in her image reflected in his shield. And he wins.[32]

Detective and spy fiction is based on this archaic mythology of the chase. Novel readers or film audiences vicariously reenact the rituals of surveillance, imagining themselves at once both the concealed watcher and the exposed watched. Anxious that an unaided body and mind might not suffice to unbalance the game in their favor, the audience in fantasy adopts the logic of the arms race and seeks prosthetic help in technology. Thus the central role played in fictions by the hardware of surveillance and counter-surveillance: *The Conversation, Blade Runner, Blue Thunder, The Silence of the Lambs* (remember the nightsight glasses), *Sneakers, Demolition Man,* and so on.[33] Thus, too, the first commandment of street tech: "Use technology before it's used on you."[34]

THE GLAMOUR OF SURVEILLANCE

Surveillance, the process by which the few monitor the many and keep records of them, is as old as agriculture and taxation. The growth since the Renaissance of bureaucratic surveillance accompanied the emergence of the nation-state, welfare state, suffrage, total war, and total law. Bureaucratic surveillance, formerly a near-monopoly of the state, has been adopted privately—since the industrial revolution to control production, and since the advertising revolution to control consumption.

The social benefits of surveillance are many and everyday. We have accustomed ourselves to sharing daily life with its apparently innocuous apparatus: forms, questionnaires, school transcripts, licenses, passport photos, countersignatures. Equally clear, though not so immediate, is its potential to inflict irreversible evil—probably with benign intent. The recent combining of electronic sensors, computers, and high-bandwidth telecoms has greatly reinforced the ability to monitor and oversee.

It is tempting to argue that social phenomena such as surveillance are driven forward by a simple coincidence of rational self-interest and technological innovation. Were this so, they could be resisted or reversed by forms of Luddism—by countering systems or by sabotaging hardware. But, as I have tried to show, systematic surveillance as a social institution also survives and flourishes on its irrational allure. The very idea of surveillance evokes curiosity, desire, aggression, guilt, and, above all, fear—emotions that interact in daydream dramas of seeing and being seen, concealment and self-exposure, attack and defense, seduction and enticement. The intensity and attraction of these dramas helps to explain the glamour and malevolence with which the apparatus of surveillance is invested, and our acceptance of it.

"I am an eye," wrote Flaubert. "I am a camera," wrote Isherwood.[35] I am a videocam.

Notes

A version of this paper was given at the first "Spaced Out" conference of the Institute of Contemporary Arts, London, 8 April 1995.

1   Paul Virilio, *The Aesthetics of Disappearance*, trans. Philip Beitchman (New York: Autonomedia, Semiotext(e), 1991), p. 65; emphasis his.

2   Critical Art Ensemble, *The Electronic Disturbance* (Brooklyn, N.Y.: Autonomedia, 1994), p. 69. *Telematics* is the study of the combination of telecommunications and computational power, whose recent increase has brought about the so-called information revolution.

3   Oscar Newman, *Defensible Space: People and Design in the Violent City* (London: Architectural Press, 1973), pp. 126–128, 182–185, recommends that to counter vandalism and crime, public housing should be designed to encourage "territoriality" on the part of tenants and their "natural surveillance" over public and semipublic space. He makes only passing (approving) reference to electronic surveillance: closed circuit TV cameras linked to home sets or monitored by "tenant patrols."

4   Michel Foucault, *Discipline and Punish: The Birth of the Prison*, trans. Alan Sheridan (1977; reprint, Harmondsworth: Penguin, 1991), influentially adopted the Panopticon to illustrate symbolically the mechanisms of a surveillance-driven "carceral society." Martin Jay, *Downcast Eyes: The Denigration of Vision in Twentieth-Century French Thought* (Berkeley: University of California Press, 1994), p. 381 n. 9, notes that Gertrude Himmelfarb in 1965 and Jacques-Alain Miller in 1973 had previously drawn similar lessons from the Panopticon.

5   Judith Barry, "Mappings: A Chronology of Remote Sensing," in *Incorporations*, ed. Jonathan Crary and Sanford Kwinter, Zone 6 (New York: Zone; Cambridge, Mass.: MIT Press, 1992), p. 570. The prison was Fort Leavenworth.

6   Joel Garreau, *Edge City: Life on the New Frontier* (New York: Doubleday, Anchor, 1991), p. 470, claims this half-humorously as one of the "Laws" of commercial development.

7   Robert Graves, *The Greek Myths* 2 vols. (1955; reprint, Harmondsworth: Penguin, 1960), secs. 3b, 7e, 170b.

8   Jay, *Downcast Eyes*, p. 37. See also Richard Sennett, *The Conscience of the Eye: The Design and Social Life of Cities* (London: Faber and Faber, 1991), p. 10.

9   Robin Evans, *The Fabrication of Virtue: English Prison Architecture, 1750–1840* (Cambridge: Cambridge University Press, 1982), p. 206.

10   Sigmund Freud, "Civilization and Its Discontents," in *Penguin Freud Library*, trans. under the editorship of James Strachey, vol. 12, *Civilization, Society, and Religion: Group Psychology, Civilization and Its Discontents, and Other Works*, ed. Albert Dickson (Harmondsworth: Penguin, 1991), pp. 316–20.

11   Lázló Moholy-Nagy, *Painting, Photography, Film*, trans. Janet Seligman (London: Lund Humphries, 1969), p. 38; emphasis his.

12   Nancy Knight, "'The New Light': X Rays and Medical Futurism," in *Imagining Tomorrow: History, Technology and the American Future*, ed. Joseph J. Corn (Cambridge, Mass.: MIT Press, 1986), pp. 11, 17.

13   Large-sheet glass-making, which began in the late eighteenth century, was not generally affordable until the last two decades of the nineteenth. Jeffrey L. Meikle, "Plastic, Material of a Thousand Uses," in Corn *Imagining Tomorrow*, p. 85, notes that Dupont's cellophane was introduced onto the consumer market in 1927, and their nylon in 1939.

14   Brian Horrigan, "The Home of Tomorrow, 1927–1945," in Corn, *Imagining Tomorrow*, pp. 141–142.

15   Lenin is quoted in David Lyon, *The Electronic Eye: The Rise of the Surveillance Society* (Cambridge: Polity Press, 1994), pp. 185–186.

16   Roland Barthes, *Camera Lucida: Reflections on Photography*, trans. Richard Howard (1981; reprint, London: Vintage, 1993), p. 11.

17   Jay, *Downcast Eyes*, p. 143.

18   Ibid., p. 288, quotes François George, *Deux études sur Sartre* (Paris: Bourgeois, 1976), p. 321: "L'autre me voit, donc je suis."

19   John Whalen, "You're Not Paranoid: They Really Are Watching You," *Wired*, March 1995

(U.S. edition), p. 80, cites Dynamics Corporation's "executive monitoring systems," "Peak & Spy."

20 Barbara Garson, *The Electronic Sweatshop: How Computers Are Transforming the Office of the Future into the Factory of the Past* (Harmondsworth: Penguin, 1989), p. 210. She cites (p. 222), among monitoring systems, Lanier's "Supervision IV" and Tower Systems International's "Surveillance."

21 Lyon, *Electronic Eye*, pp. 192–194, elaborates on the electronic threat to personhood. So do I in "Striking Home: The Electronic Assault on Identity," in *Occupying Architecture: Between the Architect and the User*, ed. Jonathan Hill (London: Routledge, 1998), pp. 217–228.

22 William J. Mitchell, *City of Bits: Space, Place, and the Infobahn* (Cambridge, Mass.: MIT Press, 1995), p. 74, mentions the inquisitive toilets that automatically monitor users' health.

23 Jacques Lacan, *The Four Fundamental Concepts of Psycho-Analysis*, ed. Jacques-Alain Miller, trans. Alan Sheridan (Harmondsworth: Penguin, 1977), p. 95.

24 Jay, *Downcast Eyes*, p. 365.

25 Graves, *Greek Myths*, sec. 88e.

26 Ibid., sec. 92e. The index gives one meaning of the equivalent name, Icarius, as "dedicated to the Moon-goddess Car."

27 Le Corbusier and Pierre Jeanneret, *Oeuvre Complète de 1910–1929* (Zurich: Editions d'Architecture Erlenbach, 1946), pp. 109–117, shows particularly aeronautic views of Le Corbusier's "Voisin" plan for Paris. Hugh Ferriss, *The Metropolis of Tomorrow* (1929; reprint, Princeton: Princeton Architectural Press, 1986) shows similar views of a future New York.

28 Jean Baudrillard, *Simulations*, trans. Paul Foss, Paul Patton, and Philip Beitchman (New York: Semiotext(e), 1983), pp. 54–55; emphasis his.

29 Mike Davis, *City of Quartz: Excavating the Future in Los Angeles* (New York: Vintage, 1992), p. 231.

30 *Voyeur* (Philips, 1993), interactive video.

31 Harold Evans, *Pictures on a Page: Photo-Journalism, Graphics, and Picture Editing* (London: Heinemann, 1978), back cover, reproduces the shot, credited to the Weegee International Center for Photography, and story.

32 Graves, *Greek Myths*, secs. 73g–h.

33 Films: *The Conversation*, dir. Francis Ford Coppola (Paramount, 1974); *Blade Runner*, dir. Ridley Scott (Warner, Ladd, 1982); *Blue Thunder*, dir. John Badham (Rastar/Columbia, 1983); *The Silence of the Lambs*, dir. Jonathan Demme (Strong Heart/Orion, 1991); Phil *Sneakers*, dir. Alden Robinson (Universal, 1992); *Demolition Man*, dir. Marco Brambilla (Silver Pictures, 1993).

34 Cited in Andrew Ross, "The New Smartness," in *Culture on the Brink: Ideologies of Technology*, ed. Gretchen Bender and Timothy Druckrey (Seattle: Bay Press, 1994), p. 335.

35 Flaubert is cited in Jay, *Downcast Eyes*, p. 112 n. 109. Christopher Isherwood, *Goodbye to Berlin* (1939; reprint, London: Minerva, 1989), p. 9; the book was adapted into, successively, a play (*I Am a Camera*), stage musical (*Cabaret*), and film.

Helen Thomas

8

Stories of Plain Territory:
The Maidan, Calcutta

A place, like any fact, is open to interpretation. The place to be interpreted here is a strange and special phenomenon, a vast empty plain situated right at the heart of a big city. The purpose of this collection of four stories is to explore the relationships between the intentions that defined the limits of this emptiness in the middle of Calcutta and the interpretations made of it through both representation and inhabitation. The physical nature and spatial logic of Calcutta align with specific events within its history as a postcolonial Indian city. Some of the best-known of these occurred on and around this grassy expanse at its center, known as the Maidan, a word that means "open land." Within the heaving, polluted reality of late-twentieth-century Calcutta, the Maidan lies between the banks of the Hooghly River and the principal artery of Chowringhee Road, which runs almost parallel to the water along a north-south axis. To its north lies what was known during the time of British colonization as the "Black Town," or native town, while to the south and east spread the spacious properties of the "White Town."

Interpretation enacts itself and the four stories; "Describing (Deciding)," "Knowing (Dreaming)," "Owning (Resisting)," and "Dreaming (Knowing)" are each allocated in their titles two verbs, which are acted out within the stories. The actions are not, of course, exclusive to the stories, since all of these verbs are interconnected. Describing facilitates owning, for example, while deciding, an empowered act, requires knowledge and can be an act of resistance. Dreaming is an impetus to owning, to which knowing is a means. In story 2, for example, dreaming is based on memory. Its substance, defined by the knowledge of past experience, produces feelings of nostalgia and hope in a strange place. These are the forms of dreaming here. Particular verbs take precedence, though, and their ascription to specific stories is intended to suggest an interpretation of the story's possible meaning. Knowing has two principal meanings in the stories: that which is empirical, and that which is invented through processes of acquisition and definition. In story 2 the first meaning is dominant, while in story 4 it is the second meaning that takes precedence.

Story 1 is concerned with my own position in relation to the Maidan. It is broached through questioning the processes of describing and deciding that are inevitable in writing about a place. Describing is never innocent; it is itself a form of owning. This idea is also important in story 3, where the act of resistance facilitates the condition of ownership and allows the full meaning of describing limits to come into play, as the edges of the Maidan are literally demarcated. Describing, then, can be both a literal and a conceptual means of territorialization, where description defines boundaries of knowledge. Sometimes these imaginary boundaries make contexts, or realities, for physical phenomena. Populations made into nations and separated through censuses as well as lands contained by maps are two examples discussed by Benedict Anderson in *Imagined Communities*.[1] This concept of gaining ownership and control by using description to create knowledge is discussed especially in "Knowing (Dreaming)," story 4. A story about the nineteenth-century idea of "total history," it delineates the limits of an act of description imagined to be absolute and objective in a time when the "narratives of origin, journey and destination can no longer be heroic myths of conquest."[2]

One of my aims here is to question the singular, complete, and global histories of imperialism inherent in this action, as I show that a piece of land can support multiple descriptions, each of which tells a new story. In an attempt to move beyond purely textual sources, such as letters by travelers, local histories, scholarly papers, journals, and newspapers, I have combined factual information gleaned from texts with lived experience and memory. This has been augmented by films, guidebooks, photographs, museums, paintings, and recordings. The use of evidence has been influenced by Anderson's approach in *Imagined Communities*, where he starts to uncover the power of maps, atlases, diaries, letters, and travel books. He looks at the ways that they have created the false conceptions of unity, nationhood, stability, and political division on which the dreams of imperialism have been, and still are, based.

All of the stories are connected to the idea of territory, both as a physical reality and a conceptual entity. In this sense the construction of knowledge and the dreams inherent in the acts of owning the Maidan and reclaiming it are intrinsic parts of these stories, which constantly fluctuate between the real and the imaginary. Some of these themes have already been explored in the field of literary criticism as it overflows into critiques of space and physical places. Seen from inside the imaginary world of the text, the world as represented in novels such as *Kim, Beloved, Shame*, and *The Heart of Darkness* becomes ever more enclosed. As Matthew Sparke points out, the "turn of the academic gaze from . . . the 'real world' . . . towards the . . . now seemingly more fashionable 'real book'" is increasingly common.[3] My intention here is to shift the focus slightly, from the reality represented in the imagination of the creative writer reflecting on his or her world to other sorts of invention that result from description as an act of recording, an act more directly concerned with a lived reality.

These issues are nowhere more intensely present than in Calcutta, a city produced, used, and understood in various and often very diverse ways. Its ambiguities and contradictions are concentrated within the history of the Maidan as a landscape that is neither urban nor rural. Built upon strategically advantageous but physically untenable swampy marshland, it lies on an artificially created topography of ditches and infill, constructed in defense against the invasion both of water and of living aggressors. Because of its physical location as well as its mythical status, the Maidan is a place especially susceptible to the accumulation of different explanations, meanings, and translations. It is surrounded by a city whose reason for existence is postcolonial, its origin ambiguous. Artificial from its inception, Calcutta was neither British in location nor Indian in intention. Along with Madras and Bombay, it was one of the three great Indian ports founded by the English East India Company; no substantial native settlement existed on its marshy site. So without memory or tradition connecting it to its location, the city was from its beginning a place of ambivalence and defiance. This British point of exchange, essential to Eastern trade, was a new and alien territory set up outside the control of the Moghul emperor at Delhi.

DESCRIBING (DECIDING)

Story 1

The Story of a Strange Place—the Maidan in the Mind of the Visitor in Postcolonial Calcutta of the Late Twentieth Century

Describing the Maidan required much selection. The following three stories originate in part from myths that make up our Western understanding of Calcutta. One of the most powerful myths about the city, and about India in general, is that of the Black Hole of Calcutta. This legend is fundamental to the existence of the Maidan, and only recently have different interpretations of the event been articulated. These form the basis of story 3—"Owning (Resisting)." Dreams of home, the creation of tradition, and the impetus to power ubiquitous within any process of colonization are explored in stories 2 and 4, about the never-certain relationship between dreaming and knowing. They involve my own choices and depend on the thought of others, the evidence available, and the possibilities for interpretation within my imagination. In themselves they are compounded of other people's words, images, and memories. They depend nearly always on what Salman Rushdie in *Imaginary Homelands* calls the "stereoscopic vision" of the migrant writer,[4] which can be described as a particular understanding, neither of here (London) or there (Calcutta), of the present or the past. For him and for many whose voices are present here, it is a fiction of memory produced from an experience of more than one homeland.

A strange place—not street, square, or contained park—the Maidan fascinated me though I visited it only briefly. At first sight empty, it is sparsely populated by various artifacts: a few buildings, some monuments, and along the riverbank many water tanks and ghats, which give access to the water for ritual bathing and serve as a place to land. Each one of these tells a particular tale about the Maidan's origin and meaning, and springs from a different moment of its past. A history is a description that presents and interprets collected evidence. Its form is determined by two factors—the evidence available and what the person creating it is able to see in this evidence before consciously selecting from it. The sources are varied. The initial catalyst for the present investigation came from personal observations, but the evidence is amassed from the imaginations of others. The necessary information was available principally in institutions set up by the British to record and know their empire, and thus it is highly selective—as are the imperial histories of India. By making histories of a particular place that is rarely described in itself—the Maidan usually exists only as a backdrop to its most important artifacts, Fort William and the Victoria Memorial—I intend to question how these "true" histories on a larger scale were constructed. Hidden in the gaps—between what is represented in official histories, atlases, and national legends, whose intentions and imaginary limits construct particular visions of the city, and the subjective observations that create different types of evidence—are keys to other stories.

My interest in the stories behind the physical existence of the Maidan was provoked by the two images reproduced here, which highlight different scales of inhabitation and gather within them the space of the Maidan and its means of confinement (explored below). Their nature as evidence—both tangible and as memory of experience—gave them added significance. There was something immediately discordant and provocative about the space they represented; it seemed to lie in the contradiction between the alien character and original reasons for the existence of particular artifacts and place-names and the ways in which those places and artifacts have been interpreted and appropriated. On the one hand, these intentions are legible through the logic of the spatiality of division of an English Victorian city. These separations include those between classes and functions produced by zoning, as well as the gendered divisions between public and private, home and work. On the other hand, an alternative reading is offered in the much more cohesive indigenous semirural spatiality, which is evident in the way that the public places of this English city, the streets and parks, are used for private domestic rituals and events by the different inhabitants of the city. Subsequently large parts of the city do not appear urban. Special words label particular types of participants in this strangely nonurban condition such as *bidesia* (a migrant living within the physical interstices of Calcutta) and *muflisia* (someone existing within a street economy that is entirely local).[5] The use of the spaces of the Maidan was consequently not in-

8.1 | Edge 1: Land. Calcutta from the Hooghly.

8.2 | Edge 2: Sea. Chowringhee from the Maidan.

terpreted as singular, transparent, or functional; rather it seemed various and ambiguous, opaque in the sense of being difficult to classify and define. Gillian Rose's comment that cultural difference "is not about mapping diversity across the territory of Western space, but rather about moments of opacity,"[6] can be applied to the Eastern/Western space of the Maidan—a place Eastern in location, Western in origin.

The Maidan can be understood, then, as a hybrid space, an idea discussed by various writers, including Fredric Jameson, Ed Soja, and Homi K. Bhabha. Sometimes it is referred to as "third space," one that is produced out of a multiplicity of imaginations and interpretations and has no single meaning, existence, or origin. Born of a simultaneous superimposition of different cultural systems, it is produced by a friction between intention and interpretation. It is a place where "overlap and displacement of domains of difference," in Bhabha's phrase,[7] is particularly intense. Each of the stories told here uncovers a different aspect of the Maidan and its interpretation as a material space, as part of a dream, and as a place of resistance. They are full of unresolvable ambiguities that arise principally from disparities between purpose and definition, evident in areas such as land ownership and use, and from the impossibility of applying simple terms such as *colonizer* and *colonized*.

As the stories are told and read, it becomes clear that the Maidan was and still is a fundamental part of Calcutta. Always contained within its physical borders, edges, and horizons, it sustained and gave meaning to the material and intellectual invention of the city. The limits of the Maidan, both physical and conceptual, are treated repeatedly within the stories. Sometimes they are boundaries defined from within; sometimes they are interfaces with wildness, with the city, with the uncontrollable—the full against its emptiness. These edges define the places that can lie beyond and thus embody hopes of resistance and change. Bhabha notes, "The beyond is neither a new horizon, nor a leaving behind of the past[.] . . . [W]e find ourselves in the moment of transit where space and time cross to produce complex figures of difference and identity, past and present, inside and outside, inclusion and exclusion."[8]

DREAMING (KNOWING)

Story 2

The Story of the City of Palaces—the Edges of the Maidan in Colonial Calcutta of the Eighteenth and Nineteenth Centuries

Arriving in Calcutta in the eighteenth century, the stranger from Europe would be immediately confronted with the distant edges of the Maidan. The story of the "City of Palaces" engages with the dreams about Calcutta that lived in the European mind, and with the means by which they were produced. From its foundation by Job Charnock in 1690, and throughout its existence as a colonial port, Calcutta was a place of pure invention, a place home to no one. It was an English fantasy where the inhabitant, whether Indian or British, was always a stranger in a foreign town. The simple dualities of native and colonizer inadequately describe the population of a city that contained Portuguese, Armenians, Jews, Parsis, and Chinese as well as Bengalis and British. Feelings of separation, danger, and strangeness were not particular to one race alone; but it was the British who most convincingly made concrete their denial of vulnerability and their confirmation of permanence.

The Maidan would have been a spacious and beautiful sight for the traveler arriving by ship at Chandphal Ghat, or by land across the pontoon bridge in the approach from Delhi; it would already be present in the traveler's imagination because of the picture books circulated at home in England. Images of Calcutta were available during the eighteenth and nineteenth centuries in England through representations made by Thomas and William Daniell for *Oriental Scenery* between 1786 and 1793 and by William Baillie, who painted twelve views in 1794. All of the images were picturesque views of the city, either looking over the Maidan from the river toward the City of Palaces, as it was known, or focusing on its principal buildings. A series of paintings made of the Black Town by Baltazard Solvyns between 1757 and 1790 were not so widely disseminated. It was the vision across the double artifice of the Maidan that presented the bravest and most picturesque face of the city. A contemporary observer praised the fringes "absolutely studded with elegant . . . garden houses," creating an illusion that provoked Kipling to advise: "if you can get out into the middle of the Maidan you will understand why Calcutta is called the City of Palaces."[9]

Since the city had no single cultural origin, the opportunity for invention produced a landscape picturesque in character. It was inhabited by neoclassical buildings, derived from an architecture rooted in the ancient cities of Greece and Rome. This architecture was deliberately different, clearly marking Britain's presence in India; but the adoption of standard European forms was also due partly to convenience. Many early colonial churches were based on the church of Saint Martin-in-the-Fields, London, for example. Its plans were published in 1728 by James Gibbs, pattern books made them readily available to engineers, whose principal interest was not design. The most dominant presence at the edge of the Maidan was the Calcutta Government House, built for Lord Wellesley in 1803. It was not a reproduction but rather an enhanced version of the eighteenth-century baronial seat of Keddleston Hall in Derbyshire. An extra story gave it a greater bearing, and its interiors—more magnificently and splendidly decorated than those of its original—became the focus of Calcutta's high society. Keddleston Hall itself was designed by Robert Adam in the 1760s, and its model was supposed to be particularly suitable to the climate of Calcutta. Apparently it allowed maximum ventilation for cooling and dispersing the foul vapors of the river, which were understood to be very unhealthy. Its presence and references to good taste and scholarly pretensions from home also gave it the gravitas necessary to represent the power and authority of Government and Empire.

By the end of the first decade of the nineteenth century, the boundaries of the Maidan formed part of a series of vistas focused on Government House. Official buildings along the Esplanade to the north, and grand private houses along Chowringhee Road to the east, were part of an urban landscape in appearance both classical and imperial—a monument to British control to be seen and, more important, experienced. This new community did not escape criticism. Walter Hamilton was skeptical of the climatically inappropriate Grecian style in 1820, while Emma Roberts in 1835 described Chowringhee as a "confused labyrinth" surrounded by savage jungle, morasses, and wildernesses.[10] The exaggeration and parodying of a remembered reality inherent in this self-conscious drama revealed, in the creation of a physical environment, an ambiguous relationship to the climatic, cultural, and historic reality of Calcutta's geographical location.

Calcutta was a beginning, rarely an end in itself. For traders and seamen, goods and adventurers it existed as a point of exchange with a vast interior. The hinterland of Calcutta, served by the river Hooghly and the Ganga, covers about half a million square miles. As an interface between the distant metropolitan center of London and its unknown territory, it was a place inhabited by many whose sole intention was to amass a fortune. A semblance of splendor and extravagance, as well as an emphasis on outward appearance, was natural. In order to feel at home, and combat feelings of separation and transience, the British created their domain in the manner of home. Their simulated physical environment was to be larger than life, their daily ritual to be more desirable, comfortable, and luxurious.[11]

The Maidan was their principal recreation ground, and in many parts dress codes prohibited entry to lower castes. Among the private clubs and pleasure grounds were large tanks of water called *lal dighees*, essential for both draining the land and providing drinking water. Carefully watched over by armed guards, like many of the tanks throughout the city, they were privately owned. Water was both a precious commodity and a deadly foe. The salt lakes lying immediately east of the city symbolized to the British the disease and contamination of the foreign land.[12] The contaminated air that blew west was as dangerous as the crocodiles, the unpredictable currents, and the frequent tidal bores—waves usually ten feet or more in height that rush up the river Hooghly almost half the days of the year. For the European the spaciousness of the plain offered a protected and safely artificial form of nature pushing against the wild foreignness beyond. Although strange tales of fishing by the natives following a gale, when fish fell with the rain, and sightings of exotic birds and boar hunting are among events of the Maidan recorded in various diaries and letters,[13] it contrasted vividly with the tiger-ridden jungle and marshland that surrounded the city outside the Maratha Ditch (an ineffective defensive construction described below in "Owning [Resisting]").

Bordering on a denial—where, as Gail Ching-Liang Low puts it, "white (w)as the invisible norm"[14]—the images of power, civilization, and familiarity constructed by the British around the Maidan were based in the urban and corresponded to what Bhabha calls a "desire for a reformed, recognisable Other."[15] To the native imagination, however, the origin of Calcutta was rural. The social and cultural reality of the city was subsequently played out in a double-sided game of mimesis between the metropolitan center and the newly invented place. The Maidan holds an example of a literal formal hybridity in the Ochterlony Monument constructed in 1828. This Greek column on an Egyptian base with a Turkish cupola is used by the police as a watch tower during rallies on the Maidan. This juxtaposition of multiple communities and various imaginative capacities[16] within Calcutta was what enabled new, fantastic spaces such as the Maidan—which was neither rural or urban, entirely public or private—to be transformed into something complex and opaque in meaning.

The concept of the urban as civilized and civilizing predominated in the eighteenth century both in Europe and its colonies. By the nineteenth century, however, an ambivalent attitude toward the idea of the city as a place of civilization was gaining strength, and Calcutta did not escape. Its reputation as a center of squalor and degradation grew, and it became famous as a place of chaos, crowds, death. Once the City of Palaces, it became Rudyard Kipling's "City of Dreadful Night." The Other city (Black Town) so carefully hidden in images of the City of Palaces (White Town) started to emerge from its concealment, threatening the illusion of permanence and total control. In 1857 the First Indian War of Independence (or the Indian Mutiny), while barely affecting Calcutta, shocked the complacent British; as Franz Fanon observed "the colonised man is an envious man. And this the settler knows very well; when their glances meet he ascertains bitterly, always on the defensive, 'They want to take our place.'"[17] This jealously guarded place was that of the civilized, the privileged; its Other—the splendid, the cruel, and the sensual—lived in the imaginary space of the East, which, Edward Said points out, provided the West with "one of its deepest and most recurring images of the Other."[18] This space was not necessarily geographically defined, as we have seen: the Orient and the Occident could exist on the same piece of territorialized land. Such density of place is clearly evident within the various interpretations of the legend of the Black Hole of Calcutta, the story of the inception of the Maidan born out of this repulsion from and fascination with the Other.

OWNING (RESISTING)

Story 3

The Story of the Black Hole of Calcutta and Two Fort Williams—the Origins of the Maidan in Colonial Calcutta at the Middle of the Eighteenth Century and Beyond

An irresistibly horrible story within the English imagination, the myth of the Black Hole of Calcutta marks the beginning of a history of ownership and resistance embodied in the space of the Maidan. It is often understood to symbolize a moment of fundamental change in the British attitude toward India and its territory. In both its origin and its ownership, the Maidan is particularly evocative of this shift from colony to empire, from pure commerce rooted in Leadenhall Street to political domination; and its creation was a direct consequence of the legendary night of 20 June 1756 in the "Black Hole" of old Fort William. As is true of all legends, the story of the Black Hole of Calcutta has more than one version. To the British it was a barbaric incident. The inscription on a commemorative monument expresses their intense emotions in sympathy for the victims: "The monument we here behold with pain, is there a heart can from a sigh refrain?"[19] Rajat Kanta Ray, in his essay *"Calcutta of Alinagar,"* tells the story from the other side.[20] In his more contemporary interpretation the nawab had good political reasons for the attack, since Fort William was a threateningly subversive presence within the Moghul Empire. Not only was its physical strength increasing, but it was also acting as a refuge for Moghul fugitives and giving security (in the sense of both investment and protection) to local merchants of various cultural backgrounds. The nawab expected the British to act as subjects of the Moghul Empire, not to create an alternative autonomous state within it.

In 1756 Bengal was still ruled by Moghul viceroys or nawabs, who headed a vulnerable urban Muslim aristocracy in a Hindu countryside. Alivardi Khan, the nawab of Bengal since 1740, died and was succeeded by his grandson Siraj-ud-Daula, aged only twenty. The land of India at that time was the sole property of the Moghul emperor, but it was controlled by the zamindar, who would act as a middleman between the tenant peasant and the emperor. The difference between the rate of taxes set by the zamindar and the fixed sum returned to the emperor's coffers could be a substantial amount of money. By the time Siraj-ud-Daula came to power, the British had bought zamindar rights to thirty-eight villages in and around Calcutta. The White Town (of the British) was a mile long and a quarter of a mile wide, and a Black Town, a circle roughly a mile and a quarter across, lay beyond it. Although they were not protecting territorial rights, the British were careful to guard their valuable trading post within the cantonment at Fort William, which bounded several warehouses and a large tank of rainwater. The threat of the Seven Years' War, far away in Europe, led them to increase the strength of the fort against the French, who were also trading in Bengal; these actions aroused the suspicions of the nawab.

On the day before the monsoon broke, the nawab marched on Calcutta. As his men scaled the walls of the fort, Governor Grant and the majority of the European inhabitants escaped down the river, leaving behind a small number of British. Taking only their watches, buckles, and jewelry, the nawab's men put their captives into the fort's punishment cell, called "the Black Hole." Accounts of what happened next vary. Geoffrey Moorhouse tentatively puts the number of those entering the Black Hole at 146, with 23 leaving it alive, the next morning; the rest were suffocated by the intense heat and humidity. He observes, "It was a brutal age all round[;] . . . the same week had seen these captives decapitating their own servants."[21]

Overnight a transformation of names and identity occurred. Allinagore was the name given to the newly Moghul town by Siraj-ud-Daula. The event held immense symbolic power for the British, for whom it confirmed their worst prejudices. Allinagore, or Alinagar, was "the space of the Other . . . always occupied by an *idée fixe*, despot, heathen, barbarian, chaos, violence."[22] The town reverted to "Calcutta" six months later, retaken by Robert Clive for the British. He went on to eliminate the French as viable competition, and brutally exacted huge sums of money in compensation from the new puppet nawab in Murshidabad. His retribution was not complete, however, until he had also vastly increased the territory directly under British control by annexing the zamindar rights to nine hundred square miles of land south of Calcutta, known as the twenty-four Parganas.

The village of Govindapur was drained and cleared of the tiger jungle and its scattering of native huts, as the site for the new Fort William moved south to cover the Govindapur Kali Temple. The fort, an example of French military architecture of the eighteenth century, was designed by Georges Coleman. Octagonal in plan, it has five regular faces inland and three river-bound faces that vary with the requirements of topography and defense. Its presence above ground is diminished by the use of large ditches, but it is described variously as being like a small city, much too large for defense requirements, and the finest fortress outside Europe.[23] Completed in 1773, it was intended to house the entire British community, but by 1780 only members of the military were allowed to live within its walls. It was surrounded by the vast defended space of the Maidan plain, which covered a ground surface of two square miles.

The Maidan became a military territory, and its roads still remain the property of the Ministry of Defense. From its center, its physical boundaries were delineated by the reaches of the outer limits of gunfire; its edges became determined by both natural and constructed means. In 1772, one year before the completion of the new fort, Warren Hastings was appointed the first governor of Calcutta, an office he held office until 1785. This signified an important change in governance of the city, which moved from the East India Company to the British government, and it marked the beginning of a new attitude toward the land and people of India. During his stay in Calcutta, Hastings was instrumental in constructing an identity for the Maidan. The river lay to its west, and along its banks lined with ghats, he constructed a promenade for ladies, called the Strand. To the north was the site of the old fort, which became the customs house and remained an administrative center of the White Town. The Chowringhee jungle bounded the south and east sides, until the City of Palaces started to replace it.

The encroaching villas slowly moved toward the outer boundary of the lines of defense that contained the city proper, known as the Maratha Ditch; begun in 1743, it was never completed. The Maratha Ditch was built to defend the town from the threat of the tribe of the Marathas who were terrorizing north and west India during the early eighteenth century, threatening the Moghul Empire and political stability. The threat never became substantial in Bengal, and the ditch was subsequently left unfinished. It served to mark the outer limits of Calcutta during the nineteenth century and was partly paved in 1799 for the Circular Road skirting the city. In 1893 it was completely filled in for the laying of the Harrison/Mahatma Ghandi Road.

The Maidan plays a fundamental role in Calcutta's history of ownership, maintained through separation. Its existence was essential in creating and sustaining the spatial and cultural distances initiated in the old layout of the city. The new Fort William shifted the focus of the White Town to the plain, with its cantonment at the center. The principal public buildings stood along the Esplanade facing the Maidan. They were turning their backs on the Black Town that stretched from the bazaar to the north, itself symbolic of unnatural chaos and the danger of infection and disease contained in the unknown world of the native. Hygiene and discipline became principal justifications for segregation.[24] In 1805 Henry Roberdean reported that "Black Calcutta does not at all interfere with the European part, a great comfort, for the Natives are very dirty and their habitations are straw huts."[25] But when considering the idea of spatial separations in Calcutta, we must also acknowledge the overlaps that occurred. As discussed above in "Dreaming (Knowing)," Calcutta's population did not consist simply of mutually exclusive British and native peoples. The mix was far more complex. Different communities sometimes inhabited specific areas, and developed their own spatialities, but the properties of wealthy natives were distributed throughout the north and south of the city. Contrary to what one might expect, for example, Clive's house was situated in the north at Dum Dum. As the north took on the character of the "Black Town," superimposed on it, large estates were subdivided many times into a type of slum called *bustees*, rather than being kept intact as garden houses.

The role of the Maidan was ambiguous in this process of spatial division within the city during the eighteenth century. As a regulatory space of control, defense, and segregation, it was a brutal assertion of conquest and power. At the same time it was a place for sports, leisure, and exhibition, principally of the upper classes. It was beginning to have an important presence in the minds of all Calcuttans, however, including the inhabitants of the more ambiguous Grey Town that was developing to the west. The physical differences between British and other territories were not just spatial; they were material as well. A notion of permanence essential to British buildings was inherent in their *puckah* construction, a term that defined a durable masonry structure built from of a mixture of brick dust, molasses, and hemp. The native buildings tended to be far more ephemeral and vulnerable to the exigent Calcutta weather; they were made of *cutchah*, a mud and thatch combination. The British evidently considered permanence and display in furnishing their interior spaces as well. This was quite different from the more minimalist, flexible approach to inhabiting the Indian interior, where functions were not fixed and spaces both domestic and public remained far more fluid in definition and use.

These physical separations were reflected culturally and intellectually—both within the British attitude toward India, as seen in a clash between tradition and reform,[26] and in the inherent differences between the indigenous and the colonizing inhabitants of Bengal. The East India Company's intellectual history of rule traditionally is viewed as having two phases: the "Orientalist," instigated by Warren Hastings and discussed at great length by Edward Said in *Orientalism*, and the "Anglicist," instituted by Hastings's successor, Lord Cornwallis. Hastings valued and promoted knowledge of Indian languages, law, culture, and tradition as different from but valid alternatives to their Western counterparts. The Asiatic Society, which he set up in 1783 on the borders of the Maidan, promoted and maintained the concept of "the Orient" as understood throughout the eighteenth and nineteenth centuries. The Anglicist phase, which reacted against this belief in the value of "native" learning, was grounded in an intention to reform and reconstruct Indian society along Western lines—in other words, to "civilize" it. At the same time Cornwallis introduced fundamental changes into the form of rule of Bengal that were very British in conception, including a replacement of zamindar rights by rights of land ownership. This Eurocentric ideal was based on a belief that there can only be one standard of rationality and civilization, naturally Western in origin.

The Anglicist approach was vulnerable in its rigidity, which made it incapable of assimilating the complex nature of reality in the Indian city. Within this weakness lay the roots of resistance, both political and cultural, to domination by the British; such resistance became more noticeable within the city of Calcutta and the Maidan in particular. The street names used demonstrated one subtle form of opposition emerging. Originary names came from villages, natural forms, and local families. During the British Empire, streets named after soldiers and civil servants represented municipal history but following Independence, congressmen, national heroes, and cultural references became the points of reference for street names.[27] Spaces like the Maidan began to be appropriated more and more for popular use. The railings surrounding part of the Maidan were finally removed in the middle of the nineteenth century, allowing access to all.[28] Markets and rallies sprang up, as did religious celebrations, such as the celebration for the goddess Kali reported by Bishop Heber in his diaries of 1824.[29] Sports such as football, which involved Indian players and Bengali teams, were established on the Maidan as early as the 1880s. Its size and position—at the center of the city, close to the seats of power—also made the Maidan an optimum site for strikes.[30]

While the ways that the Maidan was used and inhabited clearly manifested resistance, there was no accompanying self-conscious production of the physical environment, in the form of buildings and metropolitan plans for urban reform.[31] It was not until the early twentieth century that some attempt was made to deal with the urban problems stemming from the inequality of the city's social divisions, and even that came from the outside. Patrick Geddes made several plans for Calcutta that attempted to deal at a local scale with the problems of the *bustees* as social units. The Metropolitan plans produced by the Calcutta Improvement Trust in 1911 took a very different approach; they were more concerned with cutting

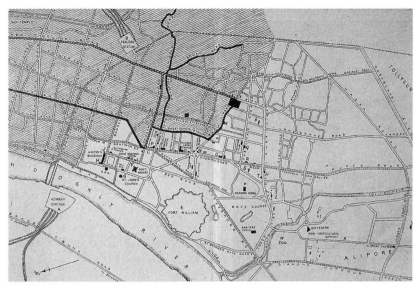

8.3 | The divided city: map of Calcutta.

8.4 | Existing edges: Calcutta.

straight roads through the city, "solving" problems of poverty through displacement.[32]

An intellectual resistance began to be manifest at the beginning of the nineteenth century in what is referred to as the Bengal Renaissance. Bengali artists and writers began to express the ambiguity of the relationship between European and Indian culture that underlies much artistic production in Calcutta. This movement, which stemmed from the Orientalist legacy of the city's complex origins, rose from the urban middle class, called the *bhadralok*. Distanced from popular culture, its members, like the Orientalists, dreamed of a mythical past and at the same time criticized Hindu practices such as suttee. Many of the heroes of the Bengal Renaissance had some connection to the Orientalist Fort William College set up by the governor-general, Lord Wellesley (1797–1805). By the middle of the century, however, the interests of the bhadralok were changing. In 1861 a Society for the Promotion of National Feeling rejected all that represented the English and cultural oppression, from the English language to Western clothing, food, games, and medicine; by the end of the nineteenth century, this intellectual resistance was beginning to be perceived as a threat by the British. Division of the land became again the means to control, and in 1905 the British drew a line down the middle of the map of Bengal that dispersed and isolated the potentially volatile bhadralok.

KNOWING (DREAMING)

Story 4

The Story of the First Partition of Bengal—the Victoria Memorial on the Maidan in Imperial Calcutta at the Beginning of the Twentieth Century

The significance of Calcutta had fundamentally changed by the turn of the twentieth century. No longer simply a port whose rights as a trading post had to be defended, it had become the focal point of a vast territory and its population, an empire. It could no longer be controlled at a distance simply by the military force that, principally for economic reasons, had protected the forts; to preserve this empire, the British turned to mechanisms based on the ownership of knowledge rather than of territory. This far more abstract system allowed a small number of people to govern and, more important administer India from the Writers' Buildings around the site of the old Fort William.

In 1899 Lord Curzon arrived in a restless Calcutta as viceroy of India, intent on implementing British control through rigorous administration. In order to maintain stable and secure conditions both for the British living in India and for those back in London depending on India's trading potential, he needed to adjust the balance of power, which was becoming increasingly vulnerable under attack by the bhadralok. He was forced to this realignment by the inevitable tension of empire, identified by Bhabha as straining "between the synchronic panoptical vision of domination—the demand for identity, stasis—and the counter-pressure of the diachrony of history—change, difference."[33] By the time Curzon arrived, the territory of

Bengal had incorporated a number of provinces. Beside Bengal proper it included Bihar, Chota Nagpur, and Orissa; its total population was 78 million. Each province was distinct historically, subracially, and culturally.

Curzon's Partition of Bengal in 1905 used the territory of Bengal itself, or rather its division, as a means of control through separation. In "Dreaming (Knowing)," this device was discussed at the scale of the city; here, the scale is much vaster. The diversity of Bengal's people and cultures created an administrative nightmare for a system based on the collection and classification of information—which provided the ostensible reason for the first partition. But this version of the story ignores the political goal whose achievement Curzon believed fundamental to the continuance of the empire: the isolation of the bhadralok, trapped by the very cultural hybridity of the city. East Bengal was principally Muslim, and Bengal in the west Hindu. In Calcutta the Hindu bhadralok found themselves outnumbered by Oriyas from outside Bengal and by Hindus with whom they shared nothing but religion. They were therefore separated from most fellow Bengalis and bhadralok, and surrounded by people of alien traditions with whom they could not communicate. The partition was a success.

These invisible mechanisms of control that were so useful to Curzon—the maps, censuses, and museums discussed by Benedict Anderson in *Imagined Communities*—developed from the search for a knowledge and understanding of the indigenous culture initiated by the Orientalists. Subverted in intention and form, however, this knowledge became a means for domination, and authority was maintained by creating an image of India defined through Britain's presence there. A facet of this phenomenon has already been explored in "Dreaming (Knowing)"; the reverse side is described by "Knowing (Dreaming)." Here the story is about a quest for knowledge bound up with the hopes of an empire. Dreams for a lost future are embodied in the solitary existence of the Victoria Memorial, placed squarely within the spaciousness of the Maidan and visible from afar.

In the same way that the military rule represented by Fort William was no longer the means to controlling the territory of Bengal, the Maidan no longer described in itself British authority. Now opened up to all of Calcutta's inhabitants, it became the site for the last great effort by the British in Calcutta to assert, through the building of a permanent monument, their position of governance. The foundation stone of the Victoria Memorial was laid in 1906 by George V. Designed by the then-president of the Royal Institute of British Architects, Sir William Emerson, it was constructed grandly in the classical style and clad in white marble. While splendid, the museum was also a physical incarnation of another facet of British influence—the production and maintenance of information as fragments of knowledge—which was a vital part of the institution of empire. British control was manifest first through the act of defining the nature of knowledge, and then in becoming its guardian: collecting, categorizing, and distributing that knowledge. As an archive of Calcutta's past and present, the Victoria Memorial collection itself was produced for the British imagination; *no more of its place than* like the buildings at the edges of the Maidan, it was an invention, a fantasy of knowledge generated from a nineteenth-century positivism. Paintings describing the authority of the British in India, room upon room of samples of Bengal's produce for trade, and tableaux of various indigenous living conditions indicate the limits of the "universal knowledge" contained by the British narrative of India. This final public display of artifacts represents a very particular understanding of India; and in displaying the desperate splendor of an unstable empire, it held within itself the seeds of modernity. The desire for a utopia conceived of as universal and justified through the momentum of "civilization" was enacted in an impulse to determine history and make the future known.

In this pursuit of separation and distance, begun in the eighteenth century and driven by a desire for permanence and stability precisely when it became impossible, the British lost Calcutta. Another (British) interpretation is that Calcutta lost the British. Following the partition, which was partially revoked as the British lost heart, the Maidan was flooded by riots. The Indian capital was transferred to a reinvention of the traditional center of Indian sovereignty, New Delhi, in December 1911. Dreams of power, total knowledge, control, and permanence represented in the presence and history of the Maidan were lost to Calcutta forever as it moved beyond its hybrid origins to become a place in its own right, looking for means to define its own contemporaneity and memory.

Notes

1   Benedict Anderson, Imagined Communities: Reflections on the Origin and Spread of Nationalism, rev. ed. (London: Verso, 1991).

2   Gillian Rose, "An Interstitial Perspective," Environment and Planning D: Society and Space 13 (1995): 366.

3   Matthew Sparke, "White Mythologies and Anaemic Geographies," Environment and Planning D: Society and Space 12 (1994): 108.

4   Salman Rushdie, Imaginary Homelands: Essays and Criticism, 1981–1991 (London: Granta, 1991), p. 19.

5   For definitions and discussion of the multivalent inhabitation of Calcutta's streets, see A. Kidwai, "Calcutta in 1901," in Calcutta, ed. J. S. Grewal (Chandigarh: Urban History Association of India, 1991), pp. 40–45.

6   Rose, "An Interstitial Perspective," p. 369.

7   Homi K. Bhabha, The Location of Culture (London: Routledge, 1994), p. 2.

8   Ibid., p. 1.

9   Eliza Fay, Original Letters from India, 1779–1815 (1925, reprint, London: Hogarth Press, 1986), p. 71; Rudyard Kipling, From Sea to Sea: Letters of Travel (London: Macmillan, 1899), 2:211.

10   Quoted in P. T. Nair, Calcutta in the Nineteenth Century (Calcutta: Firma KLM Private, 1989), pp. 222, 606.

11   Accounts of daily lives can be found in a variety of sources. See, for example, P. T. Nair, Calcutta in the Eighteenth Century (Calcutta: Firma KLM Private, 1984), and Nair, Calcutta in the Nineteenth Century.

12   See C. Furedy, "From Wasteland to Wastenot Land," in Calcutta Psyche, ed. Geeti Senthe (New Delhi: India International Centre, 1991), pp. 146–152.

13   See Nair, Calcutta in the Eighteenth Century, and Nair, Calcutta in the Nineteenth Century.

14   See Gail Ching-Liang Low, White Skins/Black Masks: Representation, Colonialism, and Cultural Cross-Dressing (London: Routledge, 1996), pp. 195–200; quotation, p. 196.

15   Bhabha, The Location of Culture, p. 86.

16   Among those discussing such imaginative capacities is Gayatri Spivak, who examines the fundamental and often unconscious differences between how a monotheist and a polytheist understand the world; see "Asked to Talk about Myself," Third Text, no. 11 (summer 1990): 12–3.

17   Franz Fanon, The Wretched of the Earth, trans. Constance Farrington (Harmondsworth: Penguin, 1963), p. 30.

18   Edward Said, Orientalism (London: Penguin, 1978), p. 1.

19   Quoted in Nair, Calcutta in the Nineteenth Century, p. 311.

20   See Rajat Kanta Ray, "Calcutta of Alinagar," in Grewal, Calcutta, pp. 16–28.

21   Geoffrey Moorhouse, Calcutta (New Delhi: Penguin, 1971), p. 44.

22   Bhabha, The Location of Culture, p. 101.

23   Nair, Calcutta in the Nineteenth Century, pp. 11, 102, 429.

24   Low discusses the British obsession with purity and hygiene in colonial Calcutta; see White Skins/Black Masks, pp. 158–168.

25   Roberdean, a bureaucrat, is quoted in Nair, Calcutta in the Nineteenth Century, p. 54.

26   Sumanta Banerjee discusses these polarized attitudes toward Indian culture in the nineteenth century in "Elite and Popular Culture in Nineteenth Century Calcutta," in The Parlour and the Streets (Calcutta: Seagull Books, 1989), pp. 147–199.

27   P. T. Nair, History of Calcutta Street Names (Calcutta: Firma KLM Private, 1987).

28   Nair, Calcutta in the Nineteenth Century, p. 918.

29   Ibid., p. 389.

30   In his portrayal of the dispossessed of Calcutta, Dominique Lapierre describes various

events on the Maidan, including a rickshaw pullers' strike and a palanquin bearers' strike, reported to have taken place as early as 1827; see The City of Joy (London: Century, 1985), p. 179.

31   See Ashish K. Maitra, "Calcutta," Architecture and Design, May–June 1989, pp. 21–43, for a discussion of the role of architecture in the cultural history of Calcutta. See also Kulbhushan Jain, "In Search of Indianness." Indian Institute of Architects' Journal January 1991, pp. 23–29; and Shireesh Deshpanole, "Search for Identity," Indian Institute of Architects' Journal, June 1987, pp. 29–34.

32   This history of infrastructural intervention is discussed in Norma Evenson, The Indian Metropolis: A view toward the West (New Haven: Yale University Press, 1989).

33   Bhabha, The Location of Culture, p. 86.

Shirley Wong

9 Colonialism, Power, and the Hongkong and Shanghai Bank

For over a century, the headquarters buildings of the Hongkong and Shanghai Bank served as prominent symbols of the central business district of Hong Kong. There were three purpose-designed buildings built at fifty-year intervals—in 1886, 1935, 1986—each on the same site fronting the harbor.

As headquarters of the most important financial institution in Hong Kong, these buildings embedded in their built forms social relations and meanings unique to the colonial setting of Hong Kong at particular moments in time. To understand what was expressed architecturally, we must consider what contributed to these forms in the first place; and the power structure of colonialism provides one means of entry into such an investigation. Although "power" by itself did not contribute directly to built form, it was the underlying force that acted on physical manifestations as its impact was channeled through various participants in the building process. To analyze the power structure of colonialism involves the unfolding of relations that operated in a hierarchical spatial order: the power structure within the colony, the power structure between the core and the periphery, and the power structure between the empire and the world at large. These relations did not operate independently but reinforced each other. Together they mapped out the overall mechanism through which colonialism was instituted and sustained.

This chapter looks at the earliest headquarters building of 1886 and unravels how class and race relations were expressed architecturally, focusing in particular on the "power structure" within the colony: that is, the dominance-dependence relationship between the Europeans and the Chinese. It examines first the characteristics of one of the main elements of the dominant group—the merchant community, whose members were the clients of the headquarters project and the main users of the building—and second the relationship between the two cultural groups in terms of the means of control, both within the Bank and in the society as a whole. Finally, it highlights the context in which this dominance-dependence relationship was grounded and which determined how it was expressed in the headquarters building.

The 1886 headquarters building was commissioned in 1882 when the scheme prepared by Clement Palmer of the architectural firm Wilson and Bird won the public competition launched by the Bank.[1] A local contractor called "Tai Yick" was used, and the building took four years to complete at a cost of HK$300,000.[2] The site was rectangular in shape, with a frontage of 125 feet and a depth of 225 feet, and stood on reclaimed land along the *praya* (embankment).[3] The building consisted of two separate volumes linked together: that facing the harbor with arched verandahs and shuttered windows shared the uniform classical architectural language adopted by other waterfront properties, while the landward portion looking into Queen's Road featured a massive dome surmounting the banking hall, which was wrapped with a screen of gigantic granite columns.

TAIPANS

The grandeur of the 1886 headquarters reflects not just the prosperous state of the Bank and its ability to afford such extravagance but also the nature of the European executives as a class. Chief executives in trading houses were known as *taipans*—they formed not only the clientele of the Bank but also its board of directors. After all, it was they who resolved to build a new headquarters, formulated the brief for the design competition, and subsequently

9.1 | Hongkong Shanghai Bank, 1886. View from southwest, showing dome and colonnaded banking hall (PH140.1.5).

selected the winning entry.[4] The Hongkong and Shanghai Bank, founded in 1864, was in effect a merger of the banking interests of established agency houses. Its boardroom was an arena in which taipans from major merchant houses with a fair share in the China trade got together; ten different firms were represented in 1882, including all the big names, such as Jardines Matheson, Peninsular and Oriental, Gilman, Siemssen, David Sassoon and Sons, and Russell and Company.[5]

Class Consciousness

Among the social characteristics of the taipans that had a significant impact on the headquarters building was class consciousness. Very few Europeans in nineteenth-century Hong Kong came from a truly upper-class or aristocratic background. The majority were from the middle or lower middle classes, but they all enjoyed a social status and a standard of living far beyond anything they could command at home.[6] For most of the early traders and civil officers, their time in the East was merely a period of transition and their ventures in Hong Kong were only a means of moving up the social ladder back home. With the help of a hierarchy created by the colonial government and an unlimited supply of Chinese subjects, they detached themselves from their humble origins and acted out the kind of class position they aspired to obtain in Britain.[7]

One of the outward signs of class consciousness was an emphasis on rank and position. Those who had gained high social status in the expatriate community wished to emphasize that they had no connections with those beneath them. The taipans despised the clerks and shopkeepers who, in turn, despised the seaman and soldiers. The merchants divided themselves into "seniors" and "juniors" and, except in business matters, maintained a wide distance between each other.[8]

This concern was expressed through the vertical spatial division in the 1886 headquarters. Bedrooms on the first floor were allocated for junior European staff,[9] while those on the second floor were reserved for European staff with a higher ranking. All top-floor rooms enjoyed unobstructed views, as this floor was above the roof line of the adjacent buildings; not only were they "spacious, lofty and well lit,"[10] but some even had views across the harbor. Views from first-floor bedrooms, by contrast, were obstructed by the city hall to the east, by the Chartered Bank to the west, and by the dome over the banking hall to the south. No bedrooms on this floor had a praya view—only the drawing room and the dining room,[11] which were used by both the senior and junior European staff.

The hierarchical vertical separation was taken to extreme in the residences of the managers who lived in separate houses in the Peak district of the city.[12] The accommodation for Chinese servants was down in the basement, separated from the European staff's living quarters.[13]

Division within the European staff according to rank and position was also expressed in the horizontal layout of the plan. There was a close correlation between depth and seniority: the further one proceeded from the main entrance at Queen's Road, the nearer one approached the core of power. The chief manager's office was right at the end of the east side of the corridor, opposite the boardroom. Next door was the office of the submanager, the second man from the top of the power structure. Adjacent to the submanager's office was the correspondents' room, where the "semi-seniors" such as the assistant chief accountant and subaccountant worked. This room was linked by a passage to the east side of the general office in the banking hall where the European junior clerks were, but it was also separated from that general office by the strong room. The gap between the junior staff and the senior staff could not be transgressed, and there was probably no better way to maintain this gap than by the physical interposition of the strong room, which was built with walls 2.5 feet thick and equipped with fire- and burglar-proof doors.[14]

Class identity was also reinforced by the interior furnishings. The marble fireplaces in the bedrooms reminded the European staff of their newly acquired status and the grandeur that came with it. The electric bells fitted in all rooms signified the luxurious lifestyle built on the services provided by an abundant supply of local servants. Finally, there was also a grand staircase linking the residential quarters and the ground floor, and the very act of ascending it fostered an elevated self-image.

Another outward sign of class consciousness was the display of wealth. An extraordinary degree of conspicuous consumption was found among the expatriate community in nineteenth-century Hong Kong, manifested particularly in their housing. Victoria, the European commercial sector of Hong Kong, was called "the city of palaces" in the 1880s because of its extensive *hongs* and elegant residences, and Governor William Des Voeux (1887–1891) pointed out that the city "savoured more of fashion and expenditure" than any other colony he had seen.[15]

The Hongkong Bank headquarters was built in keeping with the general extravagant style of the city as a whole. The very high specification of the materials used included granite facing for the whole building and solid granite columns throughout carved into the Doric, Corinthian, and Composite orders. Teak also appeared extensively in architraves and paneling.[16] Although granite and teak were widely used in prominent public buildings in nineteenth-century Hong Kong, here the intricacy of their decoration and their sheer quantity clearly indicated that cost was not to be considered. The headquarters building also featured such inherently expensive materials as stained glass for the circular windows below the dome and marble for fireplaces in the banking hall and in the bedrooms.[17]

Another way of displaying wealth was by providing a high standard of comfort. A pendant Wenham gas burner, introduced into the colony for the first time, was used in the banking hall to light the area.[18] Supplies of hot and cold water were available in all bathrooms[19]—a great luxury in the nineteenth century, particularly given the most basic problems of water supply that other areas in Hong Kong were battling. Furthermore, each contained a large bath, described by early newspapers as "most comfortable looking."[20]

Political Dominance

The second characteristic of the taipans expressed in the 1886 building was their close link with politics. The taipans had firmly established their political legitimacy in Hong Kong by increasing their representation in the colony's highest administrative bodies—the Legislative Council and Executive Council—and by influencing government officials who were allowed to engage in private business and earn fees from hongs.[21] According to a saying popular in the nineteenth century, Hong Kong was ruled by the Jardines, the Jockey Club, the Hongkong and Shanghai Bank, and the governor, in that order of importance.[22] Although a Chinese elite gradually emerged in Hong Kong from the 1850s onward, they were not a rival pressure group that could challenge the influence of taipans on politics.

Since those in the merchant community had no political rivals, they exercised their domination over the dependent group in other ways, one of which was through architecture. It was therefore hardly surprising that the Bank desired a headquarters building that reflected the kind of dominance the merchant community as a whole, and the Hongkong Bank in particular, commanded in nineteenth-century Hong Kong.

Its height was one basic way in which the Bank expressed its imposing presence. The headquarters building was taller than nearly all other buildings along the waterfront when it was completed in 1886; while most were only three stories, the Hongkong Bank was four, one above the roof line of the others. The height was further exaggerated by the central tower that sat over the projecting entrance bay. The differential was particularly obvious to viewers approaching the city, as in those days all came by sea: the waterfront premises would be observed at a distance and hence read in context. On the Queen's Road side, the 100-foot-high dome surmounting the banking hall,[23] together with the screen of gigantic columns wrapping around it, dominated even the three-story buildings nearby.

9.2 | Hongkong Shanghai Bank, 1886. Northern facade facing the harbour.
Photograph taken ca. 1900, after completion of praya reclamation (PH140.1.11).

The status of the Bank was further signified by an elevated entrance. The main entrance was reached by ascending one flight of granite steps—first to the verandah formed by the colonnade and then to the level of the entrance door. The same message was also conveyed through the immense space in the banking hall under the large octagonal dome. To the users of the Bank, the whole spatial experience of climbing the stairs and discovering this imposing space in the banking hall acted to confirm what they should already have realized: the unrivaled power enjoyed by the Bank.

The sense of solidity and strength evoked by the granite used in the building reinforced this dominance. Moreover, granite had long been associated with important government buildings such as the Flagstaff House and the Government House, which were themselves symbols of power; the headquarters building drew on these associations as well.

CONTROL

Upholding the dominance-dependence relationship was the key to sustaining the power structure within the colony. It required not just physical or overt aggression but other means of control that, though less explicit, were nonetheless powerful and persuasive. These included both maintaining the distance between the two cultural groups through social and spatial segregation and reinforcing the hegemony of English over Chinese through the language used in education. The fundamental notion underlying and justifying these measures was "Orientalism"—embedded within which is a focus on the basic distinction between the "Orient" and the "Occident," as well as the belief that certain territories and people long for domination.[24]

Social Segregation

A real sense of separateness was cultivated in nineteenth-century Hong Kong through the government policy of nonintervention and nonconsultation toward the Chinese. They were, for example, encouraged to establish their own policing system and the government made no effort to seek their opinions on public affairs.[25] Segregation by race appeared to be the norm of the day: the use of the city hall library and museum was restricted to Europeans on Sundays and at certain hours during the week; the Yacht Club, like other specialized clubs, did not allow Chinese crewman to take part in its championship races; and the Hong Kong Club rigidly excluded Chinese, Indians, and women.[26]

This phenomenon was manifested in the 1886 headquarters in the verandah, which ran around the whole building. As an architectural device, the verandah combined climatic adaptation with the purpose of upholding social distance. Underlying its use was an idea of the "tropics," perceived by Victorian Englishmen as a zone not just climatic but also cultural, with potentially threatening lands and people that were nevertheless susceptible to control. Originated from the "bungalow" in colonial India, the encircling verandah shaded the main structure and provided a space for carefully regulated intercourse with the hostile world.[27]

Two huge internal buffer zones also expressed social segregation. The first was a massive space underneath the dome in the banking hall, which separated the general offices of the European staff to the east and the Chinese staff to the west. These offices all had broad counters in front of them, bending inward and following the octagonal shape of the dome.[28] The open space was about 50 feet across at its widest point, and its sheer size not only helped maintain the social distance between the staff but also helped eliminate any possible mingling between the European and the Chinese customers. The second buffer zone was a 20-foot-wide corridor separating the European half and the Chinese half of the adjoining offices, which was in turn expressed in the praya elevation as a projected central bay.[29]

The desire to maintain social distance was reflected as well in the use of a thick, concrete ceiling to separate the Chinese employees' living quarters in the basement from the European staff's living quarters on the

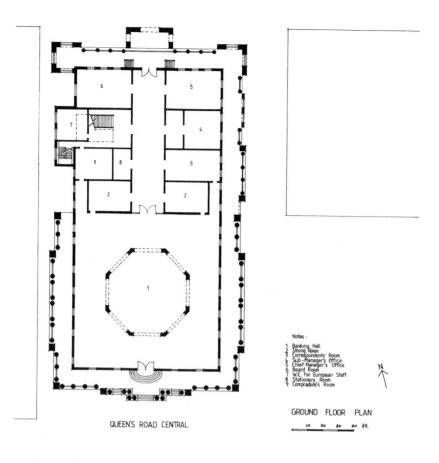

QUEEN'S ROAD CENTRAL

Notes :
1 Banking Hall
2 Strong Room
3 Correspondents' Room
4 Sub-Manager's Office
5 Chief Manager's Office
6 Board Room
7 W.C. for European Staff
8 Stationery Room
9 Compradore's Room

GROUND FLOOR PLAN
10   20   30   40 ft.

9.3 | Hongkong Shanghai Bank, 1886. Ground floor plan (author's reconstruction).

upper floors. The concrete ceiling was also intended to contain a fire if one broke out in the basement, where the kitchens were located. This separation was also expressed externally in elevation: instead of being built in brick and clad with polished granite, the basement was built in solid granite blocks with a rusticated surface and iron bars on the windows.[30]

Spatial Segregation

The two cultural groups were also kept apart through spatial segregation. A clear separation in the city between the European commercial sector and the native quarter was artificially constructed through the government's land sale policy and other regulations. The east-west boundary of the European commercial sector from Ice House Street to Bonham Strand was formed after the first land sale in June 1841.[31] At the same time, a land allocation scheme was set up for the island, and areas to the east of the European sec-

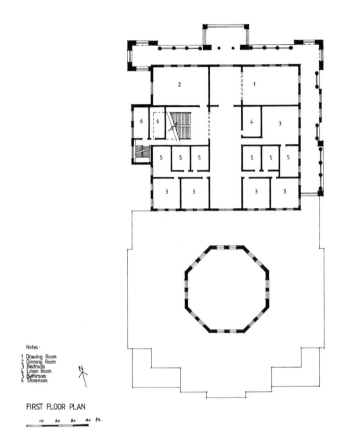

Notes :
1 Drawing Room
2 Dinning Room
3 Bedroom
4 Linen Room
5 Bathroom
6 Storeroom

FIRST FLOOR PLAN

10   20   30   40 ft.

9.4 | Hongkong Shanghai Bank, 1886. First floor plan (author's reconstruction).

tor were marked out as bazaars for the Chinese.[32] Legislation was passed in 1877 and 1888 to prevent natives from infringing on the European quarter and to create residential reservations south of Hollywood Road and in Caine Road, where Europeans desired exclusive control.[33]

In the 1886 headquarters building, spatial segregation operated horizontally in the office area and vertically in the living quarters as outlined above. In addition, utilities were segregated. Newspapers reported that there were "well fitted lavatories for the European clerks," implying that these lavatories were not to be used by the Chinese clerks who worked at the other side of the banking hall. Furthermore, in a large European kitchen in the basement only "European" food for the European staff was prepared; Chinese cooks and other Chinese employees cooked for themselves in a separate Chinese kitchen in the basement, "fitted with inexpensive and primitive appliances."[34]

Moreover, there was a segregation of circulation and entrances. The back staircase on the west side of the building linking the basement and the upper floors kept local servants off the grand staircase. There were side entrances to the basement from the Queen's Road and from the praya,[35] similarly indicating that Chinese coolies and servants were not allowed to share the main entrance door with the European taipans.

Thus spatial segregation within the headquarters building was a microcosm of the system operating in the city as a whole. Its location underscored the sense of separation between the Bank as a key member of the dominant group and the natives. The headquarters was positioned not at the heart of the European commercial sector but at its fringe, further away from the native quarter than any other plot in the sector.

Segregation of the Chinese Elite

The relationship between the two cultural groups was not just one of complete isolation. A Chinese elite class gradually emerged in the 1850s and began to find their way into the intermediate zone. It included wealthy Chinese merchants who capitalized on the sharp rise in the demand for Chinese products overseas caused by the mass emigration following the Taiping Rebellion.[36] An English-educated Chinese elite acted as middleman between the governing and the governed—a group to which the compradores belonged. The compradore system enabled the dominant group to exercise power over the dependent group while maintaining social distance; in the positioning of the compradore's office in the headquarters, we see a spatial representation of how the mechanism worked.

The compradore was responsible for recruiting and guaranteeing all Chinese employees, which explains why his office was next to the back staircase linking the servants in the basement and the European staff upstairs. But he also functioned as a business assistant whose responsibilities included overseeing all business transactions relating to Chinese merchants, handling all cash, validating the bullion, and managing the exchange business among gold, silver, copper coins, and different treaty port silver dollars.[37] Because of the large sums of funds he handled, the second compradore of the Bank (1877–1892) was required to provide a security of HK$300,000,[38] a sum equal to the total cost of the 1886 headquarters building. The compradore was directly answerable to the chief manager,[39] which in theory put him on equal status with the semi-senior European staff of the Bank. That the head compradore's room was in the office area behind the banking hall is consonant with this rank. Yet his office was segregated from all European staff—it was located on the west side of the corridor, next to the lavatories for European clerks and behind the stationery room;[40] thus he might not even have direct access to the corridor that divided the west side from the east side where the offices of European staff were all located.

Segregation of the compradore is also evidenced in the written and visual documents kept or produced by the Bank. No names of Chinese employees, not even the head compradore, appeared in the staff lists.[41] Chinese staff in Hong Kong were not included in staff photos; it was not until 1928 that the compradore department was photographed—but separately from the European staff. The first photograph featuring both European and Chinese staff together was taken in 1935.[42]

THE WIDER CONTEXT

While the power structure within the colony is the focus of the above analysis, it is by no means the only force shaping the built form of the 1886 headquarters. The power relationship between the core and the periphery provides a key for understanding other contributing factors. As already noted, the headquarters site stood at the eastern edge of the European commercial sector, an area produced by the continuous land reclamation along the praya in the nineteenth century. Reclamation in Hong Kong has to be understood in the light of the colonial government's land policy, which was driven by the need to offset Britain's military expenses and to surrender strategic sites to the military authorities. Most waterfront properties in this sector were three-story buildings with arched verandahs, a strong rhythm in facade composition, and an essentially "European" feel evoked by a classical architectural language. These premises, which fronted the praya in a straight line with a highly uniform appearance, formed a powerful context for the headquarters building and provided an architectural vocabulary for its praya facade.

The 1886 headquarters can be read on a global as well as urban scale. Since the dominance-dependence relationship within the colony was sustained by the power of the empire at large, the meaning embedded in the 1886 headquarters cannot be fully decoded without examining the building in a world context. The headquarters building was not just a symbol of the client's financial strength; it was also a manifestation of the Bank's connection with the British government, and with the empire as a whole. That connection made possible a continual increase in profits from 1864, when the Bank was formed, to 1886, when the headquarters was completed—despite the political and economic chaos in China and in the region as a whole.

Most of the Bank's revenue came from loans to China. The Foreign Office continually supported the Bank's forwarding of these loans, as the financial dependence of an indigenous government on a European banker could prove politically advantageous.[43] Furthermore, the British government had deposited with the Bank the Treasury chest: the fund for payments to government employees at the consular ports in China and Japan. The Bank therefore had ample silver coins to make short-term loans at a high rate of interest to provincial authorities in China.[44] Income also came from the Bank's branches worldwide, whose opening coincided with a period of unprecedented expansion of the British Empire in Asia. There were seventeen such branches by 1883, all at ports connected with China trade, some of which were British colonies.[45]

The Hongkong Bank was not just a local bank serving local merchants. Its biggest "client" in the loan business was imperial China, and its strongest ally was the British government. The headquarters building physically expressed this link with the empire by its classical architectural style, which would be readily perceived as bearing an imperial imprint. When finished in 1886, it was more elaborate, both in form and in level of detailing, than any government building in Hong Kong. After all, the government buildings represented only the British administration in the colony of Hong Kong, whereas the headquarters building manifested in its built form the political ambition of the British Empire toward China.

Within the next hundred years, two more new Hongkong Bank headquarters were built on the same site. Featuring neoclassical composition and art deco motifs, the 1935 headquarters was described by the local press as "the most dramatic and successful skyscraper in the East."[46] The 1986 headquarters received worldwide attention for its high-tech image and its exceptionally high cost. The analytical framework used to examine the 1886 headquarters can also be applied to the 1935 and the 1986 headquarters. Collectively, the three headquarters show the developing relationship between colonialism and built form over time; changes in their built form reflect changes in the nature of colonialism and in power relations at every level. The 1886 headquarters building is but the first stage of this process.

Notes

1 "The New Buildings of the Hongkong and Shanghai Bank," *Daily Press*, 14 August 1886.

2 "The New Buildings of the Hongkong and Shanghai Bank," *China Mail*, 9 August 1886; "New Buildings," *Daily Press*, 14 August 1886. The contractor is named in the Hongkong and Shanghai Banking Corporation, "Board Minutes (Extracts)," 15 February 1883, Hongkong Bank Archives.

3 See the map showing the Victoria seafront between 1843 and 1855, with proposed reclamation schemes, in T. R. Tregear and L. Berry, *The Development of Hong Kong and Kowloon as Told in Maps* (Hong Kong: Macmillan, 1959), p. 8; and *Plan of Victoria 1866* (Hong Kong: Public Record Office, 1866), no. 242. The dimensions are given in "New Buildings," *Daily Press*, 14 August 1886.

4 The Hongkong and Shanghai Banking Corporation, "Board Minutes (Extracts)," 27 September 1881 and 30 November 1882, Hongkong Bank Archives.

5 See the list of the Bank's 1882 board of directors in Frank King, *The Hongkong Bank in Late Imperial China, 1864–1902: On an Even Keel* (Cambridge: Cambridge University Press, 1987), p. 363.

6 Henry Lethbridge, *Hong Kong, Stability and Change: A Collection of Essays* (Hong Kong: Oxford University Press, 1978), pp. 10, 181.

7 Wai-Kwan Chan, *The Making of Hong Kong Society: Three Studies of Class Formation in Early Hong Kong* (Oxford: Oxford University Press, 1991), p. 34.

8 Colin Criswell, *The Taipans: Hong Kong's Merchant Princes* (Oxford: Oxford University Press, 1981), pp. 103–104.

9 "New Buildings," *China Mail*, 9 August 1886; "New Building," *Daily Press*, 14 August 1886.

10 "New Building," *Daily Press*, 14 August 1886.

11 "New Buildings," *China Mail*, 9 August 1886.

12 The Hongkong and Shanghai Banking Corporation, "Board Minutes (Extracts)," 2 October 1883 and 21 January 1886, Hongkong Bank Archives.

13 "New Buildings," *China Mail*, 9 August 1886; "New Building," *Daily Press*, 14 August 1886.

14 This and the following description of the plan and furnishings appear in "New Building," *Daily Press*, 14 August 1886.

15 L. N. Wheeler, *The Foreigner in China* (Chicago: S. C. Griggs, 1881), p. 242; William Des Voeux, *My Colonial Service* (London: John Murray, 1903), 2:199.

16 "New Buildings," *China Mail*, 9 August 1886; "New Building," *Daily Press*, 14 August 1886.

17 "New Buildings," *China Mail*, 9 August 1886; "New Building," *Daily Press*, 14 August 1886.

18 "New Building," *Daily Press*, 14 August 1886.

19 "New Buildings," *China Mail*, 9 August 1886.

20 "New Building," *Daily Press*, 14 August 1886.

21 Chan, *Making of Hong Kong Society*, pp. 28–29.

22 Criswell, *The Taipans*, p. 222.

23 "New Building," *Daily Press*, 14 August 1886.

24 Edward Said, *Culture and Imperialism* (London: Chatto and Windus, 1993), pp. 8–10. On Orientalism more generally, see Edward Said, *Orientalism* (London: Routledge and Kegan Paul, 1978).

25 For details of the government policy, see Elizabeth Sinn, *Power and Charity: The Early History of Tung Wah Hospital* (Hong Kong: Hong Kong University Press, 1990), pp. 2–29.

26 Criswell, *The Taipans*, pp. 104, 174, 214.

27 Thomas Metcalf, *An Imperial Vision: Indian Architecture and Britain's Raj* (London: Faber and Faber, 1989), pp. 5–6.

28 "New Building," *Daily Press*, 14 August 1886.

29 I have deduced these measurements from my reconstruction of the floor plans of the 1886 headquarters.

30 "New Building," *Daily Press*, 14 August 1886.

31 The boundary was evident in the *Map of Victoria 1856*, where lot numbers of the land sold were shown ([Hong Kong: Public Record Office, 1856], no. 203). For details of the land sale, see E. J. Eitel, *Europe in China* (1895; reprint, Oxford: Oxford University Press 1983), pp. 172–174.

32 Roger Bristow, *Land-Use Planning in Hong Kong: History, Policies, and Procedures* (Hong Kong: Oxford University Press, 1984), p. 23.

33 "Dispatch from J. M. Price, Surveyor General, to the Earl of Carnarvon, Secretary of State for the Colonies, on 8 May 1877," in London-House of Commons, *Hong Kong: Restrictions upon the Chinese* (25 August 1881); Bristow, *Land-Use Planning in Hong Kong*, p. 30.

34 Quotations from "New Building," *Daily Press*, 14 August 1886.

35 "New Buildings," *China Mail*, 9 August 1886.

36 K. C. Fok, *Lectures on Hong Kong: Hong Kong's Role in Modern Chinese History* (Hong Kong: Commercial Press, 1990), p. 101.

37 For details of the compradore's function as a business assistant, see Carl Smith, "Compradores of the Hongkong Bank," in *Eastern Banking: Essays in the History of the Hongkong and Shanghai Banking Corporation*, ed. Frank King (London: Athlone Press, 1983), pp. 93–94; Yen-Ping Hao, *The Comprador in Nineteenth Century China: Bridge between East and West* (Cambridge, Mass.: Harvard University Press, 1970), pp. 73–74.

38 Smith, "Compradores of the Hongkong Bank," p. 97.

39 Ibid., p. 94.

40 "New Buildings," *China Mail*, 9 August 1886; "New Building," *Daily Press*, 14 August 1886.

41 The Hongkong and Shanghai Banking Corporation, "Staff List, 1864–1891," compiled by Catherine King, Hongkong Bank Archives, S1.10.

42 Staff photographs in the Hongkong Bank Archives, PH140.10.

43 David McLean, "International Banking and Its Political Implications: The Hongkong and Shanghai Banking Corporation and the Imperial Bank of Persia, 1889–1914," in King, *Eastern Banking*, pp. 4, 7.

44 Maurice Collis, *Wayfoong: The Hongkong and Shanghai Banking Corporation* (London: Faber and Faber, 1965), pp. 60–61.

45 Ibid., p. 55.

46 "The New Hong Kong Building Opened," *Hong Kong Daily Press*, 11 October 1935.

Part II

Filtering Tactics

"Transform the world"—all well and good.
It is being transformed. But into what?
Here, at your feet, is one small but crucial
element in that mutation.

Henri Lefebvre
"Notes on the New Town" (trans. John Moore)

Iain Borden

10

Another Pavement, Another Beach: Skateboarding and the Performative Critique of Architecture

Considering the unknownness of the city means not only thinking about ways of knowing it but also, as Steve Pile makes clear in chapter 15 of this volume, contemplating how the city will always in part remain unknown to us. One such zone of the unknown is not geographic or social, but temporal: the future. Given that we can barely begin to understand the present, and that our world is full of hesitancies and contradictions, how can we even begin to know how the urban will be constituted next year, next decade, or next millennium? While the answer is, of course, that we cannot know such things, we can still try to glimpse, prefigure, or even affect the way the future unknown city might operate. Such actions should then not project into the future a finite and definitive model, a kind of a priori decision taken on behalf of our future selves, but should be, following Henri Lefebvre, a direction, a tendency—and, above all, it should be at once theoretical and practical.[1] Furthermore, this combination of the theoretical and the practical does not necessarily mean a schism between the two, a joining that ultimately keeps each term separate from the other. On the contrary, we must invoke a dialectic of the two such that "[l]anguage and the living word are components of a praxis," resisting the fetishization of language in order to "go beyond the active word, to find, to discover—to create—what is yet to be said."[2]

This chapter explores a particular urban practice—that of skateboarding—for its implicit yet ongoing tendency to critique contemporary cities for their meanings and modes of operation, and to prefigure what a future unknown city might be. As one skateboarder declares, "Skating is a continual search for the unknown."[3] The abstract space of capitalism harbors many contradictions, not the least being the simultaneous dissolution of old relations and generation of new relations; abstract space is thus destined not to last forever, and already contains within itself the birth of a new space—Lefebvre's putative *differential space* in which sociospatial differences are emphasized and celebrated.[4] Skateboarding, I propose, is a critical practice that challenges both the form and political mechanics of urban life, and so in its own small way is part of this birth of differential space. Through an everyday practice—neither a conscious theorization nor a codified political program—skateboarding suggests that pleasure rather than work, use values rather than exchange values, activity rather than passivity are potential components of the future, as yet unknown, city.[5]

ZERO DEGREE ARCHITECTURE

During the 1970s and early 1980s, skateboarders first undertook a series of spatial appropriations, rethinking the suburban drive as ocean surf, taking over schoolyards and drained swimming pools, and, in the purpose-built skateparks, producing a super-architectural space in which body, skateboard, and terrain were brought together and recomposed in an extraordinary encounter. And skateboarders relived photographic and video images of themselves, making the body into a mediated entity and, conversely, the image into a lived representation. But from the early 1980s, the focus of skateboarding has shifted, becoming more urban in character, directly confronting not only architecture but also the economic logic of capitalist abstract space. It is on this street-skating that I focus here.

Around 1984, Los Angeles skaters began the first radical extensions of skateboarding onto the most quotidian and conventional elements of the urban landscape. Using as their basic move the "ollie," the impact-adhesion-ascension procedure by which the skater unweights the front of the skateboard to make it pop up seemingly unaided into the air, they rode up onto the walls, steps, and street furniture of the Santa Monica strand and Venice boardwalk.[6] In the words of Stacy Peralta, skateboard manufacturer and ex-professional skater, "Skaters can exist on the essentials of what is out there. Anything is part of the run. For urban skaters the city is the hardware on their trip."[7] *Public Domain* and *Ban This*, the videos Peralta produced and directed in 1988–1989, show skaters in the streets of Los Angeles and Santa Barbara: jumping over cars; riding onto the walls of buildings, over hydrants and planters, and onto benches; flying over steps; and sliding down the freestanding handrails in front of a bank.

The first thing to note about this new kind of skateboarding is that it is no longer situated in the undulating, semi-suburban terrain of the Hollywood Hills and Santa Monica canyon, no longer among the moneyed detached villas and swimming pools; it has come downtown, to the inner city. In the words of one skater, "I realised that I would have to leave the hills and open countryside to progress in skating. Towards the urban jungle I headed. . . . Bigger and more varied types of terrain were my driving force."[8] And this is a process that has continued; today it is not only the downtown streets of New York, Washington, San Francisco, and Philadelphia that are the most intense skate scenes, but also those of London, Prague, Melbourne, Mexico City, and other cities worldwide. The new skateboarding sites are not private houses or suburban roads, hidden from public view, but university campuses, urban squares, public institutions and buildings, national theaters, and commercial office plazas, as well as the more quotidian spaces of streets, sidewalks, and car parks; they range from specific sites—such as, for example, the Annenberg Center for Performing Arts in Philadelphia—to any parking lot or bus bench in any city worldwide.

All these are appropriations of places, not dissimilar to the 1970s appropriations of schoolyard banks and backyard pools; but here, like Paul

Virilio's call for an inhabitation of the "critical spaces" of hospitals, theaters, universities, factories, and so on, skaters undertake a "counter-habitation" of habitually uninhabited but nonetheless public spaces.[9] Skaters exploit the ambiguity of the ownership and function of public and semipublic space, displaying their actions to the public at large. But why is this, and what does it mean for the experience of urban architecture?

Cities offer more opportunities for those who live in their cores and concentrated heterogeneous social spaces than for those who live in the suburbs; the rich architectural and social fabric of the city offers skateboarders a plethora of building types, social relations, times, and spaces, many of which do not necessarily require money to access or at least visit them. As a result, city dwellers are less compelled than suburbanists and potentially more adaptive, even when without economic privilege. Lefebvre notes,

> [E]ven when he is not wealthy the city dweller reaps the benefits of past glories and enjoys a considerable latitude of initiative, the make-believe existence of his environment is less fictitious and unsatisfactory than that of his suburban or new-town counterpart; it is enlivened by monuments, chance encounters and the various occupations and distractions forming part of his everyday experience; city make-believe favours the adaptation of time and space.[10]

But the decision about which spaces and relations to enter into is not easy, and for any metropolitan dweller it is ultimately conditioned by a whole range of conditions, tied not just to location and finance, but also to time, friendship, gender, race, age, culture, and ideology. In particular, it is difficult to make such decisions based on any sense of urban *style*, for while industrialization and commercialization pervade every aspect of urban life, we have little language or style of experience beyond the formal "styles" of architectural physicality and the commodified "lifestyles" of fashion, food, and the like. Analytically, this is in part due to a theoretical inheritance from Marx, who tended to reduce urbanization to organization and the demands of production, and so ignored the possibilities of adaptation to the city.[11] Socially, it means that we have no *language* of urban living, and instead we are surrounded by an emptiness filled by signs. Skateboarding, as we shall see, offers a partial glimpse of a counter future to this condition, a creation of the city by those engaging directly with its everyday spaces.

> The productive potential expressed and realized in industrial production might have been diverted towards that most essential of productions, the City, urban society. In such a city, creation of creations, everyday life would become a creation of which each citizen and each community would be capable.[12]

As part of their own participation in realizing this "productive potential," skaters recognize that architecture has no innate or fixed meaning, and they are thus free to reinterpret it as they will: "The corporate types see their structures as powerful and strong. I see them as something I can enjoy, something I can manipulate to my advantage."[13] It is sometimes argued that the most effectively appropriated spaces are those occupied by symbols (such as gardens, parks, religious buildings), appropriation offering the chance to invert social relations and meanings and so create a kind of heterotopic space.[14] To this end, skaters and other subversive or countercultural urbanists such as graffiti artists certainly do occasionally work against highly symbolic monuments—for example, one of the favored highly visible locations for Norwegian skaters is along the raised walkways and outside the central doorway of the immense Rådhus (City Hall) in Oslo.[15] Similarly, Czech skaters utilize the space around the National Theater in Prague,[16] London skaters have since the 1970s done the same around the high-cultural South Bank Centre,[17] and Parisian skaters are often to be seen in and around the high architecture *folies* of Parc La Villette designed by Bernard Tschumi.[18]

But it is in the open, public space of streets and squares that countercultural and counterspatial activities most readily take place, as these are the spaces as yet not dominated by the high ideologies and powers of the state—a point that Lefebvre notes in his little-read yet highly informative study of the events of Paris in 1968.

> It was in the streets that the demonstrations took place. It was in the streets that spontaneity expressed itself. . . . The streets have become politicized—this fact points up the political void prevailing in the specialized areas. Social space has assumed new meaning. This entails new meaning. This entails new risks. Political practice transferred to the streets sidesteps the (economic and social) practice which emanates from identifiable places.[19]

Skateboarders implicitly realize the importance of the streets as a place to act; rather than gravitating toward ideologically frontal or monumental architecture, skateboarders usually prefer the lack of meaning and symbolism of more everyday spaces—the space of the street, the urban plaza, the mini-mall—just as graffiti artists tend to write on out-of-the-way (not always very visible) sites. In part this reflects their desire to avoid social conflict, but it is also an attempt to write anew—not to change meaning but to insert a meaning where previously there was none.

What then are these other kinds of spaces, those without explicit meaning or symbolism? Most obviously, they are the left-over spaces of modernist town planning, or the spaces of decision making (typically the urban

10.1 | Harry, ollie over roundabout, Between Towns Road, Oxford (1995).

plaza) that symbolize not through overt iconography but predominantly through their expansivity of space. Lefebvre characterizes these, after Roland Barthes, as a kind of spatial degree zero: zero points of language (everyday speech), objects (functional objects), spaces (traffic circulation, deserted spaces in the heart of the city), needs (predicted, satisfied in advance), and time (programmed, organized according to a preexistent space). "Zero point is a transparency interrupting communication and relationships just at the moment when everything seems communicable because everything seems both rational and real; and then there is nothing to communicate!"[20]

Architecturally, the city is reduced to the status and form of an instrument, passed over by a capitalist and state rationality that prefers to operate at national or international scales.

> The statutes of urban "zones" and "areas" are reduced to a juxtaposition of spaces, of functions, of elements on the ground. Sectors and functions are tightly subordinated to centres of decision-making. Homogeneity overwhelms the differences originating from nature (the site), from peasant surroundings (territory and the soil), from history. The city, or what remains of it, is built or is rearranged, in the likeness of a sum or combination of elements.[21]

The new town and the reconstructed old city alike are reduced to the legibility of signs, their spaces optimized for the function of decision making.

For the experiencer of such architecture, there is a similarly reductive effect. In Barthes's concept of "zero point," elaborated in *Le degré zéro de l'écriture* (1953), the neutralization and disappearance of symbols is justified by the writer claiming to state simply and coldly what is, as if merely a witness.[22] In terms of architecture, the lack of discernible qualitative differences, and the corresponding surfeit of instructions and signals, is rendered as a feeling of monotony and lack of diversity, the urban having lost the characteristics of the creative oeuvre and of appropriation.

> There is a poverty of daily life as nothing has replaced the symbols, the appropriations, the styles, the monuments, the times and rhythms, the different and qualified spaces of the traditional city. Urban society, because of the dissolution of this city submitted to pressures which it cannot withstand, tends on the one hand to blend with the planned land use of the territory into the "urban fabric" determined by the constraints of traffic, and on the other hand, into dwelling units such as those of the detached house and the housing estates.[23]

The metropolitan dweller and architect alike become simply witnesses to the functioning of the city, in which exchanges of decisions and commodities dominate social relations and uses. The experience of urban space is reduced to that of the modern museum, where constraints on the bodies of visitors create a kind of "organized walking" in which route, speed, gestures, speaking, and sound are all controlled.[24]

This does not mean, however, that passivity and ennui are the only possible responses to such reductive architecture. Resistance to zero degree architecture takes place outside of the buildings themselves, in the streets, as some counter the everyday, routinized phenomena of privatized urban space and the commodification and pacification of urban experience by enacting a different space and time for the city. "Formerly abstract and incomplete, the dissociations now become complete. Projected onto the terrain, it is here that they can transcend themselves—in the streets. It is here that student meets worker, and reason reduced to a function again recovers speech."[25]

Skateboarders target the spaces and times of the urban degree zero, reinscribing themselves onto functional everyday spaces and objects. One has observed, "[Skateboarding] is a challenge to our everyday concepts of the functions of buildings, and to the closed world we create for ourselves out of this massively unlimited city."[26] For example, a handrail is a highly functional object; both the time and nature of its use are fully programmed. If there is

10.2 | Danny Barley, switch 180 to smith grind on handrail, 1996.

a meaning at all in a handrail, then it is directly related to function: that of safety. The surprise of the skateboarder's reuse of the handrail—ollie-ing up onto the rail, and sliding down its length sideways, weighted perilously on the skateboard deck as it at once balances and moves along the fulcrum line of the metal bar—is that it targets something to do with safety, with everyday security, and turns it into an object of risk, where previously it was precisely risk that was being erased. The whole logic of the handrail is turned on its head. More usually, however, such an object has no apparent history or wider cultural or social meaning outside of the use for which it is intentionally designed and provided. In place or on top of this absence, skateboarding inscribes a new meaning; where previously there was only the most banal of uses, skateboarders create not just a change of use but an *ex novo* act. The "meaning" of the skateboard move, then, in part takes its power and vitality from its coming out of the blue, an unexpected and sudden eruption of meaning where society had previously been content to say nothing. Skateboarding is a critique of the emptiness of meaning; skateboarders realize that "Empty of cars, car-parks have only form and no function."[27]

RHYTHM AND URBAN SENSES

If the meaning of the architecture of the new town and reconstructed postwar city is at zero point, what then does skateboarding address? What is the ground on which it acts? The answer lies less in the realm of culture of meaning than in that of physical and sensory rhythms.

While cities are made from social relations as conceived and constructed by thought, they are not, and cannot be, purely ideational. As "*urban* is not a soul, a spirit, a philosophical entity,"[28] the city is the immediate reality, the practico-material of the urban; it is the architectural fact with which the urban cannot dispense. And of course this "architectural fact" necessarily takes on a certain form, which in turn poses certain constraints and conditions—but also specific opportunities in time and space. Lefebvre notes, for example, the remarkable architecture of stairs in Mediterranean cities, which link spaces and times, and so provide the rhythm for space and time of walking in the city.[29]

What then if we applied the same "rhythmanalysis," to use Lefebvre's term,[30] to modern cities, to the architecture of the zero degree city. What kind of rhythm and experience do they presuppose? This is exactly the condition for urban skateboarders, who are both presented with, and exploitative of, the physical space-times of modernist urban space. Skateboarders address the spaces of the modern metropolis: the spaces of the square and the street, the campus and semipublic buildings. Beyond these spaces being functional, each corresponding to a particular activity or ideological purpose, they are also conceived of primarily as objects in space, as dispositions of three-dimensional form (each modulated according to its own programmatic and aesthetic concerns) in a universal, abstract space. Space here is at once homogeneous and—subjected to the various technical forces and resources available—more or less capable of being fragmented into any subdivision, plot, or architectural component that might be wished of it. "What then is the principal contradiction to be found? Between the capacity to conceive of and treat space on a global (or worldwide) scale on the one hand, and its fragmentation by a multiplicity of procedures or processes, all fragmentary themselves, on the other."[31]

Skateboarders treat space exactly as conceived of and presented in this form of architectural urbanism. First, space becomes a uniform entity, a constant layer through the city that can be utilized, in this case, as a surface on which to skate. All elements of the city are thus reduced to the homogeneous level of skateable terrain. For the skateboarder, "[a]nything is part of the run": "Buildings are building blocks for the open minded."[32] Second, skaters follow the homogeneity-fragmentation contradiction of abstract space by oscillating from this macro conception of space to the micro one of the architectural element; they move from the open canvas of the urban realm to the close focus of a specific wall, bench, fire hydrant, curb, or rail.

> Bumps, curbs and gaps. The street is really universal.[33]

> From a perfect bank, to a smooth marble step, to a lamp post: movement around lines and shadows. An unusual arrangement of street furniture can be inspiration for radness.[34]

The spatial rhythm adopted is that of a passage or journey from one element to another, the run across the city spaces interspersed with moments and momentary settlings on specific sites. This is not an activity that could take place in a medieval, Renaissance, or early industrial city. It requires the smooth surfaces and running spaces of the paved, concrete city ("the polished marble planes of [Mies] van der Rohe's plazas are Mecca to Chicago's skateboarders");[35] and, above all, it requires the object-space-object-space rhythm born from a fragmentation of objects within a homogeneous space. For the skateboarder, the "primary relationships are not with his fellow man, but with the earth beneath his feet, concrete and all."[36]

Rhythmanalysis does not refer only to space, however; it also involves the rhythm of time. The temporal rhythms—the various routines, cyclical patterns, speeds, durations, precisions, repetitions—of the city, as well as its spaces, offer a frame for skateboarders. Here it is the essentially fragmentary temporal use of urban space that skateboarders respond to, ex-

Iain Borden

10.3 | Arron Bleasdale, 1996.

10.4 | Frank Stephens, blunt on bench 1995.

ploiting the streets, urban plazas, and street furniture that others rarely use
in any constant manner for long periods. For the zero point architecture of
the new town and decision-making center, skaters interweave their own
composition of time into that of regular temporal patterns, such as waging
a fast assault on a handrail outside a bank, adding a speeding skateboard to
the slower pattern of those walking on the sidewalk ("skating past all the
business-suit lames that slog gloomily down the sidewalk, barely lifting
their feet, like they're kicking shit with every step),"[37] or staying longer in
an urban plaza as others hurry through. (I see this last kind of temporal tactic most evenings outside Euston Station in London, where a few skaters often spend an hour or so riding over its planters, benches, and low walls,
while commuters rush through to their transport connections.) For the more
contested terrains of postmodernity—such as the shopping mall or privatized public space—a different temporal tactic has to be used. In particular,
skaters exploit the highly bounded temporality of, for example, a privatized
office district by stepping outside of its normal patterns of use. In places in
London like Canary Wharf or Broadgate—both versions of privatized urban
space, with very precise patterns of usage—skaters, conduct their own activities in the hours of the weekend or evening, when the office workers are
absent. This appropriation of the unused time of a particular urban element
is also applied to smaller, less spectacular parts of the urban street; the bus
bench outside of rush hour, or the department store car park outside of shopping hours, can be the focus of skateboarders who take advantage of the few
minutes or hours in which it otherwise lies dormant.

Micro experience is also part of rhythmanalysis—the relation of the
self to the city's physical minutiae that are not always obvious to, or considered by, the dominant visualization of the city on which we most commonly
depend. "These are my streets. I know every crack of every sidewalk there is
down here."[38] For skaters this involves hearing; when traveling at speed the
skater, like a cyclist, responds to the more obvious sounds of the city, such
as a car accelerating or a police siren from behind, and to the noises of a car
door, people talking, and footsteps. In particular, the sound of the skateboard over the ground yields much information about the conditions of the
surface, such as its speed grip, and predictability. More important, micro
rhythmanalysis involves a sense of touch, generated either from direct contact with the terrain—hand on building, foot on wall—or from the smoothness and textual rhythms of the surface underneath, passed up through the
wheels, trucks, and deck up into the skater's feet and body. Here such elements as the smoothness of pure tarmac or concrete, the roughness of met-
aled road, or the intermittent counterrhythm of paving slab cracks all
combine to create a textual pattern bound into the skateboarder's experience

of urban space. The compositional sound rhythms—the monotonal constancy of the subtle roar of tarmac, the silence-click-silence-click of paving slabs, combined with the intermittent pure silences when the skateboard leaves the ground through an ollie, and the sudden cracks as it once again hits terrain and elements—are a feature of this urban space.

The skateboard run, with its patterned moves, junctures, noises, and silences is thus at once an exploitation and denial of zero degree architecture, exploiting its surfaces and smoothness while using its roughness and objectival qualities to create a new appropriative rhythm quite distinct from the routinized, passive experiences that it usually enforces. Street skateboarding is "a total focus of mind, body and environment to a level way beyond that of the dead consumers interested at best in money, beer and 'the lads.'"[39] The "new school" skateboard—with its light deck, small wheels, and equal front-back orientation specifically designed for street skating[40]— is a tool in hand for this rhythm, a tool that is also absorbed into the new rhythmic production of super-architectural space.

As this last point suggests, it is not only the city that is reengaged in the intersection of skateboard, body, and architecture. The construction of the body too is changed. In terms that recall Georg Simmel's identification in the modern metropolis of a fundamental reorientation of the physiology and psychology of its inhabitants—an "intensification of nervous stimulation which results from the swift and uninterrupted change of outer and inner stimuli," or what David Frisby calls "neurasthenia"[41]—Lefebvre notes that

> The physiological functions of the "modern" man's nervous and cerebral systems seem to have fallen victim to an excessively demanding regime, to a kind of hypertension and exhaustion. He has not yet "adapted" to the conditions of his life, to the speed of its sequences and rhythms, to the (momentarily) excessive abstraction of the frequently erroneous concepts he has so recently acquired. His nerves and senses have not yet been adequately trained by the urban and technical life he leads.[42]

For skateboarders, like all metropolitan dwellers, modern urban conditions produce new kinds of sociospatial conditions, impacting at psychological and formal as well as social levels. In Lefebvre's consideration of events, unlike Simmel's, the new kind of person this creates is not yet fully evolved, not fully adapted. In particular, modern individuals cannot abstract out the concept from the thing, for these are mixed together in their perception, creating a confused unity in which relations, order, and hierarchy are lost. This is a state of "deliberate semi-neurosis," partly playacting and "often little more than an ambivalent infantilism."[43]

We might speculate then that this "ambivalent infantilism" is exactly the condition of skateboarders, faced with the intense conditions of the modern city. And in terms of epistemology, or more precisely in the context of many skaters' lack of codified sociopolitical awareness, such conjecture would be largely correct. But the very same condition also contains the seeds of resistance, critique, and creative production. As Lefebvre notes, that the modern individual is not yet "fully adapted" suggests that a process of evolution is under way; elsewhere he is more explicit about this, seeing it as involving a transformation and development of our senses. It is then in lived experience, rather than abstract theoretical knowledge, that the skateboarder's adaptation can initially be seen.

> The activity which gives the external world and its "phenomena" shape is not a "mental" activity, theoretical and formal, but a practical, concrete one. Practical tools, not simple concepts, are the means by which social man has shaped his perceptible world. As regards the processes of knowledge by means of which we understand this "world[,]" . . . they are our senses. But our senses have been transformed by action. . . . Thus it is that our senses, organs, vital needs, instincts, feelings have been permeated with consciousness, with human reason, since they too have been shaped by social life.[44]

Such concerns directly raise the question of spatiality, as Fredric Jameson does in pointing out the alarming disjunction of body and built environment in the Westin Bonaventure Hotel in Los Angeles, where postmodern hyperspace "has finally succeeded in transcending the capacities of the individual human body to locate itself, to organize its immediate surrounding perceptually, and cognitively to map its position in a mappable external world."[45]

The skateboarder's highly developed integrated sense of balance, speed, hearing, sight, touch, and responsiveness is a product of the modern metropolis, a newly evolved sensory and cognitive mapping; the aim is not only to receive the city but to return it to itself, to change through movement and physical energy the nature of the *experience* of the urban realm.

> A feel of rhythm and an aroma of sweat overcome my senses on this Wednesday evening as the popping sound of wooden tails and the connection of metal trucks to metal coping takes place.[46]

One step ahead of the pedestrian or static eye, the architects and the artists, the people who look at shapes and patterns around themselves and see beauty in these things people have created from pattern and relationships of shapes to shapes and people to shapes. To us these things are more. These things have purpose because we have movement as well as vision.[47]

In this, skateboarding is part of the untheorized element of praxis: that which focuses on the development of a sensuous enjoyment of the object (rehabilitating the world of senses as practical-sensuous, through the immediate sensing of art, cities, buildings, objects of common use, landscapes, and relationships) and on the recognition of particular needs (here the need for activity, muscular extension, direct engagement with objects).[48] The result: "It's better than drugs. You won't believe the adrenalin. The feeling of accomplishment is insane."[49] The skateboarder's senses are thus historically produced, both through the historical constraints of the city and in engagement with the present and future opportunities of the city. These senses do not then represent a basic need, the satisfaction of which brings simply what Lefebvre calls "momentary relief to constant struggle,"[50] but a historically produced capacity to enjoy and reproduce the city. They are a sensory and spatialized version of the Althusserian concept of ideology as the imaginary representation of the subject's relationship to his or her real conditions of existence.[51]

It would be wrong to see skateboarding as some kind of nostalgic return to a prior physicality, rather it is a new physicality of enjoyment latent in the possibilities of modern architecture. Whereas, for example, the oldest towns of England are, because of their medievalist architecture and urban fabric, "crap to skate,"[52] the modern architecture of the new town offers surface (concrete not cobbles), expansivity (squares not alleys), urban elements (fragments in space, not modulations of space), and, above all, public space, semi-public space, and certain private spaces that can be appropriated. To give one precise example of skateboarding's engagement with this architectural possibility, the small wheels of new school skateboards are intended to exploit the smoothness of terrains while increasing the height of the ollie move, and thus are born from the level horizontality of the pavement and, simultaneously, aimed at a denial of that horizontality. The city offers at once precise hard-faced objects, a precise delineation of where particular functions take place, and, simultaneously, an ambiguity of meaning, circulation patterns, control, and ownership. It is this modern city that skateboarding is at once born from and working against. "Two hundred years of American technology has unwittingly created a massive cement playground of immense potential. But it was the minds of 11 year olds that could see that potential."[53]

PERFORMATIVE CRITIQUE

Many questions are raised by all this, not least as to how skateboarding, by virtue of using architecture without participating in its productive or exchange functions, might reassert use values over exchange values and so, implicitly, mount a critique of labor and consumption in capitalism. How does this relate to the subcultural values of skateboarding, through which its practitioners construct a kind of romanticist, generalized opposition to society and so create a social world in which self-identifying values and appearances are formed in distinction to conventional codes of behavior?[54] What of skateboarders' attitudes and constructions of race, age, class, gender, sexuality, and, above all, masculinity? What of the global dispersion of skateboarding, and its spatially generalized activity through millions of skateboarders in just about every major and minor city throughout the world? Conversely, what of the extremely localized physical marks and striations created by skateboarding on the urban realm—the aggressive grinds of truck against concrete, board against wood, and their destructive assault on the microboundaries of architecture? What of appropriations of time and not just space, and what of skateboarders' attitudes toward history, politics, and the material constructions of the urban? What of spontaneity? What of the city as oeuvre, as the production of human beings and the richly significant play of collective creation,[55] as well as the place of love, desire, turmoil, and uncertainty? And what of spatial, temporal, and social censorship on the part of safety experts, urban legislators, and managers, who have tried to invoke laws of trespass, criminal damage, and curfew to control skateboarding?

These questions must remain unanswered here; suffice it to say that skateboarding is antagonistic toward the urban environment ("a skateboard is the one thing you can use as a weapon in the street that you don't get patted down for").[56] But beyond possibly causing physical damage to persons and to property (a frequent accusation), in redefining space for themselves skateboarders threaten accepted definitions of space as they confront the social, spatial, and temporal logic of capitalist space. Skateboarders take over space conceptually as well as physically, and so strike at the very heart of what everyone else understands by the city.

> Around 37th, there is a quiet garden spot where students can relax in the shade of some flowering trees and enjoy a restful moment. Be sure to do some grinds on the edge of the steps down to this place, or just drop right down them (there are only two). Do a slide or something before you go. They're in a city. Don't let them forget it.[57]

Skateboarders are part of a long process in the history of cities, a fight by the unempowered and disenfranchized for a distinctive social space of their

10.5 | Skateboarder at the South Bank, London 1996.

own. They bring time, space, and social being together by confronting the architectural surface with the body and board; as a result, they redefine the city and its architecture, their own social identity and bodies, the production/reproduction nexus of architecture, the emphasis on production, exchange, and consumption, and the lived nature of representations. This is the most overt political space produced by skateboarders, a pleasure ground carved out of the city as a kind of continuous reaffirmation of one of the central maxims of the 1968 Paris revolts: that *au dessous les paves, la plage*—beneath the pavement, lies the beach.[58]

Above all, it is in the continual performance of skateboarding—which, rather than reading or writing the city, *speaks* the city through utterance as bodily engagement—that its meaning and actions are manifested. This performance cannot be seen or understood through pure abstraction; like rhythms, skateboarding requires a multiplicity of senses, thoughts, and activities to be enacted, represented, and comprehended. Lefebvre conjectures, "Rhythms. Rhythms. They reveal and hide, being much more varied than in music or the so-called civil code of successions, relatively simple texts in relation to the city. Rhythms: music of the City, a picture which listens to itself, image in the present of a discontinuous sum."[59] Rhythms disclose things not through explanation or codified interpretation, but through lived experience. For Lefebvre, to locate and understand rhythms is to find a truly social time-space that is at once a practice, conception, and experience. Most important, because these experiencers relate the fundamental conditions of their own temporality to that of the world outside, they create an engagement between subject and object that is ultimately a lived form of dialectical thought.

> Here is found that old philosophical question (the subject and the object and their relationships) posed in non-speculative terms, close to practice. The observer at the window knows that he takes as first reference *his time*, but that the first impression displaces itself and includes the most diverse rhythms, as long as they remain *to scale*. The passage from the *subject* to the *object* requires neither a leap over an abyss, nor the crossing of the desert.[60]

Skateboarding can be seen as a kind of unconscious dialectical thought, an engagement with the spatial and temporal rhythms of the city, wherein skateboarders use themselves as reference to rethink the city through its practice. Skateboarding is not the ignorance of unthinking and unknowingness but rather an activity in which a certain newness is born from knowledge, representation, and lived experience enacted together. It is also an activity that refutes architecture as domination of the self and enables the skater to declare: "Skateboarding is my only identity for better or worse."[61] Rather than allowing architecture and the city to dictate what they are, and who urban dwellers are, the skateboarder poses the unanswerable questions "what are you?" and "who am I?" Ultimately, these are questions not for the past or present, but for the future constructedness of the as yet unknown city. They arise not as metatheory or political program, but through bodily action performed on and in everyday streets, spaces, and times—and far from diminishing, its importance, this is the very source of skateboarding's historical relevance and being.

Notes

1   See also Henri Lefebvre, *The Production of Space*, trans. Donald Nicholson-Smith (Oxford: Blackwell, 1991), pp. 419–423.

2   Henri Lefebvre, *Introduction to Modernity: Twelve Preludes, September 1959–May 1961*, trans. John Moore (London: Verso, 1995), p. 5.

3   Caine Gayle, "Multiple Choice through Words and Pictures," *Slap* 4 no. 9 (September 1995): 33.

4   Lefebvre, *Production of Space*, pp. 52, 352–400.

5   This chapter is part of a larger exploration of skateboarding and the urban realm, with particular reference to Henri Lefebvre's ideas on space, the everyday, and the urban. The body-centric space and the early history of skateboarding in backyard pools and skateparks are discussed in Iain Borden, "Body Architecture: Skateboarding and the Creation of Super-Architectural Space," in *Occupying Architecture: Between the Architect and the User*, ed. Jonathan Hill (London: Routledge, 1998), pp. 195–216.

6   *Thrasher* 9, no. 6 (June 1989): 53. On the ollie, see Siân Liz Evans, "Young, Gifted, and Board Stupid," *The Big Issue*, no. 126 (17–23 April 1995): 18.

7   Stacy Peralta, interview, *Interview*, no. 17 (July 1987): 102–103.

8   Ewan Bowman, "Comment," *Sidewalk Surfer*, no. 13 (January–February 1997): n.p.

9   Virilio is cited in Edward Said, "Culture and Imperialism," *Design Book Review*, nos. 29–30 (summer/fall 1993): 6–13.

10   Henri Lefebvre, *Everyday Life in the Modern World*, trans. Sacha Rabinovitch (London: Transaction, 1984), p. 123.

11   Ibid., pp. 134–135.

12   Ibid., p. 135.

13   Jesse Neuhaus, quoted in Leah Garchik, "The Urban Landscape," *San Francisco Chronicle*, late summer 1994, posted on *DansWORLD* Internet site, http://web.cps.msu.edu/~dunhamda/dw/dansworld.html (accessed March 1995).

14   Michel Foucault, "Of Other Spaces: Utopias and Heterotopias," trans. Jay Miskowiec in *Architecture Culture 1943–1968: a Documentary Anthology*, ed. Joan Ockman (New York: Rizzoli, 1993), pp. 422–423. On symbols, see Lefebvre, *Production of Space*, p. 366.

15   Observed in Oslo, April 1997.

16   Observed in Prague, April 1990.

17   See British skateboard magazines, passim.

18   Andreas Papadakis, Geoffrey Broadbent, and Maggie Toy, eds., introduction to *Free Spirit in Architecture: Omnibus Volume* (London: Academy Editions, 1992), pp. 18–19.

19   Henri Lefebvre, *The Explosion: Marxism and the French Revolution*, trans. Alfred Ehrenfeld (New York: Monthly Review, 1969), pp. 71–72. I thank Kath Shonfield for recommending this text.

20   Lefebvre, *Everyday Life in the Modern World*, p. 184.

21   Henri Lefebvre, "Right to the City," in *Writings on Cities*, ed. and trans. Eleonore Kofman and Elizabeth Lebas (Oxford: Blackwell, 1996), p. 127.

22   Lefebvre, *Everyday Life in the Modern World*, pp. 183–184. See Roland Barthes, *Writing Degree Zero*, trans. Annette Lavers and Colin Smith (London: Cape, 1967).

23   Lefebvre, "Right to the City," p. 128.

24   Tony Bennett, *The Birth of the Museum: History, Theory, Politics* (London: Routledge, 1995).

25   Lefebvre, *Explosion*, p. 98.

26   Tom Hodgkinson, "Rad, Mad, and Dangerous to Know?" *Midweek* (London), 18 January 1990, p. 10.

27   "Searching, Finding, Living, Sharing," *R. A. D. Magazine*, no. 79 (September 1989): 16.

28   Lefebvre, "Right to the City," p. 103.

29   Henri Lefebvre, "Rhythmanalysis of Mediterranean Cities," in *Writings on Cities*, p. 237.

30   Henri Lefebvre, *éléments de rythmanalyse: Introduction à la connaissance des rythmes* (Paris:

Syllepse-Périscope, 1992); and Lefebvre, *Production of Space*, pp. 205–207. See also Lefebvre, "Rhythmanalysis of Mediterranean Cities," pp. 217–240.

31   Lefebvre, *Production of Space*, p. 355.

32   Peralta, interview, pp. 102–103; "Searching, Finding, Living, Sharing," p. 15.

33   Matt Rodriguez, interview, *Heckler* Internet site, http://heckler.com (accessed 5 May 1996).

34   "Searching, Finding, Living, Sharing," p. 15.

35   Garchik, "The Urban Landscape."

36   Paul Mulshine, "Wild in the Streets," *Philadelphia Magazine* 78, no. 4 (April 1987): 120.

37   Brian Casey, quoted in Mulshine, "Wild in the Streets," p. 120.

38   Tony Alva, interview, *Heckler* Internet site, http://heckler.com (accessed 5 May 1996).

39   Ben Powell, "Not a Toy," *Sidewalk Surfer*, no. 3 (January–February 1996): n.p.

40   "Skateboarding FAQ," *DansWORLD* internet site, http://web.cps.msu.edu/~dunhamda/dw/dansworld.html (accessed 11 April 1995).

41   Georg Simmel, "The Metropolis and Mental Life," in *Cities and Society: The Revised Reader in Urban Sociology*, ed. P. K. Hatt and A. J. Reiss (New York: Free Press, 1951), p. 635; David Frisby, *Fragments of Modernity: Theories of Modernity in the Work of Simmel, Kracauer, and Benjamin* (Cambridge, Mass.: MIT Press, 1986), pp. 72–77.

42   Henri Lefebvre, *Critique of Everyday Life*, vol. 1, *Introduction*, trans. John Moore (London: Verso, 1991), p. 120.

43   Ibid.

44   Ibid., p. 163.

45   Fredric Jameson, *Postmodernism, or, The Cultural Logic of Late Capitalism* (London: Verso, 1991), pp. 38–45; quotation, p. 44. See also Fredric Jameson, "Cognitive Mapping," in *Marxism and the Interpretation of Culture*, ed. Cary Nelson and Lawrence Grossberg (London: Macmillan, 1988), pp. 347–360.

46   Chris Carnel, interview with Bryce Kanights, *Heckler* Internet site, http://heckler.com (accessed 5 May 1996).

47   "Searching, Finding, Living, Sharing," p. 15.

48   Henri Lefebvre, *The Sociology of Marx*, trans. Norbert Guterman (1968; reprint, New York: Columbia University Press, 1982), pp. 38–39.

49   Ben Powell, quoted in Evans, "Young, Gifted, and Board Stupid," p. 18.

50   Lefebvre, *Sociology of Marx*, p. 41.

51   Jameson, "Cognitive Mapping," p. 353.

52   "Fire and Friends," *Sidewalk Surfer*, no. 3 (January–February 1996); n.p.

53   David Hunn, *Skateboarding* (London: Duckworth, 1977), p. 6. This is an oft-quoted saying in skateboarding, and has been repeated in a number of different versions.

54   See Dick Hebdige, *Subculture: The Meaning of Style* (London: Methuen, 1979), esp. pp. 1–19; and Ken Gelder and Sarah Thornton, eds., *The Subcultures Reader* (London: Routledge, 1997), esp. Sarah Thornton, "General Introduction," pp. 1–7. On such opposition as "romanticist," see Henri Lefebvre, "Towards a New Romanticism?" in *Introduction to Modernity*, pp. 239–388.

55   Lefebvre, "Right to the City," p. 101.

56   Craig Stecyk, quoted in Trip Gabriel, "Rolling Thunder," *Rolling Stone*, 16 July 1987, p. 76.

57   Brian Casey, quoted in Mulshine, "Wild in the Streets," p. 126.

58   Rob Shields, *An English Précis of Henri Lefebvre's "La Production de l'espace,"* Urban and Regional Studies Working Paper 63 (Sussex: University of Sussex, 1988), p. 2.

59   Lefebvre, "Seen from the Window," in *Writings on Cities*, p. 227.

60   Ibid.

61   Dan Cates, "Comment," *Sidewalk Surfer*, no. 13 (January–February 1997): n.p.

Adrian Forty

11

The Royal Festival Hall—a "Democratic" Space?

The Royal Festival Hall can hardly be called "unknown." Opened in 1951, it is one of London's principal concert halls, and acoustically its best. It occupies one of the most prominent sites in the city, on the South Bank of the Thames, overlooking a bend in the river that allows it to be seen for about a mile along the north shore, from Westminster to the Aldwych; and a few years ago, an *Evening Standard* poll voted it London's most popular building. What, I imagine, appealed to most of the respondents to the poll was the foyer, which is indeed one of the most remarkable interiors to be found anywhere in Britain. Since the early 1980s, the foyer has been open all day and every day, and has become host to bars, cafeterias, salad bars, book and music stores, and art exhibitions; it is a popular venue. The foyer is a single, undivided volume that fills the entire limits of the building; and standing in it, beneath the auditorium that rests above on *piloti*, one is drawn in every direction—up, down, and laterally—by the succession of stairs, landings, and voids that fill the interior. Furthermore, in addition to this architectural tour de force, it is one of the very few large public interiors that you can be in without becoming the subject of some controlling interest; unlike the typical public spaces of modernity—shopping malls, station concourses, airports, art galleries—there is no requirement to become a consumer, no obligation to follow a predetermined route through the building to some

11.1 | Royal Festival Hall, foyer. Drawing by Gordon Cullen.

11.2 | Royal Festival Hall, foyer. Contemporary photograph.

ultimate goal. You can simply *be* in it. Indeed, I am tempted to say that the building's purpose, as a concert hall, is almost irrelevant to the qualities of the foyer; one could imagine it as part of some other sort of building—a library, say—and its effect would remain the same.

Considered as a foyer, it stands comparison with those of the great opera houses of nineteenth-century Europe—the Paris Opéra, the Dresden Zwinger—whose vast foyers dwarfed the auditoria themselves, and whose remarkable staircases allowed the bourgeoisie to see each other and be seen in public. There is a difference, though, for in the great nineteenth-century opera houses there was privilege, and those who carried the greatest prestige were immediately distinguishable from those with less by virtue of the entries, lobbies, and spaces that their wealth commanded; but in the Festival Hall, as originally built (it was altered in the early 1960s), everyone entered by the same door, took the same flight of steps to the central space of the foyer, and was entitled to circulate wheresoever they wished within. Although Gordon Cullen's drawing of the interior, produced before the building's opening, shows it populated by fur-coated and dinner-jacketed British upper-class types who may look to us like an elite, the building itself neither encouraged nor permitted social exclusivity, as its more recent history confirms. And within the auditorium itself, every seat was calculated to be acoustically on a par and to have an equally good a view of the stage. (In a rare lapse of its otherwise egalitarian principles, it was provided with boxes;

but ironically, these have the worst views of the stage of anywhere in the auditorium—and the worst of all is the royal box.) The absence of any architectural means to sustain hierarchies of social difference within has led to the hall widely being described as "democratic," and "a monument to the welfare state." How are we to interpret these remarks?

Nikolaus Pevsner, writing the year after the Festival Hall opened, described the interior staircases and promenades as having "a freedom and intricacy of flow, in their own way as thrilling as what we see in the Baroque churches of Germany and Austria."[1] Pevsner's perceptive remark draws to our attention that the foyer does indeed have the form of a church in its single unbroken volume, and that just as in a baroque church there is implied movement within, forward, sideways, and backward. And we can take this comparison further: the succession of perforated planes, landings, stairs, and balconies provides an ever-receding sense of depth, against which the outer wall of the building (much of it glass) appears insignificant, a feature which also corresponds to that of south German baroque churches. When

11.3 | Royal Festival Hall, auditorium. Contemporary photograph.

Paul Frankl, a German art historian of the generation before Pevsner, described the interiors of baroque churches, he might almost have been talking about the Festival Hall. Consider, for example, the following remark: "The less interesting the contour, the stronger is our perception of the space that fills the contour and of its continuity. The lack of emphasis of the spatial boundary also makes us aware of the continuity between the interior space and the open exterior space." Or take his comments about centrally planned churches, in which "all entrances are necessary evils. We are not supposed to enter such a church slowly and approach its centre step by step. We are supposed, as if by magic, to arrive with one bound at this central point."[2] The entry to the Festival Hall could not be better described: in its original state, before a new main entrance was created on the north, riverfront facade, the principal entrance to the Festival Hall was at ground level on the east side, through a relatively inconspicuous bank of doors. These opened to a low-ceilinged vestibule, from which a short flight of steps, also covered by a soffit, lead up to the foyer; only when one has mounted these steps, and turned ninety degrees to the right, does one see much—and then what one sees is nothing less than the entire interior volume of the foyer, opening in every direction, above, beneath, and behind. By such means, one has the impression of having "arrived with one bound" at the central point of the building.

These and other insights suggest that one may see the Festival Hall as a baroque building—though obviously it is not. My point is not to try to pursue this comparison any further, but rather to think about how one might arrive at some account of the "experience" of the building. If we are to make any sense of the claim that the Festival Hall was "democratic," we will get nowhere by examining the building itself. As a thing, the building can tell us nothing about people's encounters with it, or with each other within it; all it can tell us is about its own material existence. Its significance as architecture, its aesthetic or political being, does not reside in its concrete, steel, glass, and marble elements, nor in their combination, but in the minds of those who have gone into it. The difficulty that faces the historian is first how to discover what those experiences were, and second how to relate them to what we now see; for we cannot assume that our perceptual apparatus is the same as that of those in the past. Frankl's book *The Principles of Architectural History*, from which I have quoted, is of interest here because—though first published in 1914—it has had few successors in the attempt to provide a systematic scheme for analyzing past architecture in terms of experience.

Frankl did not use the word "experience": he took it for granted that the way to know architecture was by means of the bodily sensations, real or imagined, that one received within a building. Frankl's book was in many ways remarkably perceptive but it had no sequel, for several fairly obvious reasons. First of all, Frankl was writing in the tradition of German aesthetic philosophy, within which it was always assumed that aesthetic experience was by definition a solitary encounter between the individual subject and the work in question; it is as if in Frankl's analysis the subject was always alone in the building. While this may be a reasonable way to proceed in the study of literature, or painting, it misses a rather essential aspect of architecture, which one expects normally to be populated by more than one individual at a time. The second major shortcoming of Frankl's scheme was his neglect of who the "subject" was—of what sex, of what class, of how he or she possessed a consciousness of his or her own self. This general problem, the construction of the subject, has formed a major theme of French philosophy in the mid–twentieth century, and it will be useful to consider briefly some ideas from that source in relation to our more specific problem. However, despite these shortcomings, Frankl's book has one particular value to us now in thinking about the "experience" of architecture. In the critique of modernism by postmodernism, the former has often been criticized for its excessive concentration on utility to the neglect of "experience": the bald schematic diagrams of modernists are seen as having drained "lived experience" from architecture. But in its efforts to reintroduce "experience" back into architecture, what has tended to appear is the simulacrum of experience: a spectacle, presented in literary or cinematic terms. Frankl, for all his faults, is interesting precisely because his account of experience is embedded in the spatiality of the body of the subject—in short, *he's there*. It is the unmediated directness of this that I would like to see if we can retain.

About the Festival Hall as an object, about its making, we know a great deal.[3] But was it to see the thing, a creation of glass, concrete, and marble, that people went to it when it first opened? Bernard Levin, an enthusiast of the Festival Hall, recalls his first visits:

> I suppose it must have been the first new building of *any* kind I could remember seeing, and as I dwell on that thought, it occurs to me that I can hardly then have begun to think consciously about architecture at all; perhaps the years of the war, when buildings were being knocked down rather than put up, made the subject too remote. But the glittering brightness of the Festival Hall, and the lavish use of space in its interior, the beauty of shining new wood, metal, marble, the explosive shock of the brand-new auditorium, with those boxes that looked like half-opened drawers and the pale beauty of the sycamore baffle over the orchestra—that experience

has taken the place for me beside the first intoxicated tastings of the music itself.[4]

But if the above sounds as if Levin was indeed attracted by the physical elements of the building, what he goes on to say suggests that this was not the case:

> At the end of a concert, the audience could not bear to leave, to go from this beauty and opulence into the drab world of postwar Britain, still exhausted, shabby and rationed; we wandered about the corridors and walkways, clearly determined to remain there all night. After a few days of this, the attendants . . . improvised a solution; they went to the top of the building, linked arms, and moved slowly down from level to level, very gently shepherding us all into the main foyer, and thence, even more gently, into the reality outside.[5]

As Levin makes clear, being in the Festival Hall was better than being outside. If it was "reality" outside, what was it inside? Whatever it was, it was not an experience of atomized individuals but was in some sense social, and collective.

The question of the "I" who is the subject of all experience is a theme of Jean-Paul Sartre's major work on phenomenology, *Being and Nothingness*, first published in French in 1943. While one would hardly expect what Sartre wrote to have informed the perception of visitors to the Festival Hall, the problem on which he focuses, the constitution of the self in terms of its relation to others, can be said to be one that belonged to the period in which the Festival Hall was created. Sartre writes about the three dimensions of the body's being. The first dimension is that "I exist my body." The second dimension is that "My body is known and utilized by the Other." It is only through this second dimension that a possibility of the subject's consciousness of his or her own bodily existence can occur. The third dimension of being occurs when "as *I am for others*, the Other is revealed to me as the subject for whom I am an object."[6] In other words, only in the third dimension of being does there occur the possibility of social being, through the mutual exchange of seeing. It is a recurrent theme of Sartre's book that our only knowledge of our self is in the view that we receive back of the self from the other who sees us. "The Other holds a secret—the secret of what I am." And he continues, "the Other is for me simultaneously the one who has stolen my being from me and the one who causes 'there to be' a being which is my being." "We resign ourselves," declares Sartre, "to seeing ourselves through the Other's eyes."[7]

11.4 | Royal Festival Hall, restaurant. Contemporary photograph.

What interests me is the extent to which architecture plays a part in this reflexive perception. Obviously any public building—a railway station, for example—or even any public space—a street—can provide the setting for reflexive perception, which allows an individual, through an encounter with the other, to realize his or her own being. But the majority of public buildings in which we both see and are seen belong to someone or some agency, and one's experience of the other is always subordinate to the purposes of the owner. In the railway station, the dominant requirement is to travel; and the form of the building ensures that one does this in the manner, and in the state of mind, that has been ordained by the railway operator. Similarly in the shopping center, the primary aim of the architectural experience is to ensure that one wants as many of the commodities on sale as possible. In either case, the owners' interests are always dominant, and our experience as individuals is always marginal and alienated; in phenomenological terms, a part of our being is taken from us, but not returned. As a result, we neither appear complete to other people, nor are seen by them as complete. The Festival Hall is not like this: there, the owner of the building is none other than the subject. Whoever you are, once you enter through the original main entrance at ground level, and stand with the space unfolding in front of you, beside you, and above you, the volume is *yours* and yours alone. Of course, exactly the same experience occurs for everyone else who enters the building, and so the result is the sense of an equal right to

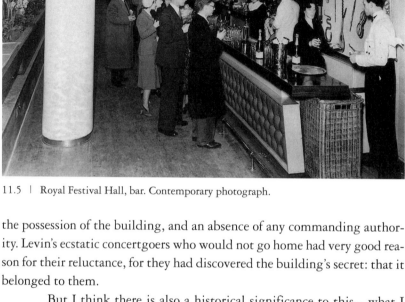

11.5 | Royal Festival Hall, bar. Contemporary photograph.

the possession of the building, and an absence of any commanding authority. Levin's ecstatic concertgoers who would not go home had very good reason for their reluctance, for they had discovered the building's secret: that it belonged to them.

But I think there is also a historical significance to this—what I have said is as true of the Festival Hall now as it was in 1951. Consciousness is historically constructed, and what a building reveals to us now is not a sure guide to the consciousness with which people in the past approached the same object. In 1951 it was still the early days of the welfare state, the purpose of which in Britain, as in other European countries, was to create a consensus between capital and labor by providing universal access to a range of social benefits and services, as well as by some redistribution of wealth and income. There was, however, no intention of removing economic inequalities in wealth and income altogether, despite a high value put on social equality. As the contemporary political theorist T. H. Marshall pointed out, consensual support for the welfare state relied on a readiness to believe that "Equality of status is more important than equality of income."[8] Recognizing the inconsistency in this, he saw that the state could only satisfactorily assure people of their "equal social worth" in the face of persisting social differences by promoting the belief that change was taking place, and that future standards of living would render social or financial differences insignificant. As Marshall put it, "what matters to the citizen is the superstructure of legitimate expectations."[9] The assurance of a sense of "equal social worth," in the face of actual and continuing social differences, was a matter that only ideology could contain.

And in this containment, architecture had special value, for architecture creates the settings in which life is lived: it is, in the French phrase, *la mise-en-scène de la vie*. The Festival Hall—paid for by the state, and an ideological project if ever there was one—was, it seems to me, a place where architectural space provided the opportunity for the individual subject to enjoy the illusion of his or her own "equal social worth" through the view of others engaged in the identical act. Levin's concertgoers would not leave because inside the Festival Hall, if not in the "reality" outside, they were, relative to one another, equal. And the glance of the woman whose eyes meet you from the bottom of Gordon Cullen's drawing likewise signals that you, too, are included in this world where privilege and hierarchy no longer exist.

It has been said that because the clientele of the Festival Hall was entirely middle class and moneyed, it is preposterous to try and understand the experience it offered as "democratic." The historian Kenneth O. Morgan has written, "It was hardly for factory workers and their families that its glossy vestibules and bars were designed."[10] Of course this is true—the notion that it was a "people's palace" was a mythology created in the last days of the Greater London Council. Its daytime use as a cultural center is a recent phenomenon; previously the doors remained firmly shut outside performance times. But to say that it was not built for factory workers and their

11.6 | Royal Festival Hall, roof terrace. Contemporary photograph.

families is to miss the point; classical music concerts appealed to the bourgeoisie and professional classes, and it was these for whom the Festival Hall was built, and it was they who went to it.[11] Yet insofar as the building caused people to see others, and through others themselves, as of "equal social worth" it can be said to have been "democratic." It offered—to the class who had least to gain from the welfare state, and were most likely to be opposed to it—the opportunity to experience the altered perception of social relations that life in a social democracy promised. As a theater of the welfare state (with an uncannily close resemblance to a Moscow Soviet workers' club),[12] it did not touch "reality"—"reality," as Levin noticed, lay outside. Like a theater, it dealt with perception and illusion, and its business was not to change the world but only to show how it might feel different.

Notes

My thanks to Brian Stater for providing some of the references, and for constructively disagreeing with me.

1   Nikolaus Pevsner, *Buildings of England: London*, vol. 2 (Harmondsworth: Penguin, 1952), p. 276; the same passage was quoted in the revised edition, Bridget Cherry and Nikolaus Pevsner, *London 2: South*, Buildings of England (Harmondsworth: Penguin, 1983), p. 347.

2   Paul Frankl, *Principles of Architectural History: The Four Phases of Architectural Style, 1420–1900*, ed. and trans. James F. O'Gorman (Cambridge, Mass.: MIT Press, 1968), pp. 47, 28.

3   See John McKean, *Royal Festival Hall* (London: Phaidon Press, 1992); and John McKean, "Royal Festival Hall: Master of Building," *Architect's Journal* 194 (9 October 1991): 22–47.

4   Bernard Levin, *Enthusiasms* (London: Jonathan Cape, 1983), p. 176.

5   Ibid., p. 177.

6   Jean-Paul Sartre, *Being and Nothingness*, trans. Hazel E. Barnes (London: Methuen, 1957), p. 351.

7   Sartre, *Being and Nothingness*, pp. 364, 354.

8   T. H. Marshall, *Citizenship and Social Class* (Cambridge: Cambridge University Press, 1950), p. 56.

9   Ibid., p. 58.

10   Kenneth O. Morgan, *The People's Peace: British History, 1945–1989* (Oxford: Oxford University Press, 1990), p. 83.

11   A 1952 Mass-Observation survey confirms that Royal Festival Hall audiences were "more often of the middle and upper classes and . . . much younger than the population as a whole." *Mass-Observation Bulletin*, no. 46 (July–August 1952): 14–16.

12   Two Soviet clubs in Moscow, the Hammer and Sickle Club (1929–1933) and the Gorbunov Palace of Culture (1930), have exteriors strikingly similar to that of the Royal Festival Hall.

Tom Gretton

12

The Cityscape and the "People" in the
Prints of José Guadalupe Posada

Archaeologists love rubbish. The spoil heaps produced by human settlements are a crucial source of information about material culture, the relationship between human aggregates and the material world: the chicken bones, the broken pots, and the abandoned half-made tools are made strange by their miraculous resurrection, but also evoke the utterly familiar experience of time wasted and things spoiled. The same goes for the archaeology of cultural constructions such as luxury or worthlessness or the exotic; the cultural dynamics of the lost city, in both its strangeness and its familiarity, can be reconstructed only through the study of its cultural rubbish. Historians of art and architecture, and even of urban form, have tended to study those aspects of the workings of the lost city that have survived precisely because they were made or received not as rubbish but as art. This chapter uses one particular form of rubbish produced by the modern or modernizing city, popular prints, to discuss some aspects of the construction and maintenance of vital forms of urban culture, such as difference and anxiety. For more than a century, almost all printed pictures of things have been so cheap and plentiful that they have been consumed as disposable in the developed world. Some of them, I have argued, have been produced and consumed specifically as rubbish; this has been a constitutive aspect of modernity.

I concentrate here on the role of printed pictures in the developing relationship between nation building, class formation, and popular culture, a focus that necessitates some close discussion of iconography and the nature of the commodities concerned. The prints are associated with the name of José Guadalupe Posada, who was born in 1852. Posada worked as an illustrator for periodicals, books, songsheets, and whatever else he was asked to do; he died in 1913, the third year of Mexico's protracted and destructive, but largely agrarian, Revolution.[1] Posada's response to the demands of representing urban existence varied with his client.[2] In illustrations for upmarket periodicals, Posada worked within an ideology of the city as a space of pleasure, spectacle, and consumption. But Posada had other clients, including the dominant producer of single-sheet imagery and cheap pamphlet literature, Antonio Vanegas Arroyo. He printed and published many different sorts of object: street-sold broadsheets, religious imagery, sheets to celebrate the days of the dead, and small paperbound pamphlets of various kinds, from songbooks to childrens' stories to cookbooks. He printed newspapers, too.

Typically, modernist imagery and modernist ideology, inheriting and developing a long Western tradition, emphasize the difference between life in the city and in the country.[3] This mutually defining pair has been loaded with changing moral, aesthetic, and political baggage, which has tended to ensure that the evolving difference between the urban and the rural has always been both clear and of fundamental cultural significance in

12.1 | "Valona dedicada a los foráneos que llegan a la ciudad de México" (Greeting-song dedicated to all the foreigners and strangers who are coming to Mexico City). This image may have been made to mark celebrations for the centennial of Mexico's independence in 1910. It is in any case unusual for a broadsheet representing Mexico as a "modern" capital, with specific monuments and locations, "advanced" street furniture, and a culture of leisure and spectacle. All this closely observed specificity shows a city displayed for and largely peopled by "foreigners," and, as such, represented as both strange and familiar to Posada's "popular" audience.

the Western world. Posada's prints worked against the grain of this powerful cultural dyad. They do this both by distributing the values we take it to polarize across the two poles and by radically reducing the difference between the poles. In these prints, ignorance, mischance, cruelty, crime, dissolute excess, violent injustice, and disruptive economic change characterize both the urban and the rural world: the cosy equation of the urban with the modern and its values, the rural with the traditional and its values, can scarcely be applied. For the most part, however, Posada's pictures reduce the experiential difference between living in the capital and living elsewhere in Mexico. We must read this intervention in the context of modernizing Mexico, as well as of other cultural forms in which the modern country-city relationship was rather more fully reproduced; but we also need to read it in relation to the specific history of the country-city polarity in Mexico.

Mexico's *pueblos*, fixed settlements with a corporate identity devised and recognized by the Spanish rulers of the New World, had long been urban in their morphology. Colonial order results from the conquest of an alien and hostile world, a conquest that is first military and then cultural, and that always moves outward from the *colonia*, the more or less fortified plantation of the European order. This is a concentrated settlement, which, because it is defined as central rather than peripheral, must in some ways be urbanistic. All such plantation settlements are thus identical remakings of civilization: colonialism entails cloning. All the chartered settlements in the New World had the potential to repeat Mexico City, itself a utopia.[4] So the European vision of a functional, morphological, and moral hierarchy of settlement, with great cities at one end and villages and farmsteads at the other, did not apply to the Spanish New World.

But this New World homogeneity between the capital and the pueblos had been breaking down for a century before Posada. In the second half of the eighteenth century, the vision of Mexico City as a utopia was quite suddenly replaced by one that gave it the modern urban vices of poverty, social and economic disorder, and disease.[5] Mexico City became the capital of a recognized nation-state in 1821: but a half century of invasions and annexations, and of civil wars over the control and role of the capital, delayed the emergence of successful representations of Mexico City as metropolis. The first half century of independence also eroded the corporate status of the pueblos, which had given them a stable civil existence, and increased the competitive pressure on pueblo culture from hacienda-based agribusiness. The pueblo had for the most part long ceased to be a bridgehead for a cultural conquest; it had become a settlement in relationships with other similar settlements, in competition with another form of rural settlement and exploitation, and in symbiotic contact with regional urban centers and even with the national capital.

In the last quarter of the nineteenth century a range of influential cultural forms, produced in Mexico City for the elites living there, came to represent the relationship between the capital and the rest of Mexico in ways that resembled the country-city division familiar to the cultural world centered on Western European cities. Such articulations of this new version of urban culture and its relationship with a rural "other" include the range of satirical and "society" illustrated periodicals produced in Mexico after 1880, the celebrated landscape paintings of Mexico City in its valley produced by José Maria Velasco, and the spectacular town planning of the Paseo de la Reforma, a boulevard that linked the edge of the old city with what emerged as a recreational park, zoo, and observatory, in the former viceregal palace/Aztec ceremonial site of Chapultepec.

Tom Gretton

—

The word *barrio* has a complex origin and sense. It comes from the Arabic, and seems always to have denoted both something like "a neighborhood," a space-and-place that is a fraction of the urban whole, and a marginal settlement, an attached but excluded populous space-and-place. In colonial Mexico, in return for military and political collaboration, certain groups of *indios* had been permitted to settle close to the Spanish towns, in a space that was neither the city nor the country but a legally constituted place of exclusion from both, with its own urban forms, its own lands, and its own organizing institutions. These settlements, and the people in them, were between the city and the country. This combination of a specific built environment and specific legal status gave colonial and early postcolonial barrios a particular form and cultural function. In the Porfiriato, the idea of the barrio as a specifiable and stable place, both integral and marginal, was swept away. "Modern" urbanization produced both chaotic sprawl and the *colonias* and *fraccionamientos*, segregated housing developments on suburban sites, catering for different status groups in different places; the poorer ones reproduced the sanitary and other shortcomings of the barrios they displaced. Though the new built environments were all in some sense "suburban," some of them became barrios, identified spaces of dependent difference from the constitutive center of the city, while others became something much more like suburbs. This cultural formation developed, in Mexico as in first world cities, with great success at the end of the nineteenth century. The suburb is indeed between city and country, but it works to exclude and dominate the city, annex and dominate the country. The suburb is not marginal; the barrio is.

But a legally defined marginality was by 1890 no longer imposed or available, so the need to make a specialized cultural space between urbane and rustic was urgent, as the insistent representation of disruptive dislocation in the urban imagery of Posada shows. Posada's pictures require us to imagine a location among people thickly settled, but not living their lives by adopting the conventional modern symbolisms of city life. The actions in Posada's prints seldom happen in the countryside, but they seldom happen in clearly delineated urban locations either. There are exceptions to this generalization: we have a handful of images of mountain, plain, or forest, and a rather larger set of images of crowds, of shopping, of the charms of sauntering, of the sociability of the *pulqueria* or of girl watching, and some images of the capital's identifiable monuments.

Any attempt to discuss the cultural politics of this imagery must address two interwoven themes: the relationship of Posada's pictures for

12.2 | "Los crimenes del Chalequero" (The crimes of "the Spoiler") Broadsheet published by A. Vanegas Arroyo, 1890. In prints such as these, clues to location are reduced: there is perhaps a waterside, and there is a building's silhouette, but despite a strong sense of space, we are told nothing about place; we cannot decide whether this is a city, its margin, or somewhere else. Dislocation is of course also represented in the severed and occluded heads.

Vanegas Arroyo to "the news" and the relationship of the bits of paper on which these pictures were printed and sold to newspapers. Everyday life and its antithesis, the world of events, are not permanent features of human existence; they have been produced in culture as part of the way that men and women have come to terms with living an urbanized, industrialized/commodified life.[6] News was most intensively produced in the newspaper, for whose triumph the development of Western cities, both as places of trade and as seats of government, has been necessary.[7] Everyday life has been produced in a range of ways, in which the regularities of wage labor and the activities of the state have been important; thus we cannot conceive of the everyday and the world of events as producing each other, without also understanding them as being the product of the development of capitalist economies and of the nation-state. "News" and "the everyday" map uncomfortably onto the categories through which these chapters interpret the city, the categories of strangeness and familiarity, but the mapping is a productive one: the newspaper is illuminated if we think of it as presenting the world as familiarly strange.

Tom Gretton

This discussion does not look at news (*noticias*) presented as such through the proper channels, nor at the everyday, but at events and presentations at the margins of "news"-ness, and thus somewhere in the middle—in the middle, in this case, not of a one-dimensional continuum but of a field. For as news and the everyday separate from each other, they also separate themselves from older ways of apprehending and giving public expression to things that happen, and of relating the ordinary to the marvelous, the ordered to the disorderly, the familiar to the strange. In Vanegas Arroyo's broadsheets, things are announced as having happened in ways that position the people who consumed these commodities at the edge of the world that the news-everyday dyad constructs. For here the concepts of news and of the everyday are not fully developed, and representations of concepts such as the *marvelous* and the *disorderly* play a significant part. These broadsheets offered accounts of events that themselves lie somewhere between the news and the everyday. An insertion into the culture of the news negotiated via such subjects and objects as these was marked as much by resistance and disruption as it was by the development of a competence to see and understand the world in these new ways.

One defining characteristic of the everyday is repetition, not just in time but also in space. First, it inscribes agents in a form of time with limited features, made of simple reiterations and cycles. Second, it inscribes the actors of the everyday among actors of the same sort. News is thus that which happens in one place (there) at one time (then); news is secondhand specificity, and depends on the cultural power to specify at a distance for a group (that is, depends on "news media") as a necessary, though not sufficient, condition of its existence. For news also has its rigorous typology; by no means everything that happens in one place at one time is news.

The murder sequence, the focus of Posada's labor for Vanegas Arroyo, is a highly charged, highly ordered, and paradoxically orderly sort of news. As it predictably unfolds from report of crime through to trial and execution, it begins and ends with the most undeniable of one-place, onetime events. Murder and execution guarantee uniqueness for the event sequence in which they are structured. But both journalistic conventions and the cyclical institutions of crime, investigation, trial, and punishment tend to reduce uniqueness, make this or that particular rupture of the everyday by the last day into an instance of a genre. At the same time, the journalist and the judiciary must represent murder as made local and anecdotal; they load the death with as much specificity (that, there, then) as possible. Both the journalist and the judge want the gory details, so it is these from which both the unrepeatable and the familiar are constructed. Posada's work tended to concentrate on the terminal points of the process, on the crime and the exe-

12.3 | "Fusilamiento del que se comió a sus hijos" (The execution of the man who ate his children). After 1891. Posada made a number of versions of the firing squad, which Vanegas Arroyo used and adapted over and over again. This is a strangely familiar image, bringing to mind Manet's *Execution of the Emperor Maximilian* as well as Goya's *Third of May*. There is no evidence to prove it, but Posada probably saw prints of both.

cution. In relation to the definition of news, and the mapping out of its limit cases, neither the murders nor the executions were specified in the imagery: we get gore, but we do not get details. The points of the sequence at which news becomes most like its antithesis, the blotting out in death of all individual particularities, are emphasized.

There are also ways in which we can consider the relationship of Posada's pictures in the sheets on which Vanegas Arroyo printed them to the newspaper, rather than to news as a cultural genre. Journals of opinion tended to have names that inscribed their readers either into measured time (*El Diario, El Diario de Hogar, El Tiempo, El Siglo XIX*), into a relationship with the constructed nation (*El Pais, El Mundo, El Universal, La Patria, El Monitor Republicano*), or into a public discourse (*El Heraldo, El Imparcial, El Partido Liberal*). To buy a paper was to buy and wear a particular sort of badge that marked one as belonging in a distinctive way to a restricted social group.

In addition, newspapers both represented an insertion into the global culture of capital and mediated an insertion into the city. They represented the connectedness of Mexico to the rest of the world, not only by reporting world news but also through such devices as carrying the address of a Paris or New York advertising and subscription agency below the masthead, or reprinting news items or caricatures from papers published in London or Chicago. Subscribers, getting their copy more or less reliably by mail, might live anywhere, and thus we are reminded of the penetration of the countryside by commodities and signifying practices derived from the city. But many Mexican men (and probably women) bought from the newsboys, and thus consumed journals as part of the experience of being at home on the modern city street. They also read regularly; buying a newspaper was a way of turning the modern, event-saturated urban world into its antithesis, daily routine. The fully developed buyer of the urban paper gets a paper on the way to work and another on the way back, pointing to a second mediation, this time between the worlds of private and public. This is a striking evolution; before woodpulp technologies made newsprint paper almost a free good after the 1870s, the raw material on which newspapers were printed was relatively scarce and expensive. Then periodicals were paradigmatically read in institutions where they could be shared: clubs, libraries, coffeehouses, and bars. Thus where once journals had been a defining feature of the public realm, now they came increasingly to define the spaces and process of the intersection of public and private.

In 1892, shortly after Posada began to make blocks for him, Vanegas Arroyo explored a way of co-opting the prestige of the newspaper as a cultural form without committing his consumers to meet the newspaper's cultural requirements of regularity and cultural location. He began to publish the *Gaceta Callejera* (*Street Gazette*), which had a numbered sequence and the same sort of masthead as a periodical. However, every issue announced below the masthead that "esta hoja volante se publicará cuando los acontecimientos de sensación lo requieran" (this newssheet [literally, "flying leaf"] will be published when sensational happenings require it). From our point of view, Vanegas Arroyo had things the wrong way around; we know that it is news that has to be produced according to the requirements of the papers. But as he and his clients saw it, the occasional newssheet option had its own advantages. It offered the possibility of building brand loyalty; it avoided the legal burdens that regular publication laid on printer and publisher alike; it marketed news in the pure state achieved by the special edition; and it did not require its purchasers to turn themselves into the sort of regular guys who bought newspapers—in fact, it offered them the option of entering the market for news in a way that worked against the classifying dynamic of the dominant news commodity.

But for the most part Posada and Vanegas Arroyo kept an even greater distance between their enterprise and the newspaper. The randomly published newssheets, the bogus news reports, the *corridos* and *ejemplos* that Vanegas Arroyo produced commodified news of and commentary on things that, it was claimed, had happened, so they were like newspapers. Through their street vendors they shared a point of sale with newspapers, and a point of origin in *los acontecimientos de sensación*. Like the newspapers, they inducted their purchasers and consumers into a commodified and ephemeral form of secular print culture. So in some respects the Vanegas Arroyo commodity offered its purchasers and consumers the chance to resemble the people who read newspapers; but it also offered the chance to be different. In buying a Vanegas Arroyo sheet you constituted yourself as an irregular guy. You refused the security, the localization, of belonging to a political opinion. You refused the classification of discourses that was laid out day by day or week by week in the journals. Instead, you supported the reconstitution of premodern oral forms, the isolated report of a happening, the playful mixing of discourses, the *corrido*, and the *ejemplo* as adequate to represent life in a world city.

12.4 | "Ejemplo: Un hijo que mata a la autora de sus dias" (Exemplary verse: A son who killed the woman who gave him life). About 1891. As in so many of Posada's images for Vanegas Arroyo, the family collapses in violence, but the location is unspecified. There is a door, but we could be in an interior or in the street. The murderous son wears an urban worker's dark shirt and boots, while his parents—he in white cotton and sandals, she with her *rebozo* flying from her neck—suggest a peasant culture. While we cannot be sure that the violence of acculturation has been projected onto a family recently arrived in the city, there is certainly enough here for us to wonder. The title given in another sheet using this image makes it the murder of a sister by a brother.

These objects represent and produce a cultural position both between the Old World and the New and at the edge of the New World. They give their consumers a way of inserting themselves into the print culture of news, but through their form they offer a way of refusing an insertion into regularity, the normal concomitant of such access. And as they co-opt, parody, ironicize, and on occasion simply refuse the discourses proper to the different sorts of reportorial genres that are invoked, these commodities construct readers who know how to read, and thus implicitly how to speak, the languages concerned, but who wear their knowledge in a "knowing" way. As these readers take on a persona, rather than a selfhood, they become both insiders and outsiders, as far as the news goes.[8]

—

My working hypothesis about the cultural dynamics of Mexico City while Posada was producing prints there is simple. At this stage in its development, Mexico City tended to attract people with a relatively high degree of "modern" cultural competence, people who had undertaken the hazardous removal to the capital generally not because they had been pushed out of their previous socioeconomic perch but because they had left it by choice—though of course agrarian change was also pushing the dispossessed and the defeated toward the cities. Mexico City had a diversified and diversifying artisan economy, and a vigorous consumer economy. At this stage its growth did not primarily result in proletarianization and impoverishment; instead the forms of labor that predominated gave rise to a relatively rich development of a politically oriented nonelite sociability in clubs and circles, rather than through proletarian unionization. It also produced a high and sharply rising literacy rate in the city, a development that must be attributed in great part to the new immigrants to the capital. However, upward cultural aspiration and upward economic mobility were, then as now, poorly correlated, as were the historical realities and the mythic structures of life in a capital city. The threat of falling added urgency and anxiety to the desire to rise; and the reality of doing neither, but of surviving conditionally on the edges of respectable competence, also needed to find its mythic forms.

In this capital city there was a successful and expanding elite, a small, diverse, and riven group of landowners and agribusinessmen, mineowners, lawyers, bond and power brokers, industrialists and traders, arrivé journalists, and senior servants of the state. There was also a middle class, in both senses. First, a group of people did white-collar jobs: teaching school, managing and running offices and small businesses, staffing telephone switchboards and shop counters; they were a potential source both of recruits for and of alternatives to the elite. Second, there was a group of people in the middle, caught between an urban culture that was symbolically the property of the symbolically stable elite and a rural culture no longer able to provide either a real or a symbolic life for them. This second sort of "middle" class includes not just the first but also large numbers of old and new artisans and sellers of old and new services. Its members found themselves looking at once up the ladder of enslaved competition for social promotion and down it, where they saw both the people whom the city and capitalism were turning into failures and the irretrievable and repulsive *campesino* existence.

In my model, the second of these versions of the middle class tries both to rise and to guard against falling in culture. On the one hand, they practice the most (s)lavish imitation they can afford, combining this with an antagonistic censoriousness of those above them as at once a hedge against and a disguise for envy. On the other hand, they join the elite in attacking popular culture, in the hope that they can sanitize the pit into which they fear to fall. The organized and self-organizing working class, as part of its making, may be observed joining this attack as fervently as any middle-class group of temperance reformers, campaigners against blood sports, or promoters of free libraries. In this case the ideological agenda is different, as imitation, antagonism, and censure are differently combined; but the action tends nonetheless to develop behaviors to which those town adjectives—*urbane*, *polite*, and *civilized*, as well as *political* and *civic*—apply. These mechanisms of emulation and discipline provide a powerful pedagogy, instilling respect for text-oriented, urbane cultural comportments.

But text-oriented urbanity must generate its own other; the litany of regret, disdain, incomprehension, and castigation that has met those commodities and comportments that are reductively categorized as modern "mass" and "popular" culture marks the process at work. In these characterizations, the ideas of disinheritance, disempowerment, and surrender predominate. From this point of view, entry into the commodity capitalism of mass culture has eliminated the possibility of independence, and radically reduced and trivialized the arena of individuation; only a full acceptance of the pedagogy as well as of the cultural satisfactions of the world of modern rationality can reproduce a space for autonomy. The Frankfurt School and their outriders, but not they alone, see mass culture, and in particular its modern "popular" sump, as pathological.

I certainly have no wish to see the cultural formation as healthy, and indeed I do not seek to look at "it" as an entity at all: I attempt to understand cultural forms and performances as adaptive, and to determine the costs and benefits of the particular adaptations that I can identify. Any characterization of a "respectable" commodified and literate urban culture requires the historian to imagine what its opposite (a commodified and literate urban culture that is disrespectful, a refusal in the city to embrace construction via the town adjectives) might have been like for those who produced themselves as unrespectable, for those participants who constituted themselves by behaving badly in class. Of course, unrespectability is in one sense a simple set of failures and omissions, such as failing not to wipe your nose on your sleeve, failing to hold down a job, omitting to finish school, or neglecting to step aside to allow a lady to pass on the street; but it must be more than that, more than a set of negatives. It is also a positive attitude toward the structures that make the ladder of emulation and discipline so compelling: not a blanket refusal to appropriate and be appropriated by them, but a practice of misappropriation.

Thus I understand that Posada, working for Vanegas Arroyo, did not offer an imagery for the most miserable and culturally disempowered section of Mexico's population, the most frightening of the occupants of the new style permeable and dispersed barrios. We should not in any case think of such men and women as being able to read or to buy the commodities on which his prints were published: Posada's social landscape, in the city but not of it, is a metaphor and an anxiety, not a market. That the hapless and violent provide the representational repertoire which, along with its distinctive "style," does so much to constitute. [. . .] this imagery surely does not result from an attempt by Posada to provide a set of actors and actions with whom his audience may identify, but it does offer more than one element from which they might fashion an identity.

In so doing, they would be refusing a specifically urban identity, an act that had two distinct advantages. First, it was a scandalous misappropriation of the pedagogy that the urban-rural dyad articulates. It used some of the tools (printed texts and images) that elsewhere were constituting people as urbanites, with all the associated "town word" values, and permitted a position in the city that was not urban in the prescribed way, that could fend off and distort the seductions and coercions of the polite and the civilized. Second, it was baffling: though itself the product of cultural reform, it produced an opacity made of what seemed to reforming eyes bizarre and repulsive. In this behavior, men and women might hide themselves, or a part of themselves, from dominating inspection.

Thus far, the active cultivation of disrespect may be understood as empowering. But the costs were very high. Respectability was a means to a relatively secure position as a member of some emerged or emergent urban social group; it also provided a simple and powerful way of severing connections with the *campesino* world, and it offered the power that "bourgeois" rationality seems indeed to have brought. Refusal of respectability entailed disruptive and subversive antagonism toward polite culture, and denied to refuseniks the possibility of recuperation by the conceptual and material power of that culture, denied them also the possibility even of an appropriation of that power (the hopes respectively of the middle and of the organized working class). It is therefore disempowering. And for city dwellers who have thrown off their location in old status hierarchies, and who refuse to be located in class, the only available model is a countermodel. They must understand their belonging with reference to a negative vision, that of the human rubbish on the edge of the city. This vision acts both as a metaphor of the consequences of refusing to insert oneself into the city and as an image of the consequences of the failure of an attempt to do so. This negatively defined, but otherwise weakly structured social position makes the prospect of real, rather than cultural, disorder in the city a terror, and the offer of an authoritarian structuration by the state attractive.

But an identity made of negations, disruptions, and anxiety is not the only resource available to the disrespectful. In Mexico, liberal discourse has always depended on the ability of a changing elite to invoke "the People," even as their political practices ensured that this category would be filled only with figures of speech, not with people.[9] Yet in the Porfirian capital, though this liberal elite dominated the production of political rhetoric and tended to use the familiar figure to disguise the protection of sectional interest, it failed to monopolize the production of political discourse; in particular, it lost control of "the People." The category became available for filling with incompatible figures of speech, and even with people.

As part of their entry into modernizing metropolitan culture, Mexican men and women came into the modern liberal hypostasis of the People, which was utterly incommensurable both with the older set of values articulated by the legally defined agrarian community (the pueblo) and with those articulated by locations in class. In the eyes of modernizing liberals, the People cannot possibly be the people of the pueblo, nor any of the urban sectional interests identified with class. For this among other reasons, the liberal invocation of the People entails the ability to represent a continuum between the city and the country, and to imagine each as coherent and homogeneous. Such is the vision imposed on the outskirts of Mexico City by the Paseo de la Reforma. It makes it possible to imagine the people as a transcendent totality, as a group not of local and particular interests in the country, and not of factional (and fractious) interests in the city. But when real people try on the People as an identity, they become not a transcendent totality but a fractional group of a particular sort. In this identity they can find a certain impermeability to the demobilizing lures and coercive disciplines of good behavior; but it also entails that at some level they accept existence as a projection of an elite figure of speech. The result is an anxiety about social location that makes passivity in the face of calls to mobilize against the existing order the rule, and mobilization on the side of the existing order a possibility.

Notes

1   Among the major secondary sources on Mexican political and urban history of the Porfiriato (the "reign" of Porfirio Diaz, effectively from 1876 to 1911) are F.-X. Guerra, *Le Mexique de l'Ancien Régime à la Révolution*, 2 vols. (Paris: L'Harmattan, 1985); A. Knight, *The Mexican Revolution*, 2 vols. (Cambridge: Cambridge University Press, 1986); J. M. Hart, *Revolutionary Mexico: The Coming and Process of the Mexican Revolution* (Berkeley: University of California Press, 1987).

2   See R. Tyler, ed., *Posada's Mexico* (Washington, D.C.: Library of Congress, 1979); J. Rothenstein, ed., *J G. Posada, Messenger of Mortality* (London: Redstone, 1989); R. Berdicio and S. Appelbaum, *Posada's Popular Mexican Prints* (New York: Dover, 1972); in Spanish, J. Soler, et al., eds., *Posada y la Prensa Ilustrada: Signos de Modernización y resistencias* (Mexico City: MUNAL, 1996). See also T. Gretton, "Posada's Prints as Photomechanical Artefacts," *Print Quarterly* 9, no. 4 (1992): 335–356; T. Gretton, "Posada and the 'Popular': Commodities and Social Constructs in Mexico before the Revolution," *Oxford Art Journal* 17, no. 2 (1994): 32–47.

3   R. Williams, *The Country and the City* (London: Chatto and Windus, 1973), offers an introduction.

4   J. Monnet, *La Ville et Son Double: Images et Usages du Centre: La Parabole de Mexico* (Paris: Nathan, 1993), pp. 19–23.

5   Ibid., pp. 30–36.

6   See H. Lefebvre, *La Vie Quotidienne dans le Monde Moderne* (Paris: Gallimard, 1968); translated into English by S. Rabinovitch as *Everyday Life in the Modern World* (London Transaction, 1984).

7   For Mexican journalism in this period, see M. del Carmen Ruiz Castañeda, L. Reed Torres, and E. Cordero y Torres, *El Periodismo en México, 450 años de Historia Mexico* (Mexico City: Editorial Tradición, 1974), and F. Toussaint Alcaraz *Escenario de la Prensa en le Porfiriato* (Mexico City: Buendía, 1989).

The words *news* and *newspapers* bring the connection between the cultural form and the commodity to mind in a particular way. In Spanish, *noticias* and *periodico* do not make the same connection, but they draw attention to other aspects of the analysis: the "public address" dimension of what in English is called news, and the crucial part played by regularity in the cultural role of the newspaper.

8   See P. Bailey, "Conspiracies of Meaning: Music-Hall and the Knowingness of Popular Culture," *Past and Present*, no. 144 (1994): 138–179; M. E. Diaz, "The Satiric Penny Press for Workers in Mexico, 1900–1910: A Case Study in the Politicization of Popular Culture," *Journal of Latin American Studies* 22 (1991): 497–526.

9   Guerra, *Le Mexique de l'Ancien Régime*, vol. 1, passim.

Revolutionary urbanists will not limit their
concern to the circulation of things and of
human beings trapped in a world of things.
They will try to break these topological chains,
paving the way with their experiments for
a human journey through authentic life.

Guy Debord
"Situationist Theses on Traffic" (1959)
(trans. Ken Knabb)

Sandy McCreery

13 The Claremont Road Situation

Claremont Road in Leyton, northeast London, was the scene of the longest and most expensive forced eviction in British history. From November 1993 until December 1994, an extraordinary performance was acted out that appeared part phony war and part pantomime, partly choreographed and partly improvised. There were, of course, occasional moments of extreme physical force, but on the whole this was a tactical contest: a game of chess in which the rules kept changing. On one side was the Department of Transport, which wanted to demolish the street in order to build the M11 motorway through the site. It was represented in the field by bailiffs, building contractors, private "security" personnel (most of whom were originally from West Africa), and very large numbers of police (on one occasion an estimated 700 officers were deployed to evict five houses).[1] On the other side was an equally mixed crew of defenders. There was a handful of longtime residents, none of whom legally owned their homes anymore as they had all sold them to the Department of Transport under compulsory purchase orders; they had just never left, or at least for no longer than it took to bank the check. Then there was a somewhat larger number of artists who had been renting some of the houses with official approval as temporary studios. These two groups were immediate victims of the motorway; their homes were being taken from them and they were not going willingly. But they did not necessarily object to road building per se, or to the use of motorcars. By far the largest number of occupants, however, were antiroad activists, opposed to any deepening of car culture, who squatted the street prior to the evictions in order to delay the new motorway and add to its expense. These were joined by some nonactive squatters who came simply because the street offered a home and plenty of entertainment, and a very large number of nonresident activists who would come up for short periods to help with particular actions.[2]

In fairness, Claremont Road had never been a particularly impressive street; it was just a single strip of about thirty late-nineteenth-century bylaw terraced houses squeezed in beside the railway. A chain-link fence delineated one side of the street and, since the 1940s, the tracks behind had been incessantly busy with the tube trains of the Central Line. You could get into the street only by turning off Grove Green Road—a street of similar houses, but one ravaged by heavy motor traffic as at some point it had been designated the A106, a major trunk road into central London. You could get out of the street only by returning onto this busy road at the other end. And Leyton had never been a particularly impressive neighborhood. Although there had once been a village core, most of the district was marshland until the railways arrived in the mid–nineteenth century; then the area was gradually taken over by marshaling yards and row upon row of monotonous terraced houses built for railway workers and others benefiting from the Great Eastern Railway's cheap workers' trains (forced on the company by the government as a condition for being allowed to build Liverpool Street Station in central London). Consequently the area was solidly working class and lower middle class, and almost all residents would have had to commute into central London to work. Leyton had very little sense of center, and it was impossible to know where it started or finished. Any fledgling sense of place had probably been extinguished by the severe bombing suffered in the First and Second World Wars.

But during 1994 Claremont Road was transformed into an extraordinary festival of resistance. The houses were pulled apart and remodeled with the original components and anything else that could be put to use. One became the "Art House," where visitors were invited to participate in, or view, a constant outpouring of murals, installations, and other artworks. There was a visitors' book, just as might be found at mainstream exhibitions. Another house, converted into the "Seventh Heaven Jazz Café," was particularly intended to attract day-trippers to the street—a means of broadcasting the message. The exteriors of almost all the others were brightly painted with various images: a floral frieze, which ran along most of the street; portraits of people in the street; dreamlike celestial horses; and political slogans. Internally, houses were transformed into a disparate collection of spaces that fused dwelling with defense. One had a deep tunnel beneath it, now a favorite device of environmental activists. The road itself was used as an enormous outdoor communal room, becoming the venue for much music and dancing. It was filled with sculptures and other structures intended to amuse or be played with, and furnished with tables and comfortable chairs. The few trees along the side of the tube tracks supported several "benders"—lightweight enclosures with walls and floors hung at startling angles. Rope netting suspended between the trees and the tops of the houses allowed flexible communication between all parts of the settlement. Rising out of one roof was a 60-foot-high tower constructed of scaffolding and other extraneous material acquired from the motorway construction site. This was Claremont Road's monument—its very own tower block and an intentional reminder to the planners of past mistakes. It was painted pink, just to upset them even more. On another roof was a fully operational gallows erected by Mick, one of the more prominent activists. He built it to symbolize the extermination of the street, but he was happy to encourage the rumor, cultivated among the bailiffs, that he would hang himself if they ever ventured to evict him.

There was no formal social organization within the street. The vast majority of residents simply got on with things, in their own time and in

13.1 | Houses, Claremont Road, 1994.

their own way. They might choose to do some barricading or might paint, tunnel, play music, make lock-ons,[3] leaflet, sculpt, keep lookout, cook, relax, or whatever else appealed at the time. And there was no hierarchy of roles, no "right" thing to be doing. Collective meals were regularly provided, but it is difficult to identify exactly how the supply was maintained. Certain individuals seemed to just take it on themselves to cook, without being asked and without expecting recognition. Occasionally the street would attract unwelcome visitors who undermined collective efforts. These would eventually be persuaded to move on, but again no specific individuals appeared to be making the decisions; there was just a collective snapping of tolerance. A minimal amount of planning went into ensuring that non-resident activists would be attracted and find it easy to participate. Saturdays, for example, tended to be for barricading and Sundays for partying.

Lacking any apparent internal authority, Claremont Road must have appeared potentially volatile, and the authorities applied their force with due caution. But they also, on occasion, betrayed a grudging respect for the activists' endeavors. It would have taken an extremely cold heart not to be affected by Claremont Road. Among all the shambolic disorder of the place there was a surprising sense of harmony, a unique balance of collective purpose and individual expression. And the creative diversity of that expression could be inspiring. These people were clearly enjoying fulfilling, purposeful lives. And the apparent futility of it all added extra poignancy. No one was under any delusion that this was going to last—the motorway would, eventually, be built. Most of the houses had deteriorated well beyond

Sandy McCreery

13.2 | Bender structure, Claremont Road, 1994.

13.3 | Tower structure, Claremont Road, 1994.

13.4 | Fortified home, Claremont Road, and Circus Bus.

the possibility of cost-effective repair even before the activists had begun their precarious remodeling; indeed, a favorite catchphrase in the street was "it's all got to go." There was something akin to a poetic sense of tragedy about Claremont Road, and even the most callous of bailiffs must have felt hesitant about rushing toward the bitter end. By suffusing the place with imaginative creativity, the people of Claremont Road produced a vision of an alternative way of living that turned the authorities into the vandals.

The street was also a place of obvious good humor. The activists constantly ridiculed both the authorities and themselves with wit and sensitivity. The security men, for example, tended to receive sympathy rather than mockery for their poorly paid and often dispiriting jobs. And there was some two-way banter between these groups. When activists chanted "Homes not Roads!"—an established cry of road protest—their opponents responded with "Soap not Dope!"; this in turn was quickly returned as "Dope not Soap!" Humor can be disarming. It is difficult to maintain one's guard against someone who irritates one moment and amuses the next. The activists constantly kept the police and bailiffs second-guessing, and for their part the authorities could seek to maintain some sense of order only through a humorless, obsessive application to the job. The playful cheek of Claremont Road turned the authorities into the fanatics.

But this is not to suggest that Claremont Road humor was simply cynical posturing. Activists generally *were* having fun, and it was their intention not simply to antagonize but also to demonstrate that there were other, possibly more rewarding, ways of living. Their real battle was not with the individuals engaged to evict them but with "car culture." They generally believed that the superficial appeal of motorcars had seduced society into making catastrophic and irreversible decisions. For them the car was fundamentally destructive; it destroyed the environment, living places, and the possibility of a rich social life within those places. Motorcars were all about selfish insularity; they provided individual benefits, but at enormous social cost. And if drivers were unaware of or unconcerned by these costs, that was generally because they had used their cars to distance themselves from society. Motorcars insulated their inhabitants from both the irritations and joys of collective existence. They made life more controllable and more controlled. They numbed the intensity of life, and in the process they destroyed the places in which rewarding communal life might otherwise exist. The purpose of Claremont Road was to demonstrate just how great this loss could be, and that the freedoms of the motorcar were illusory. The financial costs and regulations that came with motor dependency tied people to a life of mundane conformity. And without them it was possible

13.5 | Rust in Peace, Claremont Road.

to live a more playful, exploratory, expressive, imaginative, and humorous social existence.

The activists of Claremont Road described their playful, nonviolent approach as "fluffy," and their literature and surroundings were filled with reminders of the need to "stay fluffy," no matter how trying circumstances might become. And tactically it worked. The police, anxious to avoid inflaming passions further, avoided surprises. The activists almost always received a tip-off before an eviction (there were also numerous hoaxes), and the authorities would rely solely on their weight of numbers. These authorities were deliberate and methodical in their actions, an approach that tended to exaggerate the cultural contrasts between themselves and the Claremont Roaders. The two groups became almost self-parodies of their respective character roles: one uninspired and conformist, the other inventive and independent. The whole procedure began to resemble an elaborate staged performance, and one that was particularly long-running and financially extravagant. In the annals of road protest, Claremont Road was a triumph.

But for anyone with an awareness of 1950s and 1960s experimental architecture, possibly the most striking thing about Claremont Road was the extent to which it physically resembled the situationist projects of Constant and Yona Friedman.[4] The scaffolding towers, rope net planes, and elevated "benders" particularly recalled Friedman's "Space City" proposals. And the antiroad activists' actions were remarkably consistent with those advocated by the Situationists and by Henri Lefebvre. Admittedly, many of these tactics were subsequently embraced by various countercultural movements not necessarily aware of their provenance. But their employment at Claremont Road went far beyond what might be expected to have occurred through some gradual percolation of ideas in the field. We are faced here not with similarities but with duplications. Claremont Road witnessed probably the most complete exposition of situationist techniques ever seen in Britain (certainly in the previous twenty years). For the resident activists had not just grafted moments of political engagement or radical gesturing onto otherwise conventional lives. Rather, they had allowed themselves to be totally absorbed into a radically alternative culture. Every moment of every day amounted to a political act. They lived revolutionary lives, actively seeking to transform their world, and, in the true situationist manner, had fun doing so. It is tempting to imagine that both Lefebvre and Guy Debord would have felt vindicated by Claremont Road in the autumn of 1994.

Although Lefebvre and the Situationists advocated similar tactics for revolutionary living, they came to these from quite different directions. And neither had particularly emphasized roads in their analyses of capitalist culture. Equally, it is safe to assume that the Claremont Road activists had not been reading a great deal of radical French theory from the 1960s. Yet somehow all three, following different lines of thought, had arrived at essentially identical proposals. In this chapter, I contend that their congruence is more than mere coincidence and that, if we look more deeply into the ideas of Lefebvre and the Situationists, we can discover at their root a common understanding of a space/place dialectic. Nowhere is this rendered more apparent than in the conflicts surrounding road building. Also, by constructing a Lefebvrian/situationist analysis of road building, we can shed new light on the processes that underlay the events at Claremont Road.

Like many of their contemporary Marxist thinkers, Lefebvre and Debord were principally concerned with identifying the mechanisms by which capitalism, contrary to the predictions of Marx, had maintained its hold on society. Although they conceived of it somewhat differently, they both emphasized the increasing alienation of life under capitalism: the production of a "culture of separation."[5] For Lefebvre, separation was principally the result of applying scientific rationality to life: the breaking down of all areas of human experience into "knowable" intellectual categories. He related this to the calculation required in the search for profit. In other words, it was a particular consciousness that he identified, a way of thinking that both underpinned and was promoted through capitalism, and that was increasingly made concrete through its projection onto the built environment through functional modernist planning. Many of these concerns are particularly elegantly expressed in Michel de Certeau's famous reflection on the view of Manhattan from the top of the World Trade Center.[6] Certeau holds that "the 1370 foot high tower continues to construct the fiction that . . . makes the complexity of the city readable" and that "the fiction of knowledge is related to this lust to be a viewpoint and nothing more."[7] Knowledge demands detachment from everyday life, and thus it is never complete. Yet it is this viewpoint, this detached mapping, that modernism sought to build.

The situationists, in contrast, tended to stress commodification: the packaging of everything into salable units. Beginning with Marx's view that industrial capitalism destroys creativity in labor, they claimed that alienated toil was returned to the workers as products sold with a false promise to make them whole once more. Capitalism had produced a "spectacle" of material wealth in the face of psychic poverty. Atomized individuals are forced to simulate their subjectivity through objects, and what should be authentic everyday experiences are repackaged as parts of mediated lifestyles. The situationists argued that people thus become spectators of their own lives, striving fruitlessly toward the seemingly whole lives acted out by media celebrities on the spectacular stage of commodity abundance. Culture becomes nonparticipatory, and individuals no longer construct their own lives. Sadie Plant uses the example of football to illustrate this process: what was once a mass participation sport became a mass spectator sport in which the supporters' true desires are lived by others, and their sense of identity is acquired through commercial relations with a particular club.[8] For the situationists, the culture of separation meant exactly that: people are separated from their work, from each other, and from themselves.

Both Lefebvre and the situationists saw fragmentation as a weapon in the service of capitalism. Lefebvre stressed the extent to which everyday life and everyday spaces were becoming increasingly ordered, structured, and controlling. The power of the detached knowing gaze that mapped the city became concretized into the urban grid. Rational classifications and intellectual distinctions solidified into sociospatial boundaries. And this physical "knowledge as power" served as a new reality that could once again be mapped, then projected in increasingly solid, immutable, unquestionable forms. In the process, everything becomes more and more profoundly banal. Bored individuals are rendered incapable of creatively imagining any kind of alternative life. As life is objectified, so individuals are subjected to it.

The situationists also made much of the disempowering effects of separation, and particularly emphasized the addictive nature of the spectacle: it has the power to transfix and placate, and it induces dependent behavior.

As the carrot of material affluence, the promise of fulfillment, is dangled in front of workers' eyes, they seem prepared to surrender more and more of themselves to alienated drudgery. And as alienation deepens, so the search for wholeness in the form of commodities becomes ever more fervent. More and more areas of life become reified, and the possibility of authentic pleasure becomes more and more remote. There is little choice but to conform to the demands of the workplace in order to pay for spectacular pleasures.

We can thus speculate that Lefebvre and the situationists might have interpreted the building of an urban motorway, such as that resisted at Claremont Road, somewhat differently. What Lefebvre may have seen primarily as an outcome of a supposedly rational division of social space into functional parts, the situationists would probably have understood as an attempt to speed up the circulation of commodities—a deepening of the alienating spectacle. Undoubtedly they would have agreed that the motorway was symptomatic of the culture of separation, and therefore implicated in capitalism's hold over society.

But where they were really on common ground was in their advocacy of certain tactics to undercut capitalism's power. Both Lefebvre and the situationists argued that the key step was to begin living a richer, less alienated, more participatory culture—what Lefebvre described as a "new romanticism."[9] This was a mental nomadism that denied the separation of knowledge, experience, and imagination into distinct intellectual categories, a new exploratory consciousness that would revel in the human potential for emotional intensity. Through a fusion of art into everyday life, people should rediscover their ability to control their own lives. And this was also a spatial issue. For although they tended to disguise it under abstract theorizations, both Lefebvre and the situationists shared the belief that capitalism's objectification of space had destroyed the places in which such a way of being might otherwise naturally occur. Space had come to be seen as an absolute, as no more than a mappable field of geometrical coordinates all equally emptied of human content. They might have argued over whether the change derived from the desire to rationally "know" space or from its commodification into equally exchangeable plots; but Lefebvre and the situationists agreed that in the fight against capitalism, place had to be reasserted over space. That this was their guiding purpose needs to be stressed, if only because it is so often overlooked. Lefebvre's "science of space" was intended as a fundamental challenge to the conventional knowledge of space.[10] He adopted terminology that would overwrite the scientific conceptions he opposed, presumably with the intention of removing them from social discourse. Otherwise he might have described his project with greater sincerity as the "science of place" or the "culture of space." His aim was to write the richness of human experience back into our understanding of space, to deny the abstract boundaries of the map. And this is exactly the intention of a "situation," which the situationists defined as "a moment of life concretely and deliberately constructed by the collective organisation of a unitary ambience and a game of events."[11] It was the momentary construction of a shared atmosphere, a dynamic sense of place.

In some respects these distinct conceptions of space and place can be traced back to Marx. In economic terms, Marx had conceptualized capitalism as essentially a temporal process, to which space was largely irrelevant. Distance from the market was unimportant; it was the time it took to get there that mattered. For capitalism as an economic process, space was simply an obstacle to be overcome. But in political terms, Marx saw space as crucial (although he did not dwell on it), for it was through place that class consciousness—and therefore the potential for political resistance—developed. He believed nineteenth-century capitalism had laid the seeds of its own downfall by developing railways, for political

> union is helped on by the improved means of communication that . . . place the workers of different localities in contact with one another. It was just this contact that was needed to centralize the numerous local struggles, all of the same character, into one national struggle between classes. . . . And that union, to attain which the burghers of the Middle Ages, with their miserable highways required centuries, the modern proletarians, thanks to railways, achieve in a few years.[12]

But whereas in his day railways were bringing cities and labor associations together, in this century roads have allowed them to be blown apart. If the political potential to overthrow capitalism depends on place-bound political allegiances, then in the anonymous space of free-moving individuals there can be no revolution. This, then, was the crucial issue for Lefebvre and the situationists. Capitalism had survived because during the twentieth century its production of space had triumphed over place. The power of economics had undermined the economies of politics. And it is hard to imagine a context in which this conflict between space and place appears more immediate than when a planner draws the line of a new road through your house.

Place is lived space. If the space that capitalism produces is rational, ordered, mappable, controlling, anonymous, banal, and fragmented in its totality, then places are experiential, natural, transitory, confused, contested, unique, historical, and holistic. To encourage greater awareness of place, the situationists developed the *dérive*, "a technique of transient passage through various ambiences."[13] This often involved purposeful disorientation to subvert "knowable" space (by, for example, following the map of one area of the city while in another) and to allow a spontaneous drifting that focused on bodily and psychological encounters, thereby exploring the richness of human places replete with memory, myth, and imaginative possibilities. But to actually reassert place, to contest the capitalist production of space, Lefebvre and the situationists advocated the self-conscious construction of new subjective environments—an unfolding of art through space. This would involve the spatial exploration and celebration of the essentially subjective unalienated areas of life, such as humor, creativity, play, imagination, street life and carnivals, passion, history, spontaneity, and bodily pleasures. Space would thus be saturated with Lefebvre's "new romanticism"; it would be "appropriated" from capitalism.

Such an appropriation of space through the construction of situations is precisely what occurred at Claremont Road in 1994, and events there graphically illustrate the space/place dialectic. For had the area not already been rendered anonymous and banal, then the activists would not have been able to impose themselves upon it so emphatically—place could not have been so effectively reasserted over space. Certainly the view of the Department of Transport seemed to be that no one cared about Leyton. Although it housed many people, no one appeared to "live" there. Building a motorway through the area should have been conflict-free. But the Department of Transport made a tactical mistake; as it bought up the houses along the route, instead of demolishing them immediately, it made them available as temporary studios through Acme, a charity dedicated to finding space for artists. These people began, initially without purpose, to practice exactly what Lefebvre and the situationists had been preaching: they explored their creative potential through their environment. An embryonic sense of place developed, which provided the seeds of later resistance. The authorities presumably employed West African security guards partly in an attempt to mitigate against this strategic error. Besides being cheap to hire, these people were also perceived by the authorities to be culturally distant, literally dis-placed, and therefore were expected to be less sensitive to the unique ambience being developed.

Claremont Road demonstrated that situationist tactics can be extremely effective. It exposed the space/place dialectic so thoroughly that no one needed to be steeped in French cultural theory to recognize these as the fundamental issues being contested. This shows that Lefebvre and Debord, writing largely before the era of mass car ownership, had remarkably prescient insight; their arguments have proved valid. But it also reveals something of a historical oversight, for they did not sufficiently emphasize the pivotal role that roads would play in the unfolding of the space/place dialectic. During most of this century, roads have been the principal means through which space has been produced. To an extraordinary degree, they have made possible the spatial expansion and deepening of capitalism.

In his celebrated essay "Notes on the New Town," Lefebvre portrayed roads as the outcome of the rational division of space under capitalism.[14] Of course, this is only part of his story, one side of the dialectic—and one that would carry greater weight in a French context. For places can, and do, resist the production of space. The British experience has shown that road building has been fundamentally opportunistic. Roads have gone where space could dominate place with minimal resistance. And Claremont Road shows that sometimes the planners have misjudged. But the greater fault in Lefebvre's account of the new town is its failure to consider the extent to which roads have been desired *in themselves*, not as a consequence of modernist planning but as a guiding purpose.

The emotional thrill that motorcars offer in terms of speed and mobility, celebrated to great effect by the Futurists, was a major impetus behind the modernist schemes of Le Corbusier and his followers. This was made explicit in the foreword to *Urbanisme*, when Le Corbusier recalled a formative encounter on the Champs Élysées:

> I was assisting at the titanic reawakening of a comparatively new phenomenon[,] . . . traffic. Motors in all directions, going at all speeds. I was overwhelmed, an enthusiastic rapture filled me[,] . . . the rapture of power. The simple and ingenious pleasure of being in the centre of so much power, so much speed. We are a part of it[,] . . . we have confidence in this new society. . . . Its power is like a torrent swollen by storms; a destructive fury. The city is crumbling, it cannot last much longer; its time is past. It is too old. The torrent can no longer keep to its bed.[15]

And in Britain the view was being perpetuated by the architects Alison and Peter Smithson—among many other modern urbanists—just prior to the motorway proposals that eventually destroyed Claremont Road. In their 1957 "Cluster City" essay, the Smithsons quoted Le Corbusier—"when night intervened the passage of cars along the autostrada traces luminous tracks that are like the trails of meteors flashing across the summer heavens"—and acknowledged that they "still respond to this dream."[16] And in that vein they later asserted that the "first step is to realise a system of urban motorways. Not just because we need more roads, but because only they can make our cities an extension of ourselves as we now wish to be."[17] These are subjective, not objective, responses to motorcars. But they greatly assisted the road-building lobby, and thus the further expansion of capitalism.

The first wave of road building in Britain during the 1930s was principally intended as a measure to relieve unemployment. And as such it was very efficient—the roads were on edge-of-town green-field sites and almost all of the spending involved went directly toward hiring unskilled labor.[18] But these roads also allowed capitalism to develop enormous swathes of suburbia, complete with entirely new levels of mass consumption.[19] The second wave followed government recognition around 1960 that unless new, particularly urban, roads were provided, there would never be sufficient demand for motorcars to support Britain's motor industry. So roads were seen as economically desirable, not just because they allowed the circulation of goods already demanded but also because they stimulated entirely new patterns of consumption.[20] By the mid-1980s, some estimates suggested that as much as half the world's measured economic activity might be concerned with making, fueling, maintaining, and administering motor vehicles. It has transpired that the motorcar is perhaps the most powerfully narcotic product that capitalism has produced, precisely characterized by Debord as "the pilot product of the first stage of commodity abundance."[21] For not only have motorcars themselves become increasingly socially necessary, but as the places of social relations have been broken down to accommodate them, so too, in the view of the road activists (and we can presume Lefebvre and Debord would have concurred), emotional dependency on commodities has increased. Roads and motorcars deepen the reification of capitalism, the culture of separation.

Antiroad activists in Britain are now in particularly good humor. A recently elected Labour government that is known to actively research public opinion before forming policy has just cut the road-building program even further. Less than a quarter of the new roads proposed five years ago are still proceeding. The actions on Claremont Road and several other prominent sites, such as Twyford Down, Fairmile, and Salisbury, appear to have demonstrated the political effectiveness of appropriating space. But capitalism is hardly teetering on the edge of collapse, and the road activists may be tempted to overestimate their influence. David Harvey has argued convincingly that capitalism has now effectively dominated space—that global compression of space and time is sufficient to largely free capitalism from locational constraints. And with this, place, or at least simulated hyperplace, has gained new (economic) importance.[22] The dialectical balance is swinging back. For this locational freedom no longer depends so much on the ability to circulate commodities as on information and "pure" electronic spectacle. Fifteen years ago the ten largest global corporations were all either oil companies or automobile manufacturers. They are now being supplanted by the information technology giants. As we enter cybercapitalism, the economic phase of road capitalism appears to be fading. The Claremont Road situation was perhaps the first of its kind. It may also have been the last.

Notes

1   Conversation with Patrick Field, February 1997.

2   Much material for this study was supplied by Christine Binney, who lived at Claremont Road, and Patrick Field, who was a consistent visiting activist.

3   "Lock-ons" are devices by which activists could attach themselves to secure objects in the street such that the authorities would have extreme difficulty releasing them. Two varieties in particular were perfected at Claremont Road. The simpler one of these was a four-inch pipe inserted between two sides of a chimney stack. Two activists could each place an arm down the pipe and handcuff themselves together. Separating them without injury then required the piece-by-piece demolition of the chimney—a precarious and time-consuming operation. The more elaborate method involved securing a shackle in concrete beneath the road surface. A large, thick steel plate with a hole just large enough for an arm to be passed through would then be placed over the shackle. If an activist lay on the steel plate with a wrist attached to the shackle, extensive excavation of the road under the plate was then required in order to cut him or her free.

4   I use here *Situationist* when referring to members of the Situationist International (SI) and their ideas, and *situationist* when referring to similar thinking by individuals not actually members of the SI.

5   Guy Debord, "Separation Perfected," chapter 1 of *The Society of the Spectacle*, trans. Donald Nicholson-Smith (New York: Zone Books, 1994), pp. 11–24.

6   Michel de Certeau, *The Practice of Everyday Life*, trans. Steven F. Rendall (Berkeley: University of California Press, 1984), pp. 91–110.

7   Ibid., p. 92.

8   Sadie Plant, *The Most Radical Gesture: The Situationist International in a Postmodern Age* (London: Routledge, 1992), pp. 67–68.

9   Henri Lefebvre, "Towards a New Romanticism?" in *Introduction to Modernity: Twelve Preludes, September 1959–May 1961*, trans. John Moore (London: Verso, 1995), pp. 239–388.

10   Henri Lefebvre, *The Production of Space*, trans. Donald Nicholson-Smith (Oxford: Blackwell, 1991), pp. 1–67.

11   "Definitions" (1958), in *Situationist International Anthology*, ed. and trans. Ken Knabb, (Berkeley: Bureau of Public Secrets, 1981), 'Definitions' from Internationale Situationiste no. 1 (June 1958) p. 45.

12   Karl Marx and Friedrich Engels, *The Communist Manifesto*, trans. Samuel Moore (Harmondsworth: Penguin, 1967), p. 90.

13   "Definitions," p. 45.

14   Lefebvre, "Notes on the New Town," in *Introduction to Modernity*, pp. 116–126.

15   Le Corbusier, *The City of To-morrow and Its Planning*, trans. Frederick Etchells, 3d ed. (London: Architectural Press, 1971), pp. xxii–xxiv.

16   Alison and Peter Smithson, "Cluster City," *Architectural Review* 122 (November 1957): 333–336.

17   Alison and Peter Smithson, *Ordinariness and Light* (London: Faber and Faber, 1970), p. 145.

18   Sandy McCreery, "From Moderne to Modern: An Ideological Journey along London's Western Avenue from the 1930s to the 1970s" (M.Sc. thesis, University College London, 1992).

19   David Harvey, *The Urban Experience* (Oxford: Blackwell, 1989), pp. 17–58.

20   McCreery, "From Moderne to Modern."

21   Debord, *Society of the Spectacle*, pp. 123–124.

22   David Harvey, "From Space to Place and Back Again: Reflections on the Condition of Postmodernity," in *Mapping the Futures: Local Cultures, Global Change*, ed. Jon Bird et al. (London: Routledge, 1993), pp. 3–29.

14 Sally R. Munt

The Lesbian Flâneur

I haven't been doing much flâneuring recently. It's 1993, and six months ago I moved from the British coastal town of Brighton, where I'd lived for eight years, to the Midlands city of Nottingham, chasing a job. A four-hour drive separates the two, but in terms of my lesbian identity, I'm in another country. Geographically, Nottingham is located in the exact center of England: the land of Robin Hood. This local hero is mythologized in the region's heritage entertainment—next to the (fake, nineteenth-century) castle, one can purchase a ticket for the Robin Hood Experience. Nottingham, formerly a hub of urban industry, is nostalgic for a time when men were men, and codes of honor echoed from the heart of the oak, to the hearth, to the pit. D. H. Lawrence is this city's other famous son. English national identity is thus distilled into a rugged romanticized masculinity, an essence of virile populism that is potently enhanced by its attachment to the core, the fulcrum, of England. Its interiority is endemic to the boundaries that entrap it; in its corporeality it is the heart, the breast, the bosom, and to each tourist is offered the metaphoricity of home.

Brighton is on the edge: thirty miles from France, this hotel town is proud of its decaying Regency grandeur, its camp, excessive, effeminate facades. It loves the eccentricity of Englishness, but laughs at the pomposity of England. Brighton looks to Europe for its model of bohemia, for it is just warm enough to provide a pavement culture to sit out and watch the girls go by. Brighton, the gay capital of the South, the location of the dirty weekend, has historically embodied the genitals rather than the heart. Its sexual ambiguity is present on the street, in its architecture, from the orbicular tits of King George's Pavilion onion domes to the gigantic plastic dancer's legs that extrude invitingly above the entrance to the alternative cinema, the Duke of York's. Aristocratic associations imbue the town with a former glory. Its faded past, its sexual history, is a memory cathecting contemporary erotic identifications as decadent, degenerative, and whorelike. The stained window of nineteenth-century permissiveness filters my view of Brighton. Promenading on a Sunday afternoon on the pier, loitering in the Lanes, or taking a long coffee on the seafront, ostensibly reading the British broadsheet the Observer, the gaze is gay. Brighton introduced me to the dyke stare; it gave me permission to stare. It made me feel I was worth staring at, and I learned to dress for the occasion. Brighton constructed my lesbian identity, one that was given to me by the glance of others, exchanged by the looks I gave them, passing—or not passing—in the street.

It's colder in Nottingham. There's nothing like being contained in its two large shopping malls on a Saturday morning to make one feel queer. Inside again, this pseudo-public space is sexualized as privately *heterosexual. Displays of intimacy over the purchase of family-sized commodities are exchanges of gazes calculated to exclude. When the gaze turns, its intent is hostile: visual and verbal harassment make me avert my eyes. I don't loiter, ever; the surveillance is turned on myself, as the panopticon imposes self-vigilance. One night last week, I asked two straight women to walk me from the cinema to my car. The humiliation comes in acknowledging that my butch drag is not black enough, not leather enough, to hide my fear.*

As I become a victim to, rather than a possessor of, the gaze, my fantasies of lesbian mobility/eroticism return to haunt me. As "home" recedes, taking my butch sexual confidence with it, my exiled wanderings in bed at night have become literary expeditions. As I pursue myself through novels, the figure of the flâneur has imaginatively refigured the mobility of my desire. These fictional voyagers offer me a dreamlike spectacle that returns as a memory I have in fact never lived. Strolling has never been so easy, as a new spatial zone, the lesbian city, opens to me.

The flâneur is a hero of modernity. He appeared in mid-nineteenth-century France and is primarily associated with the writing of the poet Charles Baudelaire, whose best-known depiction of him is in the essay "The Painter of Modern Life" (1863). The flâneur appears successively in the criticism of the German Marxist and founder of the Frankfurt School Walter Benjamin, in the 1930s. The economic conditions of rising capitalism that stimulated his appearance resulted in the rise of the boulevards, cafés, and arcades, new spaces for his consumption of the city-spectacle. Neither completely public nor completely private, these voyeuristic zones were home to the flâneur, engaged in his detached, ironic, and somewhat melancholic gazing. He was also a sometime journalist, his writings on the city being commodified as short tableaux in the new markets for leisure reading. His origin—in Paris, that most sexualized of cities—traditionally genders his objectification as masculine, his canvas, or ground, as feminine.

The movement of Baudelaire's writing can be characterized as literary flâneuring on the streets of Paris, his poetry an attempt to depict the trajectory of the modern hero, the flâneur. This urban epistemologist accumulates his identity in part by the appropriation of the prostitutes who pervade his texts. The flâneur is the dandy on the move, applying his dry observations to the passing tableaux of the city. He is the active agent, and the city a sexualized woman—a prostitute—to be consumed. Elizabeth Wilson has taken issue with the dominant feminist opinion that this flâneur is essentially male, and she inserts the presence of women as subjects in this urban narrative. She also directs us to acknowledge the figure's insecurity, marginality, and ambiguity, rejecting the preferred version of the flâneur's voyeuristic mastery: "The flâneur represented not the triumph of masculine power, but its attenuation. . . . In the labyrinth, the flâneur effaces himself, becomes passive, feminine. In the writing of fragmentary pieces, he makes of himself a blank page upon which the city writes itself. It is a feminine, placatory gesture."[1]

During the 1920s, homosexuality was located in New York in two identifiable spaces, Greenwich Village and Harlem. Homosexuality was made permissible by journeying to a time-zone happening; one experienced a present event rather than taking one's preformed sexual identity, intact and inviolate, to the party. Social mobility was a prerequisite for sexual experimentation—the bourgeois white flâneurs who went "slumming" in Harlem paid to see in the exoticized black drag acts and strip shows,[2] a voyeuristic legitimation of their own forbidden fantasies. Flâneuring invokes seeing the turf of the city as an exotic landscape, reveling in the emporium of the spectacle; and thus discursively it is an activity developed out of the nineteenth-century colonialist project of conquest and control. It is at least notionally an imperialist gaze.

Is the flâneur someone to be appropriated for our *post*modern times? I don't wish to rehearse the arguments concerning whether the flâneur is a good or bad figure, partly because they tend to be articulated within a heterosexual paradigm, relying on heterosexual discourses of the city. I'm interested in this observer as a metaphor, offering at once a symbolic hero and antihero, a borderline personality in a parable of urban uncertainty, angst, and anomie. Within the labyrinth, the process of making up meaning in movement becomes the point, and perversely too the pleasure, as we become lost among the flowing images. It's possible the flâneur is a borderline case, an example of a roving signifier, a transient wildcard of potential, indeterminate sexuality, trapped in transliteration, caught in desire. Is the flâneur a transvestite? Can s/he be a cross-dressed lesbian?

What can we learn of spatial relations from the deployment of the flâneur by marginalized identities (in my particular example, lesbians)? How do we read the ambivalence and contradictions expressed in those appropriations? One way of exploiting the metaphor of the flâneur is to examine how it is possible to deconstruct the gender polarity active/masculine, passive/feminine through its installation in lesbian cultural history. Second, we are able to see how the flâneur, like the dandy, is not only gender-flexible but also conveniently expropriatable to class formulations. Wilson argues that the flâneur is "subtly déclassé."[3] "Racing" the flâneur is not so easy: his home in white European culture means he was exportable to the colonies, and therefore assimilable to other local narratives, but work has yet to be done on discovering an indigenous equivalent.

The most visible gay culture of the early-twentieth-century United States was largely male, working-class, and assembled around immigrant neighborhoods of New York City. George Chauncey's fifty-year history of gay New York makes the point that gay sexuality was very much in and of the streets, in part, like working-class culture in general, because of the economic and spatial limitations of the tenements. Enclaves of lesbians interacted with their gay male counterparts, congregating in the speakeasies, tearooms, and drag balls of Harlem and Greenwich Village during the 1920s. These were different worlds of homosexual identification, divided by race and class. Greenwich bohemian life tolerated a degree of sexual experimentation that conferred on the area an embryonic stature as erotica unbound (a construction much enhanced during the 1950s and 1960s with the Beat homosexuals Allen Ginsberg and William Burroughs). Lesbian and gay clubs in the Village were founded on the "Personality Clubs" of the bohemian intelligentsia. Chauncey describes the sexual "free zone" of this apparently utopian space: "The gay history of Greenwich Village suggests the extent to which the Village in the teens and twenties came to represent to the rest of the city what New York as a whole represented to the rest of the nation: a peculiar social territory in which the normal social constraints on behavior seemed to be suspended."[4]

As Harlem had functioned as the mecca for black people, now Greenwich Village became the Promised Land for (mainly) white homosexuals. Chauncey makes the point: "In the 1920s Harlem became to black America what Greenwich Village became to bohemian white America: the symbolic—and in many respects, practical—center of a vast social experiment."[5] These new gay and lesbian identities were predominantly urban, emanating from the social geographies of the streets, built out of this moment of mutable space. In Harlem, black lesbian culture centered around the clubs, mainly those featuring powerful blues singers such as Ma Rainey, Bessie Smith, and Gladys Bentley. Harlem represented the potential dissolution of a strictly regulated ideal of chaste black bourgeois female sexuality, imported from the South to working-class lesbians. Many of these African American women had friendship networks that held house parties where lesbians would pay a small entrance fee for food.[6] But during this period some working-class black and white lesbians would come together and meet in the clubs. Greenwich Village and Harlem had their own specific internal social fracturings around class, gender, and race.

The Second World War created unprecedented mobility for lesbians and gay men,[7] who relocated to military centers in cities in their tens of thousands. Resisting the small-town suburban conformity of the United States of the 1950s, men and women were again drawn, or driven, to cities as places to express their "deviant" sexuality.[8] The anonymity of the city made a gay life realizable in a repressive era. This odyssey is well represented in the lesbian novels of the period.[9] Nightclubs were a visible site for women interested in "seeing" other women, and it is in the literature of the 1950s and 1960s that the bar becomes consolidated as the symbol of home.[10] Lesbian/whore became a compacted image of sexual consumption in the popular dime novels read by straight men and lesbians alike. The lesbian adventurer inhabited a twilight world where sexual encounters were acts of romanticized outlawry, initiated in some backstreet bar and consummated in the narrative penetration of the depths of mazelike apartment buildings. She is the carnival queen of the city—"Dominating men, she ground them beneath her skyscraper heels"[11]—a public/private figure whose excess sensuality wistfully transcends spatial and bodily enclosures. This modernist nightmare of urban sexual degeneracy is crystallized in the identification of the city with homosexuality. Lesbian-authored fictions of the period set in the Village, like Ann Bannon's *Beebo Brinker* series (1957–1962), though less sensationalist syntheses of the available discursive constructions of "lesbian," still depend on that myth of the eroticized urban explorer.[12] Transmuting in more liberal times into the lesbian sexual adventurer, this figure can be recognized in diverse texts, from Rita Mae Brown's post–sexual revolution *Rubyfruit Jungle* (1973) to the San Franciscan postmodernist porn parody *Bizarro in Love* (1986).[13]

In this outline of the flâneur I have tried to gesture toward both the textual history of the form and its echo in the narratives of lived identities. As a cultural form, its status as "myth" as opposed to "lived experience" is irreducible. The flâneur is an incongruent and complex figure suggesting a number of antitheses: motion/stasis, mastery/fragility, desire/abstinence, complacency/alienation, presence/intangibility. Singularly perhaps the flâneur is a symbol of urbanity. When Walter Benjamin described flânerie as going "botanizing on the asphalt,"[14] his turn of phrase hinted at a gender ambiguity facilitating a reading of this poet as less—or more—than male. The lesbian flâneur is one step from here.

The lesbian flâneur appears as a shadow character or a minor theme in a number of recent novels, and I want briefly to offer examples of her appearance as a structuring principle in four New York fictions: a stanza of a poem by Joan Nestle; a short story, "The Swashbuckler," by Lee Lynch (1985); *Don Juan in the Village*, by Jane DeLynn (1990); and *Girls, Visions, and Everything*, by Sarah Schulman (1986).[15] Within contemporary lesbian writing we encounter a specific, even nostalgic, image of the stroller as a self-conscious lesbian voyeur. The years of feminist debate engrossed with the political acceptability of looking are the background to these lesbian vindications of the right to cruise:

New words swirl around us
and still I see you in the street
loafers, chinos, shades.
You dare to look too long
and I return your gaze,
feel the pull of old worlds
and then like a femme
drop my eyes.
But behind my broken look
you live
and walk deeper into me
as the distance grows between us.

Joan Nestle's first stanza from "Stone Butch, Drag Butch, Baby Butch" ends with the comment "Shame is the first betrayer."[16] The extract epitomizes the mechanisms of a necessarily coded visual exchange in a potentially violent, dangerous, and sexualized arena, the street. The punning title of the collection is *A Restricted Country*, and the spatial penetration of the poem recalls this analogy between the streets and the lesbian body. Inside/outside dichotomies break down as both locations become colonized. A subculture made invisible by its parent culture logically resorts to space making in its collective imagination. Mobility within that space is essential, because motion continually stamps new ground with a symbol of ownership.

Is the butch dandy strolling through the doors of the bar just a romanticized inversion of heterosexual occupation? The flâneur may not have to be biologically male for the gaze to enact masculine visual privilege. The politics of butch/femme and their relation to dominant systems of organizing gender relations have been bloodily fought over,[17] and while I am sympathetic to claims that butch and femme constitute new gender configurations that must be understood within their own terms, they are not intrinsically radical forms springing perfect from the homosexual body. Nor are they naive forms in the sense that they express a naturally good, pure, and primitive desire. Nestle's poem is interesting in that it represents the push/pull, utopian/dystopian contrariety of the ambivalent flâneur, balancing the temptation and lust for the city (embodied as a woman) with the fear of connection and belonging. Note that the narrator of the poem initiates the glance, then returns the gaze, and then becomes the owner of a "broken look." The butch penetrates with her gaze ("walk deeper into me") an assumed femme who is only "like a femme." Evading categorization, this almost-femme narrator is the one who closes the stanza by rebuking invisibility and averted eyes. Who is claiming the gaze here? We can assume only that it is a woman.

The poem describes movement: both characters are in motion on the street, and the looks that they exchange have their own dynamic rotation. Images of mobility are particularly important to lesbians *as women* inhabiting the urban environment. Feminist struggles to occupy spheres traditionally antipathetic to women go back to the imposition of post–industrial revolution bourgeois family divisions into spaces marked male (public) and female (private). This ideological construction disguises the fact that the domestic space, the "home," as Mark Wigley has written, is also built for the man, to house his woman:

> The woman on the outside is implicitly sexually mobile. Her sexuality is no longer controlled by the house. In Greek thought women lack the internal self-control credited to men as the very mark of masculinity. This self-control is no more than the maintenance of secure boundaries. These internal boundaries, or rather boundaries that define the interior of the person, the identity of the self, cannot be maintained by a woman because her fluid sexuality endlessly overflows and disrupts them. And more than this, she endlessly disrupts the boundaries of others, that is, men, disturbing their identity, if not calling it into question.[18]

The familiar construction of woman as excess has radical potential when appropriated by the lesbian flâneur. The image of the sexualized woman is double-edged, a recoupable fantasy. Swaggering down the street in her butch drag, casting her roving eye left and right, the lesbian flâneur signifies a mobilized female sexuality *in control*, not out of control. As a fantasy she transcends the limitations of the reader's personal circumstances. In her urban circumlocutions, her affectivity, her connections, she breaks down the boundary between Self and Other. She collapses the inviolate distinction between masculinity and femininity. Her threat to heteropatriarchal definitions is recognized by hegemonic voices; hence the jeering shout "Is it a man or is it a woman?" is a cry of anxiety as much as aggression. The answer is neither and both: as a Not-Woman, she slips between, beyond, and around the linear landscape. The physiology of this flâneur's city is a woman's body constantly in motion, her lips in conversation.[19]

Like Nestle's protagonists in the poem, Lee Lynch proffers a working-class hero:

Frenchy, jaw thrust forward, legs pumping to the beat of the rock-and-roll song in her head, shoulders dipping left and right with every step, emerged from the subway at 14th Street and disappeared into a cigar store. Moments later, flicking a speck of nothing from the shoulder of her black denim jacket, then rolling its collar up behind her neck, she set out through the blueness and bustle of a New York Saturday night.[20]

Perhaps the name "Frenchy" gives it away—this short passage previews a parodic portrait of the bulldagger as Parisian flâneur, complete with portable Freudian phallus (the cigar), given a sexualized ("blue") city to penetrate. The fetishized butch drag—the black denims, blue button-down shirt, sharply pointed black boots, garrison belt buckle, and jet-black hair slicked back into a bladelike D.A.[21]—constitute the image of the perfect dag. The text foregrounds the plasticity of the role by camping up Frenchy's Casanova, gay-dog, libertine diddy-bopping cruising. The sex scene takes place next to some deserted train tracks, a symbol of transience, traveling, and the moment. This generic butch then catches the subway home. On the journey toward home this flâneur *undresses*. In a classic scene of transformation, she makes herself "old maidish, like a girl who'd never had a date and went to church regularly to pray for one."[22] In a concluding twist, the short story ends with a classic revelation—she goes home to mother. Fearful that the sex smell still on her will be detected, Frenchy slips quickly into "the little girl's room" to sluice away her adult self.[23] In the metaphors of change that structure this story, both the closet and the street are zones of masquerade.

The lesbian flâneur appears in a more extended narrative as the main protagonist in Jane DeLynn's episodic novel *Don Juan in the Village*. Thirteen short scenes of conquest and submission structure this narrator's sexual odyssey. Kathy Acker has called the book "a powerful metaphor of our intense alienation from society and each other. An intriguing portrayal of that strange and trance-like locus where lust and disgust become indistinguishable,"[24] a comment that both recalls the flâneur's anomie and highlights the way in which her space is so sexualized. As does "The Swashbuckler," this novel problematizes the predatory erotics of the stroller by using irony, encouraging a feminist critique of the excessively cold and exploitative sexual consumption of women by the conventional flâneur. In *Don Juan in the Village*, although the protagonist is ostensibly writing from Iowa, Ibiza, Padova, Puerto Rico, or wherever, her actual location is immaterial. The text employs the American literary convention of the traveler in search of (her)self. Delivered with irony, she is a manifest tourist whose every foreign nook temporarily begets a colony of New York City—specifically a Greenwich Village bar, the topos of urbane lesbian identity, the flâneur's café. Her butch diffidence and boredom unsuccessfully screen a deluded, tragicomic, self-conscious sexual desperation. Her targets invariably fail to be compliant, and each escapade is a testimonial to her perpetual frustration. This is one moment of supposed sexual triumph: "As I slid down the bed I saw the World Trade Center out the window, winking at me with its red light. I was Gatsby, Eugène Rastignac, Norman Mailer, Donald Trump . . . anyone who had ever conquered a city with the sheer force of longing and desire."[25] She is going down on that most evasive of spectacles, the gay Hollywood film star. The star, very politely, but very succinctly, fucks her and dumps her. *Don Juan in the Village* depicts the solitary flâneur stalking the city with the torment of Tantalus in her cunt. Although the narrator confers upon herself the gaze, she is unable to see it through, or through it. DeLynn's flâneur wears the melancholy of the disappointed desire, searching the labyrinthine city for a vast, unfulfilled promise.

Finally, Sarah Schulman's second novel, *Girls, Visions, and Everything* (1986), recalls the quest of the American hero/traveler Sal Paradise in Jack Kerouac's *On the Road* (1957): "Somewhere along the line I knew there'd be girls, visions, everything; somewhere along the line the pearl would be handed to me."[26] The pearl, a symbol of female sexuality, is something the active masculine narrator seeks to own. This predatory macho role is located historically in the flâneur; it is the story of an alienated, solitary sexuality voyeuristically consuming the female body as a ri(gh)te of passage. Modeling herself on Paradise/Kerouac, protagonist Lila Futuransky undertakes an adventure similarly self-exploratory, but based on the *female* experiences that urban travel offers. Her likeness to Sal/Jack is her dream of being an outlaw, reconstructed by a feminist consciousness. Lila's trip is a constant circling between compatriots. Living on New York's Lower East Side, she walks the streets, marking out the geography of an urban landscape punctuated by a city mapped out with emotional happenings. Locations are symbols of connection, and constant references to crisscrossing streets remind the reader of the systematic patterns of neighborhood, in antithesis to the standard early modernist images of alienation. *Girls, Visions, and Everything* is about Lila Futuransky's New York, "the most beautiful woman she had ever known."[27]

A sardonic wit suffuses Schulman's novel, but there is also melancholic sadness: a sense of decaying nostalgia for a mythical "home," for streets filled with sisters and brothers sitting languid on the stoop, swapping stories and cementing *communitas*. This is the feminization of the street, the underworld with a human face, with its own moral and family code. It is rich kids who beat the gays and harass the poor, the prostitutes, and the pushers. The lesbians are on the streets, working the burger bar, cruising the ice cream parlor, and clubbing it at the Kitsch-Inn, currently showing a lesbian version of *A Streetcar Named Desire*. Lila meets Emily here, performing as Stella Kowalski. The romance between Lila and Emily is the main plot development in the novel, structuring its five parts. The final chapter sees Lila torn between the "masculine" desire trajectory of *On the Road* individualism and the "feminine" circularity and disruption of affective liaisons. Her friend Isobel urges Lila not to pause: "you can't stop walking the streets and trying to get under the city's skin because if you settle in your own little hole, she'll change so fast that by the time you wake up, she won't be yours anymore. . . . Don't do it buddy" (p. 178).

The text's constant engagement/disengagement with change and transformation is signified by the urban landscape, which is out of control. Even the protective zones are folding, and yet there are pockets of resistance that pierce the city's metaphoric paralysis with parody. Gay Pride is one such representation: fifty thousand homosexuals of every type parading through the city streets, presenting the Other of heterosexuality, from gay bankers to the Gay Men's Chorus singing "It's Raining Men," a carnival image of space being permeated by its antithesis. The text tries to juxtapose a jumble of readerly responses, almost jerking the reader into some consciousness of its activity of forming new imaginative space. From her position of Other, Lila reinvents New York as a heterotopia of cultural intertextuality; she *is* Jack Kerouac—the character, not the author—claiming, even as a Jewish lesbian, that "the road is the only image of freedom that an American can understand" (p. 164).

The street is an image of freedom and paradoxically of violence. The female flâneur is vulnerable—Lila walks unmolested until, near the end of the book, she is sexually harassed by Hispanics and saved from serious injury from potential queer-bashers by Ray, a black and sick drug dealer. Lila's zone is breaking down: "People's minds were splitting open right there on the sidewalk" (p. 14). The fictional worlds start clashing; Blanche DuBois appears to Emily aged eighty-five and begging for a dollar. Lila resorts to Emily with a resignation that can only be antiromance; knowing it is the wrong decision, she nostalgically laments the end of the road of selfhood: "*I don't know who I am right now*, she thought. *I want to go back to the old way*" (p. 178).

This whimsical nostalgia also highlights some disillusionment with the postmodernist models of space, wherein the public and private are collapsed onto the street, and the same space is used by different people in different ways. Hierarchies still exist. Being part of a bigger spectacle, being visible as one subculture among many, may not necessarily lead to empowerment; it may create only more competition over a diminishing resource. To the postmodernist flâneur, freedom in this space is a relative concept; the flâneur is a victim as well as an agent of it, for abstraction has its costs. His freedom is to be suspended in perpetual motion, disconnected from effective social activity, in a state of melancholic play.

Four flâneurs: Joan Nestle's butch, Frenchy, "Don Juan," and Lila Futuransky. Each is a descendant of eager European voyagers who migrated with their ticket to utopia; each with their separate feminized vulnerabilities; each a sexualized itinerant traveling through urban time and space toward a mythical selfhood, trying heroically to construct intelligibility from her experience, to collect an identity. None has the sex/gender/class privileges (fixities) of the modernist flâneur. Each of these heroes has a central ambivalence infusing her sexual wanderings, being pulled between detachment from and insertion into city regimes. Temporary, simultaneous, multiple identifications mapped out in moments, in the margins, masquerading as the male makes these flâneurs engage with the politics of *dis*location. Baudrillard's extended road-poem *America* (1988) speaks that masculine fragmentation:

> And the crucial moment is that brutal instant which reveals that the journey has no end, that there is no longer any reason for it to come to an end. Beyond a certain point, it is movement itself that changes. Movement which moves through space of its own volition changes into an absorption by space itself—end of resistance, end of the scene of the journey as such.[28]

He narrates dystopian exhaustion from the point of view of something being lost—significantly he, like Kerouac, is driving and not walking through America. But spatial reconstruction occurs in the moment of presence, however brief. The vacuum sucks us further in, but we need our fictions of consciousness or we will disappear. The tantalizing fantasy of Benjamin's "phantasmagoria" is here present for the lesbian in the urban scene, embodying melancholia and desire simultaneously. Hence, the grief of alienation is only partial; the apparitional flâneur lost in the streets also stumbles toward hope, and embodiment.

Lesbian identity is constructed in the temporal and linguistic mobilization of space, and as we move *through* space we imprint utopian and dystopian moments upon urban life. Our bodies are vital signs of this temporality and intersubjective location. In an instant, a freeze-frame, a lesbian is occupying space as it occupies her. As Susan Sontag points out, space teems with "possibilities, positions, intersections, passages, detours, u-turns, dead-ends, [and] one-way streets"[29]; it is never still. Another philosopher, Michel de Certeau, offers us the urban mise-en-scène as productive: in *The Practice of Everyday Life*, de Certeau writes about New York as a city of regeneration. Standing on the 110th floor of the World Trade Center he looks down on Manhattan and draws on Foucault's model of the panopticon. As his "view" travels down to the streets he sees a city constantly reinventing itself, and his scopic, gnostic drive falters. Taking up the position of the walker he discovers another, more anarchic spatiality. The city as concept is exceeded by the many pluralities that are generated in, of, and between it; it cannot be fully regulated. The city is a machine that produces an excess, a proliferation of illegitimacy, which discursive practices cannot contain. Pedestrian life has a singularity that escapes the cartological discipline of the architect's plans:

> The long poem of walking manipulates spatial organizations, so no matter how panoptic they may be: it is neither foreign to them (it can take place only within them) nor in conformity with them (it does not receive its identity from them). It creates shadows and ambiguities within them. It inserts its multitudinous references and citations into them. . . . These diverse aspects provide the basis of a rhetoric.[30]

de Certeau sees walking as a space of enunciation, and the pedestrian's journey, like the speech act, has an unlimited diversity. Within the city-as-text there is an antitext: "Things *extra* and *other* . . . insert themselves into the accepted framework, the imposed order. One thus has the very relationship between spatial practices and the constructed order. The surface of this order is everywhere punched and torn open by ellipses, drifts, and leaks of meaning: it is a sieve-order."[31]

The perambulations of the lesbian flâneur on the streets of the city mark out a territorial discourse—to extend the spatial analogy—of heroic proportions. Her journey from "here" to "there" invokes an active "I," a phatic statement of subjectivity and location that refuses verbal and spatial effacement. Her desire is the machine of her incarnation. *Briefly returning to Brighton for the summer, my eye follows a woman wearing a wide-shouldered linen suit. Down the street, she starts to decelerate. I zip up my jacket, put my best boot forward, and tell myself that "home" is just around the corner.*

Notes

1   Elizabeth Wilson, "The Invisible Flâneur," *New Left Review*, no. 195 (1992): 90–110; quotation, p. 110.

2   See Lillian Faderman, *Odd Girls and Twilight Lovers: A History of Lesbian Life in Twentieth-Century America* (New York: Viking; London: Penguin, 1992), pp. 62–92, and George Chauncey, *Gay New York: Gender, Urban Culture, and the Making of the Gay Male World, 1890–1940* (New York: Basic Books, 1994).

3   Wilson, "The Invisible Flâneur," p. 105.

4   Chauncey, *Gay New York*, p. 244.

5   Ibid., pp. 245–246.

6   Such friendship networks are also reported by Elizabeth Lapovsky Kennedy and Madeline D. Davis in their wonderful history of Buffalo, *Boots of Leather, Slippers of Gold: The History of a Lesbian Community* (New York: Routledge, 1993).

7   For a full treatment of this subject, see Allan Bérubé's excellent *Coming Out under Fire: The History of Gay Men and Women in World War Two* (New York: Plume, 1990).

8   Various works have charted this migration; see, for example, Peter Jackson, *Maps of Meaning: An Introduction to Cultural Geography* (1989; reprint, London: Routledge, 1992), pp. 120–130.

9   A thorough study of these texts is offered in Angela Weir and Elizabeth Wilson, "The Greyhound Bus Station in the Evolution of Lesbian Popular Culture," in *New Lesbian Criticism: Literary and Cultural Readings*, ed. Sally R. Munt (London: Harvester; New York: Columbia University Press, 1992), pp. 95–114.

10   See Katie King, "Audre Lorde's Lacquered Layerings: The Lesbian Bar as a Site of Literary Production," in Munt, *New Lesbian Criticism*, pp. 51–74.

11   Nan Keene, *Twice as Gay* (New York: After Hours, 1964), back cover.

12   See Hamer Diane, "'I Am a Woman': Ann Bannon and the Writing of Lesbian Identity in the 1950's," in *Lesbian and Gay Writing*, ed. Mark Lilly (London: Macmillan, 1990), pp. 47–75.

13   Rita Mae Brown, *Rubyfruit Jungle* (Plainfield, Vt.: Daughters, 1973); Jan Stafford, *Bizarro in Love* (San Francisco: Cheap Shots, 1986).

14   Walter Benjamin, *Charles Baudelaire: A Lyric Poet in the Era of High Capitalism*, trans. Harry Zohn (London: New Left Books, 1973), p. 26.

15   Joan Nestle, "Stone Butch, Drag Butch, Baby Butch," in *A Restricted Country: Essays and Short Stories* (London: Sheba, 1988), pp. 74–77; Lee Lynch, "The Swashbuckler" (1985), in *Women on Women: An Anthology of American Lesbian Short Fiction*, ed. Joan Nestle and Naomi Holoch (New York: Plume; London: Penguin, 1990), pp. 241–262; Jane DeLynn, *Don Juan in the Village* (New York: Pantheon, 1990); and Sarah Schulman, *Girls, Visions, and Everything* (Seattle: Seal, 1986).

16   Nestle, "Stone Butch," p. 74.

17   See, for example, Amber Hollibaugh and Cherríe Moraga, "What We're Rollin' Around in Bed With: Sexual Silences in Feminism: A Conversation towards Ending Them" (1981), in *A Persistent Desire: A Butch/Femme Reader*, ed. Joan Nestle (Boston: Alyson, 1992), pp. 243–253.

18   See Mark Wigley, "Untitled: The Housing of Gender," in *Sexuality and Space*, ed. Beatriz Colomina (New York: Princeton Architectural Press, 1992), pp. 326–389; quotation, p. 335. See also Lawrence Knopp, "Sexuality and the Spatial Dynamics of Capitalism," *Environment and Planning D: Society and Space* 10 (1992): 651–669.

19   See Luce Irigaray, "This Sex Which Is Not One" (1977), in *This Sex Which Is Not One*, trans. Catherine Porter with Carolyn Burke (Ithaca: Cornell University Press, 1985), pp. 23–33.

20   Lynch, "The Swashbuckler," p. 241.

21   As Elizabeth Lapovsky Kennedy and Madeline Davis explain, "The D.A.—the letters stand for duck's ass—was a popular hairdo for working-class men and butches during the 1950's. All side hair was combed back and joined the back hair in a manner resembling the layered feathers of a duck's tail, hence the name. Pomade was used to hold the hair in place and give a sleek appearance." See "'They was no-one to mess with': The Construction of the Butch Role in the Lesbian

Community of the 1940's and 1950's," in Nestle, *A Persistent Desire*, p. 78 n. 11.

22 Lynch, "The Swashbuckler," p. 260.

23 Ibid., p. 261.

24 DeLynn, *Don Juan in the Village*, back cover.

25 Ibid., p. 186; ellipsis hers.

26 Jack Kerouac, *On the Road* (1957; reprint, Harmondsworth: Penguin, 1972), p. 14.

27 Schulman, *Girls, Visions, and Everything*, p. 177; this edition is hereafter cited parenthetically in the text. I am aware that I am in danger of entrenching the discourse of "American exceptionalism"; concentrating my examples in New York encourages the view that it is a "special" place. It is and it isn't: the myth of New York has a political and cultural specificity in world culture and I am curious about that manifestation. For lesbian and gay people it has a particular set of meanings and associations, and to resist mythologizing New York is difficult in practice.

28 Jean Baudrillard, *America*, trans. Chris Turner (London: Verso, 1988), p. 10.

29 Susan Sontag, introduction to *One-Way Street and Other Writings*, by Walter Benjamin, trans. Edmund Jephcott and Kingsley Shorter (London: New Left Books, 1979), p. 13.

30 Michel de Certeau, *The Practice of Everyday Life*, trans. Steven Rendall (Berkeley: University of California Press, 1984), p. 101.

31 Ibid., p. 107.

The triumphs of modern industrial and
urban life arise from connections buried below
the surface of the earth.
—Rosalind Williams, *Notes on the*
Underground

Steve Pile

15 The Un(known) City . . . or, an Urban Geography of What Lies Buried below the Surface

The Unknown City is an intriguing title for a collection of chapters on the city: the city is saturated with people, their movements; millions of eyes watching the world . . . surely the city is well-known? Surely, there are no places in the city that are unknown. On the other hand, no one knows everything about the city. The question is, then, how—and why—particular urban spaces become known and unknown. So, in this chapter, I intend to examine some ways in which the city is produced as an unknown space.

There are many ways in which the city can be rendered unknown: property relationships can limit people's access to buildings and sites, thereby locking the city "behind closed doors";[1] places can be deliberately hidden from sight; things can become so familiar that they are simply overlooked; sites can be forgotten, or misrecognized, or buried under myth, or become unreal somehow, or simply have new meanings attached to them; or maybe the unknown is simply waiting to be discovered, lying off the beaten track. The city is saturated with unknowingness: the huge Crown estates of central London; the walls that surround luxury apartments in London's Docklands, with their security cameras and video entry-phones; the disused stations of the London underground, the statue of Eros (not actually Eros), Dick Whittington (and his cat), the livery companies, or the mosque in East End London that was once a synagogue that was once a church; or maybe the stormwater pumping station on the Isle of Dogs—or, as interestingly, the nondescript Telehouse in East India Dock.[2] Knowingness and unknowingness are constitutive of the city: each clads buildings in layers of visibility and invisibility, familiarity and surprise. And geography is constitutive of this (un)knowingness. Allow me to give one example.

Telehouse gives no indication that it houses the computers that link the financial markets of the City of London with the world of global telecommunications and financial flows. In this building, the wealth of the City of London is connected to lines of information that crisscross the globe through only a few centers. It is in these places that certain groups control flows of commodities and money around the world. Even while they actually have no idea what is going on, people in these centers of interpretation read the runes in the flashing screens of numbers and gamble away obscene amounts of money. Appropriately, Telehouse seems disconnected from its locality, sited in a lonely place, yet its anonymous architecture is "styled" on a similar building in New York.[3] These connections (and disconnections) are at once hidden and visible: the building is simultaneously unknown and known. Indeed, it is only when what goes on inside the building is known that the building becomes the site of unknown transactions—but most people wouldn't give it a second glance. I would like to argue that the important thing about the "unknown city" is not so much that there are parts of the city that are unknown, but that urban space vacillates between the reassuring solidity of knowingness and the sinister voids of unknowingness; in this, the city becomes—in the phrase of the earlier project out of which this book grew—strangely familiar.

The editors of *Strangely Familiar* argued, in their introduction, that

> understanding cities and architecture—and communicating that understanding—involves telling real stories about real places. . . . By using a narrative format, a route is provided which can introduce the unexpected and unfamiliar. . . . If you dig beneath the surface then you discover the unexpected. This process can reintroduce the city to the urban dweller, offering an opportunity to discover something new, and through their own agendas and perspectives find a new mapping and a new way of thinking about cities. The strange becomes familiar and the familiar becomes strange.[4]

Through telling new stories the unknown, undiscovered city can be laid open to critical scrutiny, to new urban practices, new urban subversions. This is a geographical enterprise, about exploration and mapping, about a cartography of hidden or unexplored places: real places in the map of power relations that make, and are made by, city form and urban life. The agenda is radical in its intent, but I would like to suggest that the unknown is not so easily known—it may be all too visible, right in front of our eyes, buried in the underlying infrastructures of everyday lives, so intrinsic we hardly even feel its presence anymore. And when we do, do we really want to know?

UNCANNY CITIES

Exploring the unknown city is a political act: a way of bringing to urban dwellers new resources for remapping the city. Nevertheless, the unknown might resist such attempts at disclosure. It could be that what is really unknown about the city has been known all along. Indeed, sometimes the discovery of the unknown can be quickly repressed. Let me relate a real story about a real place; the story is not mine.

Freud was once walking in Genoa:

> As I was walking, one hot summer afternoon, through the deserted streets of a provincial town in Italy which was unknown to me, I found myself in a quarter of whose character I could not long remain in doubt. Nothing but painted women were to be seen at the windows of the small houses, and I hastened to leave the narrow street at the next turning. But after having wandered about for a

time without inquiring my way, I suddenly found myself back in the same street, where my presence was now beginning to excite attention. I hurried away once more, only to arrive by another *détour* at the same place yet a third time. Now, however, a feeling overcame me which I can only describe as uncanny, and I was glad enough to find myself back at the piazza I had left a short while before, without any further voyages of discovery.[5]

What had Freud found that was so strange and, yet, so familiar? Ostensibly, he had discovered an uncanny city.[6] Freud had also mapped the limits of his desire, marking out his desire to know and his fear of knowing. The well-heeled bourgeois man had walked the streets only to find himself the streetwalkers' object of . . . attention? amusement? seduction? Of course, Freud is hardly the first, nor last, bourgeois man to be caught in his desire and fear (of streetwalking). Yet while we may find it difficult to sympathize with Freud's predicament, this particular story has something to tell us about knowing the unknown city. The story contains several elements: an unknown provincial town, (supposedly) deserted streets, walking, an unknown quarter, an unknown street, a street of known quality *judging by the women there*, (nothing but) painted women, his presence, excitement, returns, repetitions, helplessness, and the strangely familiar. It is this blend that makes, for Freud, an uncanny urban geography of the city. Indeed, Anthony Vidler argues that the uncanny is a specifically urban and spatial "dis-ease."[7]

But only in this story does Freud give the uncanny a personal setting. It is, therefore, surprising that so little critical attention has been paid to it. Mostly, the story is recounted as a tale of getting lost or as the fear of continuous repetition. Thus, it seems to be about the way in which desire shifts into fear, where Freud's unconscious desire for the women shifts into the fear of the exposure of that desire by the women. Rarely is the sexual ambivalence of Freud's detour seen as constitutive of the story: this is a story not just of Freud's fear of helpless repetition, but of his helplessness in the face of fear *and* desire: that is, Freud wanted both to leave and to return to that narrow street. Freud's trip suggests that desire and fear are inextricably intertwined—not in a static way that produces a fixed pattern of repetitions but in dynamic ways, so that repetitious patterns are both the double of the other and also different enough to fool, and so that these patterns are both situated and expressed spatially—here, on the streets.

Freud's discussion of the uncanny suggests that its significance lies in the shift between the familiar and the unfamiliar, the known and the unknown. It is this displacement that produces feelings of uncanniness: "this uncanny is in reality nothing new or alien, but something which is familiar and old-established in the mind and which has become alienated from it only through the process of repression."[8] The estrangement of the familiar implies that something hidden or secret, which had been previously repressed, has come to light. Something repressed, something unconscious, has surfaced into the object, into a feeling of dread or of horror. According to Freud, people defend themselves against traumatic or uncomfortable experiences by repressing the event or idea into the unconscious. If the unconscious is a place where disturbing material is kept away from people's knowledge of it, then that material's sudden eruption into people's experiences of familiar objects is certainly going to involve feelings of dread and horror.

For Freud, the uncanny is related to some very specific repressed experiences: first, to traumatic events occurring in childhood and, second, to the never-quite-abandoned belief in superstitions.[9] In particular, uncanniness is linked into a matrix involving the female body, the fear of castration, and the masculine gaze. So, for Freud, uncanniness is linked to boy's feelings about women's genitalia—both as an archaic site/sight of desire and the site/sight of evidence of castration. The uncanny, therefore, problematizes sexual identity by playing out both a desire to be (w)hole and a fear of being punished; it interrupts the masculine phantasm of self-identity, the fantasy that masculinity is a sexual identity independent of femininity and women's bodies. Characteristically, however, Freud does not have anything to say about how girls or women might experience uncanniness. This, of course, is a serious problem for psychoanalytic theories and practices, but my point here is that masculine sexual identities and experiences are constitutively ambivalent, fragile, and apprehensive.

In his story about walking through Genoa, Freud seems to be saying that he is afraid of women's sexuality and is afraid that they will castrate him. Freud is also saying that he is helplessly compelled to put himself in the place of women's sexuality, to reenact his fear of castration. His ambivalence, his desire and his fear, reach such a pitch that he can hardly contain himself. Uncannily, he revisits the place he finds both unknown and too well known: that is, strangely familiar. I would like to argue that Freud's uncanny story of the city represents something specific about the ways in which the city might be experienced as unknown. From this perspective, it is possible to suggest that the unknown city might be a city that should have remained hidden or secret; but such a suggestion ought to be immediately countered with the idea that there is, somewhere, a desire to know about this repressed world. Even more important, it may be that what we think of as being unknown about the city is secretly already known.

Indeed, the "un"-knowingness of the city may be the way in which the city works: there are many things that lie repressed below the city, away from our "knowledge"—and it is on these veiled, invisible, hidden, secret spaces that modern urban life rests. Awkwardly.

UNDERGROUND CITIES

So far, the unknown city I have discussed is a psychological affair. The urban geography of connections that lie buried, unknown, beneath the city are unconscious connections between everyday events and objects and the events and objects of childhood desires and fears. Thus, there is an urban geography of ambivalence: of desire and fear in the streets, as people move through them, crossing from one (familiar) place to another (strange) place. Journeys around the city are not always above ground, not always in full view. Instead, the city can become unknown as things are driven below the surface, repressed, openly buried.

According to Henri Lefebvre, there was a pit at the center of medieval Italian cities, into which rubbish was thrown, that also symbolized a connection to an underground world.[10] This pit was called the *mundus*. It was

> a sacred or accursed place in the middle of the Italiot township. A pit, originally—a dust hole, a public rubbish dump. Into it were cast trash and filth of every kind, along with those condemned to death, and any newborn baby whose father declined to "raise" it. . . . A pit, then, "deep" above all in meaning. It connected the city, the space above ground, land-as-soil and land-as-territory, to the hidden, clandestine, subterranean spaces which were those of fertility and death, of the beginning and the end, of birth and burial. . . . The pit was also a passageway through which dead souls could return to the bosom of the earth and then re-emerge and be reborn. As locus of time, of births and tombs, vagina of the nurturing earth-as-mother, dark corridor emerging from the depths, cavern opening to the light, estuary of hidden forces and mouth of the realm of shadows, the *mundus* terrified as it glorified. In its ambiguity it encompassed the greatest foulness and the greatest purity, life and death, fertility and destruction, horror and fascination.[11]

Surface and depth are counterposed through the spaces of the city and the body, each holding its own truth about life and death—simultaneously terrifying and glorified, the pit is also uncanny (in Freud's terms). And the pit introduces further narrative about the city: the underground connections that lie beneath the city tell of other ambiguities and ambivalences, bound up in life and earth, purity and foulness. Now, Lefebvre's analysis may not hold for cities elsewhere, but it does show that the spaces of the city are as much real as imagined, that the spatialities of the body are bound up in the production of urban spaces,[12] and that there are very strong emotional investments in the spaces of the city. The underground links one place to another in unseen, perhaps even unconscious, ways; but the underground is also the clandestine infrastructure without which the metropolis could not function. It may well be that looking into "the pit" will enable further explorations of the unknown city.

Beneath the city, there are connections that make the city work. These connections are not, however, innocent of power relations. The subterranean city becomes the site both of concrete connections within the city (and beyond) and of symbolic (even mythic) relationships between the city and the earth. Of course, as Lewis Mumford and Rosalind Williams have argued, the idea of the underground city has been the focus of both utopian and dystopian visions of urban futures.[13] But there is a stronger sense that metropolitan life is predicated on the technologies of the underground: real limits are imposed by the movement of water, sewage, electricity, information (via telephone lines), and people through, and beyond, the metropolis. Richard Trench and Ellis Hillman observe,

> Every time we turn on the tap, pull the chain, pick up the telephone, there is an underground movement: a gurgle of water, an impulse along a wire. Sometimes we are conscious of this movement; more often we are not. As we bask in the electric sunshine of our city surface, we are quite unaware of the subterranean labyrinth honeycombing the ground beneath our feet.[14]

The idea of the subterranean labyrinth gives a kind of mythic quality to the city under the city: a honeycomb of rat runs, a series of tubes and holes that hold, hide, and move those things "civilization" would rather not admit (to). Away from the glare of enlightenment, the repressed infrastructures of the city write themselves into the soil. And it is in the earth that the unknown traces of urban civilization might be found: as Williams reminds us, "the subterranean environment is a technological one—but it is also a mental landscape, a social terrain, and an ideological map."[15] Even so, the subterranean is also a space of burial, of loss of another kind, of death, of decomposition.[16] Below the sun-blessed surface is an entombed world of shrouded truths and meanings.

The development of the underground city involves a double-edged sword of progress (just as the unconscious involves the tension between opposing elements; just as the uncanny involves the play of the familiar and the strange): technologies capable of building the city underground are simultaneously destructive and creative.[17] In order to enable the metropolis to function, to clean its streets, to rid it of disease, and to allow ease of movement of goods, information, and people, there are a vast array of underground systems. As much as progress was measured in the size and spectacle of large buildings, grand projects, wide boulevards, so under the streets lay railways, sewers, gas and water pipes, pipes for compressed air and telephone (telecommunication) cabling. As architectural and urban design render the city on the surface known and transparent through spatial practices such as urban planning, streets are repeatedly dug up, reburied, and scarred by the doctoring of the city's intestinal world. The city is indeed built on networks of information, money, and people, but these do not exist in cyberspace: they are encased in iron and plastic under the ground.

Skyscrapers and trains are often the desired epitomes of the stainless (steel) success of the city: Kuala Lumpur celebrates its place in a global network of cities by putting up the Petronas towers; London and Paris move ever closer through the channel tunnel. Yet these triumphs have a fearful underground life: excavations and tunneling remain dangerous activities. Under solid ground, there is a world riddled with dangerous voids. The building of the metropolis is as destructive as it is creative, but its destructiveness, its dangers, and its wastes are openly buried, so that these are no longer discernible. Perhaps what we do not want to know about the city is that it creates new risks: the car crash in the tunnel, the breakdown in telecommunications, the fire in the underground station. The sense that the city is an orderly, unified system is bolstered by casting the unwanted into the pit; but the underground is an unmapped space, a map without clear passageways, a fragmenting and fragmented space of hidden infrastructures of power.

UNDERCOVER CITIES

Metropolitan life is often depicted as chaotic and disorderly—a place where unexpected, unpredictable encounters might lead to dreadful dangers (even while these encounters might be desired). The city becomes a space of paranoia, where unknown people are out to kill or harm, where there are undercurrents of crime and violence, with an underworld, an underclass. Buried below the civilized surface of urban life, there are spaces of secrecy: secret organizations inhabit the city, undercover; some are even supposed to serve and protect.

At Vauxhall Cross, there is a spectacular building, devised by architect Terry Farrell (see figure 15.1). This building is home to a government department: the secret service—MI6 (*MI* stands for "Military Intelligence"). Before we look at the building more closely, perhaps it would help to give a little background. While the British government has publicly admitted the existence of MI5,[18] MI6 does not officially exist. In part, this is probably because MI6 is responsible for protecting national security against external threats from foreign countries and organizations, which means, in effect, it must secretly gather information on and in other people's countries. It is hardly surprising that the British government would not want to admit to spying on other people. But we ought to be surprised to

15.1 | Vauxhall Cross, designed by Terry Farrell and Partners.

find that the new headquarters of its spy organization is a "post modern" "landmark" that will contribute to the "new look of London" (all expressions used by Kenneth Powell to describe the building).[19]

There is an obvious paradox here: what is a top secret organization doing in a highly visible building?[20] I do not have the answer, but there may be clues if we look at the facade of the building—if we look at the cover of the undercover city. The MI6 building is located on the Albert Embankment, on the south bank of the Thames, opposite the Tate Gallery. A riverside walk in front of the building gives the public access to the river and the stunning views of the Houses of Parliament and the sweep of the Thames.

When I visited the building, there were people on both sides of the Thames taking pictures of it. I was, as it were, not alone. Indeed, when I went into the building to ask about it, the staff there were very helpful—and they did not seem at all surprised by my questions about the building, referring me to Powell's book about the architecture, *Vauxhall Cross*. The building certainly is an attraction. Then again, so are the people who look at it: as you walk around, cameras whirl about, tracking every footstep. So, the paradox mentioned above seems to work out this way: first buy a spectacular building that attracts casual (and not so casual) attention, then cover the building in surveillance and antisurveillance equipment to watch those who come to look at it and to stop the onlookers from seeing too much. I find this economy of surveillance curious—and increasingly disturbing.

There is a fairly long story behind Vauxhall Cross, but it is enough to say that Terry Farrell produced a number of designs before the British government's Property Services Agency (PSA) agreed to buy the building—partly because the end users (MI6) had distinct requirements, including cellular offices, computer rooms, archive stores, and covered parking. Throughout these negotiations, certain principles kept the look and integrity of the design together. In particular, Farrell balanced the use of "solids" and "voids" to convey a sense not only of lightness and of air, but also of enclosure and of a human scale. It is this use of solids and voids that I will focus on, mainly because it might tell us something about the undercover city.

According to Powell, "the division between solid and void, precast and glazed cladding, on the exterior of the building is equally logical, reinforcing into three stepped blocks and the taut balance between monumentality and lightness which is the essence of the scheme."[21] Thus, the building embodies the idea of solids and voids, while meeting the requirements for enclosed and secure office spaces. The question is why solids and voids might be a "logical" extension of MI6's needs. Further, it might be asked why MI6 might agree to this balance between monumentality and lightness. Perhaps, then, "the essence of the scheme" says something about the essence of the secret service. Of course, monuments (even light ones) are associated with power. Certainly, for Lefebvre, the monument is one technique through which space is produced by power relations.[22] For him, monuments not only materialize power relations into space, but they also make that space mean something. In this way, those with power attempt to both localize and dramatize the meaning of space, partly by giving it an identity (perhaps in opposition to anarchy).

From this perspective, lightness and monumentality say something significant about the spatiality of power relations. We can infer that the power relations embodied at Vauxhall Cross are *simultaneously* "solid" and "void," both monumental and light. Thus, bland descriptions of the building, strangely, become sinister: "Superficially . . . the image of the building is one of strength: a portal guarding the way across the bridge. It provides an anchor, a point of identity in the midst of visual anarchy."[23] Architectural space is (hardly) a "superficial" representation of the strength and authority of both MI6 and secrecy in British society, yet the character and significance of this secrecy are quite unknown; this secret security seems to be very fragile, requiring a guard(ship). MI6 functions, almost, like a social unconscious: secretly making connections that cannot be explicitly examined, erupting into public life in unexpected ways—perhaps even organizing a "dirty tricks" campaign against Harold Wilson. Or, maybe, MI6 performs the role of a social superego, constantly vigilant of transgression against the state of affairs, a moral watchdog with deadly teeth. Either way, the building acts as a point of identity within anarchy. But it is designed on principles which suggest that identity is something that has to be constantly achieved in the face of oppositional tensions: between open and closed, between solid and void, between uncovered and covered-up, between life and death. If Vauxhall Cross conveys a sense of place, then this sense could be that this most visible of monuments renders space unknown, or it could be that we do not know what happens behind closed doors . . . or that we should be worried by the unknown effects of fixing identity through strength and authority.

We are still no nearer understanding the central paradox of secrecy/visibility embodied in the building. On the one hand, is unlikely to be a surprise to the world of spies that MI6 exists and therefore is hardly a threat to national security that this unknown organization should house itself in a spectacular monument (to the cold war?); on the other hand, inconsistencies still hang over the building, and I would like to finish with one more. When Farrell's designs for the building were originally valued, the cost was put at around £54 million. After discussions with the PSA, the

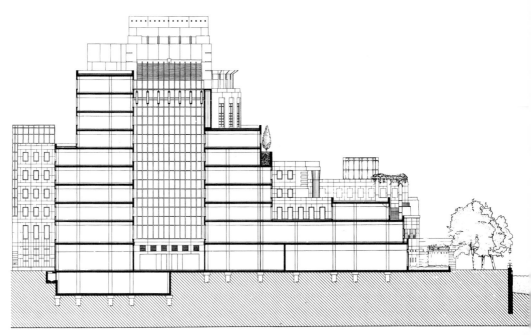

15.2 | Vauxhall Cross: longitudinal section.

agreed price—after adjustments for MI6's special design needs (which, I
guess, must have included greater security of fuel supplies, enhanced
bombproofing of walls and windows, electronic and acoustic countermea-
sures, and so on)—was £130 million. Despite the developer's (successful) attempts to keep the building on budget, estimates of the total cost of the
building vary between £240 million and £250 million.[24]

    Now, the building was always intended to have a second "fit" to in-
stall the "more complex" requirements of MI6; but I would like to know,
what cost the extra £110–120 million? Some have speculated that a secret
underground tunnel was built to connect MI6 with the MI5 building at 60
Vauxhall Bridge Road. If you visit the area, you might think this unlikely,
especially since the MI5 building has become available for rent. Perhaps, instead, the additional money was used to build a citadel, deep under the building's foundations. Of course, Farrell's longitudinal section for Vauxhall Cross
gives no indication that this might be the case. It shows only one basement,
which is supposed to house plant machinery (see figure 15.2). If this seems
far-fetched, remember that there are (huge) underground citadels underneath not only MI5's building in Curzon Street but also Whitehall (of which
the Cabinet War Rooms form only a small part) and various tube stations.

Could it be, though, that this extravagant and highly expensive building is simply camouflage—an excessive cover to disguise a deeper undercover world?

SOLIDS, VOIDS, AND TRACES OF THE UN(-)CITY

In this chapter, I have suggested that the unknown city can be thought about in many different ways. I have explored just a few—all related to a kind of underground or repressed urban life. I have touched on Freud's uncanny experience of walking through Genoa, looked into the underground systems that underlie and underpin modern urban life, and puzzled over the mystery of the highly visible cover of an undercover organization. These stories are interwoven, and I would like to conclude by pulling together some of the threads.

One thread is that there is no such thing as the known or the unknown city. The idea that either exists is a diversion: it is clear that spaces and places in the city are both known and unknown, both real and imagined—and they are known and unknown through the specific practices, discourses, and narratives that call them to mind, or bring them into (in)visibility. It is clear that the MI6 building both does—and in a very material way—does not exist. What goes on behind its closed doors, I can only guess at. Yet it writes itself through its building onto the face of London: simultaneously there and not there, as much solid as void. The building materializes identity, a sense of place, a city; its solids and voids are occupied by people who replicate and reproduce power relations that are simultaneously concrete and vacuous. The building houses "techniques of spatial occupation, of territorial mapping, of invasion and surveillance," which are the all-too-well-known "instruments of social and individual control";[25] it thereby dramatizes both the thereness and the not-thereness of power relations.

A further thread is that there is something "unconscious" about city life. This is not to reduce the city to unconscious motivations, but to say that everyday experiences are not simply rational nor fully knowing nor cold-blooded. An emotional life lies at the heart of the city—and the city can become a strange, pleasurable, hostile place through our reactions to its buildings (irrespective of conscious designs).[26] It is these unconscious reactions that inform Freud's uncanny experience. Desire and fear, of course, play a large part in urban lives: the city provides ample opportunities for expressing the passions. However, Freud's uncanny return to the place of desire and humiliation tells not of the presence either of desire or of fear, but of the way in which desire and fear are bound up one in the other. The unknown streets of known quality speak of the intermeshing of desire and fear:

they are both present and absent. The presence of one allows the other space, each becoming solid and void in the presence/absence of the other. If that sounded mystical, then how about this? Freud could only recognize the "known" quality of the "unknown" street once fear of the (un)known quality of the (sexed) female body had been shifted and sifted by desire into a fear of the (seemingly) known quality of the (apparently prostitute: supposedly aggressive) women. Through desire for and fear of the female body, the street becomes at once recognizable and unfamiliar. Freud was compelled to reenact his movement through the streets not because fear and desire were separate, but because they were bound up in each other; and it is this dynamic that bound him into helpless repetition. In this regard the city is not of unknown quality: it is, in part at least, built on the fragility and ambivalence of dominant masculinities and subversive femininities.

In each of these stories about the un(known) city is a sense of movement: unseen, hidden, closed off—for one reason and another. These movements are relayed at different scales: the walker on the streets, the movement of services (water, gas, sewage) through networks under the city, and the interconnections between and beyond cities through secret networks of information. None of these movements is "free," either in the sense of being able to go anywhere anytime, or in the sense of lying outside the infrastructures of power, infrastructures that enable as much as control movement. These movements create a porous city, whose boundaries are perpetually and necessarily crossed. But some boundaries are not meant to be crossed. And these boundaries are warily policed: as Freud becomes self-aware and alarmed, so the women become aware of, and "excited" by, Freud; as MI6 watch the edges of their building, people pass in and out constantly. Sometimes, in the shift from one place to another, something is revealed about the un(known) city—as Freud discovered on his street walk.

The un(known) city, furthermore, has required some digging beneath the surface to find the truth that lies below. However, depth models of knowledge remain obstinately difficult: truths are also to be found (as well as hidden) in surfaces, in facades, in the way things appear. A constant referral to subterranean processes carries the manifest danger of missing the obvious. And I would like to end this chapter on one obvious point: whatever is known and unknown about the city is produced and reproduced through power relations and resistance to authority, domination, and/or exclusion. But there is no map of the un(-)city; there is no map of power relations or of the memories of everyday struggles in the face of violence and oppression. The connections I have traced between the unconscious, the uncanny, the underground, and the undercover are the faded marks left by intersecting relations of power; traces are produced by the vacillation between the known and the unknown. This suggests that what passes under cover of the term *power* is as much solid as it is void, as much familiar as it is strange. What is normally called power is fragile, contingent, arbitrary; it is at its most barbaric when under threat, and needs to be believed to be effective. Is this why MI6 sits in its highly visible building—because now we *know* it is there (even though what it does is unknown)? And is it an exaggeration to say this is also a matter of life and death? Possibly. But from the familiar and the strange, specters of power appear to haunt the un(-)city.

Notes

1   "Behind Closed Doors" was the title of a *Time Out* special issue on what it described as "London's most private parts" (front cover, 10–17 August 1994).

2   These examples may be followed up in books by Andrew Duncan, *Secret London* (London: New Holland, 1995); William J. Fishman, Nicholas Breach, and John M. Hall, *East End and Docklands* (London: Duckworth, 1990); and Stephanie Williams, *Docklands*, ADT Architecture Guide (London: Architecture Design and Technology Press, 1990).

3   See Williams, *Docklands*, p. 136.

4   Iain Borden, Joe Kerr, Alicia Pivaro, and Jane Rendell, introduction to *Strangely Familiar: Narratives of Architecture in the City*, ed. Borden, Kerr, Pivaro, and Rendell (London: Routledge, 1996), p. 9.

5   Sigmund Freud, "The 'Uncanny'" (1919), in *Penguin Freud Library*, trans. under the editorship of James Strachey, vol. 14, *Art and Literature: Jensen's "Gradiva," Leonardo da Vinci, and Other Works*, ed. Albert Dickson (Harmondsworth: Penguin, 1985), p. 359.

6   For outstanding readings of architectural practices and the uncanny, see Anthony Vidler, *The Architectural Uncanny: Essays in the Modern Unhomely* (Cambridge, Mass.: MIT Press, 1992), and of the uncanny and urban practices, see Jane M. Jacobs, *Edge of Empire: Postcolonialism and the City* (London: Routledge, 1996).

7   Vidler, *The Architectural Uncanny*, p. 6.

8   Freud, "The 'Uncanny,'" pp. 363–364.

9   Vidler, *The Architectural Uncanny*, p. 79.

10   In part, my essay is "secretly" a response to one of Lefebvre's provocative assertions about psychoanalysis and the existence of an underground or repressed life to cities. See Henri Lefebvre, *The Production of Space*, trans. Donald Nicholson-Smith (Oxford: Blackwell, 1991), p. 36, and my brief reference to this in Steve Pile, *The Body and the City: Psychoanalysis, Space, and Subjectivity* (London: Routledge, 1996), p. 152 n. 8. Explaining the whole of modern urban life through the workings of the unconscious mind is, of course, intolerably reductive, but it may be

the case that there is an underground and repressed urban life and that this is strangely known.

11   Lefebvre, *Production of Space*, p. 242.

12   On this point see also Richard Sennett, *The Flesh and the Stone: The Body and the City in Western Civilisation* (London: Faber and Faber, 1994).

13   See Lewis Mumford, *The City in History: Its Origins, Its Transformations, and Its Prospects* (Harmondsworth: Penguin, 1961), and Rosalind Williams, *Notes on the Underground: An Essay on Technology, Society, and the Imagination* (Cambridge, Mass.: MIT Press, 1990).

14   Richard Trench and Ellis Hillman, *London under London: A Subterranean Guide*, new ed. (London: Murray, 1993), p. 7.

15   R. Williams, *Notes on the Underground*, p. 21.

16   Vidler, *The Architectural Uncanny*, pp. 117–146.

17   R. Williams, *Notes on the Underground*, chapter 3.

18   MI5 is tasked with internal security and intelligence gathering, and it has recently taken a role in countering the activities both of the Irish Republican Army and of organized crime and drug syndicates.

19   Kenneth Powell, *Vauxhall Cross: The Story of the Design and Construction of a New London Landmark* (London: Wordsearch, 1992), pp. 25, 10, 60.

20   Somewhat bizarrely, it is well known that this building is the headquarters of the British secret service. In the James Bond movie *Goldeneye* (1995), there are external shots of the Vauxhall Cross building. Similar images appear in Patrick Keiller's film *London* (1994), at a point when the narrator says that an air of secrecy pervades London life. It would be interesting to know whether MI6 permitted pictures of the building to appear in these films. More paradoxically, the latest Bond movie, *The World Is Not Enough* (1999), was refused permission to use exterior shots!

21   Powell, *Vauxhall Cross*, p. 75.

22   Lefebvre, *Production of Space*, chapter 3.

23   Powell, *Vauxhall Cross*, p. 79.

24   It sickens me to think that this building should cost about the same to build as four hospitals.

25   Vidler, *The Architectural Uncanny*, p. 167.

26   See Vidler, *The Architectural Uncanny*.

*All these elements of the general spectacle in
this entertaining country at least give one's
regular habits of thought the stimulus of a
little confusion and make one feel that one is
dealing with an original genius.*

Henry James
Transatlantic Sketches (1875)

*What, then, is the Dutch culture offered here?
An allegiance that was fashioned as the consequence, not the cause, of freedom, and that
was defined by common habits rather than
legislated by institutions. It was a manner of
sharing a peculiar—very peculiar—space at
a particular time{,} . . . the product of the
encounter between fresh historical experience
and the constraints of geography.*

Simon Schama
*The Embarrassment of Riches:
An Interpretation of Dutch Culture
in the Golden Age (1988)*

Edward W. Soja

16

On Spuistraat: The Contested Streetscape
in Amsterdam

In Amsterdam in 1990, I dwelled for a time on Spuistraat, a border street on the western flank of the oldest part of the Inner City. Squeezed in between the busy Nieuwezijds Voorburgwal (literally, on the "new side" of the original settlement, in front of the old city wall) and the Singel (or "girdle," the first protective canal moat built just beyond the wall), Spuistraat runs roughly north–south. It starts near the old port and the teeming Stationsplein, where the Central Railway Station sits blocking the sea view, pumping thousands of visitors daily into the historic urban core. At its halfway point, Spuistraat is cut by Raadhuisstraat, the start of the main western boulevard axis branching off from the nearby Royal Palace (once the town hall, or *raadhuis*) and tourist-crammed Dam Square, where the city was born more than seven hundred years ago in a portentous act of regulatory tolerance (granting the local settlers toll-free use of the new dam across the Amstel River, Amstelledamme becoming Amsterdam).

After passing the old canal house where I lived, the street ends in what is simply called Spui, or "sluice," once a control channel connecting the Amstel and the older inner-city canal system with the great bib of concentric canals that ring the outer crescent of the Inner City, or, as it is popularly called, the Centrum. The Spui (pronounced somewhere in between "spay" and "spy") is now a short, broad boulevard lined with bookstores, cafés, a university building, the occasional open-air art fair, and the entranceways to several popular tourist attractions, ranging from the banal (Madame Tussaud's) to the enchanting (the Begijnhof and, just beyond, the Amsterdam Historical Museum). The "city museum" offers the most organized introduction to the historical geography of Amsterdam, with roomfuls of splendid imagery bringing to life what you see first on entering: a panoramic model that sequentially lights up the city's territorial expansion in stages from 1275 to the present. Just as effective, however, as a starting point for an interpretive stroll through Amsterdam's Centrum is the Begijnhof, or Beguine Court.

The Begijnhof is a small window onto the Amsterdam *mentalité*, that bewildering Dutch mix of the familiar and the incomprehensible that so attracted Henry James in the 1870s and later inspired Simon Schama's brilliant portrayal of the "moralizing geography" of Dutch culture in its seventeenth-century Golden Age, *The Embarrassment of Riches*. One enters the Begijnhof through an arched oak door off Spui square, an innocently unmarked opening to an enticing microcosm of civic refuge and peaceful respite in a cosmopolitan Dutch world of ever-so-slightly repressive tolerance. Before you is a neat quadrangle of lawn surrounded by beautifully preserved and reconstructed seventeenth- and eighteenth-century almshouses, nearly every one fronted with flower-filled gardens. A restored wooden

16.1 | Begijnhof, Amsterdam.

house dates back to the fifteenth century, one of two survivors of the many fires that burned down the old city (and the original Begijnhof) before the more substantial Golden Age. The other survivor is located in a different kind of refuge zone along the Zeedijk, today known as the "boulevard of junkies," the tolerated and planned resting place for the city's residential corps of aging hard-drug users.

There are also two small churches in the Begijnhof, one dating back to 1392 but built again in 1607 and known since as either English Reformed or Scottish Presbyterian. Here the fleeing English Pilgrim Fathers prayed before setting sail on the *Mayflower*, comfortable in their temporary but dependable Dutch haven. On one of my visits, the church was filled with the concerted voices of the Loyola College choir from New Orleans, singing American spirituals to the passersby. The other church, a clandestine construction in 1665, was originally a refuge for Catholic sisters escaping post-Reformation Calvinist religious purges. One of its stained-glass windows commemorates the epochal "wafer miracle" of 1345, an event that boosted Amsterdam into becoming a major medieval pilgrimage center and began its still-continuing and far-reaching internationalization.[1]

The Beguine Court was originally founded one year after the miracle as a sanctuary for the Beguines, a Dutch lay sisterhood whose members sought a conventlike life but with the freedom to leave and marry if they wished—an early marker of the many Dutch experiments with what might be called engagingly flexible inflexibility. Today, the Begijnhof continues to be home to *ongehuwde dames* (unmarried ladies) who pay a nominal rent to live very comfortably around the lawned quadrangle and proffer their services to the ill and the elderly. Despite the flocking tourists, it remains a remarkably peaceful spot, a reflective urban retreat that succeeds in being both open and closed at the same time, just like so many other paradoxical spaces and places in the refugee-filled Amsterdam Centrum.

I lived just around the corner in another of these artfully preserved places and spaces, a relatively modest variant of the more than six thousand "monuments" to the Golden Age that are packed into the sustaining Centrum, the largest and most successfully reproduced historic inner city in Europe. With a frontage that seemed no wider than my driveway back home in Los Angeles, the building, like nearly all the others in the Centrum, rose four stories to a gabled peak embedded with a startling metal hook designed for moving furniture and bulky items by ropes in through the wide windows. Given my sizable bulk (I stand nearly two meters high and weigh more than an eighth of a ton), I had visions of having to be hoisted up and in myself when I first saw the steep, narrow stairwell (*trappenhuis*) to the first floor. But I quickly learned to bow my head and sidle in the doorway.

Golden Age taxation systems encouraged physical narrowness and relatively uniform building facades up front, squeezing living space (and stimulating expansive creativity in interior design) upward and inward from the tiny street- or canal-side openings. The patient preservation yet modernization of these monuments reflects that "original genius" of the Dutch to make the most of little spaces, to literally produce an enriching and communal urban spatiality through aggressive social intervention and imaginative grassroots planning. In many ways, the preservative modernization of the cityscape of the Centrum has been an adaptive feat on a par with the Dutch conquest of the sea.

Simon Schama roots Dutch culture in this moral geography of adaptation, an uncanny skill in working against the prevailing tides and times to create places that reinforce collective self-recognition, identity, and freedom. "Dutchness," he writes, "was often equated with the transformation, under divine guidance, of catastrophe into good fortune, infirmity into strength, water into dry land, mud into gold."[2] In Amsterdam, perhaps more so than in any other Dutch city, these earthy efforts to "moralize materialism" moved out from the polderlands to become evocatively urban, not through divine guidance as much as through secularized spatial planning, enlightened scientific management, and an extraordinarily committed civic consciousness that persists to the present. The canal house simulates this rootedness, enabling one to experience within it the very essence of a livable city, the agglomeration of individuals into socially constructed lifespaces that are always open to new possibilities even as they tightly enclose and constrain. The lived spaces of the Centrum are popularly designed to make density beautiful as well as accommodating, to flexibly enculturate and socialize without imprisoning, to make the strange familiar, and to add somehow to one's regular habits of thought that entertaining stimulus of a little confusion.

To live in a canal house is to immediately and precipitously encounter Amsterdam. The past is omnipresent in its narrow nooks and odd-angled passageways, its flower-potted corners and unscreened windows that both open and close to the views outside. Everyday life inside becomes a crowded reminder of at least four rich centuries of urban geohistory being preserved on a scale and contemporary intensity that is unique to Amsterdam. At home, one is invited daily into the creative spatiality of the city's social life and culture, an invitation that is at the same time embracingly tolerant and carefully guarded. Not everyone can become an Amsterdammer, but everyone must at least be given the chance to try.

The prevailing atmosphere is not, however, that of a museum, a fixed and dead immortalization of the city's culturally built environment. The history and geography are remarkably alive and filled with the urban entertainment that makes Amsterdam so attractively familiar and yet so peculiarly incomprehensible; neat and clean and regular but curiously tilted, puzzling; an island of mud not quite entirely turned into gold but transformed enough to make one believe in the creative alchemy of Amsterdam's modestly democratic city builders. From my vantage point on Spuistraat a moving picture of contemporary life in the vital center of Amsterdam visually unfolded, opening my eyes to much more than I ever expected to see.

The view from my front windows affirmed for me what I continue to believe is the most extraordinary quality of this city, its relatively (the Dutch constitutionally refuse all absolutes) successful achievement of highly regulated urban anarchism—another of the creative paradoxes (along with the closely related "repressive tolerance" and "flexible inflexibility") that two-sidedly filter through the city's historical geography in ways that defy comparison with almost any other polis, past or present. This deep and enduring commitment to libertarian socialist values and participatory spatial democracy is openly apparent throughout the urban built environment and in the social practices of urban planning, law enforcement, popular culture, and everyday life. One senses that Amsterdam is not just preserving its own Golden Age but is actively keeping alive the very possibility of a socially just and humanely scaled urbanism. Still far from perfection itself, as the Dutch never cease telling you, Amsterdam is nonetheless packed with conspicuously anomalous achievements. There is little or no boosterism, no effort to proclaim the achievements or to present them as a

16.2 | Spuistraat, Amsterdam, 1995.

model for others to follow. Instead, there is again, *pace* Schama, an unadvertised "embarrassment of riches," modestly reproduced as in the past on the moral ambiguity of good fortune.

There are many ways to illustrate this peculiar urban genius. The view through my Spuistraat window will do for a start. Immediately opposite, in a building very much like mine, each floor is a separate flat and each story tells a vertical story of subtle and creative city-building processes. It was almost surely a squatter-occupied house in the past and is probably one now, for Spuistraat has long been an active scene of the squatter movement. On the ground floor is an extension of the garage offices next door. There is a small "No Parking" sign on the window, but nearly always a car or two is parked in front. Our ground floor, in contrast, is a used book shop, one of the many dozens densely packed in this most literate of Centrums, the place where Enlightenment scholars from Descartes to Voltaire, Montesquieu, and Rousseau first found the freedom to have their works published and publicized without censorship.

One cannot avoid noticing that the automobile is an intruder in the Centrum. Spuistraat, like so many others, is a street designed and re-designed primarily for pedestrians and cyclists. Alongside the busy bike path there is a narrow one-way car lane and some newly indented parking spaces, but this accommodation to the automobile is tension-filled and wittily punctuated. The police are always ready to arrive with those great metal wheel clamps and the spectacle of their attachment usually draws apprecia-tive, occasionally cheering and laughing, crowds of onlookers. Traffic is nearly always jammed, yet (most of the time) the Dutch drivers wait pa-tiently, almost meekly, for they know they are guilty of intrusion and wish to avoid the steel jaws of public sanction. I was told that the city planners have accepted the need to construct several large underground parking garages in the gridlocked Centrum, but only with the provision that for every space constructed below ground, one space above is taken away.

On the first floor of the house across the way were the most obvi-ously elegant living quarters, occupied by a woman who had probably squatted there as a student but had by now comfortably entered the job mar-ket. She spent a great deal of time in the front room, frequently had guests in for candlelit dinners, and would occasionally wave to us across the street, for my wife, Maureen, and I too had our most comfortable living space just by the front windows. On the floor above there was a young couple. They were probably still students and still poor, although the young man may have been working at least part-time, for he was rarely seen, except in the morning and late at night. The woman was obviously pregnant and spent most of her time at home. Except when the sun was bright and warm, they tended to remain away from the front window and never acknowledged any-one outside, for their orientation was decidedly inward. The small top floor, little more than an attic, still had plastic sheeting covering the roof. A single male student lived there and nearly always ate his lunch leaning out the front window alone. His space made one wonder whether the whole build-ing was still a "squat," for if he was paying a nominal rent, one would have expected the roof to have been fixed, in keeping with the negotiated compromises that have marked what some would call the social absorption of the squatter movement in the 1980s. Civic authorities have actually issued pamphlets on "how to be a squatter" in Amsterdam, still another example of creatively regulated tolerance.

This vertical transect through the current status of the squatter movement was matched by an even more dramatic horizontal panorama along the east side of Spuistraat, from Paleisstraat (Palace Street) to the Spui. To the north (my left, looking out the front window) was an informative sequence of symbolic structures, beginning with a comfortable corner house on Paleisstraat that had been recently rehabilitated with neat squatter rentals (another contradiction in terms?) above. Below was a series of shops also run by the same group of rehabilitated and socially absorbed squatter-renters: a well-stocked fruit and vegetable market/grocery selling basic staples at excellent prices, a small beer-tasting store stocked with dozens of imported (mainly Belgian) brews and their distinctively matching mugs and drinking glasses, a tiny bookstore and gift shop specializing in primarily black gay and lesbian literature, a used household furnishings shop with dozens of chairs and tables set out on the front sidewalk, and finally, closest to my view, a small shop selling handcrafted cloth hats for women.

This remarkably successful example of gentrification by the youthful poor is just a stone's throw away from the Royal Palace on the Dam, the focal point for the most demonstrative peaking of the radical squatter movement that blossomed citywide in conjunction with the coronation of Queen Beatrix in 1980. A more immediate explanation of origins, however, is found just next door on Spuistraat, where a new office/construction site has replaced former squatter dwellings in an accomplished give-and-take trade-off with the urban authorities. And just next door to this site, even closer to my window, was still another paradoxical juxtapositioning, one that signaled the continued life of the radical squatter movement in its old anarchic colors.

A privately owned building had been recently occupied by contemporary squatters, and its facade was brightly repainted, graffiti-covered, and festooned with political banners and symbolic bric-a-brac announcing the particular form, function, and focus of the occupation. The absentee owner was caricatured as a fat tourist obviously beached somewhere with sunglasses and tropical drink in hand, while a white-sheet headline banner bridged the road to connect with a similar squat on my side of the street, also bedecked with startling colors and slogans and blaring with music from an established squatter pub. I was told early in my stay that this was the most provocative ongoing squatter settlement in the Centrum. It was

16.3 | Spuistraat, Amsterdam, 1995.

scheduled to be recaptured by the authorities several days after my arrival, but when I left the situation was unchanged, at least on the surface.

The view south, to my right, on Spuistraat presented an urban trajectory dominated by much more traditional forms of gentrification. Some splendid conversion, using fancy wooden shutters, modernized gables (no hook here), and vaulted interior designs, was transforming an old structure for its new inhabitants, who were much more likely to visit the boutiques and gourmet restaurants in the vicinity than the shops up the road. The transition quickened in a little restaurant row that ranged from what was reputed to be the best seafood place in Amsterdam and one of the grandest traditional centers of Dutch cuisine (called the Five Flies and fed daily by busloads of mainly Japanese and German package-tourists), to a variety of smaller cafés, Indonesian restaurants (considered part of Dutch cuisine), and fast-food emporia selling tasty bags of *frites*.

By the time you reach the Spui on foot, the street scene is awash again with activity and variety. A large bookstore shares one corner with an international news center, spilling over onto the sidewalk with newspapers, magazines, and academic journals from around the world as well as pamphlets, flyers, and broadsheets announcing more local events. There are beer pubs nearby, as well as an American-style cocktail bar and several representatives of the astonishing variety of specialized Amsterdam cafés. Tourist guidebooks list many different café types, each with its own internal variations: white, brown, and neo-brown; cocktail bars, gay bars, beer cafés, student cafés (differentiated by dress codes and academic disciplines), literary cafés, chess cafés, ping-pong cafés, theatrical cafés, high-tech cafés, 8 to 2 cafés, discotheques, and night pubs.

One of the Centrum's best known "white cafés" (just drinks) is located where Spuistraat meets the Spui. It is beginning to lose its yuppie edge, however, to the stand-up, quick service, "old-style" café next door, much better able to quench the growing thirst for nostalgia. Nearly adjacent but stoically distanced is a famous radical café, where an older clientele sits and glares at the sipping elites across the way. The dense territorialities here are invisible to the casual visitor and they may be blurring even for the Dutch, as the cosmopolitan mixture of Amsterdam takes over, globalizing the local street scene.

Just around the corner are a few of the Centrum's hash coffee shops, perhaps the best known of Amsterdam's almost infinite variety of meeting places. Their heady smoke flows out to fill the nostrils of passersby. While living on Spuistraat, I had the good fortune to be taken on an amazing tour of the entire inner Centrum by Adrian Jansen, author of a fascinating analysis of the geography of hash coffee shops in Amsterdam.[3] Jansen is the Baudelaire of the Centrum, a geographer-flâneur of the inner spaces of the city. He reads the Centrum on foot—he reputedly does not even own a bicycle—and writes on such topics as "Funshopping" and the Dutch taste for Belgian beer and beer halls. In his treatise on cannabis in Amsterdam, which ranges from Fellini-esque poetics to stodgy classical location theories (e.g., Hotelling's famous "ice cream vendor" model), Jansen describes life in Siberia, the name of a hashish coffee shop he took me to on our foot tour.

> Compared to the "Tweede Kamer," "Siberia" is a much larger coffee shop. Not only does it offer a large variety of soft drinks, but they also serve excellent coffee. The espresso machine guarantees high quality, as it does in most coffee shops. The table football game is in constant use. Some people come in to play cards. Others play a kind of home-made skill game, in which a bicycle bell sounds if someone is not doing too well. Not every visitor buys hashish or marijuana, and not everyone pays. A man, clearly on his way home from the beach, orders yoghurt and disappears soon after eating it. Two men from Surinam enter. One has a story about his jacket being stolen. He asks the coffee shop owner for a loan, since he and his friend want a smoke. He gets it, but the shopkeeper makes him

promise to return the money tomorrow. (I have reason to believe that the two use hard drugs as well. They are often to be seen at the "Bridge of Pills," a spot near my home where hard drugs change hands. Their hollow cheeked faces show small inflammations.) Hashish and marijuana are offered here in prepacked quantities; in small bags worth ten or 25 guilders. The ten guilder bags appear to be the most popular. The shop owner turns to me and says, "Hey, tell me, what do you think is the best coffee shop around?" A difficult question.[4]

My journey with Jansen opened up many spaces I would never have seen on my own, or with any other tour guide. Thank you, Adrian. Here's to your health.

Back on Spuistraat, the panorama being explored seems to concentrate and distill the spectrum of forces that have creatively rejuvenated the residential life of the Centrum and preserved its anxiety-inducing *overvloed* (superabundance, literally "overflood") of urban riches. At the center of this rejuvenation has been the squatter movement, which has probably etched itself more deeply into the urban built environment of Amsterdam than of any other inner city in the world. To many of its most radical leaders, the movement today seems to be in retreat, deflected if not co-opted entirely by an embracing civic tolerance. But it has been this slightly repressive tolerance that has kept open the competitive channels for alternative housing and countercultural lifestyles, not only for the student population of today but for other age groups as well. It has also shaped, in distinctive ways, the more "acceptable" gentrification process and helped it contribute to the diversity of the Centrum rather than to its homogenization, although this struggle is clearly not yet over.

This contemporary residential rejuvenation of Amsterdam requires some geohistorical explanation. Decentralization in the 1930s began emptying the inner city of offices and manufacturing employment, and postwar suburbanization continued the process in a heightened flow of residential out-migration not just to the polycentered urban fringe but beyond, to such new towns as Almere and Lelystad, planned and plotted in hexagonal lattices on the reclaimed polders of isotropic Flevoland. As has happened in every century after the Golden Age, the continued life and liveliness of the Centrum was threatened by exogenous forces of modernization. A turning point, however, was reached in the 1960s, as cities exploded all over the world in often violent announcements that the postwar boom's excesses were no longer tolerable to the underclasses of urban society. A contrapuntal process of urban restructuring was initiated almost everywhere in an effort to control the spreading unrest and to shift economic gears so that the expansionary capitalist momentum might be recovered.

The contemporary residential rejuvenation of Amsterdam's Centrum, more effectively than in any other place I know, illustrates the power of popular control over the social production of urban space in general and, in particular, over the ongoing process of urban restructuring. It has been perhaps the most successful enactment of the anarcho-socialist-environmentalist intentions that inspired the urban social movements of the 1960s to recover their "right to the city," *le droit à la ville*, as it was termed by Henri Lefebvre, who visited Amsterdam many times and whose earlier work on everyday life inspired the Amsterdam movements.[5] Lefebvre was particularly influential in the COBRA (Copenhagen-Brussels-Amsterdam) movement that formed in 1949 to reject the arrogantly rational modernization of state planning in the immediate postwar period and to release the pleasure of art in popular culture and everyday life. COBRA disbanded in 1951, but its inspiration continued to live on, especially in Amsterdam.

More familiar contemporary paths of urban restructuring can be found in and around Amsterdam, but the Centrum's experience verges on the unique. Uncovering this uniqueness is difficult, for it has been overlain by more conventional wisdoms, right and left, that see today only either a continuation of "creatively destructive" decentralization emptying the urban core of its no-longer-needed economic base (and hence necessitating more drastic forms of urban renewal to fit the core to its new role); or the defeat and co-optation of the most radical urban social movements by the governing powers (leading too easily to a sense of popular despair over what is to be done in these once radically open but now closing spaces of resistance). Both views can be argued with abundant statistics and effective polemics; but when Amsterdam is seen from the outside, in a more comparative and global perspective on the past twenty-five years of urban restructuring, a third view emerges.

In 1965, while Watts was burning in Los Angeles, a small group of Amsterdammers called the Provo (after their published and pamphleted "provocations") sparked an urban uprising of radical expectations and demands that continues to be played out on Spuistraat and elsewhere in Amsterdam's "magical center" of the world. The Provos became active in the previous summer and had rallied their famous "happenings" nearly every Saturday evening around *Het Lieverdje*, a bronze statue of a smiling street urchin that still stands in Spui square. At first the movement focused, with conscious irony, on an antitobacco campaign (the statue had been donated by a local cigarette manufacturer), but soon the Provos' provocations spread to antiwar, antinuclear, and antipollution protests.

Their "White Bikes Plan" (whereby publicly provided bicycles would be available for free use throughout the city) symbolized the growing resistance to automobile traffic in the Centrum that would far outlive the plan itself. Today, the network of bicycle paths and the density of cyclists is probably the most extensive and highest in any major industrial or even postindustrial city; urban planners routinely publicize their distaste for automobile traffic while flexibly accommodating its inevitability; and the people continue to take free public transport by simply not paying on the subway, tram, or bus. If the free riders are caught (by characteristically soft enforcers, usually unemployed youth hired as fare checkers), they make up names, for the Dutch were unique in pre-1992 continental Europe in having no official identification cards. Driving licenses, the universal stamp and regulator of personal identity in America, are nearly superfluous in the Netherlands and certainly not open to easy inspection. Integration into the European Union is today forcing the introduction of identity cards, but depend on the Dutch to find ways to keep them out of sight.

The Provos concentrated their eventful happenings in both Dam and Spui squares and managed to win a seat on the city council, indicative of their success in arousing wider public sympathies. Their artful challenges to hierarchy and authority lasted for only a few years, but they set in motion a generational revolution of the "twentysomethings" (my term for the youthful households composed mainly of students between the ages of twenty and thirty that today make up nearly a quarter of the Centrum's population) that would dominate the renewal of the Centrum over the next two and a half decades. In no other major world city today are young householders, whether students or young professionals, in such command of the city center.

After 1967 the movement was continued by the Kabouters (Sprights or Gnomes), who not only promoted a complete ban on cars in the Centrum but also developed plans for a full-scale greening of Amsterdam, with city-based farms, windmill-generated electricity, more open-space greenbelts, and special ministries for the elderly and the poor. In 1970, the "Orange Free State" was declared as an alternative popular government rallying around the last Provo city councillor, a key figure in the movement who was named ambassador to the "old state" and who would sit again in the 1980s on the Amsterdam City Council as representative of perhaps the most radical anarchist-Green party in Europe. A few years ago, when it came time to assign a council member to oversee the still-being-negotiated plans to construct a luxury office and upscale housing development in the old Oosterdok waterfront—Amsterdam's anticipated version of London's Docklands or New York's Battery Park City—the same radical anarchist environmentalist became the obvious choice. No better symbol can be found of the continuing impact of the twentysomethings: compromised to be sure, far from having any absolute power, but nevertheless aging with significant virtue, commitment, and influence.

The final renewal came with the full-scale squatter or *kraken* movement, beginning in 1976. The squatters launched their famous "No Housing No Coronation" campaign in 1980 and, for a few days, occupied a building near Vondel Park, declaring the site "Vondel Free State." Armed with helmets, iron bars, and stink bombs, the Vondel Free State squatters were eventually defeated by an army of 1,200 police, six tanks, a helicopter, several armored cars, and a water cannon. After 1980, the movement did not decline so much as become a more generalized radical pressure group protesting against all forms of oppression contained within what might be called the specific geography of capitalism, from the local to the global scales. Squatters, for example, merged into the woman's movement, the antinuclear and peace movements, and the protests against apartheid (a particularly sensitive issue for the Dutch) and environmental degradation (keeping Amsterdam one of the world's major centers for radical Green politics), as well as against urban speculation, gentrification, factory closures, tourism, and the siting of the Olympic games in Amsterdam.

The greatest local success of the squatter movement was ironically also the cause of its apparent decline in intensity and radicalness. This was to keep the right to accessible and affordable housing at the top of the urban political agenda by, in Virginie Mamadouh's words, "convincing the local authorities of the urgency of building more housing for young households and of prohibiting the destruction of cheap housing in the central city for economic restructuring, gentrification, or urban renewal."[6] Nowhere else did so much of the spirit of the 1960s penetrate so deeply into the urban planning practices of the 1980s and 1990s.

The population of Amsterdam peaked around 1965 at over 860,000. Twenty years later the total had dropped to a little over 680,000, but the Centrum had already begun to grow again; and, after 1985, so has the city as a whole. Many factors affected this turnaround, but from a comparative perspective none seems more important than that peculiar blend of democratic spatial planning and regenerative social anarchism that has preserved the Centrum as a magical center for youth of all ages, a stimulating possibilities machine that is turned on by active popular participation in the social construction of urban space. As the prospects for urban social justice seem to be dimming almost everywhere else today, there remains in Amsterdam a particularly valuable embarrassment of geohistorical riches.

Edward W. Soja

Notes

This essay has been extracted from "The Stimulus of a Little Confusion: A Contemporary Comparison of Amsterdam and Los Angeles," a chapter in my *Thirdspace: Journeys to Los Angeles and Other Real-and-Imagined Places* (Oxford: Blackwell, 1996), pp. 280–320. That chapter, in turn, was based on an original version published by the Centrum voor Grootstedelijk Onderzoek (Center for Metropolitan Research) of the University of Amsterdam in 1991.

1   The "miracle" apparently occurred when a sick man, unable to swallow the communion bread, spat it into a fireplace where it remained whole and unburned. The site of this holy event is commemorated under a small glass window embedded into the sidewalk near where the fourteenth-century Chapel of the Holy City formerly stood.

2   Simon Schama, *The Embarrassment of Riches: An Interpretation of Dutch Culture in the Golden Age* (Berkeley: University of California Press, 1988), p. 25.

3   A. C. M. Jansen, *Cannabis in Amsterdam: A Geography of Hashish and Marijuana* (Muiderberg: Coutinho BV, 1991).

4   Ibid., p. 14.

5   See Henri Lefebvre, "Right to the City," in *Writing on Cities*, ed. and trans. Eleonora Kofman and Elizabeth Lebas (Oxford: Blackwell, 1996), pp. 63–181.

6   Virginie Mamadouh, "Three Urban Social Movements in Amsterdam: Young Households in the Political Arena between 1965 and 1985," revised version (September 1989) of a paper presented at the conference "The Urban Agglomeration as Political Arena," Amsterdam, June 1989, p. 15.

Lynne Walker

17

Home and Away: The Feminist
Remapping of Public and Private
Space in Victorian London

The West End of Victorian London is normally understood as the center of the world of work and of institutions of power, "the masculine domain of modern, public, urban life" from which women were excluded.[1] But viewed in another way, through the experience of the independent, middle-class women who lived and worked there, this highly masculinized terrain can be remapped as a site of women's buildings and places within the urban center, associated with the social networks, alliances, and organizations of the nineteenth-century women's movement. This focus on a single strand is not intended to overshadow other readings of the sexed city, but instead adds another layer to the meanings of its diverse gendered spaces and their occupants.

Between 1850 and 1900, members of Victorian women's groups and circles experienced and reconceived "London's heavily patriarchal public and private spheres" in new ways that offered women opportunities for "control over their social actions and identity."[2] Normally, the identity of Victorian women was closely bound up in the home and their removal from public life. The "ideal divide"[3] that separated the legitimate spheres of men and women was deeply drawn between the public (masculine) world of remuneration, work, and recognition and the private, (feminine) domestic realm of home and family responsibilities, which were undertaken for love rather than money. Ideologically, the stakes were high; social stability, the good order of society, and even human happiness were perceived to be dependent on woman's presence in the home.[4]

At midcentury, middle-class woman's place in the home distinguished respectable femininity in opposition to the prostitute, the fallen woman of the streets, whom Henry Mayhew called the "public woman."[5] But in part responding to changing connotations of public in relation to woman and in part constituting new definitions of *public* and *woman*, independent middle-class women in London were able to take up public roles without losing respectability and at the same time change the nature of home and domesticity to include their work. Leaders of the women's movement who lived in London, such as Barbara Leigh Smith Bodichon, Dr. Elizabeth Garrett Anderson, Emily Davies, Emily Faithfull, and Millicent Fawcett, were able to build identities as respectable women with roles and activities linked to the public realm. Working from home or in premises nearby, philanthropists, reformers, and professionals used their London homes as political bases from which to address the wider world of public affairs.

This juxtaposition of home and work made the home a political space in which social initiatives germinated and developed. As we shall see, feminists such as Emmeline Pankhurst and Barbara Bodichon adapted their family homes for meetings and other events associated with women's rights, while the offices of related women's organizations, clubs, and restaurants were located within walking distance of their homes in Marylebone and Bloomsbury. This "neighborliness" was, on the one hand, the social glue of the women's movement in central London; on the other, it generated sites for political activities as well as providing easy access to the public realm on their doorstep. The apparatus of their "staged identities" as white, middle-class, British women[6]—the well-ordered home, the "good" address at the heart of London and of empire, the round of formal introductions, social calls, and duties, as well as a sense of neighborly connection for those who lived nearby—supplied the private, social matrix for public, political action. In addition, the presence and proximity in the city of feminist activists—such as Dr. Elizabeth Garrett Anderson, Barbara Bodichon, and Emily Davies in Marylebone and Emily Faithfull, Rhoda Garrett, and Millicent Fawcett in Bloomsbury—facilitated projects that developed from feminist concerns for women's education, employment, health, and financial and personal independence. These independent middle-class women were well-placed to cross and redraw the boundaries between public and private. As this chapter will explore, they devised tactics based on necessity and opportunity: working from home, gaining access to the professions, providing accommodation for their own needs (most notably in housing, health, and women's clubs and organizations), and appropriating space for women on the less-familiar ground of public institutions.

For these women in the late-nineteenth-century city, the intersection of gender, space, and experience produced control, or at least a sense of control, of social actions and identity. The positions that they took up remained deeply contested and within certain boundaries, but opportunities for developing new identities that differed from the social norm were offered at various sites in the city, both public and private. Moreover, not only were their groups and networks critical to the successful struggle for women's rights, but their socially lived identities were partly defined by the spaces they occupied, and in turn their presence produced the social spaces and buildings that they occupied—a process that was cumulative and reflexive, a process taking place over time, producing, and being produced by and within, dynamic gendered space.[7] In this sense, late Victorian women were producers as well as consumers of the built environment. Their presence helped determine the spaces provided, the building types constructed, the needs that were represented, and, most important, how it felt to be in public space: the ideas people received about themselves and the representations they were able to make when using architecture and the public realm.

WORKING FROM HOME

An important tactic that women adopted to negotiate a public presence was to work from home. In her many campaigns and projects, the artist and feminist Barbara Leigh Smith Bodichon operated from her house in Marylebone, which in 1855, in the early years of the organized women's movement, provided a meeting place for the group that petitioned in support of the Married Women's Property Bill.[8] From there, the first petition for female suffrage was assembled and dispatched to John Stuart Mill at the Houses of Parliament; it was delivered by Emily Davies and Elizabeth Garrett (Anderson), who had been recruited into the women's movement over tea at 5 Blandford Square.[9]

Later, Davies and Bodichon worked successfully for women's admission to university examinations and together produced one of the central achievements of nineteenth-century education: Girton College, Cambridge, which opened in 1873. For this venture, Bodichon's house was again called into action as an examination hall for the first candidates and later functioned as a place of entertainment and moral support for Girton students.[10] Elizabeth Garrett Anderson herself gained personal support, introductions, and encouragement at Bodichon's house for a career in medicine, helping her to become England's first female physician. After qualifying, she followed a pattern similar to Bodichon's, setting up both her home and place of work over the years on various sites in the West End.

After their first meeting, Bodichon sent Davies and Elizabeth Garrett Anderson off to the *English Woman's Journal*, the voice and center of the women's movement, which then had an office on Prince's Street, Cavendish Square. Bodichon funded the journal and was a founding member of the Langham Place group, as the network of women who wrote for the journal and were associated with its related projects were known (after its most famous site). In three different locations in the Oxford Street area (Prince's Street, Langham Place, and Berners Street) and in various combinations, a loose alliance of associated groups were housed with the *English Woman's Journal* (later the *Englishwoman's Review*), including the Society for Promoting the Employment of Women (SPEW), the Ladies Sanitary Association, the National Association for the Promotion of Social Science, and the Ladies' Institute.[11] That these organizations drew on the identity of the journal, and each other, as well as enjoying the advantages of a central site and a familiar place, is demonstrated by the way they either stayed with the journal over the years or spun off into nearby streets.

Like education and property rights, employment for women was a major theme of the movement; the Society for Promoting the Education of Women took practical steps to help women gain marketable skills and find jobs. Like the National Association for the Promotion of Social Science, SPEW helped direct women into new fields; for example, the Ladies Tracing Society (established 1875) provided training and employment in an office in Westminster for women to copy architectural plans.[12]

Members of the Langham Place group collaborated on projects that were motivated by feminist politics, philanthropy, and business necessity, and these mutually beneficial activities were developed and facilitated by the proximity of home and work. A resident of Bloomsbury (10 Taviton Street), the printer and philanthropist Emily Faithfull served on the women's employment committee of the National Association for the Promotion of Social Science. She established the Victoria Press in Bloomsbury (Great Coram Street) with the feminist and SPEW member Bessie Rayner Parkes, who edited the *English Woman's Journal* (which the Victoria Press published).[13]

Unlike Emily Faithfull, who followed her profession on a number of sites a short walk from home, Emmeline Pankhurst on moving to London in the 1880s initially made arrangements similar to those of earlier generations of women: she put home, work, and family together by living over the shop. After three years of selling arts and crafts products on the Hampstead Road,[14] Emmeline Pankhurst and her family moved to Russell Square (number 8, demolished; now the location of the Russell Hotel). There, she again combined public and private space—but this time to political ends, adapting her house for meetings of the Women's Franchise League (an organization that, contrary to its name, addressed a variety of social and political problems and included men among its members). In Russell Square, Mrs. Pankhurst gave birth to her fifth child, directed the upbringing of two other leaders of the Edwardian suffrage movement (her daughters Christabel and Sylvia) and received a stream of highly politicized visitors, described by her son Richard Pankhurst as "Socialists, Anarchists, Radicals, Republicans, Nationalists, suffragists, free thinkers, agnostics, atheists and humanitarians of all kinds," from Louise Michel (*La Petrouleuse*) to William Morris.[15]

A stone's throw from the Pankhursts' was 61 Russell Square (now the Imperial Hotel), the home (1881–1891) of Mary Ward, the writer and philanthropist who founded and built the Passmore Edwards Settlement in nearby Tavistock Place.[16] A great believer in higher education and a member of the council of Somerville Hall, Oxford's first college for women, from its opening in 1879, she nevertheless later became an active antisuffrage campaigner and suffragists' bugbear.[17]

Like her neighbor Mrs. Pankhurst, Mary Ward worked from home. From a small study, she produced her best-selling book *Robert Elsmere* (1889), about a clergyman who refound his lost faith through social work with the London poor. This successful novel signaled the building of the Mary Ward Settlement House, a local project that combined religious belief, philanthropy, and public service. By 1914, there were two dozen settlement houses in London where middle-class young men lived and worked to help the poor. At the heart of the settlement movement was the idea that by bringing the classes together, the perceived social crisis in the cities would be addressed and ultimately the nation regenerated. Having imbibed the settlement idea at Oxford, and following Keble College's Oxford House and Toynbee Hall in the East End, Mary Ward established her settlement house after two earlier false starts (also in Bloomsbury). A powerful committee that included the feminists Frances Power Cobbe, a member of the Langham Place Circle, and Beatrice Potter (Webb) helped set up the Mary Ward settlement, which accommodated an ambitious social program to meet the needs of the local working-class community and provided living quarters for the idealistic middle-class residents. These young people had come to share their lives in a way that would, they believed, heal class divisions and create a better urban environment for all.[18]

ACCESS TO THE PROFESSIONS

Women's struggle for access both for training and membership in the professions can be (re)mapped in the streets and buildings of the West End. University College, London, the Architectural Association, Middlesex Hospital, the Royal Institute of British Architects, and the University of London—all located in central London—were among the institutions that blocked or resisted women's medical or architectural education; and all eventually responded to pressure from women to open their doors.

Among the many women seeking a route into professional training and practice were Agnes and Rhoda Garrett,[19] who pioneered interior design and decoration from their studio/home at 2 Gower Street, Bloomsbury. The Garretts were cousins and members of the famous family that included Agnes's sisters, Dr. Elizabeth Garrett Anderson and Millicent Garrett Fawcett, leaders of the nineteenth-century women's movement and both clients of the design firm. For Agnes and Rhoda Garrett, like many women in what Deborah Cherry calls "the arena of high culture,"[20] design and the campaign for women's rights were a joint project. Their agenda included the entry of women into the professions, as well as full suffrage and the repeal of the Contagious Diseases Acts of the 1860s. Rhoda Garrett published "The Electoral Disabilities of Women" and, according to Ray Strachey, was an effective, impressive speaker on behalf of women's rights.[21] At the same time, the cousins' design book, *Suggestions for House Decoration in Painting, Woodwork, and Furniture* (1876)—one of many advice and information books written by women for women in the late nineteenth century—claimed a substantial role for interior designers, and indeed for themselves, in the design process.

ACCOMMODATING WOMEN

Among feminist priorities in the last quarter of the nineteenth century was the provision of respectable accommodation for single middle-class women working in the city. Agnes Garrett and her sister, Dr. Elizabeth Garrett Anderson, were directors of the Ladies' Dwellings Company (LDC), which built the Chenies Street Chambers, around the corner from Agnes's house in Gower Street. Aimed at accommodating professional women at a moderate cost, Chenies Street Chambers (1889) and York Street Chambers in Marylebone (1891) were the most successful and architecturally ambitious schemes of their kind in central London, while other similar residential projects flourished in the affluent inner suburbs of Kensington, Chelsea, and Earl's Court.[22]

In Chenies Street, co-operative principles applied: individual households retained their privacy but combined to pay the costs and share mutual facilities for cleaning, cooking, and laundry. Individual flats were of two, three, and four rooms, and although meals could be taken communally in the basement dining room, each accommodation was self-contained with either scullery or kitchen and toilet, larder, cupboard, coal bunker, and dust chute. R. W. Hitchen's system of silicate cotton and plaster slabs was employed for sound and fireproofing. Rents were ten to twenty five shillings per week, plus ten shillings for dining room and caretaker charges.[23] These arrangements suited residents such as Olive Schreiner, the South African feminist who wrote *The Story of an African Farm* and *Woman and Labour* and lived in Chenies Street in 1899,[24] and Ethel and Bessie Charles, the first women members of the Royal Institute of British Architects, who ran their architectural practice from the York Street flats.[25]

Feminist networks extended to male allies such as the architect of Chenies Street Chambers, J. M. Brydon, who trained Agnes and Rhoda Garrett and supported Ethel and Bessie Charles for membership in the RIBA.[26] While the access of middle-class women to design was restricted, as clients and patrons their participation was welcomed, which empowered many women in the public sphere. Through Elizabeth Garrett Anderson, Brydon was employed again for two other important women's buildings: the Hospital for Women (opened 1890), on Euston Road, and the London School of Medicine for Women (opened 1898), on Hunter Street near Brunswick Square. These women also relied on networks of kinship and patronage. Commissions for interiors and furnishings were forthcoming from

17.1 | Elizabeth Garrett Anderson's Hospital for Women.

Agnes's sister and Rhoda's cousin, Millicent Garrett Fawcett, in Cambridge and in London, and from Elizabeth Garrett Anderson for her own flat in Upper Berkeley Street; they also designed furniture for their Beale cousins' new country house, Standen, in Sussex. It was the intervention of Florence Nightingale, Barbara Bodichon's cousin, that ensured the funding and completion of Elizabeth Garrett Anderson's hospital on Euston Road.[27] As late as the 1920s, the architect Ethel Charles was designing a decorative scheme for paneling the library of her soldier brother at Camberley.[28]

An effective practitioner of doorstep philanthropy and one of the key members of the campaign for a Married Woman's Property Act to secure property rights for middle-class women was Octavia Hill. Unlike many of her feminist contemporaries, she had known financial insecurity personally and experienced firsthand the dire living conditions of the poor in the homes of toyworkers whom, to earn her own living, she had taught. Although her philanthropic schemes extended throughout London and her principles of housing management were widely influential, Octavia Hill's first experiment in architectural and social reform was undertaken in 1864 about a hundred yards from her own house in Nottingham Place (number 14), Marylebone, at the inappropriately named Paradise Place (now Garbutt Place).[29] By the early 1870s, her most ambitious program to date was only a short walk away in St. Christopher's Place, off Oxford Street, and involved the refurbishment and partial rebuilding of Barrett's Court, which was purchased with the assistance of Lady Ducie and of Mrs. Stopford Brooke.[30]

WOMEN'S CLUBLAND IN MAYFAIR

Women's place in the public sphere was supported and encouraged by clubs for women, which became a prominent feature of the West End in the second half of the nineteenth century. They provided feminists both access to the city, and thus a base from which to promote their agenda, and the facilities, elsewhere lacking, to meet women's basic needs. The Ladies' Institute was one of the first nineteenth-century clubs where women could eat, read, and meet their friends when away from home.[31] Nevertheless, even in the early clubs, membership and location rarely crossed class lines. Some clubs, such as the New Somerville, the Victoria, and the Tea and Shopping, were located in Oxford Street and Regent Street; but in the main, women's clubs were off the main thoroughfares, clustered in the streets of Mayfair associated with small, exclusive shops and elegant eighteenth-century mansions.[32]

Around 1900, the highest concentration of clubs was in Dover Street and its continuation, Grafton Street, the Pall Mall of women's clubland. As Erica Rappaport has pointed out, the trend was from earlier, consciously feminist, political clubs to later, more social, apolitical ones. The idea of private clubs for women was developed by female entrepreneurs, feminists, and philanthropists; it was popularized at the beginning of the twentieth century by the department stores, most notably Debenham and Freebody, Harrod's, Selfridge's, and Whiteley's. The Ladies' Institute, a feminist innovation; its latter-day incarnation, the Berners Club; and, most prominently, the Pioneer Club were, however, models for dozens of clubs that were set up for middle- and upper-class women who were away from home working, shopping, or enjoying other urban pleasures.[33]

Located on various Mayfair sites over the years, the most long-lived of all the women's clubs is the University Club for Ladies (today the University Women's Club), with a membership profile in 1898 of "graduates, undergraduates, students, fee lecturers, and medical practitioners."[34] In addition to meeting the needs of women in the city, feminist clubs provided a private space within the public sphere that produced public women. Their identity was formed through shared social interactions in a supportive and stimulating network, and forged in debate and discussion on a wide range of subjects. At the feminist Pioneer Club, a public identity, negotiated across gender and class, drew on the status and respectability of their location in a grand townhouse in aristocratic Mayfair and on representations of femininity in architecture, design, and fashion. The decorative language of

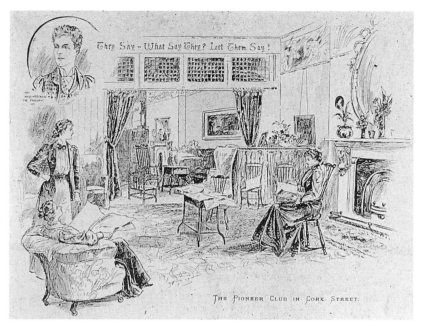

The PIONEER CLUB IN CORK STREET.

17.2 | The Pioneer Club, Cork Street, London.

the "Queen Anne" style employed at the Pioneer Club was perceived as most appropriate for the modern independent woman and for her femininity. The decorated interiors and their generous spaces were considered by contemporary observers to be elegant, refined, and suitably domestic for their female occupants. At the same time, other signifiers of class and rank, such as the oriental carpets and old oak furniture found in the houses of the rich in the West End, were used or referenced by the club and were valuable for creating a respectable (classed) identity.[35] Both the deeply contested position that these feminists took up in the late nineteenth century and the protection the new boundaries provided are represented in the motto inscribed on the drawing room walls: "They Say—What Say They? Let Them Say!" This inscription expressed feminist defiance within the Pioneer's fashionable, decorative interior, which smacked of modernity but negotiated their radical, outspoken sentiments and position through traditional signifiers of the dominant class.

Often modeled on the club's founder, Mrs. Massingberd, the identity of a feminist public woman was also produced and reproduced at the Pioneer Club through dress codes, demeanor, and bodily presentation:[36] short hair, upright posture, tailored frocks, badges (inscribed with their membership numbers), the use of nicknames, and abstinence from alcohol were the norm.

FAMILIAR GROUND

As one retraces the sites and spaces of Victorian London, new meanings can be read from familiar buildings and greater texture can be given to a new social mapping of the city. At the British Museum, for example, women readers were a feature of both the old library and of the domed Reading Room that opened in 1857.[37] Many were involved in systematic programs of self-education or in professional research and writing; among them were Eleanor Marx, who lived near the museum, and Clementina Black, who campaigned for equal pay and improved living conditions for working women and who supported herself through her research and writing at the museum, while sharing a bedsit with her sister across Tottenham Court Road on Fitzroy Street.[38] Two rows of ladies-only seating were provided in the Reading Room until 1907, but they were treated as unnecessary and generally were unoccupied.[39] In the museum itself, the expertise and authority of women guides were accepted by visitors, who were taken around the exhibits by peripatetic women lecturers.[40]

SPACE FOR WOMEN

The buildings and places, both public and private, that were the arena of women's groups and networks and the sites and spaces of lived female identities in London constitute a different mapping of the city. However, drawing out a single narrative strand from the larger urban fabric is problematic; it highlights women's presence and achievement and perhaps thereby blunts the critique of sexual difference, which accounts for their absence. Certainly, the focus on one group of women (i.e., those associated with the women's movement) does eradicate, if only temporarily, the representation of the experience of other numerous and diverse urban women, also users and producers of the spaces of the West End. There were working-class women, many of whom lived and toiled in their thousands as servants in the great houses of the West End; street sellers and entertainers; barmaids and female drinkers; prostitutes and performers; middle-class proprietors of shops—more than forty women shopowners were listed in Regent Street alone in 1891;[41] lower-middle-class and working-class shop assistants in the burgeoning department stores of Oxford Street and Regent Street; many kinds of students and lesson takers and teachers; and thousands of visiting consumers, both foreign and domestic.[42] Sheer numbers, or at least critical mass, were important to women's identity and experience of the city, and to their impact on spatial definitions and material culture; but in late-nineteenth-century London, class divisions remained as strong as gender bonds.

—

Unlike the usual architectural history of London, which focuses on architects and their monumental buildings, an approach that retraces and remaps the sites and spaces of the nineteenth-century women's movement prompts narratives of women's lives and experience. It takes us into the domestic sphere; into the gendered spaces of Victorian architecture; to sites of long-demolished buildings associated with the suffrage movement, philanthropy, women's education, and entry into and employment in the professions; and to a variety of architectural and social projects devised by women clients and patrons.

Although using the home for political ends was not new—it was familiar from antislavery campaigns[43]—the politicized home was a powerful political space for women. By blending public and private spheres through the conjunction of home and work, these women created new social spaces that challenged the traditional division between the public male institutions and the private female place of home.

While the home became both center and origin of women's organizations and networks, the activities of these nineteenth-century feminists were not, as we have seen, restricted to domestic space or identities. Public space, such as the offices of the *English Woman's Journal* and its associated organizations, was claimed and utilized to promote feminist goals and projects; by extension, such claiming normalized women's presence in the city. This concentration of women in the city, combined with their privileged backgrounds and positions, helped secure access to the public sphere and facilitated women's participation in public life and the development of a public ideology for women.

Lynne Walker

Notes

1   Lisa Tickner, *The Spectacle of Women: Imagery of the Suffrage Campaign, 1907–14* (London: Chatto and Windus, 1987), p. 14. Tickner discusses the challenge of Edwardian suffragists to this masculine domain. For the purposes of this paper, the boundaries of the West End are Regents Park (N). Haymarket/Piccadilly (S), Marble Arch (W), and Holborn (E). Compare, for instance, P. J. Atkins, "The Spatial Configuration of Class Solidarity in London's West End, 1792–1939," in *Urban History Yearbook, vol. 17, 1990,* ed. R. Rodger (Leicester: Leicester University Press, 1990), pp. 36–65.

2   Iain Borden, Joe Kerr, Alicia Pivaro, and Jane Rendell, introduction to *Strangely Familiar: Narratives of Architecture in the City*, ed. Borden, Kerr, Pivaro, and Rendell (London: Routledge, 1996), p. 12.

3   Griselda Pollock, "Modernity and the Spaces of Femininity," in *Vision and Difference: Femininity, Feminism, and the Histories of Art* (London: Routledge, 1988), p. 68.

4   See Leonore Davidoff and Catherine Hall, *Family Fortunes: Men and Women of the English Middle Class, 1780–1850* (Chicago: University of Chicago Press, 1987), and, e.g., Leonore Davidoff, Jean L' Esperance, and Howard Newby, "Landscape with Figures: Home and Community in English Society," in *The Rights and Wrongs of Women*, ed. Juliet Mitchell and Ann Oakley (Harmondsworth: Penguin, 1976), pp. 139–175.

5   Henry Mayhew, *London Labour and the London Poor* (1861; reprint, New York: Dover, 1968), 4:218. Also see Lynda Nead, *Myths of Sexuality: Representations of Women in Victorian Britain* (Oxford: Blackwell, 1988), and Judith Walkowitz, *City of Dreadful Delight: Narratives of Sexual Danger in Late-Victorian London* (London: Virago, 1992).

6   "Staged identities" is Jane Beckett's phrase.

7   See Shirley Ardener, ed., *Women and Space: Ground Rules and Social Maps*, rev. ed. (Oxford: Berg, 1993); Doreen Massey, *Space, Place, and Gender* (Cambridge: Polity Press, 1994); Henri Lefebvre, *The Production of Space*, trans. Donald Nicholson-Smith (Oxford: Blackwell, 1991); John Urry, *Consuming Places* (London: Routledge, 1994); and Jos Boys, "Is There a Feminist Analy-

sis of Architecture?" *Built Environment* 10, no. 1 (1984): 25.

8   Frances Gandy, Kate Perry, and Peter Sparks, *Barbara Bodichon, 1827–1891* (Cambridge: Girton College, 1991), p. 3. For Bodichon's role in art and women's culture generally, see Deborah Cherry, *Painting Women: Victorian Women Artists* (London: Routledge, 1993).

9   Jo Manton, *Elizabeth Garrett Anderson: England's First Woman Physician* (London: Methuen, 1987), pp. 48–49.

10   Gandy, Perry, and Sparks, *Barbara Bodichon*, p. 5.

11   I have found or checked the street addresses mentioned in the 1850–1900 volumes of *Kelly's Post Office Directory*.

12   "Lady Plan Tracers," *Englishwoman's Review* 7 (15 May 1876); 223–224.

13   B. C. Bloomfield, *Dictionary of National Biography: Missing Persons* (Oxford: Oxford University Press, 1993), p. 220.

14   Richard Pankhurst, *Sylvia Pankhurst: Artist and Crusader* (London: Paddington Press, 1979), p. 13.

15   Ibid., p. 15.

16   The Passmore Edwards Settlement was renamed the Mary Ward Centre in 1920, but it is often referred to as the Mary Ward Settlement House or simply Mary Ward House. Mary Ward wrote her novels under her married name, Mrs. Humphrey Ward.

17   John Sutherland, *The Mary Ward Centre, 1890–1990*, published lecture (ca. 1990). Sutherland also wrote *Mrs. Humphry Ward: Eminent Victorian, Pre-eminent Edwardian* (Oxford: Clarendon, 1990).

18   Adrian Forty, "The Mary Ward Settlement," *Architects' Journal*, 2 August 1989, pp. 28–48.

19   See Moncure Daniel Conway, *Travels in South Kensington* (London: Träbner, 1882), pp. 166–71; obituaries of Rhoda Garrett in the Fawcett Library (e.g., *Englishwoman's Review* 13 [15 December 1882]: 547–548); and Judith Neiswander, "Liberalism, Nationalism, and the Evolution of Middle-Class Values: The Litera-

ture on Interior Decoration in England" (Ph.D. diss., University of London, 1988).

20 Deborah Cherry, "Women Artists and the Politics of Feminism, 1850–1900," in *Women in the Victorian Art World*, ed. Clarissa Campbell Orr (Manchester: Manchester University Press, 1995), p. 49.

21 Ray Strachey, *Women's Suffrage and Women's Service: The History of the London and National Society for Women's Service* (London: London and National Society for Women's Service, 1927), p. 12.

22 "Old Maid, Answers . . . Ladies Dwellings," *Queen* 88 (4 October 1890): 507. For more on homes for working women, see Lynn F. Pearson, *The Architectural and Social History of Cooperative Living* (London: Macmillan, 1988), esp. pp. 45–55.

23 *Builder* 57 (9 November 1889): 332 (illus. p. 333).

24 Anna Davin, *Feminist History: A Sponsored Walk* (London: Community Press, 1978), p. 8. I am grateful to Jane Beckett, who recommended this publication, and to its author, who generously shared her copy with me.

25 See architectural drawings by Ethel and Bessie Charles, inscribed with their work/home address, British Architectural Library, RIBA Drawings Collection, Royal Institute of British Architects, London.

26 Conway, *Travels in South Kensington*, p. 170; Ethel Charles, RIBA Nomination Papers (1898), British Architectural Library, London.

27 Manton, *Elizabeth Garrett Anderson*, p. 286.

28 The scheme is now in the RIBA Drawings Collection.

29 Gillian Darley, *Octavia Hill: A Life* (London: Constable, 1990), pp. 91–93.

30 Ibid., pp. 132–143.

31 "19, Langham Place," *London Illustrated News*, 28 January 1860, clipping in City of Westminster Archives Centre. Set up by Bessie Parkes in Prince's Street, the Ladies' Institute moved with the journal to Langham Place, where it expanded with the addition of a luncheon room.

32 For street addresses and dates, see Lynne Walker, "A West-End of One's Own: Women's Buildings and Social Spaces from Bloomsbury to Mayfair" (November 1996), notes of an architectural walk organized by the Victorian Society (GB).

33 Erica Rappaport, "Gender and Commercial Culture in London, 1860–1914" (Ph.D. diss., Rutgers University, 1993), esp. pp. 170–198.

34 Lists of a dozen clubs with addresses and other details, reproduced from *Queen*; in Rappaport, "Gender and Commercial Culture," fig. 2. On clubs, see also Elizabeth Crawford, *The Women's Suffrage Movement: A Reference Guide, 1866–1928* (London: UCL Press, 1999), pp. 117–130.

35 For more on the decoration of the Pioneer Club, see Rappaport, "Gender and Commercial Culture," p. 186; she cites *The Young Woman* 4 (1895): 302 and *The Lady*, 6 April 1895, p. 585.

36 Jane Beckett and Deborah Cherry, "Sorties: Ways Out from behind the Veil of Representation," *Feminist Art News* 3, no. 4 (n.d.): 4. On Mrs. Massingberd and her club, see "Women's Clubs in London. III.—The Pioneer," *Queen* 94 (23 December 1893): 1081.

37 Engraving by H. Melville after T. H. Shepherd, *London Interiors* (1841), and *Graphic*, 16 January 1875; reproduced in Felix Barker and Peter Jackson, *London: 2000 Years of a City and Its People* (London: Macmillan, 1974), p. 303, figs. 7 and 6, respectively.

38 Davin, *Feminist History*, pp. 7, 10.

39 Barker and Jackson, *London*, p. 302.

40 Engraving in *Graphic* 1881; reproduced in Alan Bolt, ed., *Our Mothers* (London: Victor Gollancz, 1932), p. 155.

41 *Kelly's Post Office Directory*, entry for Regent Street, 1891. These shopowners included a chiropodist, a decorative artist, a photographer, a restaurant owner, numerous milliners, court dress- and glove-makers and makers of stays and mantles, as well as agencies owned by women for governesses, schools, and domestic staff.

42 See Mica Nava and Alan O'Shea, *Modern Times: Reflection on a Century of English Modernity*

Lynne Walker

(London: Routledge, 1996), pp. 38–76; Elizabeth Wilson, *Adorned in Dreams: Fashion and Modernity* (London: Virago, 1985), and *The Sphinx in the City: Urban Life, the Control of Disorder, and Women* (London: Virago, 1991); Walkowitz, *City of Dreadful Delight*; Rappaport, "Gender and Commercial Culture"; and Orr, *Women*. For theoretical reorientation, see Amanda Vickery, "Golden Age to Separate Spheres? A Review of the Categories and Chronologies of Women's History," *Historical Journal* 36 (1993): 383–414.

43 Lynne Walker and Vron Ware, "Political Pincushions: Decorating the Abolitionist Interior, 1790–1860," in *Domestic Space: Reading the Nineteenth-Century Interior*, ed. Inga Bryden and Janet Floyd (Manchester: Manchester University Press, 1999).

Part III

Tactics

18 Brief Encounters

a conversation with Alicia Pivaro

THEATERS, GARDENS, ROME, LONDON

As students of Bernard Tschumi at the Architectural Association [AA] we investigated what architecture meant as well as how it worked. Conceptual art and performance art—which could generate strong meanings out of relatively little—were very influential. In particular, most of our work had an art influence where there were strong metaphors for being in space; they addressed the body as an important component of the space you were in. Many of the projects were about devices which could reveal such ideas. For example, a housing project was a grid of blocks that were mirrored and cut through by a neon cross—which amplified the awareness of being in a particular place against the continuous texture of the city.

Some years later I became very interested in theater and gardens, which were both, in a sense, metaphors for experiences and real places. The theater relies heavily on conceptual strategies linking the stage and the auditorium, which was a formalization of the far more individual experiences that happen in gardens. The gardens around Rome, Siena, and Florence provided a highly mutated classical situation enabling the discovery of an existential quality beyond history.

Then there was Rome—I did not see it as just a collection of fabulous buildings with baroque city jammed between, but also a very sexy city. The obvious activities of the city—the shops, houses, and offices—were threaded with an additional layer, with other undercurrents that were erotic, sexy, and transgressive, and which in some way converted the spaces. The Piazza Navona was in fact an amazing theater of people—at night it was a huge melting pot for pickup and exchange. In other words you could read Rome as Fellini had in *La Dolce Vita*—that the coming together of a contemporary world of desire and gratification could make use of the baroque city in a way that was never intended. Such experiences helped me understand what I was interested in—about gardens, about spaces and cities, which most books merely describe in formal ways.

At this time we were also working under the waning influence of utopian architecture, of Superstudio and Archizoom, who had driven the tendencies of Archigram to a limit of a bland inevitability. This had converted the discussions that had been traditionally associated with architecture through the ages into new ironic possibilities. Therefore London, which was by no means Rome, became the focus of both the AA and our early work. The same sorts of things were beginning to happen whereby huge quarters of the city were losing their original interiors and had become ambiguous ruins—for example, Docklands. This change, in conjunction with shifts in street culture (which was no longer about glamour and

18.1 | Nigel Coates, *Prison Park,* 1974.

18.2 | Mark Prizeman, *The Chemical Works,* 1982.

aspiration but which had begun to regain a dystopian grit), became more and more important.

From a milieu of abstract investigations, I became more confident in encouraging the students to feed their work with what they were interested in, what they could see around them. There were components of the decayed city, technology, elements of disconnection and dysfunctioning places. There were lots of things you could do anywhere whether they were legal or not—changes to the postindustrial city had enabled a power to be taken back into your own hands (although inevitably as a power is gained another is also lost). One of the first projects I set in 1981 was *Giant-Sized Baby Town,* a title reworked from a BowWowWow song. It suggested that London's Isle of Dogs was a posttypical bit of the city, and that in some way it engendered the sort of clashes that could enable a lifestyle attitude to be expressed. By bringing together notions of work and home, the projects used the factory as a metaphor that undid the traditional relationship between the home and public space.

The next year we focused on Surrey Docks and on the more obvious pairing of art and science. Projects looked at different levels of art and culture, at institutional intentions that set down markers for certain kinds of collective activities with a cultural or leisure dimension. Overlaying this with a scientific vision of the electronic nomad—whether you were unem-

18.3 | NATO, no. 1 (1983), cover.

ployed and had a computer or video camera—possibilities were filled out, as in the pre-NATO [Narrative Architecture Today] project Albion.

All these things came together with an increasing enjoyment in the discord, decay, and juxtapositions of a city that had its sense ripped out of it, but retained a lot of artifacts. These artifacts in themselves contained a rich history—from rope making to shipbuilding to the connections with the rest of the world—and from here duplicitous scales emerged, from the imaging of spaces in terms of what they feel like, and what happens in them (as a moviemaker would imagine them), to having a global overview. Such contrasts were often deliberately ridiculous, such as thinking—because we were trying to influence the culture of architecture more than the specific future of a place—about what happens if Surrey Docks occupied half of the globe. We knew what would really get built would be a tacky mess.

DISCORD, DIFFERENCE, MOVEMENT, NARRATIVE

In the NATO period there were certain ingredients—in the organization of space, the understanding of the use of a place, its relationship with the older fabric of the city, and the kinds of illusion that the environment could make. Things from quite different sources could come together—all based on bringing the user into some *friendly zone of discord* so that questions were asked. Teaching, I thought, must have the same approach, since it is not about showing people what to do, but about creating an intellectual environment, a doing environment, stimulating quite radical juxtapositions, that can then be passed on through the building into the user.

Generating such an attitude is more difficult in our society than in say a city like Tokyo—a place where the old rules are so imprinted on people's minds that to transgress them is relatively obvious. I prefer places that are chaotic rather than cities like Rotterdam where everything is in place. At first Paris seems obvious too, but there is always something interesting behind the grand facades—the passageways and places where things have gone slightly wrong. Some cities have evidence of instinctual definitions of space where paths turn into roads across an unplanned landscape. These are all characteristics of Arabian cities: the capital of Yemen, Sana, is incredible for the earthy directness of its labyrinth of towers in symbiotic harmony with tumultuous activity.

For our early work, the entropic condition of Japanese cities provided a real testing ground. The layering and distortion of these cities is almost baroque. Tokyo is strikingly intense, a clashing of city material which adds up to a consistency of inconsistency; a twenty-story building next to a small wooden house, that is the condition. It rejects all the traditional thrust of trying to organize cities. For some of our Japanese projects we developed this feeling of the baroque, as a sensibility, as Deleuze describes it—as curiously modern, sensuous, granular, fluid, and mobile.

The question of difference is fundamental in this. A city ought to be a place which encourages the acknowledgment of differences, not necessarily addressing particular bits to particular people, but at least asking questions, being playful enough to permit the other. How to reconcile the

18.4 | Sana, Yemen.

18.5 | Caffe Bongo.

mass and substance of architecture with this kind of event is difficult, but any space will have components that can be used to amplify a sense of unexpected connection—and that can happen on lots of different scales. Our own office, for example, is an old industrial space. The rigid organization of desks emphasizes this, but we introduced blue sails, pushing the inside out and allowing the outside to come in. They are a parenthesis of the space that indicates a dynamic of observation, signs of movement, so as you walk through a building you feel a part of something else.

There is a way of generating a process of design that is to do with moving through space, and being a figure in a space. This can bring about quite different ideas that begin to modulate and therefore design that space. We don't work from the plan but from situations that are set up; we then start to interpret the situations from a pragmatic point while searching for what they allude to. In a small theater project in Poland we wanted to add a vital sense of the present. By repeating the proscenium arch on the outside of the building—so that you enter through it—a component of the inside is exported to set up a tension in space and meaning. For me a narrative component is derived from the thing itself. In other projects the tension is created by the character of spaces rubbing up against one another, where each space may be affiliated to very different things. In the National Centre for Popular Music in Sheffield, the main museum is housed in four drums, and between them is a cross. The building comes together like a piece of machinery, the intention being that the cross is the connection to the streets and passages, a continuation of the genetic coding that forms the street pattern of the city. While the drums are more industrial in character, more static—you enter each of them as into a cave. It is a very simple idea, but it sets up a complex dynamic. While designing I didn't really understand this complexity—I was working intuitively. My hunch was that the enclosed qualities of the domes would be very appropriate for the museum, when offset and emphasized by the open, elevated, free-flowing cross shape.

This sort of duplicity in form, through what it feels like, makes the experience at once familiar and not familiar, somehow commonly unfamiliar. This leads to what *narrative* architecture is really about. It is not an architecture that tells stories, so much as an architecture that has additional fragments of choreography and insinuation that contradict the first-order vocabulary. The museum and other current projects are more abstract with their narrative. Today, our work is getting cleaner. It doesn't have this sense of collage that our work may have had before, but the transformational mechanisms and illusions are there—just simplified. To strip down is a process of amplification, and the way things work on the mind and body are far

18.6 | National Centre for Popular Music, Sheffield. Image by Branson Coates.

18.7 | Jigsaw, Kensington High Street, London. Drawing by Nigel Coates, 1988.

more important than what they look like in a photo. This is more of a cinematic sensibility than one of the frozen image.

But in some of our earlier work there was an overriding desire to assault the senses. For example, the Katharine Hamnett shop was very piled on—a plethora that doesn't seem to work anymore. Similarly, Jigsaw in Knightsbridge used the Italian palace as a narrative, which seemed to be the right concept for that part of town. In some way you had a feeling that the place was attracting you and involving you, distracting you, and turning around what you are actually there for—the clothes. Many people go into a shop, dive at the rails, and won't have a clue where they are but they take the environment in peripherally. These shops were formed around the idea of places in the city that are stimulating but at the same time familiar. In some odd way you belong, which contrasted with straight chic or minimalism. This attitude comes from never seeing architecture as a cultural end in itself—it is always contingent. Not to see it as such is out of tune with the way people use the city—which is all sorts of signs threaded together from the car dashboard to the views from the top of a bus, hoardings, closed-down shops, people . . .

REFERENCE, IDENTITY, CHANGE, MEANING

In Japan, we did not set out for people to really understand our references. As we were just pillaging our own toolbox, never intending our work to be read as one meaning, we were creating environments rich and stimulating enough to be interpreted differently by whoever went to them. In a curious way this sort of multiplicity was exactly right for Japan. People didn't really know what the bits meant, but they knew that there was something they liked about how they added up. We were one of few practices building in Japan who had looked around at the sense of what made a Japanese town— and took the mishmash in. When many Japanese architects were going on about purity and Zen, creating little islands of contemplation, effectively turning their backs on the city—we enjoyed the fact that there were electrical cables hung festively along every street, massive zebra crossings, traffic then people switching, choreographed chaos.

As in London, the people and the traffic are the blood pulsing through the city. But many historic cities have had their centers cleaned up and "heritagized"—and so have had that very vital sense taken away, suppressing the chance danger and unpredictable experience that makes the essence of the urban experience.

Duplicitous by nature, the city is something you can never know or understand completely, can never want to predict. Like us, the city constantly wrestles for control and the loss of it, always wanting something new to happen while wanting security to preside. This I see as an existential parallel to the practice of architecture. The way we are now is so very interesting in that the environment is becoming more and more contrived and controlled, but we are far more capable now of thinking laterally, of interacting in between our thoughts, expression, and desires, of being attuned to a much more intangible environment, through information space, markets, clubs, and music—even relationships are much less prescribed. I just think that all this can influence the culture that you work with in architecture and if it doesn't—if you try to tidy up—it falls back into the same old form.

Whilst in buildings as well as cities there must be components for orientation, there must also be a sense of getting lost—traditionally an anathema to architects who always strive to make things clear. I put my own identity in my work to a huge degree—there is a deliberate ambivalence in finding sources in things I like. If you are completely detached from what you do, and don't use your own experiences as a laboratory, then that touch isn't there. But at the same time I always undo that part, so that I can let go. Our work sends out different signals for different people. My sexual orientation is not fundamentally important in our work—except that maybe an understanding of duplicity provides something extra. There are components of the masculine and feminine in what I do—never meant specifically for men or women—that indicate a sense of evolution, towards confounding interpretation. This may not always be obvious, it may be that I'm as chauvinistic as Le Corbusier was, but that is not what I'm trying to do. I try to include elements of self-criticism and retreat.

Architecture is a public art, a setting up of frameworks which are never absolute in use or interpretation. Each project is different. I don't mind that some of the interiors in Japan no longer exist. Some things come together at a time, cause a stir, then conditions change. I think that is all part of the way cities evolve. What is important is to do with what the original project intended. Like Rachel Whiteread's *House*—we knew it was going to be demolished, and its passing reinforced what was important about it: it is a memory.

I never want to build monuments. I have an excitement for the way that places are, and therefore try to extrude what is there and then pile in narrative metaphors for what it is, building up a condition which isn't just read once but also has a sense of the way it is used and added to. There is a need for architects to bring together conflicting layers of signs, layer components that set off triggers, generate erotic conditions in space. But for me these conditions are always familiar—the hallucinating effect of nightclubs, the way Soho has changed, ships and the Thames and its bank (HMS *Belfast* is the best building in London). They create a frisson in a place, in small scale and large scale with a constant switching of effects. The cultural role of architecture has huge potential, but people will become more interested in architectural expression only when it comes to parallel something intimate in their lives.

装置はいかにして都市生活に飲みこまれ、
どろどろに消化されながら同時に発展していくのだろうか
とりわけハードコアなテクノポリス、東京で未来の
A&V生活を想像することは、不気味に刺激的である。
ロンドン気鋭の建築家ナイジェル・コーツが描いてみせる
我らがハイファイ・ライフの行く末、とくと御覧あれ。

18.8 │ "Gamma Tokyo" design for cover of *Brutus Magazine.* By Nigel Coates.

18.9 │ *Ecstacity,* exhibition installation, Architectural Association, London, 1992.

18.10 | Alexander McQueen fashion show, Royal Agricultural Show.

18.11 | "Bridge City" for Habitable Bridge competition. By Branson Coates, 1996.

Note

This text is an edited version of an interview of
Nigel Coates by Alicia Pivaro, conducted in the
summer of 1997.

The power of a work of art derives from
its economy. Whether simple or complex,
the work of art must be efficient.

Carl Andre
interview with Paul Sutinen (1980)

19 Live Adventures

Urban art projects can embody a critique of the physical and institutional spaces in which they are located. But they also involve urban forms of practice, and this too is part of the critique. The three projects discussed here are marked for us by an increased inclusion of the processes surrounding artistic production within the artwork itself; the involvement of people from a range of organizations in realizing the work, together with the role of viewers as participants, has meant that beyond their physical presence, these works constitute live interventions into systems or situations.

In our own practice, we began operating without a studio for economic and logistical reasons; but over time this rootlessness has come to inform our operations in more profound ways. Because our work can take place anywhere, we are more able to respond to the very particular qualities of a site. For us, the artists' studio space has never been essential as a creative locus. Realizing our work brings us into contact with bureaucratic systems, and consequently administration is an essential part of our practice. We move around the city—usually on foot, tracing more or less purposeful connections between London sandwich bars, public libraries and park benches, stock photo agencies, toolshops, and light industrial units. Walking in the city brings a direct physical aspect to the understanding of distance, topography, and scale that has formed an important element of our installations.

In its finished form, our work is often sculptural, yet the way it is conceived relates in part to the juxtapositions of collage that stem from our background in photography and graphic media. We use images principally in two ways: practically, to plan and visualize projects in advance and to document them on completion; and theoretically, as ready-made elements incorporated into the substance of the work. In our finished work we present rather than represent.

By relocating industrial and consumer goods, often through single gestures, our projects have become involved in complex situations. The titles we choose are taken from a diverse range of sources within the public domain, and often in current use. We use titles not to describe but to add another element, which can gradually bring meaning.

While our work is to some extent identifiable by technique and formal devices, its key feature is a critical engagement with the prevailing ideas and attitudes that underlie consumer culture within late capitalism. Familiar yet evolving urban forms such as shopping centers, business parks, and road networks continually offer new manifestations of those ideas and attitudes.

This choice of subject matter and our mode of dealing with it has been a response to living and working in the city; in particular, we are interested in how patterns of social, political, and economic organization

19.1 | *Camelot:* in progress.

19.2 | *Camelot:* overview

19.3 | *Camelot* at night.

manifest themselves in the spaces and boundaries of the urban environment. Thus, rather than attempting to produce our observations from a traditionally "oppositional" viewpoint, our work aims to connect different values and ideas so as to encourage a certain reflective skepticism toward individual actions and their collective results. Our work combines these social concerns with certain formal and conceptual art-historical references in order to aestheticize a "twisted critique" of the sites and contexts we engage with. While our formal concerns fuse with an ideological engagement, we also hope to retain an element of good humor.

CAMELOT

Camelot was a site-specific installation produced for *City Limits*, a group show curated by Godfrey Burke and organized by Terry Shave, head of fine art at Staffordshire University, in September 1996. The show consisted of an exhibition in the university galleries and several new site-specific commissions around the city of Stoke-on-Trent. When we visited, we intuitively decided to work on one of the most neglected public sites.

The site in Albion Square is distinct yet typical of those found in many other cities: a poorly planned intersection of heavy flows of foot and vehicle traffic. Although the site marks the entrance to Hanley town center, it is defined only by three irregularly shaped patches of trampled grass, flanked with anti-pedestrian brickwork, and cut off by traffic on either side. Rather than using a public art commission to superficially enhance the site, we decided to produce something that would engage with the very conception of "public." In one sense, our piece—*Camelot*—was a literal interpretation of the "city limits" theme, as it aimed to provoke reflection and debate on the physical and social boundaries that often determine the patterns of city life. *Camelot* used 120 meters of 3-meter-high steel palisade security fencing to deny people access to these small, neglected fragments of public urban land.

By reinforcing the boundaries of these grass verges with an excessive display of authority, we raised the status of the land through its enclosure. In the context of the contemporary debate around security and access within town centers, *Camelot* explored the political notion of the "tragedy of the commons"—that is, the tendency of resources not under private ownership to fall into neglect. While construction work was taking place we encountered a great deal of very real—at times threatening—anger from local people passing by or visiting the piece. Through many discussions, it became apparent that the neglect of this site was held to be symptomatic of a lack of communication between the electorate and their representatives on the town council.

A related photographic work exhibited in the university gallery referred to the more subtle ways of channeling movement around the privileged lawns of the "ivory towers" of Oxbridge colleges. No security fences are required here. Instead, time-honored codes of conduct dictate who is entitled to walk on the grass. Few members of the public would risk the embarrassment of rejection from the quadrangle: spaces such as these have, since antiquity, challenged visitors to rank themselves according to the hierarchy of English social class and academic status.

The project title, *Camelot*, referred to the phenomenally successful United Kingdom National Lottery, an institution on which many artistic and cultural projects are increasingly financially dependent. The lottery organizers' choice of "Camelot" evokes a mythical "golden age" of English history, when the court of King Arthur established fair play in a feudal society through the code of chivalrous behavior. Perhaps the old idea that only an accident of birth separates the prince from the pauper underlies today's popular interest in the journey from rags to riches through the luck of the draw.

A particularly positive aspect of our *Camelot* was that it raised the status of the site and triggered debate; the resulting publicity focused attention onto the local authority council. We will be interested to see how the site will be permanently improved when funds are made available.

PARK IN THE PARK

Across Two Cultures: Digital Dreams 4 in Newcastle-upon-Tyne, November 1996, was a conference and exhibition programmed by Lisa Haskel and curated by Helen Sloan that explored the links between scientific and artistic practice. We worked with London-based architects and town planners West and Partners, the Ordnance Survey, the National Remote Sensing Centre, and aerial photographers to produce *Park in the Park*—exhibited in a new and as yet unoccupied office development on Newcastle's Quayside.

This project questioned whether the "purity" of scientific knowledge becomes compromised through its translation into public policy or goods and services for the market. City planners, policy makers, and corporate strategists now have access to precise and detailed scientific data as a result of combining satellite remote sensing and aerial photography with geographical information systems. However, the technologies' potential for radical planning could be better used for long-term solutions to the problems posed by unlimited demand for finite resources. *Park in the Park* foregrounded the relationship between consumer demand, land use, and urban planning.

19.4 | *Park in the Park:* installation.

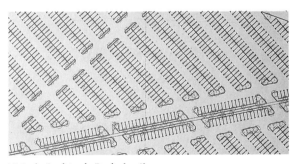

19.5 | *Park in the Park:* detail.

19.6 | *Park in the Park:* installation.

Official projections up to the year 2025 forecast that car traffic in the United Kingdom will continue to grow steeply;[1] yet according to conventional wisdom, increased demand must be accommodated. *Park in the Park* critiqued this short-term technocratic approach by proposing the conversion of Newcastle's Leazes Park into a vast pay-and-display car park. This strategic plan to increase private car parking at the expense of public green space aimed to provoke questions on where the limits are for car use.

The installation explored these ideas through cartography because through interpreting and communicating complex information, map drawing combines editorial skill, artistic judgment, and scientific rationale. Maps make visible, and even reproduce, certain aspects of the social relations of power, such as how property and mobility are manifested in land use and transport. Maps and plans are central to the whole process of land development, from identifying a new business opportunity, through gaining planning permission, to construction and end use.

West and Partners was briefed on the project and spent several weeks designing a fully functional car park, complete with coach and disabled parking provision, landscaping, and modifications to the local road network. The design was realized with a combination of recently launched Ordnance Survey *Superplan* data and in-house CAD software.

The core of the work, which combined these urban designs with digital maps, aerial photographs, and satellite images, was produced to "lock in" to the context in which it was exhibited: the expansive empty spaces of the new Quayside office development. To engage with the site, which offered far more floor than wall space, maps were produced to a very large scale, resulting in 5-, 3-, and 1-meter squares. These were positioned on the floor, forming echoes between various grid systems—relating the tiles of the aerial photographs and Ordnance Survey maps to the standard carpet tiles on the floor and to the tiled suspended ceiling. Rather than forcing the digital maps to fit the grid of the building, we aligned them due north. This combination of formal decisions put viewers in a privileged position—looking down on the ground plane, easily able to identify and orient themselves in relation to features in the cityscape—and encouraged them to make links between the bland, detached exhibition space and their own mental map of the city.

NEW HOLLAND

While *Park in the Park* challenged viewers with a scenario in which consumer demand could push the urban landscape to a new extreme, the final project discussed here used ideas about the urbanization of the countryside as a main point of entry. This came through *East* 1997, an international group show curated by Lynda Morris at Norwich School of Art in association with the Sainsbury Centre for Visual Arts, University of East Anglia. We were invited by Nicola Johnson and William Jeffett to produce a site-specific installation at the the Centre, which was designed by the architects Foster Associates to house the Sainsbury's art collection. Norman Foster had insisted that the building should relate to the scientists of the University of East Anglia: "The site chosen terminates the major linear sequence of university buildings—being adjacent to the School of Biological Sciences at the end of the cranked teaching block and related to what is seen as the 'domestic' scale of Norfolk Terrace."[2] Another aspect of the site is that the Sainsbury Centre is set in an artificial landscape: a former golf course complete with lake created from a flooded gravel pit. Similarly, what appears to be a lawn immediately in front of the center is in fact a Dutch-built "green roof" covering the Crescent Wing galleries underground—also designed by Foster—and creating an apparent fusion of architecture and landscape.

New Holland grew out of a consideration of the relationships between architecture, economic activity, and cultural responses to the landscape in a consumer society. The installation consisted of a new steel structure based on an industrial/agricultural building, positioned outside the main entrance to the Sainsbury Centre. In size and proportion— $10 \times 20 \times 33$ meters—the structure referred to a "Bernard Matthews" turkey breeder unit, though it had neither doors nor windows. The heavy mechanical beat of a blend of rap, house, and garage music from CD compilations could be heard pumping out from the darkness inside.

On one level, *New Holland* exploited tensions between English romantic representations of landscape, exemplified by Henry Moore's nearby sculpture, and the realities of modern industrial agriculture as experienced in Norfolk's intensive turkey farms. The structure was at once entirely appropriate yet uncomfortably out of place in its physical and institutional context.

Spatially, the work simultaneously divided and linked the Sainsbury Centre and the Henry Moore "reclining figure" sculpture. Foster's building, which proposes a technocratic patriarchy, and Moore's vision of nature as "Mother" signify two sides of modernist ideology in architecture and agriculture. Positioning our work outdoors questioned the Centre architecturally and institutionally, yet the piece was not created in terms of a simple opposition: instead, *New Holland* occupied a space of controlled rebellion.

Architecturally, the barn's system-built construction methods and materials addressed Foster's award-winning structure, with its rationale of

19.7 | *New Holland:* in progress.

19.8 | *New Holland:* overview.

19.9 | *New Holland:* overview.

the "well-serviced shed." (Coincidentally, the Bernard Matthews turkey farm we visited when researching *New Holland* links with Foster's references to aviation in the Centre, as this "farm" is located on a former U.S. air base, with the barns built directly on the old runways.) Visitors approaching the Centre were confronted with a bland but imposing structure clad entirely in nonreflective, polyester-coated pressed steel (as preferred by planning committees). The structure referred primarily to a modern farm building, but it would be equally acceptable in a retail park or industrial estate. In the beautiful grounds of the Sainsbury Centre it could be seen as the "country cousin" at a smart garden party, or yet another infill development in an unspoiled rural idyll.

The house and garage music further played on the notions of rebellion in the piece, with the mechanistic succession of repetitive beats evoking the now-traditional invasion of the countryside for weekender raves, while at the same time considering the absorption of youthful dissent into the blind hedonism of mainstream consumer culture. Parallels emerged between the barn's containment of music related to black culture and the Sainsbury Centre's containment of ethnic (African, Oceanic, pre-Columbian, and oriental) objects: in each structure, the cultural product could be grasped as representative of some "primitive other."

As well as being the name of a leading manufacturer of farm machinery, the title "New Holland" called to mind historic links between the Netherlands and East Anglia, including patterns of trade and the engineering methods used to reclaim land from the sea.

—

As is evident from these three projects, it is important that all our finished installations have a material presence and be experienced in a particular context. Each piece is manifested as physical objects positioned in real space, but each is the result of a process of interaction with a wide range of systems and organizations, from local turkey barn builders to the National Remote Sensing Centre. This way of working not only gives us a continually changing insight into some of the forces shaping the built, natural, and social environment, but it also exposes our emerging ideas to indifference, criticism, and the test of relevance to "everyday life." We are constantly surprised and reassured at the amount of time given to us by people who have no direct connection to the art world.

Our works are of course realized within a capitalist economy: the material objects we use and the spaces into which we place them are inevitably part of the commodity system. Yet even though producing these works has involved commercial transactions, and each addresses issues at the intersection of economics and culture, they have resisted commodification because of their specificity to a particular site. Because each was a temporary intervention into a social system and physical space, we have been allowed a degree of "freedom" from official and institutional restraint that is highly uncommon for works on permanent public display.

Ultimately, these projects have articulated elements from the commodity system, before dispersing them back into it; the works' unrehearsed and live realization in public spaces involved a degree of social interaction that connected the sites to wider ideological forces.

Notes

This chapter is based on a presentation given at the "Parallel Spaces" conference, Institute of Contemporary Arts, London, 5 July 1997, programmed by Lisa Haskel.

1   Royal Commission on Environmental Pollution, *Eighteenth Report: Transport and the Environment* (London: HMSO, 1994), p. 19.

2   Andrew Peckham, "This Is the Modern World," *Architectural Design* 49, no. 2 [A.D. Profile 19: Foster Associates' Sainsbury Centre] (1979): 6.

20 ^{Fat}

It's Not Unusual: Projects and Tactics

Fat's architecture is generated via the use of familiar icons that are altered and collaged together to create new environments, in which the elements are recognizable yet uncanny. Rather than creating idealized urbanisms that look to mythical utopias of the past and present, Fat's urban projects attempt to deal with and give creative and critical expression to the economic, social, and urban realities of the twentieth-century city. These architectural projects are informed by urban art events that appropriate familiar urban sites—such as the bus shelter, the billboard, and the "for sale" sign—to promote work that invites the active participation of the viewer and exploits the idea that the urban environment is experienced as movement between sites as well as a series of urban spaces.

JUST DO IT

The art events that Fat instigates aim to set up structures within which both the artist and viewer can participate in a more proactive and thereby critical way. The tactics employed in the projects attempt to penetrate the mythology that currently protects the business of contemporary art production and consumption. Mythologies that stem from a historical tradition are inbred in fine art education, nurtured in the media, and confirmed in the institution/gallery in its promotion of the artist as individual genius/product. Fat aims to force a critical debate between the general public and artists, one that is more usually only voiced in a reactionary vein in response to sensationalist tactics. Fat rejects the sensational because it remains generally unreadable, or readable on only a few levels and therefore exclusive. Members of Fat are not cultural terrorists. To explode myths and address core issues Fat works, controversially, from the inside out. Utilizing the tactic of leaching—intervention and recoding within existing structures such as the media, advertising spaces, prestigious/exclusive art events, urban transport systems—we aim to explore, challenge, and possibly explode current notions of what is perceived to be art and to oppose traditional conceptions of authenticity, authorship, and value endorsed by the art world.

THE EXPLODED GALLERY—FAT AT THE LIMIT
OF ARCHITECTURE

Gallery is, of course, a far from neutral term, describing a far from neutral space. The space of the art gallery is a dependent territory of the institution—which acts by conferring cultural and economic status on the objects and events occurring within its jurisdiction. When the boundary that marks the perimeter of the gallery is erased, the seal that prevents the contamination of the art space from external influence is broken.

Now Fat is not interested in destroying the gallery. Through a series of urban art projects, members are proposing architecture at its very limit—an architecture that arises out of provisional and negotiated relationships between objects, environments, and programs. It is an "extended architecture," in which the architecture resides not in the making of boundaries but in the relationships between event (function) and territory (space). These projects construct new urban experiences by the redistribution of the gallery program through a variety of existing urban situations. The program either becomes a device used to slice through the city (*Outpost*), making a new set of connections between its previously unconnected parts (the go-go bar, the National Gallery, a Burger King), or is parasitically attached to existing forms of urban program (the "for sale" sign, the bus shelter, the advertising site). The projects are sited outside the gallery so that we can explore how the meaning and significance of a work of art are read against the context in which it is experienced. A number of artists involved in the projects subvert the conventional identification of "artists" as a small number of "inspired" individuals.

Fat aims to invest architecture with a critical agenda that draws on current conceptual tendencies in fine art as well as on contemporary architectural practice and theory. Through a critical analysis of architectural rep-

20.1 | Fat, installation for *Fused* at the Royal Institute of British Architects, London, 1997.

20.2 | Fat, 1997.

resentation, ideology, and iconography, the work of Fat raises relevant cultural questions about the current limits of architecture and the means of its production. Recent built projects have explored the contemporary possibilities of architecture with respect to both program and expression.

OUTPOST

Fat has staged three *Outpost* events, two within the 1993 and 1994 Edinburgh Festivals and the third at the 1995 Venice International Art Biennale. Both the Edinburgh and Venice international festivals were chosen because as established prestigious events, they guaranteed that Fat's challenge to conventional cultural ideology would come to the attention of a large, international, and diverse audience, including the media. *Outpost* consists of a massive collectable exhibition of artworks. Those taking part in the project each produce one hundred business card–sized artworks, together with a corresponding number of signature cards. These artworks are then dispensed, free of charge, from gravity-loaded dispensers in diverse locations around the city. The locations range from private and national galleries to contexts less associated with the consumption of art, such as Burger King franchises, go-go bars, newsstands, parks, and so on. The viewer then compiles his or her own exhibition by retrieving the cards from the venues and, if desired, the corresponding signature card from the *Outpost* sales desk. The cards can be collated in the *Outpost* collectors album.

20.3

20.4 | Fat, *Outpost Venice Biennale,* 1996. One thousand artists from thirty countries produced 200,000 pieces of artwork.

THE MIRACULOUS TRANSFORMATION OF SPACE BY EVENT

The six to ten seconds on 22 November 1963, during which John Kennedy was struck by gunfire, are the most intensely studied few seconds in history. There are eighty-two still and movie photographers known to have been in Dealey Plaza during the assassination. Attempts have been made to identify every person appearing in each frame of film, and their histories have been investigated by federal commissions, criminal and civil courts, the mass media, and, most significantly, by an assortment of private citizens who are not satisfied by the official accounts.

NEW CHOPPER

The crisis of late postmodernism: media, size, style, content. Rather than being a limitation, the required business card–size of the *Outpost* artwork and the artwork/signature separation encourage a conceptual response. Rejecting the macho premise that big art is best art, the idea becomes (bigger than) the artwork. The divorced signature encourages the audience to explore the relationship between the image and signature cards; and rather than a pure statement of authorship, the signature card becomes essential to and the "other half" of a specific work. Artist response: image cards display mounted medical dressings with seemingly random dates—the corresponding signature cards reveal the childhood incident that required the dressing: "New Chopper Christmas 1968."

MULTIPLE NARRATIVES

Just as conspiracy theory explodes the myth of a single linear history, architecture can be seen as not the fastidious refinement of an abstract language but the site of collisions between competing ideologies. Architecture becomes a trip across the wavebands, samples of disassociated, but recognizable, story lines. A single narrative thread is lost, thereby making possible multiple readings. Despite their questioning of the official or the proper, when taken individually conspiracy theories represent a search for the authentic, the true story. Collectively, though, they deny the possibility of such a search.

MOD CONS

In the paranoid world of the conspiracy theorist, the elegantly positioned mezzanine level becomes the perfect sniper's nest. In *Mod Cons* familiar objects from the domestic realm are displaced around the city: shower equip-

20.5

20.6 | Domestic incidents photographed in the city, London. Fat, *Mod Cons,* 1996.

ment in the square, a welcome mat at the entrance to the shopping arcade, a bedside table in the bus stop. The municipal fountain is not so much an abstract symbol of civic pride as a nice place to take a bath.

BURGER KING VERSUS THE GALLERY

Who has a more highly developed sense of taste: the dancers in a go-go bar or visitors to the National Gallery? Where would you most like to see Damien Hirst's *Mother and Child Divided* exhibited: in a Burger King or in a post office? Or is it made specifically for the architecture of the gallery? Like all Fat art, the *Outpost* projects highlight the way in which the experience of art is affected by the context in which it is encountered. Art is consumed within architecture, whether that be the architecture of the home, gallery, street, shop, or office. *Outpost* aims to ensure a critical response to the urban context from both audience and practitioners. The sites occupied by the *Outpost* dispensers are intentionally diverse, forcing the viewer to realize that readings of the artworks will be different according to the site they occupy. The same piece of artwork is obviously construed differently when read in the Museum of Modern Art compared to a Burger King or the Casino Municipal, although its signatureless value is also equal within the different contexts. The dispensers located around the city invite the viewer to explore a prescribed route as well as to cross through different urban territories; casino, newsstand, museum. The context outside the gallery is intended to elicit a site-specific response from the practitioners, allowing them to address the urban condition outside the gallery, which in turn informs the viewer. Artistic response to context included laminated sachets of urine, symbolizing the marking of (artistic) territory.

F1

The annual arrival of F1 (Formula 1 motor racing) to the principality of Monaco provides an alternative model of urban planning. It is a temporary (and recurring) anomaly—an impossible combination of scenarios that undermine the supposedly "natural" condition of the city (the closure of the possibilities that make up the city). It is this rupture in the understanding of the city that provides an opportunity to change the relationship between the civic institution and its citizens, offering a possibility that the city is an ephemeral experience (as opposed to the permanent, the definite, and the monumental)—it is a simultaneous experience of programs, events, meanings, iconographies, and bylaws.

20.7 | Ten central London bus shelters were used as installation sites for collaborative work between musicians and arts practitioners—shelter by Beaconsfield. Fat, *Roadworks*, 1997.

ADSITE

Adsite is a project that utilizes the tactic of parasitic urban intervention. Two hundred bus shelter advertising sites within central London were hired and occupied by the work of as many artists, architects, and other practitioners. The existing London bus shelter system was chosen primarily because it was accessible both to the practitioner and to the audience; it was highly visible, occupying a site within an urban context that transcended the limitations of the traditional gallery system. *Roadworks* set out few curatorial requirements to the participants; there were no rules regarding content, the only stipulation being the prescribed size.

SOCCER CITY

The types of buildings that are admitted into the architectural canon share an abstract idea of the kind of space architecture is interested in. To contrast two examples, the art gallery (as a prime "architectural space") and the football pitch (as an "uncanonized space") display very different conceptions of what space is, or what spatial experience might be. The art gallery is a passive, contemplative, and abstract space, while the football pitch is active and dynamic. There spatial relationships ebb and flow and space is made legible, creating meanings that are experienced and seen—threat, danger, attack, promise, big, tight, pressure, open. Think of how football commentators can articulate sophisticated spatial analysis, in comparison to the difficulties (and hence the imprecise vagaries) architects have in describing the nature of their "abstract" space.

20.8 | Fat, *Soccer City,* 1995.

PANINI'S FOOTBALL '97

The *Outpost* catalogue utilizes the interactive and obsession-inducing format of the collector's album in order to encourage the viewer to make personal taste and value decisions in assembling his or her collection, which essentially becomes the exhibition. Negating the fixed format of a traditional exhibition catalogue, the album is made up of a series of diverse but accessible texts written by a variety of contributors; they range from rap rantings to academic arcana. Fifty blank pages follow the text, into which the artwork and corresponding cards, notes, and drawings can be inserted as the individual collector chooses.

COLLAPSED GEOGRAPHIES

Fat's urban art projects move art out of the contemplative space of the gallery to be experienced in the habitual space of the urban realm. Freed from the support structures of the gallery (both as social and physical institution), art is left to fend for itself, its value no longer prescribed by the regimes of liberal intellectual taste. Architecture, similarly, is already experienced in a blur of habit. Its mechanisms of order and control are all the more powerful for their supposed neutrality. Fat sees these as not simply unsavory facts to be ignored in the pursuit of a nice detail, but as points of creative departure. A running track in the office or a gallery in the park disrupts our expected readings of program and territory, pointing to possibilities of differing modes of occupation and behavior.

20.9 | Intervention challenging preconceived ideas of taste and value at Royal Academy Summer Show, London. Fat, *Red Dot,* 1995.

20.10 | Conversion of ex-Baptist chapel, London. Fat, *Chez Garçon,* 1995.

BLOOD MONEY

Outpost attempts to encourage practitioners and viewers to develop a more critical and intimate relationship with artwork by setting up structures within which participants can escape the passive roles of production and contemplation and become the real critics, collectors, and curators of the exhibition. Within these more proactive roles, participants can explore concepts such as taste, value, and the economies of art. Historical influences are impossible to escape; however, Fat would like the viewer to be free to evaluate artwork aside from economic influences enforced by a system intent on promoting certain artists' works as being in "good taste." *Outpost* addresses the "value" of artwork—the signatures are priced by the artists according to their own conceptions of value. This results in a diverse range of exchanges that include blood, money, spit, urine, kisses, and so on, according to the concept of the specific artwork. The decision as to whether they value their collected works enough to make the required exchange is left to the viewers.

DECORATIONS AND ORNAMENT

Throughout Fat projects, the main concern is with surfaces—with the meanings that are inscribed onto surfaces. From *Red Dot*—the application of small, round red stickers to the walls of the Royal Academy during the "Summer Show," where the ornamental addition of a red dot below a piece of art communicates a cultural and economic value; to *Chez Garçon*—the cladding of a stud partition with shiplap, where the surface of the partition wall gives it a meaning through its reference to particular building type and so to a range of associated environmental, geographic, and programmatic meanings; Fat is interested in the direct communication of information (as opposed to the modernist legacy of the "dumb box," which demands that one regard surface as neutral, at times able to be without meaning). Fat uses a range of tactics to this end, involving the appropriation of forms and sites and cutting or pasting alternative functions and meanings. The appropriation of the "for sale" sign as a site for the display of art has immediate consequences: the message of a familiar form of communication is altered, the nature of the art object changes through its relocation, and the experience of the street is altered as it becomes the site for a gallery.

Within *Brunel Rooms*, the program of a nightclub is combined with alternative forms and uses. A garden shed becomes a bar, a suburban living room a chill-out area; and surfaces are used to communicate meanings—the carpet linking the main room with the chill-out room patterned with running track, the cloakroom a glowing swimming pool.

20.11 | Images produced in collaboration with the residents of a London street, displayed on "for sale" signs outside the occupants' respective houses. Fat, *Home Ideals,* 1997.

20.12 | Nightclub interior, Swindon. Fat, *Brunel Rooms,* 1994–1995.

20.13 | Nightclub interior, London. Fat, *Leisure Lounge,* 1994.

Dolores Hayden

21

Claiming Women's History in the Urban Landscape: Projects from Los Angeles

Layered with the traces of previous generations' struggles to find their livelihoods, raise children, and participate in community life, the vernacular urban landscape, as John Brinckerhoff Jackson has written, "is the image of our common humanity—hard work, stubborn hope, and mutual forbearance striving to be love,"[1] a definition that carries cultural geography and architecture straight toward urban social history. At the intersection of these fields lies the history of urban space and its public meanings. How do urban landscapes hold public memory? And why should feminists and scholars of women's history struggle to create projects honoring and preserving women's history as part of public culture?

Every American city and town contains traces of historic landscapes intertwined with its current spatial configuration. These parts of older landscapes can be preserved and interpreted to strengthen people's understanding of how a city has developed over time. But often what happens is something else. Cycles of development and redevelopment occur; care is not taken to preserve the spatial history of ordinary working people and their everyday lives. Instead, funds are often lavished on the preservation of a few architectural monuments along with the celebration of a few men as "city fathers." (For example, in New York City, many buildings designed by the architects McKim, Mead, and White at the turn of the century are closely identified with an Anglo-Saxon, Protestant, male elite who commissioned the private men's clubs, mansions, banks, and other structures from which many citizens were generally excluded.) In contrast, modest urban buildings that represent the social and economic struggles of the majority of ordinary citizens—especially women and members of diverse ethnic communities—have frequently been overlooked as resources possibly suitable for historic preservation. The power of place to nurture social memory—to encompass shared time in the form of shared territory—remains largely untapped for most working people's neighborhoods in most American cities, and for most ethnic history, and for most women's history. If we hear little of city mothers, the sense of civic identity that shared women's history can convey is lost. And even bitter experiences and fights that women have lost need to be remembered—so as not to diminish their importance.

To reverse the neglect of physical resources that are important to women's history is not a simple process, especially if preservationists are to frame these issues as part of a broader social history encompassing gender, race, and class. First, it involves claiming the entire urban landscape, not just its architectural monuments, as a key part of American history. Second, it means identifying the building types—such as tenement, market, factory, packing shed, union hall—that have housed women's work and everyday lives. Third, it involves finding creative ways to interpret these modest buildings as part of the flow of contemporary city life. This means devising a politically conscious approach to urban preservation—complementary to architectural preservation—that emphasizes public processes to nurture shared memories and meanings. It also means reconsidering strategies for the representation of women's history and ethnic history in public places, as well as for the preservation of places themselves.

Early in the 1980s, when I was teaching at the Graduate School of Architecture and Urban Planning at UCLA, I founded The Power of Place as a small, experimental nonprofit corporation, to explore ways to present the public history of workers, women, and people of color in Los Angeles. It began as an unpaid effort, with a few students as interns—I also had a full-time teaching job. Los Angeles is an ethnically diverse city. It always has been, since the day when a group of colonists of mixed Spanish, African, and Native American heritage arrived to found the pueblo in 1781, next to Yang-Na. It has remained so through the transfer of Los Angeles from Mexican to U.S. rule in the mid–nineteenth century and on into the late twentieth. Residents—more than one-third Latino, one-eighth African American, one-eighth Asian American, one-half women—cannot find their heritage adequately represented by existing cultural historic landmarks. (In 1985, 97.5 percent of all official city landmarks commemorated Anglo history and only 2.5 percent represented people of color; 96 percent dealt with men and only 4 percent with women, including Anglo women.)[2] No one has yet written a definitive social history of Los Angeles. By the early 1980s, however, older works by Carey McWilliams and Robert Fogelson were being complemented by new narratives about ghettos, barrios, and ethnic enclaves, as Albert Camarillo, Mario Garcia, Vicki Ruiz, Richard Griswold del Castillo, Ricardo Romo, Rodolfo Acuna, Lonnie Bunch, Don and Nadine Hata, Mike Murase, Noritaka Yagasaki, and many others were creating accounts of Latinos, African Americans, Chinese Americans, and Japanese Americans in L.A.[3] The new work suggested the outline the urban history of Los Angeles must one day fill. As a feminist scholar concerned with the history of the urban landscape, transplanted from New England to Los Angeles, I was tremendously excited by the new, ethnic urban history, particularly by its potential to broaden my teaching in a professional school whose students were concerned with the physical design of the city, in areas such as preservation, physical planning, public art, and urban design. (I was looking for ways to enable students to take something back to their own communities.)

One of the first projects of The Power of Place in 1984 to 1985 was a walking tour of downtown Los Angeles (co-authored with then–UCLA graduate students Gail Dubrow and Carolyn Flynn).[4] Organized around the

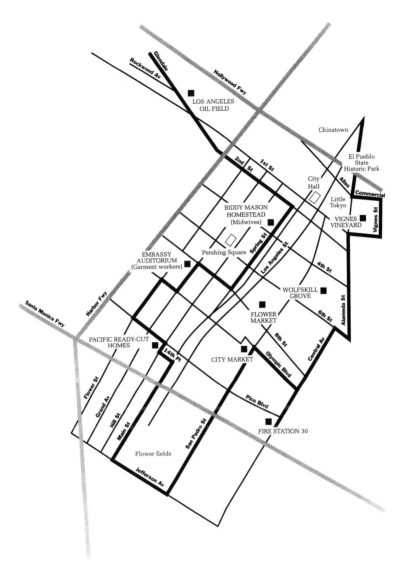

21.1 | The Power of Place, itinerary of historic places in downtown Los Angeles.

economic development of the city, the tour looked at some of the working landscapes various industries had shaped over the previous two centuries. It highlighted the city's history of production, defining its core and emphasizing the skill and energy that workers have expended to feed, clothe, and house the population. These workers included women, men, and sometimes children of every ethnic group employed in citrus groves, flower fields, flower markets, produce markets, oil fields, and prefabricated housing factories, as well as garment workers, midwives, nurses, and firefighters. The state of California's ongoing research on ethnic landmarks, eventually published as *Five Views*, was then available in manuscript form.[5] The Power of Place ran some public humanities workshops on topics such as Japanese Americans in the flower industry, and African American firefighters. The published walking tour pamphlet finally identified an itinerary of nine major downtown places (and twenty-seven minor ones): some were buildings eligible for landmark status because of their significant social history, some were buildings with architectural landmark status needing reinterpretation to emphasize their importance to social history, and a few were vacant historic sites where no structures remained but where new public art or open-space designs might be possible to commemorate the site's importance.

In 1986, The Power of Place launched into work of a much more experimental kind—combining public history and public art to commemorate an African American midwife's homestead where no historic structure remained. The site was one of downtown's endless parking lots. At that time, the Los Angeles Community Redevelopment Agency (CRA) was developing a plan for a ten-story commercial and garage building at 333 Spring Street. Because the material in the walking tour had been listed in their computer, the address popped out as Biddy Mason's historic homestead. The Power of Place was invited to propose a component for this new project involving both public history and public art. I served as project director and historian, and raised money from arts and humanities foundations. The team included public art curator Donna Graves and artists Susan E. King, Betye Saar, and Sheila Levrant de Bretteville. The first public event was a workshop in 1987, co-sponsored by the African American studies program at UCLA, and assisted by the California Afro-American Museum and the First African Methodist Episcopal Church (FAME). The team came together with community members to discuss the importance of the history of the African American community in Los Angeles, and women's history within it.

Using Biddy Mason's biography as the basis of the project was the key to finding a broad audience. One pioneer's life cannot tell the whole story of building a city. Yet the record of a single citizen's struggle to raise a family, earn a living, and contribute to professional, social, and religious activities can suggest how a city develops over time. This is especially true for Biddy Mason. Her experiences as a citizen of Los Angeles were typical—as a family head, homeowner, and churchgoer. Yet they were also unusual—since gender, race, and legal status as a slave increased her burdens.

Born in 1818, Biddy Mason was the lifelong slave of a master from Mississippi.[6] She had trekked west with his family and other slaves, including her three daughters, herding his livestock behind a Mormon wagon train, first to Deseret (Salt Lake City, Utah) and then to the Mormon outpost of San Bernardino, California. They arrived in Southern California in 1851. Biddy Mason brought suit for freedom for herself and thirteen others in court in Los Angeles in 1855. When she won her case and chose to settle in the small town of Los Angeles in 1856 as part of the very small African American community there, her special medical skills, learned as a slave, midwife, and nurse, provided entry for her into many households. She became the city's most famous midwife, delivering hundreds of babies. She lived and worked in the city until her death in January 1891.

The Biddy Mason project focused on the changing experience of being African American in Los Angeles, the problems of earning a living as a free woman of color in the city, and the nature of home as one woman created it. Although Mason at first lived with another family, and then rented on her own, the homestead she built in Los Angeles in the 1880s, a quarter century after her arrival, was a surprisingly urban place: a brick commercial building with space for her grandsons' business enterprises on the ground floor and for her own quarters upstairs, where the early organizational meetings of the local branch of the First African Methodist Episcopal Church were held.

A working woman of color is the ideal subject for a public history project because in her life all the struggles associated with class, ethnicity, and gender are intertwined. Although she herself was unable to read and write, the history of Biddy Mason was not lost. Through Mormon records of colonization, I was able to trace her journey west. Through the account of her suit for freedom in the local newspaper, I followed the legal proceedings. Some diaries and a photograph from the family her daughter married into provided personal details. Then, using work in the history of medicine concerning other African American midwives and women healers, I constructed an account of what a successful midwife's medical practice was probably like. (A few years later, Laurel Ulrich's *Midwife's Tale*, a marvelous book about a Maine midwife's diary, confirmed some of my ideas about the social importance of women's medical work.)[7] Finally, using detailed records of the built environment, I was able to unlock the narrative of how Biddy Mason created her urban homestead. The records of her property happened to be particularly significant since the growth of the Spring Street commercial district in Los Angeles between 1866, when she bought her land, and 1891, when she died, proceeded right down her street and included her property. Thus, her life story spans the wider themes of slavery and freedom, family life in pioneer times, women in the healing professions, and economic development in Los Angeles between the 1850s and 1890s.

Shaded area = site of new public art
by Betye Saar and Sheila de Bretteville

21.2 | Site plan, Biddy Mason project, 1986–1989.

The Biddy Mason project eventually included five parts. First, Betye Saar's installation, *Biddy Mason's House of the Open Hand*, was placed in the elevator lobby of the new structure. It includes a photomural and motifs from vernacular architecture of the 1880s, as well as an assemblage on Mason's life. Second, Susan King created a large-format artist's letterpress book, *HOME/stead*, in an edition of thirty-five.[8] King incorporated rubbings from the Evergreen Cemetery in Boyle Heights where Mason is buried. These included vines, leaves, and an image of the gate of heaven. The book weaves together the history of Mason's life (drawing on my research and some by Donna Graves) with King's meditations on the homestead becoming a ten-story building. Third, an inexpensive poster, *Grandma Mason's Place: A Midwife's Homestead*, was designed by Sheila de Bretteville. The historical text I wrote for the poster included midwives' architectural rituals for welcoming a newborn, such as painting the shutters of a house blue, or turning a door around on its hinges. Fourth, *Biddy Mason: Time and Place*, a black poured-concrete wall (81 feet long) with slate, limestone, and granite inset panels, was designed by Sheila de Bretteville to chronicle the story of Biddy Mason and her life, as well as the history of urban development in Los Angeles from 1818 to 1891. The wall includes a midwife's bag, scissors, and spools of thread debossed into the concrete. De Bretteville also included a picket fence, agave leaves, and wagon wheels representing Mason's walk to freedom from Mississippi to California. Both the deed to her homestead and her "Freedom Papers" are among the historic documents photographed and bonded to limestone panels. And fifth, the project included prose in a journal. My article, "Biddy Mason's Los Angeles, 1856–1891," appeared in the fall 1989 *California History*.

Everyone who gets involved in a public history or public art project hopes for an audience beyond the classroom or the museum. The poster was widely distributed. The wall by Sheila de Bretteville has been especially successful in evoking the community spirit of claiming the place. Youngsters run their hands along the wagon wheels; teenagers trace the shape of Los Angeles on historic maps and decipher the old-fashioned handwriting on the Freedom Papers. People of all ages ask their friends to pose for snapshots in front of their favorite parts of the wall. Since the project opened in late 1989, we who worked together on this project have had the satisfaction of seeing it become a new public place, one that connects individual women with family history, community history, and the city's urban landscape, developing over time.

If you lift your eyes above the wall, you will see a garment factory. The next project that The Power of Place sponsored involved the Embassy Theater as a site of union organizing and community organizing among Latina workers in the 1930s. This project was directed by Donna Graves, while I remained as president of the organization. It suggests some ways an existing architectural landmark can be reinterpreted in terms of its importance to women's history, labor history, and ethnic history. Designated a Los Angeles Cultural-Historic Landmark (as part of a real estate deal) for its

21.3 | *Biddy Mason: Time and Place,* by Sheila Levrant de Bretteville with The Power of Place.

indifferent neoclassical architecture designed by Fitzhugh, Krucker, and Deckbar in 1914, the Embassy Theater is far more important as the historic gathering place for labor unions and community organizations—including Russian Jewish and Latina garment workers, Latina cannery workers, and Russian Molokan walnut shellers. Unions, especially women's unions, met inside and marched outside the Embassy between the 1920s and the 1940s, as did El Congreso (the Spanish Speaking People's Congress), the first national Latino civil rights organization.[9] By the 1990s it had become a residential college for the University of Southern California.

The Embassy in its heyday was frequented by many of that era's most colorful organizers, including Rose Pesotta of the ILGWU (International Ladies' Garment Workers' Union), who led the 1933 Dressmakers' strike, Luisa Moreno of UCAPAWA (United Cannery, Agricultural, Packing, and Allied Workers Association), and Josefina Fierro de Bright of El Congreso. All three reached Los Angeles after epic journeys of the same proportions as Biddy Mason's—from Russia for Pesotta, Guatemala for Moreno, and Mexico for Fierro de Bright. All three experienced the height of their careers in Los Angeles, recruiting thousands of Spanish-speaking women into their organizations—but it must be added that their work was so controversial and disturbing that Pesotta resigned as ILGWU vice president and Moreno and Fierro left for Mexico during the red-baiting years.

Graves's project highlighted these three organizers. Artist Rupert Garcia created a poster with their portraits to advertise a public humanities workshop, "La Fuerza de Union," held in the historic main auditorium in the spring of 1991. Participants included two artists, Garcia and Celia Alvarez Munoz; a restoration architect, Brenda Levin; and historians George Sanchez and Albert Camarillo (Moreno's biographer), as well as union leaders, students, and retirees. (Historian Vicki Ruiz, whose wonderful book *Cannery Women, Cannery Lives* had first drawn attention to Moreno, also worked on the team briefly.)[10]

Following the workshop, Celia Alvarez Muñoz created an artist's book, *If Walls Could Speak*, which intertwined public and private story lines in English and Spanish, beginning: "If walls could speak, these walls would tell / in sounds of human voices, music, and machines / of the early tremors of the City of Angels." And on the same three pages, she wrote: "As a young child, I learned my mother had two families. / One with my grandmother, my aunt, and I. / The other at la fabrica, the factory." The endpapers were union logos, and so was the conclusion. A typical spread included historic images of Rose Pesotta with her arm around a worker, and another worker stitching a banner reading "Win the War," or Josefina Fierro organizing for El Congreso, and workers with linked arms. The small artist's book was dis-

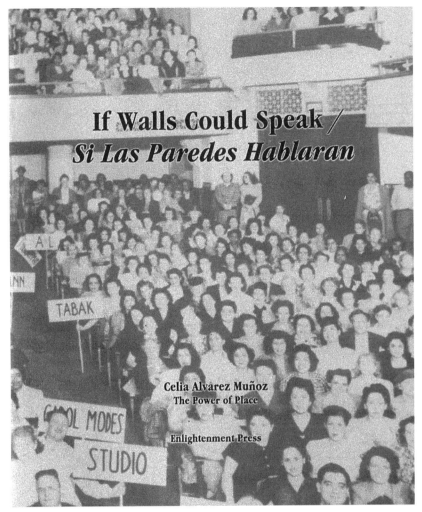

21.4 | Celia Alvarez Muñoz, artist with The Power of Place, *If Walls Could Speak/Si Las Paredes Hablaran,* 1991.

tributed free to several thousand people, including union members, retirees, and students.[11]

At the same time, architect Brenda Levin proposed the re-creation of two traditional showcases in front of the Embassy Theater to carry historical text, as well as sculptural representations of the workers' sewing machines, spools, and hammers, while union logos were to be pressed into a new concrete sidewalk. In a storefront adjoining the sidewalk, the faculty hoped to open the "Luisa Moreno Reading Room" for students interested in social history. It was a disappointment to us all that although the permanent art was fully funded, plans by the owners, USC, to sell the building prevented installation. Then the January 1994 earthquake hit the building so hard that it had to be evacuated. Another site for a permanent commemoration is preferable.

Today many of us who worked together in L.A. continue activities in other cities, but some subsequent projects in Los Angeles go on too. In Little Tokyo, a UCLA student working with me and The Power of Place, Susan Sztaray, helped plan a project for a public art sidewalk wrapping the First Street National Register Historic District. Sztaray wanted to recall the scale of small, traditional Japanese American businesses that had flourished there before the internment of the 1940s. The Los Angeles Community Redevelopment Agency took up this plan, and ran a public art competition. Working as an independent artist, Sheila de Bretteville, who designed the Biddy Mason wall, won the CRA public art commission along with artists Sonya Ishii and Nobuho Nagasawa. Construction has recently concluded. Los Angeles will then have three cultural heritage projects—one African American, one Latina, one Japanese American—in three very different kinds of settings, ranging from a lost homestead to a reinterpreted theater building to a National Register Historic district, that demonstrate some of the new ways artists can work with preservationists and historians on parts of the public landscape.

The projects I've discussed here are all located in the area of our 1984 walking tour, close to the center of downtown Los Angeles, set near the high-rise buildings of the Bunker Hill redevelopment area. They have challenged the idea that only massive commercial development can provide a downtown with an identity: The Power of Place presented an alternative account of the process of building a city, emphasizing the importance of people of diverse backgrounds and work—both paid work and work in family life—to urban survival. In a city where half the residents are women and more than 60 percent are people of color, these small projects struck a responsive chord.

The projects straddled several worlds: academic urban history and public history, urban planning, public art, preservation, and urban design. Every project had a multiethnic, multidisciplinary team. Teamwork is difficult, especially across disciplines. But there are rewards. First, public space has a resonance for local history no other medium can match. Second, locking women's history into the design of the city exploits a relatively inexpensive medium. Over time the exposure can be as great as a film or an exhibit can offer. Third, as projects like Biddy Mason and the Embassy show, when you have *one* significant public place, there is less pressure to divide history into academic categories (such as women, ethnic, or labor) that often trivialize and marginalize urban stories. The university benefits as well. A fieldwork program like The Power of Place connected students to

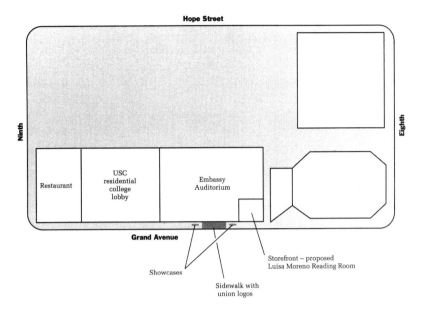

Hope Street

Ninth

Eighth

Restaurant

USC
residential
college
lobby

Embassy
Auditorium

Grand Avenue

Storefront – proposed
Luisa Moreno Reading Room

Showcases

Sidewalk with
union logos

21.5 | Site plan, Embassy project, 1989–1991.

urban history, and at the same time gave them the chance to work as interns on local projects with diverse organizations as co-sponsors.

For the city itself there are also rewards. Putting working people's history into downtown expands the potential audience for all urban preservation and public art. The recognition of important cultural heritage in diverse working people's neighborhoods can support other kinds of community organizing—including neighborhood economic development and planning for affordable housing. Teachers can bring classes to the sites to launch educational projects on women's history. Last, but not least, public space dedicated to women's history and ethnic history, especially to projects focused on working women of color, claims political territory in tangible ways. Women can meet in these historic places and work together on new issues, supported by the collective knowledge of earlier struggles. And this fosters a public realm where, at last, we as women are free to be ourselves and to see ourselves as strong and wise people, because we have represented ourselves that way.

Across the country today, I see many successful preservation projects focusing on women's history, such as the Seneca Falls Women's Rights National Historical Park. And at the same time, promoting ethnic diversity in preservation has become a goal shared by many organizations, including the National Trust for Historic Preservation; so projects involving African American, Asian American, and Latina/Latino history are receiving higher

Dolores Hayden

funding and visibility. Artists too are working on many more public projects exploring spatial history. The beginning of a new century offers many opportunities for reclaiming women's history and ethnic history in the urban landscape. Today there are hundreds of architects, landscape architects, and artists, as well as historians and preservationists, who enjoy these challenges. Finding the stories of diverse working women, and inscribing them in public space, is one small part of creating a public, political culture that can carry the American city into the future.

Notes

This chapter is based on a presentation given at the "Strangely Familiar" conference, RIBA Architecture Centre, London, January 1996. An earlier version, "The Power of Place," appeared in the *Journal of Urban History* 20 (August 1994): 466–485.

1   John Brinckerhoff Jackson, *Discovering the Vernacular Landscape* (New Haven: Yale University Press, 1984), p. xii.

2   Gail Dubrow made this count.

3   A pioneering work with a multiethnic approach is Carey McWilliams, *Southern California: An Island on the Land* (1946; reprint, Salt Lake City: Peregrine Smith, 1983). More recent overall treatments include Robert Fogelson, *The Fragmented Metropolis: Los Angeles, 1850–1930* (Cambridge, Mass.: Harvard University Press, 1967); Scott Bottles, *Los Angeles and the Automobile: The Making of the Modern City* (Berkeley: University of California Press, 1987); and Mike Davis, *City of Quartz: Excavating the Future in Los Angeles* (London: Verso, 1990). For a few examples of ethnic studies, see Rudolfo Acuna, *A Community under Siege: A Chronicle of Chicanos East of the Los Angeles River, 1945–1975* (Los Angeles: UCLA Chicano Studies Center, 1980); Richard Griswold del Castillo, *The Los Angeles Barrio, 1850–1890: A Social History* (Berkeley: University of California Press, 1979); Ricardo Romo, *East Los Angeles: History of a Barrio* (Austin: University of Texas Press, 1983); Lonnie G. Bunch III, *Black Angelenos* (Los Angeles: California African-American Museum, 1989); and Noritaka Yagasaki, "Ethnic Cooperativism and Immigrant Agriculture: A Study of Japanese Floriculture and Truck Farming in California" (Ph.D. diss., University of California, Berkeley, 1982).

4   Dolores Hayden, Gail Dubrow, and Carolyn Flynn, *Los Angeles: The Power of Place* (Los Angeles: Power of Place, 1985).

5   State of California, Department of Parks and Recreation, *Five Views: An Ethnic Sites Survey for California* (Sacramento: Department of Parks and Recreation, 1988).

6   Dolores Hayden, "Biddy Mason's Los Angeles, 1856–1891," *California History* 68 (fall 1989): 86–99, carries the full documentation.

7   Laurel Thatcher Ulrich, *A Midwife's Tale: The Life of Martha Ballard, Based on Her Diary, 1785–1812* (New York: Knopf, 1990).

8   Susan E. King, *HOME/stead* (Los Angeles: Paradise Press, 1987).

9   Mario Garcia, *Mexican Americans: Leadership, Ideology, and Identity, 1930–1960* (New Haven: Yale University Press, 1989).

10   Nicki Ruiz, *Cannery Women, Cannery Lives: Mexican Women, Unionization, and the California Food Processing Industry, 1930–1950* (Albuquerque: University of New Mexico Press, 1987).

11   Celia Alvarez Muñoz, *If Walls Could Speak/Si Las Paredes Hablaran* (Arlington, Tex.: Enlightenment Press, 1991).

Bernard Tschumi

22

Architecture and the City

an interview with William Menking

William Menking:
I want to ask you today about the relationship of architecture to the city. You claim that architects can approach the complexity of the city in three different ways, they can move a project from idea to drawing and then building, in three possible ways: firstly, by designing a masterly construction; secondly, by deconstructing what exists, by analyzing critically the historical layers that preceded it, by adding other layers derived from elsewhere, other cities, etc.; or thirdly, by searching for an intermediary, an abstract system to mediate between the site, the constraints of the program, and some other concept quite beyond the actual city or program as mediator.

How does your architecture evolve from idea, through drawings, to buildings?

Bernard Tschumi:
I try to take a position which coincides with a moment in history. For example, architects thought that they could literally start from scratch, wipe the table clean and install a new system or structure on the ground. Sometimes it is wonderfully generous, as it is with a new structure, or a mirror image of an ideological structure. But there were those, of course, who denied this attitude and talked about continuity and a seamless whole, whereby history had appeared to come to a standstill.

WM: You mean postmodernism?
BT: Well, modernism was the first attitude, the tabula rasa attitude. It was opposed to the second attitude of continuity, what is quite often a kind of blind preservation attitude, but sometimes is a slightly more intelligent way of trying to determine what is the coherent and extant system, and what is functioning within that. I questioned both attitudes, and particularly the simple addition, the collage attitude of bringing something new in relationship to something old—even if it could exist in a more interesting manner, namely playing games of disruption.

WM: But many architects work in this way!
BT: Architects are perceived as working in that way, and they try to fill that perception; it is how the media is going to give them an echo. I eventually became most interested in trying to find out what the others had missed. Somewhere you could find out what was in the things that nobody had thought about, because somehow it was hidden among the contradictions of a given program or a list of activities that you are supposed to shelter within your building: realizing that quite often it's why the art of architecture is not in producing an object to introduce form, but much more in establishing rela-

22.1 | *Parc de la Villette,* Paris.

tions between parts that nobody has thought about. And hence my interest in a program which extended the idea of the event and which is very strong in our last two or three buildings, where I feel much more like a person who has designed conditions for an event to take place, rather than someone who conditions the design or does packaging. I am not interested in packaging.

WM: Does any of this come from living in New York, where nothing ever seems to get built, where architects never get to do an urban project but only renovations—somehow only being able to make smaller decisions in the urban fabric?

BT: I would have a hard time responding to this question, because I have been here for such a long time that I am sure that there are certain things, or awarenesses, that you develop because of the place of your residence. If I think of the *Parc de la Villette* in Paris, that was a sort of tabula rasa project, although there were a number of things that already existed on that site. By choosing the smallest common denominator, the red cube, for example, that was a way to be able to insert oneself within the other huge structures—industrial slaughterhouses, canal, and urban highway. The smallest common denominator was such that it could suddenly be unbelievably strong by the sheer strength of repetition: because it is such a different site whether you come in from the museum, or the other side, or come in from the hotel site, etc. Yes, each has different scales, different perceptions. And that was a particularly conscious structure—lines of movement, paths and covered galleries, and so on. The point was that one was setting conditions for a variety of uses and especially something that I find extremely important with the work, namely the possible appropriation of the work by others. I am interested in the old Situationist word *détournement*, which is a form of disruption, subversion. I am not as interested in operating the *détournement* as in operating the condition of the *détournement*.

WM: Are any of the buildings that came after your follies, like the public housing at La Villette, Paris, in the spirit of *détournement*?

BT: No, that is another story. The slaughterhouse refit, and the public housing, and the transformation into the *City of Science* came before I arrived. Everything else came after; things like the rock concert arena or the *City of Music* building were very much a part of my role as master planner for that whole area. The housing out there was a political gesture. Within the Socialist government of the time there were unbelievable tensions between different factions: the cultural faction, the hard-core social faction, and the social housing faction, who had set 10,000 housing units at La Villette, which were of course just multiplied by the square footage, which meant there would be

22.2 | *Parc de la Villette*, Paris.

22.3 | *Parc de la Villette*, Paris.

22.4 | *Parc de la Villette*, Paris.

no park! There was quite a battle, which went all the way up to the level of President Mitterand. A sort of compromise was worked out, whereby housing would be located next to the *City of Science* and to the *City of Music*.

WM: Was this compromise in the spirit that you had proposed for the park?
BT: It was not in the spirit of anything!

WM: I understand your impulse not to want to be a master planner, but on the other hand that seems to be one of the strengths of the project.
BT: Yes, but this is a question which is bigger than oneself, and I am increasingly convinced that the architect has the ability, is the best person to have the overview. Generally the politician has one particular agenda, which is usually for two, three, four years depending on their time in power. Or you have the developer who is also thinking short term, or the social commentator. They all have very narrow agendas. The same applies to actual buildings: there are others involved—the structural engineer, the HVAC designer, for instance—but the only one that has the overall picture is the architect. That overview is the most interesting part of the work. The word project in Italian is *progetto*—you put forward into the future. That is exactly what the architect should be able to do best, and so the notion that I call "designing the condition" has always been the aim. It means that from one project to another, the architect does not follow the same strategy, because they do not function according to the same circumstances. New circumstances always require new strategies. The building which is being completed right now in the north of France, *La Fresnoy*, is also interesting for these urban notions of which we have been speaking. It happens to be a center for art and film, and the ambition is to encourage crossovers between disciplines, for the sculptors or visual artists who want to use film or video or digital technology.

WM: What is the site condition that you are dealing with in this project?
BT: It is an urban site in a working-class area of a place called Tourcoing. Like Lille and Roubaix, these are all old mining and textile towns, which today are going through profound changes because of technology, which is affecting their social makeup. What has happened is not unlike what had happened at La Villette, where an ambitious cultural program was injected into a neighborhood which had ceased to exist according to its previous logic. I have injected something with the hope that it is going to revitalize or change the nature of the area. The art and film center, which consisted of two experimental cinemas, exhibition halls, performance areas, library, and postgraduate school, was an interesting starting point for me because of that "crossover." In other words it was not the Bauhaus, where everything was

precisely categorized. Now, on the site there were some existing old ware-houses that had been used as a wrestling arena in the 1930s and an ice skat-ing rink in the 1940s, the first cinema in the region, and a ballroom, all in a completely nonarchitectural space. These conditions had quite a character, but the buildings were completely rotten and decrepit, and I was basically asked to tear it down and design a tabula rasa space. But walking through the site I was struck by the fact that those spaces, bigger actually than what we had been asked to do, were also spaces that we would not re-create, for we are in another economic logic. The notion of crossovers was fascinating, so I said "Hey, what about an architecture of crossovers," bringing things to-gether that were never meant to be together, and doing it in such a way that it is not anymore a mere style thing, or a dialectic between A and B, or trying to work in the style of. . . . There was one particular condition, which was that the warehouse roofs were leaking, and I was supposed to be designing highly technologized sound and film studios. So it occurred to me that by putting a huge roof on—in fact an electronic roof—not only would that provide the umbrella and all the technological support systems, but it would also result in an incredible residue of space 10 or 12 meters high, in between the old roof and the new one. These were not spaces that were designed, but instead were the result of the juxtapositions. This would be an enormous roof 100 meters by 70 meters, covering not only some of the old buildings but also many of the new buildings that we brought in.

WM: These leftover spaces are the central public spaces in the project?
BT: Exactly—there to be appropriated by the users, the visitors, the students. The steps over the new studios become an outdoor cinema, what one once called an architectural promenade, but suspended in the in-between spaces. These places are the sites of the crossovers, because that is what links the various functional spaces.

WM: You built bridges between the new spaces?
BT: No. Bridges are wonderful, but they are vectors, and these have their lim-itations. So we used a mix where you have both suspended catwalks and plat-forms where people can move freely.

WM: It sounds as if you have finally constructed Buckminster Fuller's dome over Manhattan.
BT: Well, it is not quite the same size. Moreover Bucky was after purity, and these spaces are not pure at all. The dome was important for what Bucky did for technology. In the case of La Fresnoy the important part is actually the gaps, or the interstices, between the existing and the designed, an approach

that comes occasionally in different manners. In the student center currently under construction here at Columbia University, which I have just designed, we were also confronted with a great variety of different activities.

WM: There were many different conditions and spaces inside and outside the campus.

BT: Yes. The location was difficult, and here we get into New York particularities. Europeans are much more relaxed about their history than Americans. You can go to Italy and see how Scarpa acted in the ruins of a castello. He put the most sophisticated modern glass and technologies inside extraordinary Renaissance palaces, combining the two with a great finesse. New York conservationists would be unbelievably upset if we ever tried to do that. If they have an old stone they want to put another old stone next to it. In the case of the Columbia scheme, there was also a master plan by McKim, Mead, and White that was very interesting, and which we decided to celebrate rather than go against. But I tried to use that tactic of judo where you use the opponent's strength against him. There are two characteristics of the master plan: between the two blocks that were suggested for the building site there is a void, and that void was the place of what I call "event." The two blocks had very different sides: one faced Broadway and the other faced inside the walled campus. This could have been a problem, because the campus is half a story higher than Broadway. It became very tempting to bring ramps and simply connect the two wings, instead of having staggered horizontal layers where you have a dynamic continuity between them. So all the activities were placed in the more generic block or wing, so that they would charge the space in between, making it not a residual space, but a highly defined space. The notion I suggest is that the architect's role, quoting Deleuze, is "actualizing potentialities," which I find extremely interesting—in other words, taking circumstances, but turning them into something altogether different.

But the more general point that interests me is that architecture is always defined as the materialization of a concept. So the questions are first of all, what is the concept, how do you derive it, and how do you actualize its potentialities? But then concepts themselves have moments which are more acute, more crucial, in any given circumstance. So generally it is the more acute places where I try to bring technological invention, probably based on the notion that our cities and our architecture have taken great leaps forward when there have been new technological developments: the department store in the nineteenth century, the railway station, the invention of the elevator, etc. Hence, in many of our projects we have been trying to push the technological envelope. In the Columbia Student Center, the ramps are covered in glass so that they are translucent and self-supporting. And we hope that will be an incredibly social place—what we called a *hub* of activities. It will be the first time in New York City that structural glass has been used in this particular way.

WM: Have you seen the new Nike Town building in New York, where escalators are not the central spaces, but only routes to selling floors—and thus not what we would like to see cities be or become?
BT: Yes, cities are such incredibly complex places, but the question is always how do you increase their complexity, not how do you centralize them, and how do you design certain buildings as urban generators?

WM: You had a very unusual site at Columbia in the history of New York because normally we have zoning, or laws that ask buildings to go in certain ways, but there is never a physical frame for the building: yet here you had a physical master plan dropped into the surrounding commercial city.
BT: Yes, you don't know how right you are. The zoning of New York is in contradiction to the McKim, Mead, and White master plan for Columbia. And we said we were going to be normative: that is, we said we would like to continue the cornice of the existing McKim buildings, so we had to go for six months through an unbelievably complicated, bureaucratic process. The zoning in this area said that you had to have a cornice at 85 feet, but the McKim cornice adjacent to this site was at 100 feet. We had to ask for a zoning variance, which meant that we had to go before community boards, which meant that anyone can protest your building.

WM: This story goes to the heart of the problem of designing in New York City, and how much education the public needs to understand the design process in this city.
BT: It is interesting, the bureaucratic code developed by the city over many years, with all its contradictions—even when there are historical and physical changes, and the code is no longer appropriate. There is a puzzle with these constraints: you are much freer to invent within that Gordian knot of impossibilities than if you ask for a variance, where you are endlessly scrutinized with all the wrong criteria. This is the fascination of the New York process.

WM: How about the Gröningen Video Gallery site, which is a lost "nowhere site," in a roundabout? Were you given that site or did you select it?

BT: Well, we were given a choice of three or four. We chose the roundabout because it *was* a nowhere site. Amusingly enough, we understood how the space worked and then we developed a pavilion, and went back to the city giving them alternative implementations on the site and said "Put it where you want." They selected this implementation as the most appropriate one. But to go back to your original point, "How do you actualize the potentialities of a site or building?" The program was to design a temporary pavilion for a video and music festival. It occurred to me that somehow the preconception that a video is something private that you watch in your living room with a VCR was not necessarily the way to go about the design for this gallery: it should have a public nature to it that could be realized. We considered a reversal and said "No: the videos will be in the open. They will be visible and people will watch them together"—and so we turned the thing around to make it a completely glass pavilion, as opposed to a box.

I was also interested in the relation between the body and the perception that you would walk through it and see each of those monitors. So there was something that could be done by simply shifting your balance as you walked. We lifted the building, and tilted it sideways, so that again your relation to the images would not be quite the normal one. We provided a situation where the viewer had a dynamic relationship to the videos. The gallery was glass, a technological invention that was not much of an invention; but we decided we were not going to use columns or steel, we were just going to use glass. If you remove the glass you have nothing left, just a slab and a structure. This meant then that the relationship between the envelope and what was happening inside became completely challenged by the fact that you would have endless reflections; at night it became unbelievably strange. The slight imbalance, or lack of balance, of the oblique structure as you walked, and then the video monitors endlessly reflecting against the columns and beams of glass, meant that your sense of space was constantly challenged. Its role in the city was extraordinary, because while it was being used, suddenly you had bizarre things, with the images dancing endlessly, and people floating in midair. Amazingly, the city decided it liked the gallery and wanted to keep it, and it became a permanent fixture, which is still used at regular intervals. They have now suggested that it could become part of various museum structures.

WM: You have also said that an architect can take what exists, fill in the gaps, complete the text, and scribble as it were in the margins, producing a complement to what is already there.

BT: This we can do occasionally, but again I would place it more in a continuity approach. But you *can* scribble like the Italians and their palazzi.

WM: You also claim that you can search for an intermediary and abstract system.

BT: Yes, that is La Villette, where the mediator is the *folie*.

WM: How do you feel about La Villette after all these years, and how it has been treated by the public?

BT: Well first it was a major effort, because it took twelve years to complete, under five different governments, from different regions. At the time people said I would only build two or three *folies*, but I didn't realize that they were right, that there was not a chance in the world. Then something fantastic occurred. The general public started to come to La Villette more and more. They did not stand around and block the project. The building was conceived more as an activator, made through the permutation of different parts, but the considerations were not part of architectural culture; they were much more part of culture in general. The intent was that by superimposition of movement and *folies* and so on, one was trying to create an incredible social thing, which it was and still is: the park receives 8 million visitors a year. But what is stunning and fascinating to me (this will never happen to any other building I design) is the difference between visiting the park on a Monday morning in November or a Sunday afternoon in July, when you have totally different perceptions. The *folies* become a mirror for your fantasies, but you find that the mirror is always throwing you different images, at different times, whether you are on your own on a foggy Monday morning, or you are surrounded by 25,000 people. So the park has been an incredible popular success, to the point where I am concerned as to whether it will survive the wear and tear.

WM: Has it gentrified the area?

BT: Oh, yes, of course! I think that was a part of the plot of the politicians who commissioned it.

WM: It seemed to be one of the strengths of the park when I first visited it that it was actually placed in a working-class neighborhood, or at least not in the center of Paris.

BT: Yes, the direct vicinity, and the French social impulse that it would have housing surrounding it that would be for different economic levels, means you have different buildings—and the housing blocks are not bad.

WM: You brought other people into the garden project?

BT: At the time there was an enormous resentment from the landscape architecture profession against an architect doing the largest park since the nineteenth century. The competition was originally for both architects and landscape architects, but suddenly an architect was in charge, and this enraged the landscape profession. I am still perceived by the landscape architects as a wolf. The park, for me, was a part of the city and it was very much a cultural construct. It was not building nature: on the contrary, within the cultural construct, I had thought about doing the so-called cinematic promenade, which was a promenade of gardens. The gardens would be placed in sequence, and then we started to invite landscape architects to do some of those gardens, but with a twist. We decided not to leave them alone but to have them work with artists, poets, philosophers, etc. The first one was the bamboo garden with Alexandre Chemetoff and Daniel Buren.

WM: Buren contributed stripes?

BT: You guessed it; but they are very subtle, in black and beige pebbles, and then the stripes continue into the concrete, the concrete shifts, and the stripes change. It is the most successful collaboration in the park. I had also the idea of inviting for that garden the philosopher Jean-François Lyotard, but Lyotard was finishing another project at the Centre Pompidou and could not participate. At this same time I was preparing the next sequence at La Villette, and for this sequence I wanted the intervention to comment about deconstruction. So having the advantage of being the master planner, I thought "Let's put Peter Eisenman and Jacques Derrida together and see what happens." But as I often say, great love affairs do not have to end up in procreation. The garden was never built, but it was an interesting collaboration.

WM: You seem to be talking in a pedagogical way: understanding the problems, and trying to not just deal with problems but to figure out ways to teach people about architectural culture in your projects.

BT: I would say I do not try to teach but to set the conditions, where people are going to learn because of those conditions that you have set forth.

WM: Do you think of yourself as a planner?

BT: Oh, yes. It's a pity that the word *planner* is so discredited today—even, it seems, among planners. Today most planners are not even planners, they are bureaucrats. These design methodologies I suggest are not unlike what I do at Columbia's architecture school, where by analogy I believe the school is like a city. It functions best when there are slight contradictions, conflicts, and nodes of irritation that are actually dynamic, and this condition produces new ideas. So I see my role as setting those things in motion. Generally, you find in institutions that when there is a conflictual situation everything freezes, and everybody tries to block everybody else, and nothing happens. But I try to keep everybody moving around all the time and not frozen on a single position—making sure the ball is moving all the time. This is what I have tried to do at Columbia—but in a more general sense, as with the best cities: and New York is one of them, despite its horrendous shortcomings, because it is moving all the time. So you try to seize the occasion, and after making major moves at the beginning, you make small moves to say "No, you can't keep the ball any longer to yourself," or you add another player who is going to make sure positions change. Because the absolute necessity is that you break through ideological positions, so that things keep moving. I would say that with architecture it is not any different: you just set things in motion, and you hope that people and situations will respond.

WM: How do you feel about architecture culture in New York and America at the moment, as opposed to Europe?
BT: It is interesting that you use the term *architecture culture*, because at the moment the architecture culture in America—that is, at academic conferences—is in good shape. I think the schools are generally speaking unbelievably good compared to the European system. The conversations that happen in the schools and the level of information is very high, but it is because we have many young architects who do not have work in their practice and so put a lot of energy into the schools.

WM: This is not a social democratic country that is letting young architects build. But not even the best New York architects get a chance to build their own city. Why can't we have brilliant new architecture here?
BT: Well I am hoping this is coming to an end with increased awareness, but my Columbia Student Center process has made me aware of certain conditions here. For one, the role of the construction industry is very strong here in the city, with its unions. Zoning codes have been evolving over a hundred years and have created a situation which is far more locked-in than what you would have in France, for instance. The amazing thing is that the architects refuse to deal with the situation. Instead of being close to the beginning of the chain of command, they have accepted being just one of many service monitors for the client and the building industry.

WM: Does any of the paper architecture that is being done in New York at the moment help convince anyone that the city needs good architecture?

BT: The problem is not to convince anybody until things are being done. You do not get a project built because people want to do you a favor, nor because people think it is the next new trend, but because it in some way provides an answer that was not provided before, and is absolutely required under the circumstances. We can take any of the projects we have been talking about—they are successful only because they hit the right button at the right time.

Note

Bernard Tschumi was interviewed by William
Menking at Columbia University in April 1997.

23

"The Accident of Where I Live"—
Journeys on the Caledonian Road

an interview with Joe Kerr

Artist Richard Wentworth has lived for twenty-five years just off the Caledonian Road, in North London. In his constant journeying along the "Cally" he has investigated, and photographed, the many singularities and irregularities—pavement bubblegum sculptures, often useless but grandly titled shops, hapless dentists, and piles of "building vomit" (the indigestible remnants of a bad postwar diet)—that for him make this decayed inner-city neighborhood an endlessly fascinating and genuinely unique fragment of the urban whole.

His photographs of the street, and the objects and people that inhabit it, illuminate his anecdotal accounts of the Cally, which together normally constitute a lecture performance of provoking originality. The following interview, which was conducted on and off the Caledonian Road, is intended partly to fix in a new and more permanent form this particular intertwining of word and image; but it also investigates how artistic practice is informed by urban experience and observation, and equally how this specific form of practice itself illuminates the understanding of architecture and of cities. Almost paradoxically, what makes Wentworth's work so original and insightful is its evocation of the surreal richness of mundanity, eccentricity, and accident that only city life, and a determinedly awkward artistic sensibility, can supply.

In particular, the perennial observation of the serial repetitions of everyday activity injects the sensation of lived time, and even perhaps of mythmaking, into the more familiar structural understanding contained in

23.1

the conventional "snapshot" image of local life. Equally the close textural and textual study of the physical fabric—the accumulated flotsam of buildings and objects, the marks of pragmatic interventions—enables Wentworth to tease out a subjective and fleeting narrative, an intense and vivid testimony to the continuous relationship between people and the architecture they inhabit. However, this is not merely an uncritical celebration of life "as it is," for part of the process is to speculate, in the most imaginative and untrammeled manner, about the causes and purposes of what might otherwise be considered to be a wholly arbitrary collection and organization of diverse objects and phenomena. It is this poetic engagement with observable reality that distinguishes this as a creative process and not merely as a task of recording, while it is the freedom from the constraints of academic convention that allows fresh insights into our discussions of urban experience.

This independence from such systems of thought permits the parameters—geographical and intellectual—of the urban study to be developed in subjective and arbitrary terms. For Wentworth, the Cally is mapped in relation to his own participation in this environment; its structure is revealed when he discerns the underlying patterns of the landscape, and it is narrated by the successive act of photography.

EXPERIENCE AND PRACTICE

Joe Kerr:
So what status do we accord "the Cally"; is it a definable concept?

Richard Wentworth:
Our habits of movement within cities are very telling—they may not be consistent but they are full of patterns based in accumulated choice and necessity. They contain preferred routes, whose whim may hinge on "the sunny side of the street," or an expectation of things or people to see or to avoid. The "accident of where I live" presents me with one very specific option—a run of nearly a mile on a single road whose various characteristics combine under the one heading, "the Cally." This mile seems to contain the most significant phrases and measures of the Caledonian Road between the two landmarks of Pentonville Prison and King's Cross Station. Somehow it's a totality, a continuum.

It occurs to me that a roll of film is similar, and unavoidably any thirty-six exposures are a kind of diary, containing all kinds of oppositions mediated in linear form, a narrative frame by frame. Perhaps the length of a film is in some apposite relation to this length of road—a "manageable"

23.2 | The parallels of art and life.

amount, readable but not epic. Terraced house construction is very similar (my street has thirty-six "exposures" on either side). There is often that sense in London of a module which has had time to develop sufficient variety, so that between any two we may compare and contrast. Just like the paving slabs of the pavement are for children, these are ways of *calibrating* our path through the city. By etymology we can extend it still further and say that this is how we gauge the *caliber* of a place.

I like my working process to be like the one which arranges the world anyway: the one which parks the cars so that they seem to have a kind of defined order about them, although you know there's no one out there with a peaked cap saying where they should be; the one that stacks up the washing-up to make a sculpture every time you do it. I am intrigued by all those practices which are actually world forming, and which in turn we respond to—how cars are parked affects how you are as a pedestrian—all those kinds of essentially urban conversations between people and objects. The problem of course is that those things that interest me are for the most part un-self-conscious; when you park the car you are not aware of making an image, but I come along and see the cars as imagery; I see three reds, a blue, two whites, a green, four blacks, and a brown, and I read it as an order, but the people who put the cars there weren't doing that.

JK: Presumably photography is an obvious way of actually making sense of that relationship between different objects in the world.

RW: I think these photographs are as near as I'll ever come to trying to pin down the moment of thinking that kind of thing, of revealing the potential of reverie.

JK: That's a very revealing idea, to talk about reverie in relation to your practice.

RW: But describing it creates one of those telling oppositions; if reverie is a beautiful engine, who would want to pin it down and reveal it? It's a typical human comedy, like saying "Aren't butterflies wonderful, so bang a nail through them and stick them in a box." But I like those spaces which seem to me to guarantee that they produce reverie, journeys sitting on the top of the bus, or speaking on the telephone: there's a completely different space that you occupy when you're on the telephone, which allows you to see the world as a sort of theater, like Jimmy Stewart does in *Rear Window*. I'm intrigued by the idea that humans are voyeuristic; it seems to me something that perhaps we ought to celebrate rather than try and prevent, because it's unpreventable. It seems to me that it's the engine of curiosity that you look, and as you look you name, and as you name you look more, and the whole process goes round.

JK: When you're actually walking on the street and seeing this striking relationship between the green and the white and the blue and the red object, to what extent is that something which just gives you pleasure for its own sake, or to what extent are you using it as a sketchbook, storing it up as something which will be useful in another place, to do something else—to make pieces, for instance?

RW: Well there's no obvious correspondence between the street and my work at all; the correspondence if there is any is that what I see on the street is a set of sympathies which I then try and allow in the work. The last thing I would want to do is to go to the studio and mimic, or mock up, or reengineer an event. I just want that apparent likeness, or banality, or set of oppositions, to come across.

JK: So why do you feel the need to create a fix of this?

RW: I feel rather ashamed, but I have realized recently that it's because I actually want to tell other people about it; it isn't enough for me to do it as an obsessive, private act. I want it to have other lives, even though if I died tomorrow nobody would know what to do with my slide photographs—most of them aren't even captioned—so I'm the only person who really knows anything about them. Some of these pictures are very articulate, and some of them are just about the voice-over, or the caption. But there is some sort of value there, and while there are comparable examples, it is not the work of Atget, it is not the work of Reyner Banham, nor is it the work of some freak in Islington civil engineering department, but it's in a space between all those, and thousands of other possibilities. Significantly, I don't actually like the transparencies as objects.

JK: But they're actually inert, except when they're being projected.

RW: Yes, and I love the idea that in much the same way the street is inert. Someone quoted Hamlet to me the other day, something like, "There's neither good nor bad till it's thought." It's only now when you look at the building opposite, which I've seen a thousand times, that you think, "Aren't the afternoon shadows amazing"; because that's a north-facing street and it aligns itself with the setting sun at this time of the year. The rest of the time you might be merely saying, "Oh they're stuccoed up to the first floor, and mostly they're painted white"; it's only where you are exhilarated that you name it.

JK: That was an intriguing list you gave of Atget, Banham, and others. So are you conscious of being in a tradition of urban commentary about lived experience, and of looking at the world in a certain way?

RW: No I don't think I am, and in a studied way I don't know anything about it, but I'm sensitive to that kind of idea. I remember that soon after leaving college, it was like throwing down a gauntlet to read Christopher Alexander's description of a newspaper-selling machine near a traffic light (I guess in Harvard); and the traffic light sequence allows you to stop at the newspaper machine, put the money in, and get the newspaper. He just pointed out that the sequence of the traffic lights gave that shop its economy. I thought this idea was just delicious, and it now seems terribly obvious, so for instance I know why the dry cleaners is by the bus stop, while ten doors up would not be a good site. I'm sure that particular dry cleaners legitimizes the incompetence of the bus service, so that people feel better about the wait, because there's a potential to do something in that space. It's not a traceable thing but I'm sure that part of that sense of waiting for the bus, the inconvenience of traveling by bus in London, is matched up with the idea "well that's all right because I can combine it with going to the dry cleaners," so that the two things are in a symbiotic relationship. Unlike nearby Logman Ltd., "specialising in water melons," who presumably doesn't need to be anywhere near any bus stop.

JK: Specializing in watermelons is a great idea, isn't it.

RW: It suggests that there are other things you can specialize in, like potatoes. . . .

And the junk shop near here, I can't stand at the bus stop without surveying it, an automatic act of dawdling.

JK: That's like shopping malls, which are designed to hold you within one space for as long as possible to maximize the probability of purchase.

RW: Well in its horrible truth I can feel that it must be so. A friend of mine who is an art director says that the length of the feature film, an hour and a half, is based on the average "bladder time."

JK: So do you sympathize with Walter Benjamin's idea that it's from the fragments, the forgotten bits, that you actually read the world? He collected detritus, and said that this was the real museum.

RW: I think that idea relates to my work in one way, which is that the physical size of the most successful things I've made is very small, and in that sense aren't in the tradition of hefty sculpture—but I always think that there's an enormous space that comes with them, which is the space of imagination. If they're any good they can provoke that; they don't need to be huge. They're not in the American tradition of "long and wide." They don't come out of minimalism, which is a branch of the American landscape tradition, simply because I don't have any experience of that. In Europe there's nowhere we can go where someone hasn't been before, and you grow up knowing that. We don't have an idea about wilderness, except in the most conceptual way.

JK: And cities aren't as morally damaging or culturally impure in the European philosophical tradition as they are in the American one either. We don't live in the land of Thoreau or Whitman.

RW: Yes, I think that's so—and anyway we no longer have the space to make such tidy-minded distinctions.

23 ON AND OFF THE CALLY

RW: As to why the Cally means something to me, I'm one of those people who lives somewhere where I would never turn left outside my house, and that means I come down here. We all have those habits of bias. So in a way I'm obliged to see it, not like those places which you live very near, but which you never see. Thus in fact I do live near to Pentonville Prison but I'm not really a witness to the prison—and obviously you could read into that a kind of psychology. It's not that I don't want to live near the prison, I don't want to acknowledge it. It's as much part of being in a city as anything else, but I would be an odd person if I constantly went out and beat the bounds of the prison.

This view of the Cally causes even me to check; it's topographically correct, as it were, but then you think, "Hey, this guy's going to die"; it's from a very high viewpoint. I was inspired by a fantastic radio broadcast by Kees Notteboum from the top of a London bus. I've used the top of the bus much more since I heard that program; he reminded me that it's a very specific kind of place.

The Caledonian Road used to be much more "butcher, baker, candlestick maker"; there was a wet fish shop here, a decent baker, Woolworth's, Boots, Tesco's, and they've all gone as they have in the whole country. But what is delightful here is that it's completely without any of the new orthodoxies of consumption—it's lost the old ones, but there's no Body Shop, no Sock Shop, no Pret à Manger, nobody wants to come here. The retail chains have somehow described an exclusion zone. The Cally hovers in the vacuum.

Surveying this, you have to ask who owns what and why. For people who think that there isn't a narrative, or that you shouldn't speak narratively, it is necessary to examine this landscape. You have here a circa 1972 conspiracy by the new middle-class occupiers of these residential streets to put barriers in the roads to make this side belong to us, and that side belong to them—just what Victorian London was like, I understand. Then you've got

23.3 | The view you can't have.

23.4

gestures to the Fire Brigade—they've put emergency access that looks like it couldn't possibly work: bollarding, some seats, private forecourts. If you came down here with a different color code for everything, this would be a psychedelic space, wouldn't it?

JK: Someone's organized this set of objects down the street, haven't they?
RW: Yes, this is the result of brief visitations by Islington Council, proposals that are completely blind in one eye, by somebody who probably just left architecture school, is still not really sure what it's all about, but who came here and laid this down.

I've often cited this particular bit of private space as not unlike the way we talk about the landscape, so that on a wet day the incredible hopelessness of this is actually very beautiful, this accumulation of knocked-up bits of mortar. It's a no-man's-land, but often when I'm walking through here I feel rather reassured; it's like the ruins of ancient Rome.

I've always felt there was something about trading on the street that was comparable to trading outside the city walls: there's always that strange collection of things that can't quite function inside the city, and part of that seems to be this collecting of fridges and freezers. A new thing that I've only seen for a year now is that you shrink-wrap them to somehow pull them back into being new, as if you've maintained a valued product, when in fact what you are doing is preventing anyone from looking inside to see if it works. Then symbolically you put the tall ones at the back and the short ones at the front and you make these walls, a process that's definitely been going on on the street for probably fifteen or twenty years (and this is done every day). These white parapets are built up each morning and dismantled at night, day-in day day-out.

JK: You've got shops here which actually want to be a market, don't they? They set out their market stall every morning.

RW: I think that is the history of the street. They say that on a Sunday before the war this was somewhere you could come and buy absolutely anything. In a way it is like a disarranged Brick Lane [a famous Sunday secondhand market]; but there is something in the street which is deeply informal, unlike Brick Lane, which has a time to begin, a time to end, it's relatively structured—all anarchy will meet there for six hours. The Cally is in a much more flexible state.

Probably the undeclared fact of the street is that these were actually gardens and got paved over—so to the general user of the street it's all pavement, but in fact you can see it contains a legal demarcation: it's got crap care of Islington Council on one side, and crap care of the shopowner on the other side. And some people colonize it this way.

I often photograph this man's wall—he always makes these patterns, tries to order materials in this way. He has to try and arrange the fridges with the bed, with the bookshelves, but he always ends up with this row of fridges and cookers. I suspect it is their cubic-ness that's doing it—it's not that it's the kitchen section. It is the kind of order which could as likely be "cooker/cooker/fridge/safe" as it could be "cooker/cooker/filing cabinet/safe/fridge"

23.5 | The city of fridges.

23.6 | Turning your trash into cash.

23.7

—because "that's how they go," as a fruit seller on the Cally once justified a rotten punnet of fruit to my wife.

And this classification also happens with the smaller-scale objects, which rattle around together under some nominal order. Probably at the small scale it guarantees a much better surrealism, this absolute stew of objects. When everything has been reduced to the scale of a shard, you get some pretty extraordinary combinations.

I think the owners, Lionel and his son Neville, may be the ultimate emblem for me: they don't live in the street, they come from Ilford every day, and they have a dog, Ben, which starts barking at Highbury Corner, it barks all the morning in the Cally, and in the afternoon it doesn't bark.

They don't have the interest, or the time, to do it otherwise—they're not antique dealers, which I think is incredibly important, and they know they're not antique dealers. They know what things are worth, within the big social-material possibility—like street sweeping; they're definitely dealing in the kind of stuff you push with a wide broom, rather than the refined, delicate stuff you'd sweep with a dustpan.

House clearance represents a very narrow vector of material. It's period limited, probably 1940s onwards, completely devoid of self-conscious value. If you want to get excited about the kind of blue china that we had the green version of when I was a child, you can. Tomorrow there'll be an Italian student who'll buy the lot and be delighted. But it's in a very narrow kind of space, and Neville uses that private space very vigorously. The display comes

23.8

zooming out in the morning and he moves it all back much more sluggishly in the evening, like packing a suitcase. Every day a percentage gets left out—which I often photograph—of failure, the invalids, the three-legged beds. My children come down here if they want a 13-amp plug and chop it off the lame fridge with a Stanley knife.

JK: This is an extraordinary arrangement of objects on the pavement!

RW: The interesting thing is about how you make an organization out of these disparate parts; we're looking at the moment at maybe basins from a builder who had gone bankrupt, weights from a weightlifter, school chairs, fridges, cookers, desks, hoovers [vacuum cleaners], old electric typewriters, all of these things which actually you can name but would never be found in that order domestically. Here there's a kind of battle to make sense of them. There are periods when he has a few boxes which he designates as the "flawed" goods and then suddenly somebody will turn up and buy the whole lot, and then for a while there'll be a chaotic period when it's all in bins. So it hasn't got a finite form. And if you ask Neville why he does it he'll tell you he does it for people's pleasure; he loves the theater of it, he's quite open about that. It sustains him in some way.

23.9

JK: But it's also an archiving process of the objects?
RW: Yes, even though if I tell him that he says, "Well I don't know, I just put them out"; but I think he knows incredibly well, but it's got nothing to do with that antique shop high self-consciousness.

JK: But objects are categorized as they would be in an antique shop, aren't they? The glasses are put together and so are the pots and the dumbbells.
RW: They are today.

There is a capacity for the Cally just to be permanently nauseated, which could obviously be traced to some economic condition, but I do sometimes imagine that round the back it is actually producing new products to spit out; but what comes out is always of a certain type and period. It's what I call the "Valor/Ascot/Raleigh/Aladdin moment," which is like a smell of "Old London"; but also for my generation it's a diagram of "the end of everything." Even though those things were made very badly, they had the illusion of British Empire competence, and we found afterwards that we couldn't do it any more. There was a skip [large trash container] here this week full of large quantities of things that had obviously been shoveled out into a garden and left. It doesn't actually take a large quantity of this stuff to fill a skip, but

23.10 | The afterlife of objects.

23.11 | Transforming the ex-Tesco's.

visually it's amazing. I don't willfully photograph skips, but that one struck me as extraordinary.

This was Tesco's and is still a supermarket, but of its own kind, which is in the process of turning itself into "student hostel with supermarket below." Part of the design seems to have been to put in regularly spaced windows on the street face, and it's been my pleasure for about a month to witness a real predicament in actually inserting one of the windows, because it collides with some bit of interior structure; and I suppose the ultimate delight is that they've actually switched the windows to open the other way round. The more I look at it, the more wonderful it seems; I mean it's very inventive, and also stubborn, which is a characteristic of the street. No matter how stupid it is they wouldn't say "Actually we won't have one there," or shift the rhythm, they just carry on in this willful way.

I am in the process of gathering up all the adjectives, and perhaps imperatives to be found in the Cally, such as *Trust* and *Hot*. There's a President motor company and a Paradise grocers and the clean is *quick* and it's the Caledonian Superstore. Although you will find these elsewhere, I think there is a kind of collective knowledge on this street, of trying for self-elevation.

THE JEWELLERS AND PAWNBROKERS

As far as I can remember the sign has always only had one golden ball, and it's funny how everyone comprehends it. I don't think it's part of any comedy; everybody just understands it's supposed to have three, and it's only got one.

23.12

23.13 | The Caf.

23.14 | The Caf.

That's part of this absent, hyperpresent thing that the street has, which is that it's either missing something, but you understand what is absent and you just fill it in, or somebody isn't very sure about it so you see things which are numbered twice or named twice, or that are incredibly assertive.

How many times does it say café and restaurant and breakfast on one frontage? Except that having gone to some considerable effort to have proper signs put up, the *E* falls off and the *U* falls off, and have been off now for six months.

It's rather charming really, "CAF RESTA RANT"!

JK: What about the possible accusation that with this work you are appropriating the city, aestheticizing it?
RW: There's a Barnet Newman quote, something about "where art goes, property follows." Given the very nature of doing what we're doing, which is to give attention to something and look at it, to turn it into an object, it seems probable to me that we're at the beginning of declaring the Caledonian Road as the Hoxton Square [a recently gentrified "artists' quarter"] of the late '90s.

EVENTUALITIES

There's something that is to do with the experience of a city which is a continuum of experience, which no amount of diary keeping, or the cinema, or photography, can convey. It is a totality of continuous knowledge; so, for instance, in the case of the supermarket window there was a hole in the wall for a month with an awkward bit of structure behind it; it contained all the builder's head scratching and worries and insecurities about what he was going to do about it, which could not be represented by taking a snapshot of it afterwards.

The pleasure of the street for me is the fact that it's out of control. It occurred to me that this is comparable to our relationship to the outdoors. Why do we go for a walk and look at the landscape, given that we don't any longer live in it or have a daily experience of it, or own it? It's like owning a cat: a half-wild furry thing, it's a kind of game with nature, it's a proposition about things beyond one's immediate control.

What I've probably done is to start to enjoy the city as a surrogate for that. Maybe there is a way you can enjoy the fear of the city, the fact that it's slightly out of control, and that people who live on the edge of the city are absolutely horrified by it and don't enjoy it the way you and I do. But because we're about as close to being in the middle as one can get without being either very poor or very rich, one gets a real sense of that pulse. It's a kind of free theater. It's completely rewarding because there are so many eventualities, and you know that you are the sole witness of those particular eventu-alities. In twenty seconds' time the next person will get a completely differ-ent palette, or rather the same palette in a different order. It's incredibly stimulating, but what I'm supposed to do with it I don't quite know!

23.15

Richard Wentworth   Journeys on the Caledonian Road

Note

Richard Wentworth was interviewed by Joe Kerr
on and off the Caledonian Road in May/June
1997.

Part IV

Tactical Filters

The event of dwelling exceeds the knowing,
the thought, and the idea in which, after
the event, the subject will want to contain
what is incommensurable with a knowing.

Emmanuel Lévinas
Totality and Infinity
(trans. Alphonso Lingis)

Iain Chambers

24

Architecture, Amnesia, and the Emergent Archaic

Writing in 1924, Walter Benjamin and Asja Lacis noted that Naples consists in a "porous architecture," for its principal building material is the yellow *tufo*: volcanic matter emerging out of the maritime depths and solidifying on contact with seawater. Transformed into habitation, this porous rock returns buildings to the dampness of their origins. In this dramatic encounter with the archaic elements (earth, air, fire, and water) there already lies the incalculable extremes that coordinate the Neapolitan quotidian. The crumbling tufo, child of the violent marriage between volcano and sea, is symptomatic of the unstable edifice that is the city. Further the use of tufo reveals a naked imbroglio in the very building of the city. Forbidden by the Spanish authorities (who were seeking to control urban development) to import building stone, Neapolitans excavated the volcanic stone literally from under their feet: casting the material once again skyward. The ground beneath the city is hollow, honeycombed with the subsequent caverns. Not only is the present-day city constructed with volatile and physically unreliable materials, its origins are also legally suspect. To borrow from the book—*Ursprung des Deutschen Trauerspiels* (1928)—that Benjamin wrote on the German baroque theater of mourning while he was on Capri and regularly visiting Naples, the city is an allegory of the precarious forces of modernity, a perpetual negation of the assumed inevitability of "progress," a continual interrogation of its foundations. Lived as a "crisis" environment, rather than a planned one, Naples remains a baroque city. Its innumerable seventeenth-century buildings are silent witnesses to the continuing disruption of linear development as urban and architectural design dissolves into sounds, streets, and bodies that do not readily bend to the modern will. The city offers the heterotopic space of many, sedimented pasts, of multiple presents . . . and diverse futures.

Walking in the city, I follow narrow alleys that turn inward toward the piazza, a church, or bring me to monuments to mortality and disaster—the decorated columns that commemorate volcanic eruptions, earthquakes, and plagues; only rarely do streets direct me toward the opening of the sea. It is as though the sea draws its energies from the darkness, the shadows, sucking the light out of things in an irrepressible self-reflection that serves to illuminate its egocentricity. The sea remains an accessory, an appendage from which fish once arrived and to which urban effluent is now dispatched.

Naples is also a vertical city. Social classes commence with one-room dwellings on the streets—*i bassi*—to arrive at the attics and terraces of the professional classes and splinters of aristocracy still clinging to the heights. The sea and sky are caught in snatches, the lateral (democratic?) view is rarely permitted; the gaze is either bounded by narrow streets or else

24.1 | Naples.

directed upward toward secular and religious authority. Space rapidly becomes an introspective expanse: the site of psychosomatic inscriptions.

Probably the aspect that most immediately strikes a visitor, a stranger, is that Naples is a city that exists above all in the conundrum of noise. Added to the constant murmur that a local *intellighenzia* spins in literary melancholia and critical conservatism around urban ruin, nostalgia, and decay are sounds that rise from the street between the interminable acceleration of scooters and angry horns: the shouts of the fishmonger; the cries of greeting; the passing trucks and megaphoned voices offering watermelons, children's toys, glassware, and pirated cassettes of Neapolitan song; the fruit seller who publicly comments on his wares and their low prices in the third person: "Che belle pesche. Duemila lire . . . ma questo è pazzo" (What fine peaches. Only two thousand lire . . . but this guy's crazy); the itinerant seller of wild berries at seven in the July morning whose high cry fills the empty alley. These lacerations of silence attest to the physical punctuation of space by the voice, the body. And it is the body that provides a fundamental gestured grammar in which hands become interrogative beaks, arms tormented signals, and faces contorted masks. A prelinguistic economy erupts in urban space to reveal among the sounds a deep-seated distrust of words, their promise of explanation and their custody of reason.

The hidden plan of the city lies in an architecture of introspection that is revealed not only in crumbling edifices and grime-coated facades, but also in the taciturn faces and skeptical sentiments of its inhabitants. Here, where the linearity of times spirals out into diverse tempos, the residual, the archaic, and the premodern can become emergent as visceral details and distortions undermine the dreamed-of purity of rational planning and functional design. In its art of getting by (*arrangiarsi*), making do, and rearranging available elements as props for a fragile urban existence, the presence of Naples on the southern edge of Europe proposes an eternal return to the enigmatic lexicon of the city, to the contingencies of an unstable language in which all city dwellers are formed and cast. So, Naples is perhaps a potential paradigm of the city *after* modernity. Connected in its uneven rhythms and volatile habits to other non-occidental cities and an emerging metropolitan globality, it proposes an *interruption* in our inherited understanding of urban life, architecture, and planning. Participating in progress without being fully absorbed in its agenda, Naples, as a composite city, reintroduces the uneven and the unplanned, the contingent, the historical. Viewed and, above all, lived in this manner, the interrogation posed by Naples returns the question of the city to the relationship between politics and poetics in determining our sense of the ethical and the aesthetic: our sense of the possible.

We all write and speak from somewhere. We have an address, a location in space, a material niche in time. Our views and voices bear the imprint of different histories; they speak out of a particular place. So, whatever I have to say on the question of architecture undoubtedly lies in my response to the ambiguous, even enigmatic, context of where I work and live: the city of Naples. At the same time, however, to nominate the site of my body, voice and thoughts, desires and obsessions in terms of a particular city is inevitably also to connect my observations to the habitat of the city as the privileged site of modern existence. Both in economic and experiential terms, it is seemingly the city that most immediately compresses history, culture, and identities into configurations that command critical attention. What is excluded from this metropolitan comprehension of our being—the nonurban worlds of nomadism, peasantry, rural life, even the suburban fringes, however populous and necessary these spaces may be for our existence (from agriculture to tourism and residence, as well as the sustenance of our imagination)—is considered to be subordinate to, if not merely an appendage of, the city.

But if Naples is unwittingly thrust into the critical and global limelight of metropolitan inquiry, it brings along its own form of disturbance, a particular contribution to the simultaneous formation of concentration and dispersal, that *unheimlichkeit* or uncanny return that eternally doubles and displaces urban geometry with the unruly histories of the repressed—perhaps the profoundest product of modern urban life.[1] Naples is frequently reviled for appearing to exist at the limit of Europe and modern urbanism, clinging intermittently to those more ordered lifestyles associated with London, Paris, Milan, and New York. Yet, in its seeming proximity to the more "typical" world cities and civic chaos of El Cairo, Mexico City, São Paulo, and Shanghai, this Mediterranean city also paradoxically finds itself drawn into proximity with the cosmopolitan composition of Los Angeles and London, as its internal history comes increasingly to be intersected by the intrusion of extra-European immigration and the impositions of global capital on its local concerns. In the space of these "new powers and expanded intercourse on the part of individuals" that, incidentally, forcefully invite us to radically rethink the spatial divisions of center and periphery, of "first" and "third" worlds, the peculiar historical configuration of a city such as Naples amounts to an insistence that cannot be readily disposed of. In its uneasy insertion into modernity and capitalism, such an insistence—and, however dramatically etched against the background of a volcano and the blue of the Mediterranean, it is by no means unique to Naples—returns to interrogate and disturb the projected homogeneity of the blueprint born in the anxious midst of metropolitan powers desirous of a seamless symmetry.[2] The plan contemplated by the eye, by the technologies of visual hegemony and their management of the indivisible nexus of knowledge and power, can be torn, punctured, or simply exceeded by further regimes of individual and collective urban sense unexpectedly confuting the administrative projection. The outcome of the struggle for a common ground of meaning, or shared frame of sense, is rarely inevitable; its politics reaches into the very heart of the matter at hand, into the very heart of our being in the city, in modern life.

In the city the perpetual myth and desire for origins, for a secure site of explanation, is constantly deferred by their being retold and rewritten. This eternal return opens up an interval in the present that permits a reconfiguration able to interrupt a further myth: that of "progress." To narrate the city in the physical passage of our bodies, to walk it and to measure ourselves with and against it, is no doubt to seek in our environs the reasoned paradigm of the ancient polis, the primary promise of the agora. But that design and desire is inevitably intersected by modern motives and motifs—speed, efficiency, rationalization: in a phrase, by the economic management of technology driven by the telos of development. Most of us do not walk the city, but ride it: in cars, subways, and buses. The crossings of these multiple metropolitan trajectories—the mythical source of its space and the modern injunctions of its organization—create a complex and composite place in which the return of the repressed inevitably bubbles up through the cracks in the sidewalk and the gaps in the highway to crease, contest, and sometimes tear the administrative and architectural will.

In this site there exists what overflows and exceeds the planned and projected structure of the city. In this unknown supplement—that both adds to the plan and threatens to disrupt it—something occurs that transgresses the instance of rationalism. For it is we who exist in this space, in this step beyond rationalization. It is in our passage through this space, whether on foot or on wheels, that the body becomes a subject, that we become who we are. We, and our myths, our beginnings, originate here, in this passage. "Building, dwelling, thinking" (so Heidegger) thus becomes a question of how to originate, how to commence, how to construct and construe our selves. Although the conditions are not of our own choosing, this is not an arbitrary act. The languages, histories, cultures, and traditions that envelop us in the city, in our daily lives, both provoke and constitute this space. It is our inhabitation of this space that configures the city. Yet, this space is simultaneously already configured, constituted, awaiting our arrival, and supplemented by a void, surrounded by the blank margins of the design and intimations of infinity—of what remains radically irreducible to the closure of the plan. It is this unrepresented, even unrepresentable, persistence that interrogates the city, its architecture, and all the disciplines that seek to delimit and determine its destiny. The response to, and responsibility for, this space invests all of us in the reconfiguration of the city, in the reconfiguration of building, dwelling, thinking, and . . . listening to this space.

With such considerations distilled from urban and Neapolitan life in mind, it becomes possible to commence formulating a wider interrogation: to ask a question of what the Japanese critic Kojin Karatani calls the "will to architecture."[3] To inquire into the desire to build—both physically and metaphysically—is, above all, to consider how the understanding of one is inextricably bound into an understanding of the other. Listening to Heidegger at this point, I desert the security of the Cartesian axiom *cogito ergo sum* for the uncertain prospect of being that exceeds my thinking the event of being—*ich bin:* "I am" now equals "I dwell."[4] From here I extend toward architecture the question, which is a particular variant on the question concerning technology (that is, the question concerning the application of technology, techniques, and art to the environment, encapsulated in the Greek word *technê*) that rises eternally in the application of historical forces, social endeavor, and individual desire to the ambience in the making of a *domus,* a habitat, a home.

Architecture as the planned and rationalized laying up, or standing reserve, of time and labor, of historical and cultural energies, as the simultaneous projection and preservation of resources, as the space of a plan, a construction, a building, is always transformed into a contingent place, into a vulnerable edifice, into a societal opening whose historical outcome no architectural drawing board can foretell. Architecture does not merely involve the physical erection of buildings; it stands out or stands forth, revealing the essence of something in simultaneously economic, political, historical, and aesthetic terms. It articulates a location among these coordinates: it both discloses and obfuscates its being-in-the-world. In these interstices it involves both a response and a responsibility.

So, a building never stands alone, is never an isolated fact. Each and every edifice, whatever the intention of the architect and the builder, evokes the connection of a community that continually frustrates "technological, calculating representation."[5] In that gap between abstract intention and corporeal investment emerges the coeval disclosure and concealment of being; and by "being" I am referring not to the abstract essence of existence or the radical will of subjectivity, but rather to the historical configuration of our lives sustained in a finite habitat between past and future, earth and sky. Buildings deploy in the most obvious manner a technology that as *Ge-stell* or enframing both stands over and challenges us, and yet reveals or exposes us to the truth of our condition.[6] The city, its buildings and architecture, is one of the fundamental modalities that enframes our paradoxical location in a closed and finite place while constituting an opening that permits the possibility of thinking at and beyond such limits.

Although our histories, cultures, memories, and subjectivities are inevitably cast in the syntax and languages of the symbolic and physical construction of our habitat, today increasingly framed by the city—itself a metaphor for the technologization of the globe—the daily prose of metropolitan life nevertheless provides us with the opportunity to think and live our condition otherwise. The question of the city, and its architecture, is a question of construction: both the physical construction that is erected and the cultural, historical, and aesthetic construction that is elaborated. So the question of architecture, together with the question of aesthetics, is also a question of ethics. Architecture, to echo the American architect Peter Eisenman, and despite Tom Wolfe's amusing but deeply disparaging and anti-intellectualist take on the question in *From Bauhaus to Our House,* is about meaning.[7] And what we understand by meaning is unavoidably tied to what we understand as the truth of our being-in-the-world.

Buildings as historical dwellings are missives of time, destined for decay. Since the European seventeenth century and the epoch of the baroque, we have become accustomed to inhabiting the potentialities of the ruin. Subsequently some of us have adopted an aesthetics that assumes that a building is never new, that its walls and decor are always already worn, baptized in dirt and grime, that there never existed a point zero or day one whence the building began; it is always and already inhabited. As the site of previous lives, the city becomes a shifting accumulation of traces, a palimpsest to be reworked and rewritten again and again. Of course others have chosen to submerge and repress such inscriptions of transition in the anonymous transcendence afforded by the flat surfaces and direct lines of an ever-new and ever-white modernism. To choose to pay heed to the former perspective, without falling into the barrenness of hapless nostalgia or stultifying historicism, means to refuse to halt in emotional thrall or resignation before the spectacle of mortality. It means, to listen to Benjamin, to seize hold of the baroque as a flash that flares up in a moment of danger to illuminate our present, permitting us to consider a relationship between buildings and memory in which architecture becomes the art of recollection that gathers together histories in its material construction and design, and reveals in the concatenation of economic, political, and cultural regimes a sense of our being.[8]

Yet it is also undeniable that much contemporary architecture—frequently self-referential in style and intent—both stands out and is framed in a context that is testimony to a waning of place, a waning that even goes to the extent of disappearing completely into the void between the freeways, the shopping malls, and the desert at the end of the West somewhere in Southern California. Here the unruly and uncanny possibilities of the city are transmuted into what Edward Soja calls *exopolis*—cities without "city-ness," capital-intensive spaces seemingly intent on confounding all attempts to transform them into the social uncertainty and cultural vicissitudes of place.[9] For to ask the question concerning architecture is to interrogate the city as the simultaneous site of memory and amnesia in an epoch that often seems intent on dispensing with civil society, that is perhaps even dispensing with democracy, as commercial imperatives and closed communities reproduce themselves in paranoid logic—strangely reminiscent of ancient hill fortresses—between the desert and the Pacific, living off the subsidized waters of the Sierras and public roadworks; all these elements are subsequently extended to anticipated global developments in the science fiction worlds of such novels as William Gibson's *Neuromancer* and Neal Stephenson's *Snow Crash*.

The waning of place is also a waning of memory.

But are there such things as building without memory? The modernism that lies at the edges of the Occident, there in the desert of Southern California, perhaps presents us with objects that embody only the transitory memory of the materials of which they are composed: glass, steel, plastic,

24.2 | Desert, California, 1991.

optical fiber, cement, tarmac, neon. In this *pragmatica desertica* critics sourly inform us that memory—too wasteful to inscribe, too time-consuming to acknowledge—is bleached out, purged. Only the bronze statue of John Wayne (from Jean-Luc Godard's favorite Ford western, *The Searchers*) in the Orange County airport foyer remains as a trace. But perhaps the apparent starkness of oblivion invites us to think again. Perhaps here memory is spatialized rather than sedimented in vertical strata. So, the seemingly memoryless city of Irvine is both doubled and shadowed by the older, largely Spanish-speaking, settlement of Santa Ana. The rational light of the former's planning and management depends on the shadows that accommodate those who service and sustain it from afar. To consider memory in spatial terms—as different, even separate, sites—is inevitably to contrast experience of the vertical city (Naples) with the horizontal one (Irvine). The former is in debt to, sometimes overwhelmed by, historicity: in Naples time is an avatar that not only reminds us of our bodies, our mortality, but devours every explanation, reason, and judgment. Irvine meanwhile is a city that apparently exists at the end of time; here explanations are not introspective (memory, narcissism) but projective (fantasy, desire). The sedimented, vertical city is governed by its foundations (mythic, historical, cultural), the other by its horizon (desert, sea, sky). One might be tempted to suggest that while one is a city the other is a settlement, hence provisional: only the freeways have a certain air of permanency. One represents time, the other represses it.

In the irreversible metropolitan disengagement of labor and locality, civic life is unchained from the immediate presence and pressures of organized production, and labor is reconfigured in other bodies (often female, nonwhite, and not of the first world) and then spatially disseminated in the fragmented immediacy of metropolitan service and leisure industries, or else removed to distanced points of transnational production in Californian strawberry fields and microchip assembly lines in Singapore. Yet the city—whether a hard historical settlement such as Naples or a flexible module such as Irvine, Orange County—continues to disclose and concurrently obfuscate such coordinates as they come to be concentrated in its language, its buildings, its daily praxis and style.

If for Le Corbusier houses are machines for living, Heidegger reminds us that machine "technology remains up to now the most visible outgrowth of the essence of modern technology, which is identical with the essence of modern metaphysics."[10] As design, project, and instrumental desire, architecture mediates the transmission of intention to realization and utility, to cultural finality and historical inscription. As such it finds itself caught in the drive to reduce terrestrial contingency to the causal and controllable logic of a transparent language in which the "political" and the "social" are fully absorbed into a regime of rationalism, today increasingly translated into the seeming soft neutrality of "information." Note that I say "rationalism," which, as the Italian philosopher Gianni Vattimo rightly points out, is not necessarily the highest form of reason.[11]

But there are limits that circumscribe the projections of such futures, both that of the desired transcendence promised by technology and that of the associated suspension of urban civics and the subsequent numbing of politics. While Southern California is among our futures, it is not necessarily *the* future. For, and here I echo both Martin Heidegger and Richard Sennett, place is not merely the product of global processing. In his famous essay "Building Dwelling Thinking," the German philosopher writes: "spaces receive their essential being from locations and not from 'space.'"[12] A location, a place, is always the site of cultural appropriation and historical transformation, the site of dwelling. It is the object of an abstract design that employs the lexicons of capitalism, technology, government, planning, and architecture—yet what emerges is never simply the alienated object of such processes but a subject who introduces agonism into the agora, constructing a particular place out of this space, confuting the regulated transparency of the plan with the opacities of the unruly event.[13]

Making such a claim is to insist on the deeply heteronomic disposition of modernity, on what lies repressed beneath the surface of a rationalist coherence. It is to engage with undoing the links of linearity and the teleology of a time called "progress," and to dwell on the emergence of the unsettling presence of what modernity represses and yet ultimately depends on: the exploitation of the forgotten, the disenfranchised, the alien, and the negated—those condemned to bear the burden of modernity in the name of progress, underdevelopment, backwardness, illegality, and the inevitable activation of the glossaries of sexual prejudice, ethnic discrimination, and racism that seek to supervise such scenes.

To directly inscribe such interruptions, such discontinuities, into the contemporary accounting of time, into the balance sheet of our modernity, returns us to the question of architecture. In his "Letter to Peter Eisenman," Jacques Derrida lists a series of relationships that in Heideggerean fashion expose architecture to the provocation of its terrestrial framing, to what both exceeds and yet envelops its discourse: architecture and poverty, architecture and homelessness, architecture and ruins. He finally returns us to the very foundations of such questioning by raising the question of the Earth and the ultimate provocation sustained by our dwelling.[14]

If language is ultimately the house of being, then it is in language that a sense of dwelling, a sense of the city, of its architecture, buildings, and streets, both endures and develops. The stones, steel, cement, and glass that seemingly furnish the conclusion of a discourse, a project, a plan, a building, a city, are merely material points of departure as architectural space is rendered into place, is transformed into historical practices and cultural apertures: into an irrepressible series of languages, bodies, acts, and provocation.

Architecture as the "spatial synthesis of the heterogeneous" is the synthesis not only of forms and materials, as Paul Ricoeur suggests,[15] but also of social, cultural, and historical forces and elements. As a text it is not merely a plot to be read, it is also a story we tell and in which we are told. So, we must bring to bear on the disciplines that think and project the city—architecture, urban planning and government, investments and speculation—a reading and listening that permits the other cities that exist within the City to come into view and hearing: the gendered, sexual, ethnic, and racial edifices that both constitute and inhabit urban space. To map the city along these lines is to supplement, and sometimes subvert, the understanding of this habitat grasped in terms of an abstract population, generic civic space, anonymous labor pool, or commercial concentration. To understand the city in this fashion is to decisively shift emphasis from the prescriptive protocols of the urban plan, the architectural project, administrative intention, and economic strategy to the inscriptive: to the city that speaks, that narrates itself in diversity.

Here, according to Lévinas, in the passage from the interdiction of the said to the exposure of saying, in the vacillation between the abstraction of the law and the unplanned event, exists the insistence of ethics where the prescriptive is rendered accountable.[16] But what does that mean: no planning, no architecture until the unplanned can be recuperated and the ethical installed? As that event can never occur, is the plan forever frozen in anticipation of the future? Is architecture now reduced to repair work, patching up the urban environment, indulging in localized experimentation, while waiting for a new mandate? Certainly it, too, has suffered the critique of its previous aspirations, a critique that in insisting on the "beyond" or supplement of totality renders irretrievable that previous project. Anthony Vidler notes:

> Here the city, as existing, stands as the object and generator of so many possible futures, each calculated according to the nature of its opposition to those futures. The architectural project, while crystallizing one or more of those futures, is then presented to the city, so to speak, as a whole, not as a replacement or substitute, as in the utopian urbanism of modernism, but as material to be submitted to the life and consuming power of the context. Apparently totalizing "types" will thereby inevitably be fragmented by the counterforce of the site.[17]

Cities, urban life, architecture, like our everyday gendered, ethnic, national, and local selves, however much they may be prescribed by disciplinary regimes and the law, are ultimately dependent on the performative event of being, on historical articulation and an ethics of becoming. The truth of our being lies in that becoming, in our listening and responding to that language. In that space, however overdetermined by the geographies of capital and corporate control—what these days increasingly stands in for institutional policies and politics—there exists the supplement of language, the cultural and poetic excess that resides in the house of being and that is irreducible to the calculating rationalism and logic of those intent on overseeing our futures. This supplement interrupts and interrogates the political desire for conclusion, universal comprehension, and a rationalist domestication of the world. Such desire is dispersed in the space between buildings, in the gap between measured words, in the silence that data fail to encode. Ultimately energies spill out in a border country of uncertainties where historical bodies and voices—moving in a mutable, here "primitive" there "cyborg," state—conjoin technology and being in a mutual interrogation; and the beguiling transparency of information and its cartographies of power is betrayed in the perpetual transit and translation attendant on our seeking other accommodations in the world. Here we exit from the confines of calculation to run the risk of thinking. To think what calculation cannot represent, what the numbers and lines repress, is to expose the plan to the incalculable risks—to the world—it hides.

Architecture as the attempt to stabilize space, to transform it into place, building, habitat, is always confronted with the instability, the narrative eruption, of social life and historical being. At this point there emerges the prospect of a "weak architecture": an architecture able to accommodate, or at least register, the interval between plan and place. Clearly this attempt seeks to weaken architectural sovereignty by turning attention away from the disposition of a homogeneous rationality through insisting on the heterogeneous histories that the construction is destined to house. The architect becomes less of a universal planner and more a caring builder: one who constructs, tends, and harbors human habitation.[18] The plan, the project, the building becomes a weaker construct—less monumental, less metaphysical in its aspirations, more modest, open, and accommodating in its response to the place in which it is destined to acquire lives, histories, memories, meanings. That calculation cannot, of course, be simply built in. The act of architecture is always a disturbance, a provocation. It radically interrupts, or more modestly reconfigures, an already existing place. Even if the imperatives of capital and the global property market could be set aside, architecture cannot withdraw from that task. But the awareness that architecture also embodies something which goes beyond its calculation, something which exemplifies and exposes that supplementary condition, and thereby always exceeds the more obvious techniques of design, engineering, and planning, paradoxically insists on its limits. Such an architecture intersects the art of rational construction, mere buildings, with the projection, and protection, of the ethical—with the question of dwelling.

Notes

1   See Anthony Vidler, *The Architectural Uncanny: Essays in the Modern Unhomely* (Cambridge, Mass.: MIT Press, 1992).

2   The quotation about "expanded intercourse" is from Karl Marx, *Grundrisse: Foundations of the Critique of Political Economy*, trans. Martin Nicolaus (Harmondsworth: Penguin, 1973), p. 540. For further critical discussion of the "center-periphery" model, see my "The Broken World: Whose Centre, Whose Periphery?" in *Migrancy, Culture, Identity* (London: Routledge, 1993), pp. 67–91.

3   Kojin Karatani, *Architecture as Metaphor: Language, Number, Money,* ed. Michael Speaks, trans. Sabu Kohso (Cambridge, Mass.: MIT Press, 1995).

4   Martin Heidegger, "Building Dwelling Thinking," in *Basic Writings: From "Being and Time" (1927) to "The Task of Thinking,"* ed. David Farrell Krell (New York: Harper and Row, 1977), p. 324. His point emerges from considering the etymology of *bauen,* "to build," and is justified as follows: "Man acts as though he were the shaper and master of language, while in fact *language* remains the master of man. Perhaps it is before all else man's subversion of *this* relation of domination that drives his essential nature into alienation."

5   Martin Heidegger, "The Turning," in *The Question Concerning Technology and Other Essays,* trans. William Lovitt (New York: Harper, 1977), p. 48.

6   Martin Heidegger, "The Question Concerning Technology," in *The Question Concerning Technology,* pp. 12–15.

7   Tom Wolfe, *From Bauhaus to Our House* (New York: Farrar Straus Giroux, 1981). For Eisenman, see his essay in William Lillyman, Marilyn Moriarty, and David Neuman, eds., *Critical Architecture and Contemporary Culture* (New York: Oxford University Press, 1994).

8   The telescoping of time in a moment of danger is a clear allusion to Walter Benjamin's "Theses on the Philosophy of History" (in *Illuminations,* ed. Hannah Arendt and trans. Harry Zohn [London: Cape, 1970], pp. 253–264), as well as to his intuitive imbrication of the baroque in his reading of modernity (see esp. *Das Pas-sagen-Werk* [Frankfurt: Suhrkamp Verlag, 1982]).

9   Edward Soja, "Inside Exopolis: Scenes from Orange County," in *Variations on a Theme Park: The New American City and the End of Public Space,* ed. Michael Sorkin (New York: Hill and Wang, 1992), pp. 94–122.

10   Martin Heidegger, "The Age of the World Pictures," in *The Question Concerning Technology,* p. 117.

11   Gianni Vattimo, "Dialettica, differenza, pensiero debole," in *Il pensiero debole,* ed. Gianni Vattimo and Pier Aldo Rovatti (Milan: Feltrinelli, 1983).

12   Heidegger, "Building Dwelling Thinking," p. 332.

13   See Richard Sennett, "Something in the City: The Spectre of Uselessness and the Search for a Place in the World," *Times Literary Supplement,* 22 September 1995.

14   Jacques Derrida, "Letter to Peter Eisenman," in *Critical Architecture and Contemporary Culture,* eds. William Lillyman, Marilyn Moriarty, and David Neuman (New York: Oxford University Press, 1994). The letter is dated 12 October 1989.

15   Paul Ricoeur, "Architecture and Narrative," in *Identity and Difference: Integration and Plurality in Today's Forms: Cultures between the Ephemeral and the Lasting,* catalogue of the Triennale di Milano, XIX Esposizione Internazionale (Milan: Electa, 1996), pp. 64–72; quotation, p. 68.

16   Emmanuel Lévinas, *Totality and Infinity: An Essay on Exteriority,* trans. Alphonso Lingis (Pittsburgh: Duquesne University Press, 1969), pp. 194–195.

17   Vidler, *The Architectural Uncanny,* p. 200. Vidler is describing the experimental architecture of Wiel Arets.

18   "Man is not the lord of beings. Man is the shepherd of Being." Martin Heidegger, "Letter on Humanism," in *Basic Writings,* p. 221.

Jonathan Charley

25

Reflections from a Moscow Diary, 1984–1994

TIMELESS LABOR

Kolya is the ghost in the landscape. The grand laborer whose handprint is buried in every meter of the railways that streak the Russian landscape, whose footprints lie underneath every metropolitan construction, and whose price of labor is embedded in every grain of dust in the industrialised world. Kolya is the grand drunk whose mouth has touched every bottle in the journey from the medieval village commune to the twentieth-century urban labor market. His is the distant voice of the dispossessed serf, the wandering free laborer, liberated from all property save his power to labor on the building sites of Russia. Kolya is the absent memory of the hero who appeared as a vagabond. Olga was his love, the idealized peasant woman without whom the migration could never have begun. She is history's prostitute, farmer, mother, and wage earner, and her story lies hidden even deeper in the matter that marks the birth of the commodity world.

THE MEMORY MAN

Crime, historical memory, and truth are held together by fragile threads that in dictatorships can wither to dust. At such moments the rule of law is reduced to its crudest form, a naked protection of ruling class interests. But let me introduce myself, I am the memory man. If you want a name, then Misha will do, although in the world I inhabit identity is an ephemeral condition.

In the depths of a Russian winter, the damp mists can seep into the bone, and by a similar process of stealth I can penetrate the unknown recesses of consciousness. In the old days they called me the policeman of the mind, the spider director of remembrance retrieval with a special brief to infiltrate the spaces of memory. As the orchestrator and obliterator of sanctioned recollections, my manifestations were varied and many. Whether eavesdropping at doors on the stair landings, swirling at the foot of Stalin's wedding cakes, or slithering up the concrete walls of the towers on the periphery, I have hovered throughout the world of matter and nonmatter, ambushing, violating, and highjacking all of the big questions concerning freedom, truth, and pleasure.

In the three decades of Stalin's rule, my tasks were relatively simple. There was only one memory, and those that remembered differently were criminals. One of my principal mnemonic devices was fear. I existed in the secret regimes of the Cheka, the GPU, NKVD, and KGB, enforcing allegiance to the institutions of family, state, and nation. But I could be subtle in my relentless quest to obscure and mask the nature of political and economic power, lurking in the texts of history books, and in the meanings attached to paintings, buildings, and other fetishes of the social world.

I enjoyed my job, erasing people from image and text, touching up photographs, writing lies, destroying monuments and building new ones. Such acts are central to the maintenance of a ruling class's hegemony, and form part of a program of legitimation organized within the culture industry that sets out to occupy the same time and space that was of symbolic value to the previous regime's attempt to appropriate the spirit.

In the 1920s I organized a general campaign of ecclesiastical destruction, seizing the sites of worship, dragging the patriarch to the ground, toppling the crosses from the cupolas, whitewashing the icons, and on one occasion turning a church into a shoe factory. I cleansed the streets of the bronzed statuesque reminders of religious and aristocratic figures and subsequently covered the city in slogans, carefully filling holes in the landscape with images of idealized hero workers. At my most profane I embalmed Lenin, and rolled back the buildings on Gorky Street, wide enough to conduct parades to his mausoleum in Red Square.

Being an aspatial and transhistorical phenomenon, I have been fickle in my alliances. But whoever has been in power, my job has been the same—to camouflage, to invert, and to invent.

FEAR

Outside of the apartment there were few public spaces or large institutions that were immune from the creeping culture of inspection and observation. Almost all institutions possessed a room known as the *spyetz otdyel*, the special department. These were the state's control outposts run by clones of Gogol's madman and inspector. Zealous bureaucrats, they were steeped in the ancient art of spying, writing reports, and reciting shibboleths. As the guardian beetles of civic order they would scuttle around the panoptican labyrinth of numbered doors, brown corridors, and whispering telephones, with an eye open for any deviation, ready on the slightest provocation to order a visit.

In the popular memory there lies a sequence of sounds. The screeched brakes. The metal steps. The crack on the door. "You are under arrest." Have I time to take a last shot of vodka? The muscle arm clicks, the steps on the stairs repeat themselves, but this time multiplied, the engine growls and the black Volga heads for the Kazan station, the introduction to the gulag, no time to flag the vodka man.

LUDMILLA IN 1932

Ludmilla gazed with astonishment as the workers pushed the architect into a wheelbarrow and carted him offsite. She had heard stories of how in the revolution of 1917 the "carting off" ceremony had been the ritual by which workers literally threw the factory managers out of the building. But this was all rather different. There had been a heated argument between state officials and the architects on one side and the building workers on the other. Many of the rank-and-file workers still felt sympathetic to the Left Opposition and Lev Davidovich Trotsky, who had been such a popular speaker in previous years at the Congresses of the Building Workers Trade Union in Moscow. The argument had started when the visiting authorities, fervent supporters of Stalin, issued thinly barbed warnings to angry workers who had objected to what they considered to be the further extension of capitalist work practices, such as one-man management and piece rates, and to the ludicrous demands for productivity increases that would have reduced the most enthusiastic of shock workers to a stooping shadow.

Everyone had laughed as the ridiculed officials brushed down their suits at the edge of the site, but Ludmilla sensed that their actions would have violent repercussions. There were stories circulating of people being arrested for what were called "anti-Soviet" activities. She was frightened not least because she was determined not to jeopardize her newly won position as a painter and decorator. Ten years before she had tried to read some of Alexandra Kollantai's articles and although she did not understand everything, she liked the talk of how life for women would be completely different under socialism. In any case it seemed to her that the dispute was more a case of boys toughing it out.

They were building a block of flats not far from the Moscow River. It was designed by a man called Golosov and was dominated by a triumphal arched entrance, flanked by statues of armed workers. Sitting high on the scaffold she was struck by how different the shapes of the constructions were, compared with those she had seen in street demonstrations and in pictures at one of the public art exhibitions in the 1920s. There she had seen paintings by women that were colorful and dynamic, if a little bit odd, and she had liked the images of shiny buildings made from concrete, glass, and steel. By comparison the heavy decorative stonework of the front wall that she was painting was rather disappointing, too solid, too sad, and far too redolent of a past that she at least would have preferred to have forgotten.

Jonathan Charley

VODKA IN THE LATE 1980s

If the cap fits let him wear it.
and when the cork flips
let them drink it to the bottom.

It is a foolish and amnesiac government that thinks it can curtail alcohol
consumption by closing down the off-licenses and bars. It is surprising in
retrospect, that this act alone in the mid-1980s, tantamount to a direct assault on the Russia soul, did not prompt an immediate insurrection. But by
then the Moscow citizen was more than used to the moral puritanism of the
Party and had invented a thousand ways of avoiding it. There are three immediate reasons why programs of enforced abstinence are doomed to failure.
In the first place, you cannot prevent the pursuit of pleasure by abolishing
the object of desire. That which is banned inevitably becomes available underground or floating in the city's unregulated interspaces. Second, a government loses immense amounts of revenue through the subsequent drop in
taxes. Third, the anti-alcohol campaign did little to address the root causes
of a history of alcoholism that had touched all sectors of the population. But
this did not deter the authorities from trying.

Badges were distributed to the youth proclaiming them to be
members of the Society of Sobriety. Stalwart Communists proclaimed the
life-enhancing properties of Soviet mineral water, and leaders in full view of
the camera proudly consumed green bottles of sparkling metal liquid. The
streets were cleared of the vodka-dispensing shot stalls, leaving behind rust-
ing soda-water machines and the odd Kvas pump. The front pages of *Pravda*
printed parables about drunk tractor drivers running their fathers over in
the fields, and along with editorials in the rest of the media chastized the
demon spirit for instigating the collapse in productivity levels and the disintegration of family life. But the fifty-ruble-a-night Militia hotels, temporary prisons for the purposes of drying out, continued to be fully booked,
and the frozen corpses of the vodka sleepers were still being picked up from
the morning streets.

Alcohol production never stopped, and a trickle continued to bleed
onto the streets with a characteristically Muscovite unpredictability as to
time and place. This made the process of procurement a tedious game of detection, one that demanded a fierce attention to duty. If you hit them at the
right time, the big shops on Stolichniye Pereulok and Prospect Kalinina
normally had something, maybe even a bottle of Cuban rum. Then there
was the *samagon*, homemade vodka that when nurtured in the hands of an
able peasant and flavored with an earthy blend of herbs and spices could

taste of Russian history—but when forced by the fists of a heretic could induce a chemical blindness.

Restaurants were a safer bet with respect to vodka but not to gangsters. Run like little fiefdoms, the grandest of these—such as the Hotel Moskva on Revolution Square; Stalin's favorite, the Aragvi; or the Ukraine Hotel—were pictures of still time and faded aristocracy. In parodies of palatial bourgeois dining rooms, penguin-suited troupes of disinterested waiters and waitresses would thread through the mirrors, red carpets, and pastel walls, dropping drinks, fish in aspic, and salads onto the table. Up on the stage a carefully sanitized cabaret would tick along to pirouetting Hula-Hoop dancing girls, flashing beneath the spinning silver ball of a seventies light show. The attached band of metronomic musicians play transcontinental easy listening, and with a twist of the imagination and several rounds of champagne and vodka chasers, the white nightmare descends; the diner rises to the dance floor and for a minute is transported to 1920s kitsch Berlin.

At the other end of the consumer hierarchy were the queues of dedicated drinkers at the perfume counter, the oral consumption of Russian eau de cologne performing the double function of getting you pissed and covering up the smell of stale urine. For casual spontaneous drinkers there were a whole number of options. One of the most reliable was to stand in the middle of the road at any time of the night making a V-sign pointed at one's own throat. This was not a gesture of violence but a message to ambulance men, taxi drivers, and opportunist militia that you needed a bottle. Buying it this way at three in the morning was expensive. But when the argument of a Russian night explodes, there is a ritual the performance of which is a necessity.

—

When the vodka has chilled and possesses the viscosity of runny honey it is ready to drink. Poured neat into 50 ml glasses, it is thrown back with a single snap of the head, but not before two plates have been laid on the table. One that displays slices of black rye bread, the other pickled gherkins. The consumption of these three items is the ignition sequence that can lead to lasting friendship but can as easily disintegrate into tears, regret, and even murder.

THE REBELLIOUS HOME
Unlike advanced capitalist nations in which the assimilation of resistance has become so common as to be unnoticeable, in the USSR the public en-

actment of difference and defiance was illegal. For decades the culture of opposition hid, revealing itself in the crowded, smoky sitting rooms of the *kvartira*, or in the timber dacha deep in the silver birch forests. It was in these irreverent dark woody spaces, filled with sofa bed, books, rugs, and paintings, that philosophy and politics could be dismembered, and sex and deviant beliefs celebrated.

At the epicenter, lit by a yellow lamp, stood the low table on which the debris of glasses, ashtrays, and *zakuski* would accumulate as the toasts flowed until everyone, and every hope, had been drunk to in a festival of daring self-affirmation.

NEW YEAR'S EVE

Vodka is the silent guest at every gathering. It was New Year's Eve in 1987, and none of the guests had arrived. Having long before spent any remaining hard currency, I stood with everyone else in the queues for vodka. Everyone, that is, except for smart people and apparatchiks, who had their own shops and contacts. The Muscovite had long since grown accustomed to waiting, but while queuing had become a daily sufferance for unconnected citizens, there was always the possibility of a surprise, which is why you never left home without a bag. A lorry might approach through the slush and mist, skid to a stop, and throw open its doors to reveal plump Hungarian chickens. But then again it might be a pickup truck carrying only cabbages, which would be unceremoniously dumped on the ground as if the driver had mistaken the people for cattle.

But on this night I was scouring one of the immense citadel estates that butt up to the circular ring road surrounding Moscow. If the sun was shining you could blink and imagine the twenty-story towers as monuments in the park; but in the depths of winter they became canyons of wrinkled sentry boxes, graveyards of accelerated urbanization. Though lacking in shops and social infrastructure they would at least possess a *Univermag* Supermarket, and it was out of the back doors of one of these that a queue had formed, snaking its way across the snow between the blocks of flats in a line that must have been anything up to a kilometer long. Word was out on the estate that a delivery truck was rumbling our way. The rumor was strong enough to make people endure what turned out to be a three-hour wait to reach the steel doors of vodka heaven. In a temperature of minus twenty Celsius, fires had been lit along its length, scattering embers of heated conversations into the snow.

As we stood sandwiched between old muzhiks, math professors, the odd babushka, and a cross-section of the unfaithful, stories and lives were exchanged at liberty, freezing breath joining one face to another. In the crystal air the metallic shotgun clang of the doors cracked over head. Murmurs quickly spread along the line that it was two bottles only. Conversations changed to bullet one-liners as the snake began to wriggle in anticipation. Ignoring the waiting queue, crews of demobbed paratroopers and determined alcoholics pushed in at the front. The militia men stood to one side with a collective shrug. With no one else likely to confront the vodka bandits it appeared for a moment that all was lost and the unthinkable had happened: the vodka would be highjacked and New Year's Eve would be sober.

But no one should underestimate the women in white coats. They appear everywhere—on hotel landings, reception desks of buildings, cloakrooms, toilets, shops, and factories. A secret army dressed in medical overalls, hair permed with a color tint, wearing black galoshes, and carrying sixteen stone, their stares alone could reduce an outlaw to apology. From behind the metal grill in what was no more than a large refrigerator they reimposed order by threatening to close up. Bruised and battered after struggling through a storm of curses and flailing arms, I reached the counter and made the purchase.

Armed in both pockets, pulling the flaps down over my ears I hurtled through the ice and slush to the metro on Yaroslavskoye Shosse with what I reckoned was just enough time to meet my friends at the Pushkin monument. There, standing on Tverskaya Ulitsa, is the figure of the deeply ponderous Ethiopian-Russian poet. Circled by benches of conversation and flower beds, this is an immemorial place of rendezvous, the prelude to a night of illicit romance and Muscovite sabotage. Such moments in Soviet life when the town was turned into a circus were moments of free time. The crowds made the task of moral observance impossible; corks popped, the caps of vodka bottles were jettisoned, and for a moment public space became public again. As momentary concessions from government, carnivals serve the function of soaking up anger, and with fireworks illuminating the squares and boulevards, the noise of laughter and obscenity crashed off the stone walls of Gorky Street past the Hotel Moskva and down toward Red Square. The Kremlin bells peeled midnight, as the iced honey warmed the body. The humming multitude erupted and a group of first-generation punks screamed "Fuck the Communist Party."

WORSHIP

1. It was Easter time in Zagorsk, one of the major spiritual homes of the Orthodox Church. In the entrance to the dark incensed gloom a generation of

solo women were writing their prayers on scraps of paper and leading them to be blessed. She must have been ninety or a hundred and fifty, and she shakingly wrote, "God save the tsar."

2. The worship of bombs is one of the worst of all surrenders. These were not firecrackers but SS20 missiles gliding past on party floats, enjoying the breadth of the boulevards that surround the inner core of the city. The audience cheered and waved flags at the weapons of mass destruction heading home to the sleeping pen.

3. The families were picnicking on the banks of the Moscow River, staring across the muddy torrent to the Beliye Dom. With mouths full of gherkin their synchronized eyes followed the missile's trajectory. "Hurrah, hurrah, another fine hit," sang the happy picnickers, as the front face of the parliament burst into flame.

1991 TELEPHONE

"Yuri Pavlovich, is that you?"

"Djonatanchick, it's good to hear your voice."

"Are you all right? What's going on?"

"Everything's fine, the tanks are rolling down the streets as normal."

MISHA'S RETURN

My years in the subconscious mind convinced me that historical memory is not a free choice—it is a loaded gun. I would only add that it is not loaded just with bullets, but with the poisons that accompany manufactured nostalgia.

MORE VANDALISM IN THE 1990s

In the *Eighteenth Brumaire of Louis Bonaparte*, Marx comments that when history repeated itself the first time, it became known as tragedy. The second time, as farce. But what does history become when it repeats itself a third, fourth, or fifth time? This is what I asked myself when the Soviet system collapsed in the 1980s. With the disintegration of the mirage of a unitary ideology, belief fragmented into a thousand claims on truth, forming a "free market" of meaning in which the notion of authentic memory was finally murdered. The question of the distortion of reality became redundant as a new virus emanated from the history machine, declaring reality to be wholly illusory. In its place a pluralist historical relativism was installed, the resting place of truth and reason, Misha's personal gift for the end of the millennium.

Far from representing the end of ideology, the pluralist ideal of history became a cover for the emergence of the class that had won the battle to control the means of communication. But media domination is never enough for a ruling class—it must always return to stamp the skyline of the capital in its own image, an infantile disorder manifest in making things bigger and in outwitting the vanquished. The reconstruction of symbolic buildings that had previously been destroyed, such as the Church of Christ the Savior, is one such example. It was first built in 1869 as a grand project to unite an insurgent people, financed by the imposition of a draconian system of taxation; it towered over the city, an affirmation of the crisis of greedy belief. This, combined with the lucrative seizure of church property, was why Stalin had it destroyed in the 1930s, although in truth among the Muscovite poor and secular it was never very popular.

As an allegory of the collision of church and state, it was intended to be replaced, after an epic architectural competition, with Iofan's Palace of the Soviets, a monumental colossus that would dwarf the world. But a combination of a cursed place and the death of its mentor left the site as a circular open-air swimming pool named after the anarchist prince Kropotkin. As if to prove how little their behavior could be distinguished from the actions of those they had conquered, the new regime of virtuous bureaucrats closed the popular pool and had the cathedral rebuilt. A symbolic anti-Soviet act, its reconstruction in the 1990s marks a key point in the manufacture of a new history that is deeply romantic in its nostalgia for a mythical Christian prerevolutionary Russia.

Just as the icons of the Orthodox Church had been whitewashed after 1917, so now it was the turn for the murals of heroic workers on gable end walls to be painted out of the city. The photographic displays of loyal deputies on the roadsides grew dusty, and the bulbs blew in the hammer-and-sickle street lamps. Ladders went up and the camouflage of red banners hanging across the boulevards were removed. In place of directives extolling the virtues of the Party and the five-year plan, new banners were erected in the same places, only this time offering stocks, shares, and instant cash. Images and statues of former heroes and heroines of the Soviet state were demolished, streets were renamed, and in a drunken orgy Dzershinsky was removed from the front of the KGB building and dumped along with the broken pieces of other leaders on a patch of grass next to the House of Art.

But Lenin still stands outside Oktyabraskaya metro, and however hard the new bureaucrats try it will be impossible to erase the historical imprint of the Soviet era on the city. The star is embossed too far up on the stone steeples of buildings and too deeply in the souls of citizens. In all of this the thirst for truth and memory is matched only by the equal and opposite desire to forget.

TRUE STORY—TEA WITH CRIMINALS

I studied philosophy at the Moscow State University and had graduated by impersonating a parrot. But philosophy is a poorly paid profession, and I opted for a career as a chauffeur. I longed for the opportunity to screech across Red Square into the Kremlin; you know the shot, it's the one where the whistle-blowing militia part the masses for a high-speed black car that hurtles through an arch and disappears into the wall. But for most of the time I was assigned to ferrying minor Party functionaries around the city, barely enduring their petty jealousies. I broke this routine up by doing a bit of taxi work, selling vodka, and ripping off tourists with crushed eggplant dressed up as caviar. When the Party collapsed I started driving for a new generation of hungry power brokers. This was more lucrative, because unlike the old guard the modern-day gangsters liked to flash their money; it was all right to be rich again, and I got to drive better cars.

But you had to be careful. During the hot summer months of the early 1990s, at five in the afternoon, it was best to avoid standing near a BMW in the center of Moscow. That was when they tended to explode. But on this particular day I was away from the bullfight, circling around the Moscow ring road in a Lada jeep, stopping off for my client to pick up pay-offs at some of the more infamous peripheral estates that punctured the July horizon. Closer to an anarchic game show than a tarmacked motorway, the ring road is a place where reason is suspended and all are invited to play chicken with the monumental trucks carrying piles of concrete and steel that career between the potholes.

Toward the end of the afternoon we turned off and plunged deep into a silver birch forest. After driving up a single-lane track for ten minutes, we came to a gate in a high steel fence flanked by soldiers. An exchange of passwords and dollars, and we crossed over a no-man's-land of stunted grass toward another armed sentry post. The same ritual took place and we entered into a little village of dachas. Scattered between the trees and joined by a tarmac road were a collection of modest single-story cottages, country retreats for the siblings and relatives of previous presidents and well-placed bureaucrats—including, it was said, a great-nephew of Lenin.

In the center of the city the Party elite crudely disguised its wealth and power by labeling it state property. Propped up by a culture of paranoia, they would rarely appear outside of iconic and choreographed spectacles.

But in their rural virtual villages, for a moment they could return to an idealized peasant world of picking mushrooms and growing cucumbers. Unlike, however, the clusters of dachas that Muscovites retreat to at the weekend, private fortified compounds like this one did not appear on maps.

I had grown to despise the parasitic habits of the old functionaries. As a boy they had tried to get me committed to a mental ward when, as a previously loyal Komsomol, I started making effigies of Brezhnev. My father's military contacts saved me. Covert in my rebellion, I drove the meat and vodka faces to all of their secret haunts; dining rooms and wine cellars hidden in mountains, luxury shops disguised as offices, bars on the thirtieth floor, and forest gambling clubs. I would usually sit in the car, chain-smoking, imagining every cigarette as a named bullet, thinking of how in the morning they would make grotesque speeches about the toiling masses. More devious than a vulture, when the time came in the 1980s to change their clothing, they were faster than the emperor.

We stopped at a recently built brick cottage. I followed my employer into a sparse whitewashed living room. Greetings were exchanged in Uzbek and we sat around the table for a tea ceremony with three newly awoken tracksuited hardmen. This was a new phenomenon, a previous generation of state criminal rulers living as neighbors with representatives of a new gang of swindlers and usurpers of power.

I was left to watch World Cup football as the balcony became a heated exchange market. Returning from outside and brandishing a sword that he had unsheathed from an imperial leather scabbard, the main tracksuit sauntered across the parquet floor toward me. "This is the parade sword of the last Tsar, have a feel." Surrounded by the remnants of the old Communist Party and representatives of the new mob, a plan began to form. Stroking the meter-long gold-plated razor blade, I could already read the headlines.

> Today in a village on the outskirts of Moscow, a maniac monarchist armed with a priceless relic from the last Tsar's armory ran amok, slaying the last remaining relatives of previous Party leaders, in what he announced as a revenge attack for the execution of the royal family in 1917. Three as yet unidentified men in blue-and-white regulation tracksuits were also found at the crime scene.

Or alternatively:

> Today in a village on the outskirts of Moscow, a maniac Communist armed with a priceless relic from the last Tsar's armory ran amok, slaying the last remaining relatives of previous Party leaders, in what he announced as a revenge attack for the execution of

the Bolshevik Party in the 1920s and '30s. Three as yet unidentified men in blue-and-white regulation tracksuits were also found at the crime scene.

SMOKING

One of the slang names for hashish in Russia was the word "plan." A smart piece of irony, since if the plan could not be fulfilled, which it rarely if ever was, you could always smoke it.

THE BABUSHKA

The fable of the Russian Babushka is endless. She sits in every eye shot. She is indeed majestic like her sister Bahiana in Brazil. Pregnant with memory, she sits in the park with her friends, guards the entrances and exits, tells the stories, and mourns for the millions dead. Now she stands at the metro selling a loaf of bread or a solitary tulip. But she has stiff competition from the professors who are there selling bouquets. Everyone waits at the foot of the grand underground.

KOLYA IN 1994

Kolya peeled away the gluey mucus that held his eyes shut. Stumbling upward his head spun with the alcohol nausea that rushed through every limb. He had never dreamed that his journey to Moscow would have ended like this, prostrate beneath the statue of Yuri Gagarin. The hangover lurked with a vengeance and Kolya became uncontrollably hungry. Searching his pockets he found one last gulp of vodka and a piece of black bread. Feeling better he squatted down on the pavement and stared up the Lenin Prospect. For a moment the spring sun seemed to pick out the gilt on horse-drawn carriages and the whole street seemed to be ablaze as he thought of god, tsars, monasteries, and peasants. He shook his head, blinked, but this time saw nothing other than the letter *B*, for Banks, BMWs, Bananas, Bullets, and Bandits.

COUPS

As sure as winter comes to the streets of Moscow, so in autumn does the Russian mind turn to revolution. At the height of the confrontation in 1991, when the general's tanks were rolling, the streets were pillaged for building materials and a series of barricades were constructed from all manner of timber, metal, and concrete. These were the last line of defense in front of the Russian parliament.

A week after the direct street confrontations had subsided, I was walking down the Prospect Kalinina, the showpiece sixties boulevard that rips westward through the city from the Kremlin. People had stopped on the bridge near the Beliye Dom where the Prospect crosses the inner ring road. Flowers, ribbons, and printed messages surrounded the photograph of a young man, flanked by a glass of vodka and some rye bread. He had been crushed by a tank in the underpass below and this was his commemoration.

In the gray rain of a Moscow autumn, the spontaneous construction of a Russian grave on a public thoroughfare spoke louder than any institutionalized act of remembrance. This was the people not the state remembering, and it should have been left, the vodka glass refilled and the bread replaced on a daily basis, until the whole construction had seeped into the pavements, permanently etched into the city's memory.

In the days of the putsch, many had lived and slept on the barricades. A large section of them remained, an explosion of strangulated debris that, had it been in a gallery, would have been hailed as an installation art masterpiece. Here, watched over by its civilian guards peering out from makeshift tents, it was an unforgettable expression of defiance. The few youths who remained told me of their campaign to have it kept as a monument, a warning beacon to anyone intent on the illegal seizure of power. Two days later in the middle of the night it was bulldozed, so as to leave no physical trace of the uprising.

Out of the shadows appeared new guards dressed in tsarist uniforms, there to protect the entrances to the Beliye Dom. The red flag slid down the mast, and the banner of the imperial Russian eagle was resurrected. From the top of the bell tower the mischievous memory man sings a lament for an older fictitious Russia, a fable in which there exists little trace of the might of a citizenry mobilized against oppression. It is at this point that memory ceases to function.

26

City Living: Love's Meeting Place

Walking through the streets of Harlem, you will see many abandoned buildings, the shadows of structures that were once strong and complete. Growing up without material privilege, I knew that material wealth ensured that one could live, work, and study in structures that would stand forever, that would shelter and abide. For those living in poverty, shelter was always something that could be taken away, that could fall down, disintegrate around you. Even though I loved clapboard houses and wooden shacks, everyone knew that concrete was the hope of lasting structures.

In small Southern towns that were the landscape of my dreaming—the only worlds I knew growing up—we all lived in houses. Many of these houses were tiny, with thin walls that just barely kept out the cold. Yet they had stood the test of time, with little upkeep. They were abiding and life would be lived in them from generation to generation. There were no apartment dwellings in the segregated all-black world of my youth, not in the black neighborhood. No matter how poor you were, no matter how destitute, there was a little shack somewhere that would offer sanctuary. Land surrounded you. The earth held you and your dwelling.

I share this to provide a background to frame my current relationship to the city. In my youth that city represented to me only the unknown, a place of mystery where one could be lost. It was impossible to lose oneself in a small town. The first American city I journeyed to was Chicago. Although relatives lived there, all I knew of it came from Carl Sandburg's poem, where it was described vividly as "hog butcher for the world." The city was too strange to enchant me. I lost my way there. Home as I understood it was a place where I would never be lost.

Cities had no magic for me. In my imagination they were places where too much was happening. All the movement of cities made it difficult for folks to find time for one another. Small towns were places where one could be recognized, where the familiar affirmed itself daily in habit, routine, predictability. After Chicago, I went away to college and lived in many small cities. There I discovered the groundedness of neighborhoods. Even if one could not know the city in its entirety, one could live in the familiar world of the neighborhood.

The first large city that I lived in was Los Angeles. When I came there to live in my early twenties, I did not know how to drive a car and thus the city was for a time always an alien place. One could never hope to traverse its many boundaries without a moving vehicle. And yet once I got behind the wheel, I would claim this city from a distance. My car was constantly breaking down and so I would see many new neighborhoods trying to find my way home. My deepest metaphor for life in the city continued to be that the city was a place where one could be lost.

Whenever I traveled to cities, I saw them as lonely places. I could not imagine life in the tall, dark apartment buildings. To me the city was a bleak place—a wilderness of concrete, high-rises, and bits of green earth here and there but not enough to let a body feel at home. The lack of visible cemeteries made the city seem all the more a place of absences and vacancies.

My first visits to New York City were always to do business. I came to give lectures. Absolutely nothing about the city charmed me. It seemed always to be a lonely place and leaving it I felt as though I was recovering some lost part of myself. In my late thirties, I moved to a small town, much smaller than the town I had been raised in. The population was below ten thousand—and it had that sleeptime feeling—a sense of languidness. It was easy for me to make a home there. My two-story wood frame "shack" with its seemingly endless small rooms, which appear to have been added as a mere afterthought, was the place I had always dreamed about. When decorating my house I chose the theme "soledad hermosa." It was my desert place, a place I could come for rest and sanctuary. Sheltered from neighbors and the street, it became a place for me to think and write, to renew my spirits.

Like all deserts, it was also at times a lonely place. And so I began to leave it to run off to the city and find spaces of connection and pleasure. It began when the artist Julie Ault came to give a lecture in our small town. We walked to the cemetery here and she insisted that there was life in the city and culture I should be involved in and know about. Naturally, I explained to her my theory that the city was really a great wilderness. Still she lured me there.

The connections I made with artists and writers in New York City seduced me—not the place but the people. When asked to consider coming to teach at City College in Harlem, I agreed. Initially, I sublet flats in Chelsea and the West Village. It was difficult for me to come to terms with living in large buildings with strangers. Practically all my life, I have lived in a world where everyone knows everyone else by name and on sight. The city made me feel lonely inside. It made me feel like a stranger.

More than any other place I have lived in, it has changed my relationship to space, compelling me to think about the connection between class status and home making. Since leaving my hometown it is the one place where a fierce system of racial apartheid seriously informs the conditions and locations in which individuals live.

Even though I work way uptown, I chose to live in the West Village. Initially, I did not think much about the issue of race. My choice was merely informed by the desire to be in a less densely populated area—one that was more neighborly, more like a small town. Buildings were smaller in the West Village and it was an easy location to catch the 1 or the 9 train to travel uptown. Like most locations where tourism is the prime industry, the West Village has a false air of friendliness. Still, it is an easier area to know. Unlike the rest of the city, which follows a grid, and streets are easy to find, the West Village makes no sense and has mazelike quality. It is truly a place where one can be turned around—lost.

After renting small flats for several years, I decided to buy a place in the Village. Whether renting or buying, any black person seeking to find a home in the West Village encounters racial discrimination. Real estate racism is fierce. When I looked at lovely places in buildings where individuals expressed fear or anxiety at the sight of a black person, I immediately crossed those places off my list. Not because I would not have been able to acquire them; I could not bear the thought of encountering racist fear every day when coming home—living in a place where I would be accepted as the "familiar other" but where people of color visiting me would be harassed by racist terrorism.

Luckily, I found a place in a small building with a motley crew of progressive individuals from diverse backgrounds, ages, sexual practices, and so on. In this one-hundred-year-old "tenement" building, the flats all have a similar floor plan, and all our bathrooms are off the kitchen as is often the case in older buildings. The dimly lit narrow hallway that leads into the building is a feature of city apartment dwellings I find depressing. Money and aesthetically pleasing decor could change that, but I seem to be the only person who cares about the hallway, who would be willing to spend money and time to make it more appealing.

By purchasing a flat, I feel that I am making a commitment to life in New York City. The ceilings of the flat are high so it appears to be larger than it really is. I bought this flat hoping to share it with a partner. And I chose to give it the theme "love's meeting place." Before I changed it around it had three large rooms, a kitchen, and bath. It was painted in dreary colors, like the vast majority of flats I have seen. Of the more than one hundred places I looked at, most were dark and filled with huge furniture. Even though the vast majority of people in New York City live in small spaces it's hard to find beautiful pieces of furniture that are not huge. When I walk into what seem like endless furniture stores and ask why everything is so big, I am told again and again that "Americans like big furniture." I have only thought of race and class as I have searched for a place to live, not of nationality, but that too determines the way individuals inhabit space.

I suppose the myth of plenty and possibility, coupled with the will to overconsume, accounts for this obsession with wanting space that is huge, wanting big furniture. Even when space is small then everyone has to pretend. When I bought my "shack" I had little money to do remodeling, so I did most of the work myself with the help of two friends. We were delighted by all the inventive ways we discovered to renew the place without having to spend tons of money.

In New York, where I make much more money than I made in my small town, I hired a team of workers to change the space. They were all Polish immigrants, and most of them spoke only a bit of English. Unlike most folks I wanted to create small private spaces instead of having two huge rooms. Years ago, when I began to think seriously about the political implications of class, I realized that class had to do with more than just economic status, that it had to do with attitudes, values, habits of being. For example, even though I had the money to buy a place I had never thought of hiring an architect to design the new apartment. When friends suggested I do this, the estimate I was given for the work was more than I could afford at the time.

My desires for the space were simple and I was able to draw plans. I wanted French doors to close off the living room and dining room. New closets were added to the bedroom. A doorway leading from the living room to the bedroom was closed off and a wall with a single French door was added to create a tiny workroom off the bedroom. Now the only door to the bedroom was through the dining area. These changes created more private spaces and made the flat more a space where two people could love and work comfortably. The dark walls were painted a color called "navaho white"—a bright color.

When the work was completed I was amazed to see a dreary place transformed into a space of light and warmth. It was awesome to see firsthand what money and a sense of style could accomplish. Constantly I feel a deep sadness about the way in which individuals without access to material privilege in large cities are confined to spaces that are aesthetically joyless.

In this new flat, "love's meeting place," I have brought only possessions that are genuinely needed and loved, keeping in mind William Morris's admonition to "have nothing . . . that you do not know to be useful, or believe to be beautiful." My sparse pieces of furniture are oak—wood that has been in every place I have ever lived. Outside on city streets, I am less a stranger for I am always coming home to a place where love is—a peaceful sanctuary where I come back to myself.

New York City is a harsh place. Unlike the small towns that have claimed my heart, it will always be a wilderness—a place where one may find beauty in unexpected surroundings, a place where the familiar must be tenderly cultivated.

Patrick Keiller

27 Port Statistics

The following paragraphs were written in the last months of 1996, during the final stages of production of the film *Robinson in Space,* for which the journeys they recall were carried out. Toward the end of a previous film, *London,* a fictitious narrator offers the ambiguous assertion, "The true identity of London . . . is in its absence."[1] "Absence of what?" the viewer might ask. One of many possible answers to this question is that London came into being and grew as a port city. Its port activity is now largely *absent,* but continues somewhere else. One of *Robinson*'s objectives was to locate some of the economic activity that no longer takes place in cities.

—

Robinson in Space was photographed between March and November 1995.[2] It documents the explorations of an unseen fictional character called Robinson, who was the protagonist of the earlier *London,* itself a reimagination of its subject suggested by the surrealist literature of Paris. *Robinson in Space* is a similar study of the *look* of present-day England in 1995, and was suggested to some extent by Daniel Defoe's *Tour through the Whole Island of Great Britain* (1724–1726). Among its subjects are many new spaces, particularly the sites where manufactured products are produced, imported, and distributed. Robinson has been commissioned by "a well-known international advertising agency" to undertake a study of the "problem" of England.[3] It is not stated in the film what this problem is, but there are images of Eton, Oxford, and Cambridge, a Rover car plant, the inward investment sites of Toyota and Samsung, a lot of ports, supermarkets, a shopping mall, and other subjects that evoke the by now familiar critique of "gentlemanly capitalism," which sees the United Kingdom's economic weakness as a result of the City of London's long-term (English) neglect of the (United Kingdom's) industrial economy, particularly its manufacturing base.

Early in the film, the narrator quotes from Oscar Wilde's *Picture of Dorian Gray:* "It is only shallow people who do not judge by appearances. The true mystery of the world is the visible, not the invisible."[4] The appearances by which the viewer is invited to judge are initially the dilapidation of public space, the extent of visible poverty, the absence of U.K.-branded products in the shops and on the roads, *and* England's cultural conservatism. Robinson's image of U.K. industry is based on his memories of the collapse of the early Thatcher years. He has assumed that poverty and dilapidation are the result of economic failure, and that economic failure is a result of the inability of U.K. industry to produce *desirable* consumer products. He believes, moreover, that this has something to do with the *feel* of "Middle England," which he sees as a landscape increasingly characterized by sexual

Patrick Keiller

27.1 | *Robinson in Space.* Sign to Toyota plant, Burnaston, Derbyshire.

repression, homophobia, and the frequent advocacy of child beating. At the same time, he is dimly aware that the United Kingdom is still the fifth-largest trading economy in the world and that British, even English people, particularly women and the young, are probably neither as sexually une-mancipated, as sadistic, or as miserable as he thinks the *look* of the United Kingdom suggests. The film's narrative is based on a series of journeys in which his prejudices are examined, and some of them are disposed of.

Robinson's interest in manufacturing, however, is rooted in his quasi-surrealist practice. Whereas *London* set out to transform appearances through a more-or-less radical subjectivity, *Robinson in Space* addresses the production of actual space: the manufacture of artifacts and the development of sites, the physical production of the visible. Both films attempt to change reality with a heightened awareness in which "I can always see how beautiful anything could be if only I could change it"—the words of the Situationist text quoted in the opening sequence of *Robinson in Space*[5]—but in the second film, the initial interest is in the production of (at least some of) this *anything.* In the history of the modernist avant-gardes, the transformation of appearances by the poetic imagination preceded the design and construction of *new things,* and the identification of modernity was the bridge

between the two. In a letter from Ethiopia, Rimbaud imagined a son who would become "a famous engineer, a man rich and powerful through science."[6]

An early motive for making the film was a curiosity about how imports of cars, electronics, and other consumer goods reached the shops (apart from the cars, one hardly ever sees them in transit), and what—if any—were the exports that paid for them; and so there is a lot of material that deals with ports.

In the Department of Transport's 1994 edition of *Port Statistics*,[7] based on figures for the twelve months of 1993, the Mersey Docks and Harbour Company (MDHC) was the most profitable port authority listed. Associated British Ports, which was not listed, declared a higher profit for 1993, but it operates twenty-two ports in the United Kingdom, including Southampton, Immingham, and Hull. The MDHC bought the profitable Medway Ports in October 1993, and operates a ferry service and a container

27.2 | *Robinson in Space.* Daewoo cars with Nosac car carrier unloading Toyotas behind, at Royal Portbury Dock, Bristol. When this photograph was taken in July 1995, there were 60,000 cars stockpiled at Portbury awaiting registration.

terminal in Northern Ireland, but nonetheless Liverpool was (and still seems to be) "the most profitable port in the U.K."

Reading these figures, I imagined there might be some exceptional reason for the MDHC's profitability—a one-off land sale, perhaps, commercial rents, or grant aid from the European Union (EU). Like many people with a tourist's familiarity with the waterfronts of Liverpool and Birkenhead, I took the spectacular dereliction of the docks to be symptomatic of a past decline in their traffic, and Liverpool's impoverishment to be a result of this decline in its importance as a port. In fact, in September 1995, when the images of Liverpool in the film were photographed, Liverpool's port traffic was greater than at any time in its history.

In modern terms, individual British ports are not very large: Rotterdam—the world's biggest port—has an annual traffic of about 300 million tonnes. In contrast the United Kingdom has a long coastline and its traffic, though greater than ever, is divided among many different ports. Since 1960, the tonnage of exports has quadrupled, increasing most rapidly in the 1970s when North Sea oil was first exploited. The tonnage of imports has fluctuated, but overall it has risen by more than 20 percent.

London is still the largest port in the United Kingdom (sixth-largest in the EU),[8] with a total of about 52 million tonnes in 1994. "London," however, consists of the Port of London Authority's entire jurisdiction from Teddington Lock to Foulness, more than seventy miles of the Thames estuary. The largest single location of port activity is at Tilbury, where the docks are now owned by Forth Ports, but Tilbury itself is not a large port. Much of the traffic in the Thames is to and from other U.K. ports, especially that in oil. The total in *foreign* traffic for London and the Medway (which is a separate entity) is exceeded by the combined total for the Humber ports of Grimsby and Immingham, Hull, and the rivers Trent and Humber.

The second-largest total tonnage in 1994 was in the Forth estuary—44 million tonnes, 68 percent more than in 1993—which is as fragmented as the Thames; there the traffic is mostly oil. Next are the port authorities of Tees and Hartlepool, and Grimsby and Immingham, each with about 43 million tonnes. In these pairs, the Tees greatly exceeds Hartlepool and Immingham exceeds Grimsby, though to a lesser extent: Grimsby handles imports from Volkswagen and exports from Toyota. The traffic in the Tees estuary is largely bulk—imports of iron ore and coal for the steelworks at Redcar, exports of chemicals from the plants at Billingham and Wilton, and oil and petroleum products. A large figure for oil exports arises from the reexport of the product of a Norwegian field in the North Sea, which comes ashore by pipeline. There is not much container or semi-bulk traffic (timber, etc.). The traffic at Immingham is also largely bulk—

imports of iron ore and coal (3 million tonnes a year, the equivalent of 10 percent of all the United Kingdom's deep-mined coal), imports of oil for the Immingham refineries, and chemicals into and out of quayside plants—KNAUF has an automated plasterboard plant at Immingham. In addition, there is some container and conventional traffic, and BMW, Volvo, and Saab import cars.

The fifth- and sixth-largest tonnages are at Sullum Voe, an oil terminal in the Shetlands, with 39 million tonnes, almost entirely outgoing crude oil, and Milford Haven, with 34 million tonnes, again almost all oil. Southampton and Liverpool each handle about 30 million tonnes. Both have large container terminals—Liverpool has a large traffic in animal feeds, a new terminal for Powergen's coal imports, and most of the United Kingdom's scrap metal exports. Southampton has a vehicle terminal—Renault, Rover, General Motors, Jaguar—and considerable oil imports.

The other two big ports in the United Kingdom are Felixstowe, which has the second-largest *non-oil* traffic after London and handles 40 percent of *all* the United Kingdom's container traffic (50 percent of its *deep-sea* container traffic), and Dover, which, despite the Channel Tunnel, still handles 50 percent of international roll-on-roll-off traffic—that is, road goods vehicles, which in the last twenty years have become such a large part of international freight.

It is presumably a mistake to assess a port's importance solely by the tonnage of its traffic—a tonne of Colombian coal is worth about £28 at the destination port; a tonne of Volkswagens, say, £12,000; a tonne of laptop computers probably not less than £250,000. Container and road vehicle loads probably always represent considerably greater monetary value than do bulk materials. On this basis, Felixstowe probably handles the traffic with the greatest value. However, given that other large ports are either fragmented (London), aggregates of two or more sites (Tees and Hartlepool, Grimsby and Immingham), or specialist in particular types of traffic (Sullum Voe is *all* oil exports, Felixstowe is *only* containers, Immingham and the Tees largely bulk), Liverpool could now be described as "the UK's largest conventional port." If Liverpool's relative importance is not what it was one hundred years ago, it is not because its traffic has declined but because there is now much more port traffic, and there are more big ports.

Certainly, Liverpool's traffic did decline. In the early 1980s, it was down to about 10 million tonnes per year, but it is now about the same as it was in the mid-1960s. What has vanished is not the working port itself, even though most of the waterfront is derelict, but the contribution that the port made to the economy of Liverpool. Of all the United Kingdom's maritime cities, only Hull, which is much smaller, was as dependent on its port for wealth. Liverpool's population in 1994 was estimated at 474,000, just 60 percent of the 789,000 in 1951. At its peak, the port employed 25,000 dockworkers. The MDHC now employs about 500 dockers (and sacked 329 of these in September 1995). Similarly, a very large proportion of the dock traffic is now in containers and bulk, both of which are highly automated and pass through Liverpool without generating many ancillary jobs locally. The Channel Tunnel enables the MDHC to market Liverpool as a continental European port for transatlantic traffic, so that the ancillary jobs it supports may even be outside the United Kingdom. Also, like any English city outside London, Liverpool is now largely a branch-office location, and long ago lost the headquarters establishments (White Star, Cunard) that made it a world city, the point of departure for emigrants from all over Europe to the New World.

Another influence on Liverpool's economy and culture has been the virtual elimination of the United Kingdom's merchant shipping fleet. According to Tony Lane, of Liverpool University's Sociology Department, although there were never more than about 250,000 seafarers in the British merchant fleet (about a third of whom were of Afro-Caribbean or Asian descent), seafarers were once the third most numerous group of workers in Liverpool.[9] The typical length of a seafarer's career was about seven years, so that at a given moment a very high proportion of men in Liverpool had at some time been away to sea. Most of the few remaining British seafarers work on car, passenger, or freight ferries, on which the majority of jobs are in catering. Apart from the decline in U.K.-owned ships and U.K. crews, modern merchant ships are very large and very sparsely crewed: there are never many ships in even a large modern port. They don't stay long, and crews have little—if any—time ashore, even assuming they might have money to spend. The P&O's *Colombo Bay,* for example, a large U.K.-registered container vessel, has a crew of twenty and a capacity of about 4,200 twenty-foot-equivalent containers (4,200 teu), typically a mixture of twenty-foot and forty-foot units, each one of which is potentially the full load of an articulated lorry. Presumably, jobs lost in port cities and on ships have to some extent been made up by expansion in the numbers of truck drivers.

Not only do ports and shipping now employ very few people, but they also occupy surprisingly little space. Felixstowe is the fourth-largest container port in Europe, but it does not cover a very large area. The dereliction of the Liverpool waterfront is a result not of the port's disappearance but of its new insubstantiality. The warehouses that used to line both sides of the river have been superseded by a fragmented and mobile space: goods vehicles moving or parked on the United Kingdom's roads at any given time—the road system as a publicly funded warehouse. This is most obvi-

27.3 | *Robinson in Space.* Maintainer depot and Truckworld, West Thurrock, Essex, near the Dartford Bridge and Tunnel, the M25 crossing.

ous on summer evenings, when busy trunk roads on which parking is permitted become truck dormitories: south of Derby, an eighteen-mile stretch of the A42 lined with lay-bys that connects the M42 with the M1, is one of these; the nine-mile stretch of the A34 between Oxford and the M40 is another. Many of these trucks are bound for the enormous warehouses of inland distribution estates near motorway junctions—*Wakefield 41,* for example, at junction 41 of the M1, next to its junction with the M62. The road haulage—or *logistics*—industry does not typically base its depots in port cities, though it is intimately linked to them: the road construction battlefields of Twyford Down and Newbury were the last obstacles to rapid road access to the port of Southampton from London (by the M3) and from the Midlands and the North (by the M40 to the A34). The relative insubstantiality of industrial development in the modern landscape seems to be accompanied by very high levels of energy consumption.

Despite having shed the majority of its dockers, the Liverpool port employer's attitude to its remaining workforce is extremely aggressive. In September 1995, two weeks after telling *Lloyd's List* that it had the most productive workforce in Europe,[10] the MDHC sacked 329 of its 500 remaining dockers after they refused to cross a picket line. Five employees of a contract labor firm had been sacked in a dispute over payment periods for

27.4 | *Robinson in Space.* Sign to Midpoint distribution park, near Middlewich, Cheshire. Tesco has a 375,000 ft² distribution center at Midpoint, built in 1993. It has 33,000 pallet positions and a holding capacity of 43 million cases, or nine days' stock for 120 stores. Each store receives between one and four deliveries per day.

overtime, and this led to the picket line that the MDHC workers refused to cross. Liverpool dockers were supported by secondary actions in New York and elsewhere, so that the giant U.S. container line ACL threatened to move its ships from Liverpool unless the lockout was ended. In other countries, even employers were shocked by the MDHC's unrestrained determination to be rid of most of their last few dockers. In July 1996, ACL carried out its threat and moved its ships to Thamesport, an independently owned container terminal within the MDHC-owned Medway Ports in Kent (ACL later returned to Liverpool). Medway Ports, which had been privatized in 1989 as a management-employee buyout, was bought by the MDHC in 1993 in a transaction that made Medway's former chief executive a multi-millionaire. Medway had previously sacked 300 of *its* dockers for refusing to accept new contracts. On dismissal, the dockers were obliged to surrender their shares in the company at a valuation of £2.50 per share, shortly before MDHC bought them for £37.25 each.

The main port of the Medway is Sheerness, which is the largest vehicle handling port in the United Kingdom, with imports by Volkswagen-Audi, two-way traffic by Peugeot-Citroën, and exports from General Motors' U.K. plants, among others. Like other modern U.K. ports, it is a somewhat *out-of-the-way* place. Opposite the dock gates is the plant of Co-

Steel Sheerness, which recycles scrap into steel rod and bar. Co-Steel, a Canadian company, is the proponent of what it calls "total team culture," in which all employees are salaried, overtime is unpaid, and union members fear identification. In June 1996, the International Labor Organization (ILO) called on the U.K. government to investigate Co-Steel's anti-union practices. On the other side of the Isle of Sheppey, at Ridham Dock (a "hitherto little-known port" which featured in the Scott inquiry,[11] and from which Royal Ordnance military explosives were shipped to Iran), there is another KNAUF automated plasterboard plant, which the 1995 Medway Ports' *Handbook and Directory* describes as "the fastest running production line in Europe." Opposite Sheerness, on the end of the Isle of Grain, is the automated container terminal of Thamesport to which ACL's ships were diverted from Liverpool. In the Medway Ports' *Handbook,* Thamesport is described as the UK's most sophisticated container terminal, "where driverless computerised cranes move boxes around a regimented stacking area with precision and speed." Thamesport's managing director insists nonetheless that "This is a people industry. The calibre and commitment of people is absolutely critical." When Thamesport recruited its 200 staff, "I did not want anyone with experience of ports because this is not a port—it's an automated warehouse that just happens not to have a lid on it."

In England, only 1.1 percent of employees work in agriculture, but the United Kingdom grows far more food than it did a hundred years ago, when the agricultural workforce was still large. In 1995, unemployment in Liverpool was 14 percent. On Teesside, which is arguably "the UK's biggest *single* port," is British Steel's plant at Redcar, as well as Wilton, the huge chemical plant now shared by ICI with Union Carbide, BASF, and DuPont. British Steel is now the world's third-largest steel producer, with substantial exports, and the chemical industry is one of the United Kingdom's most successful, with an export surplus of £4 billion. Nearby is the new Samsung plant at Wynyard Park. Despite this concentration of successful manufacturing industry and the port, unemployment in Middlesbrough, on Teesside, is 17 percent: the highest in the country. Wages in some parts of the United Kingdom are apparently now lower than in South Korea.

In the 1980s there were attempts to assert that the future of the United Kingdom's economy lay in services, and that the imbalance in imports of manufactured goods that characterized the Thatcher years could be sustained through increased exports of services (particularly "financial services"). In fact, because of the virtual disappearance of the merchant shipping fleet, the service sector's share of exports has actually declined since 1960, and imports of cars, electronics, and other *visible* items (there are few toys, for instance, not now marked "made in China") are balanced by exports not of services but of other manufactured items, in particular intermediate products (for example, chemicals) and capital goods (power stations, airports). These strengths seem to match the financial sector's cultural preferences: chemical plants are capital-intensive, but do not involve the risks and ephemerality of product design; exports of capital goods are, by definition, financed by other people's capital. The United Kingdom is good at low-investment craft-based high technology, but not at high-investment mass-production high technology, unless it is owned and financed elsewhere (the United States, Japan, South Korea, or Germany). The United Kingdom's most extensive indigenous high-technology industry is weaponry, in which investment is supported by the state. It appears that the decline in manufacturing industry that has been so widely lamented, typically by design-conscious pro-Europeans who grew up in the 1960s (like myself), has been a partial phenomenon.

27.5 | *Robinson in Space.* British Steel works, Redcar, Teesside. The works produce 70,000 tonnes of steel per week, much of which is exported. British Steel is now the third-largest steel producer in the world, after Nippon (Japan) and Pohang (South Korea).

The United Kingdom's production of *desirable* artifacts is certainly lamentable (and confirms the stereotype of a nation run by Philistines with unattractive attitudes toward sex), but any perception of the demise of manufacturing industry based on its failure to produce technologically sophisticated, attractive consumer goods is bound to be overstated. Most U.K. manufacturing is unglamorous—intermediate products and capital goods are not branded items visible in the shops. Intermediate products, in particular, are often produced in *out-of-the-way* places like Sheerness or Immingham—places at the ends of roads. The United Kingdom's domestically owned manufacturing sector is now small, but its most successful concerns are efficient, highly automated, and employ only a few people, many of whom are highly specialized technicians. The United Kingdom's *foreign-owned* manufacturing sector employs comparatively larger numbers of people in the production of cars, electronic products or components, and other visible, but internationally branded, items: many GM cars built in the United Kingdom are badged as Opels, Ford now produces Mazdas (Ford owns 25 percent of Mazda) at Dagenham, and the United Kingdom now has export surpluses in televisions and computers. The big export earners in manufacturing, like the ports, have a tendency to be invisible.

The juxtaposition of successful industry and urban decay in the landscape of the United Kingdom is certainly not confined to the north of the country. A town like Reading, with some of the fastest growth in the country (Microsoft, US Robotics, Digital, British Gas, Prudential Assurance) offers, albeit to a lesser degree, exactly the same contrasts between corporate wealth and urban deprivation: the United Kingdom does not look anything like as affluent as it really is. The dilapidated *appearance* of the visible landscape, especially the urban landscape, masks its prosperity. It has been argued that in eighteen years of Conservative government the United Kingdom has slipped in a ranking of the world's most prosperous economies in terms of gross domestic product (GDP) per head, but it is equally likely that the position has remained unchanged. In any case, this is a ranking among nations all of which are becoming increasingly wealthy. If the United Kingdom has slipped in this table, it has not slipped nearly as much as, say, Australia or Sweden, or even the Netherlands. The United Kingdom's GDP is the fifth largest in the world, after the United States, Japan, Germany, and France. What has changed is the distribution of wealth.

In the United Kingdom, wealth is not confined to a Conservative *nomenklatura,* but the condition of, say, public transport or state-sector secondary schools indicates that the governing class does not have a great deal of use for them. People whose everyday experience is of decayed surroundings, pollution, cash-starved public services, job insecurity, part-time employment, or freelancing tend to forget about the United Kingdom's wealth. We have been inclined to think that we are living at a time of economic decline, to regret the loss of the visible manufacturing economy, and to lower our expectations. We dismiss the [Conservative] government's claims that the United Kingdom is "the most successful enterprise economy in Europe" but are more inclined to accept that there might be less money for schools and hospitals, if only because of the cost of financing mass unemployment.

There is something Orwellian about this effect of dilapidated everyday surroundings, especially when they are juxtaposed with the possibility of immediate virtual or imminent actual presence elsewhere, through electronic communication networks and cheap travel. Gradually, one comes to see dilapidation not only as an indication of poverty but also as damage inflicted by the increased centralization of media and political control in the last two decades.

In the rural landscape, meanwhile, the built structures at least are more obviously modern, but the atmosphere is disconcerting. The windowless sheds of the *logistics* industry, recent and continuing road construction, spiky mobile phone aerials, a proliferation of new fencing of various types, security guards, police helicopters and cameras, new prisons, agribusiness (BSE, genetic engineering, organophosphates, declining wildlife), U.K. and U.S. military bases (microwaves, radioactivity), mysterious research and training centers, "independent" schools, eerie commuter villages, rural poverty, and the country houses of rich and powerful men of unrestrained habits are visible features of a landscape in which the suggestion of *cruelty* is never very far away.

In their book *Too Close to Call,* Sarah Hogg and Jonathan Hill describe the strategy behind the 1992 Conservative election campaign.

> Throughout the summer [of 1991], Saatchi's had been refining their thinking. Maurice Saatchi's thesis went like this. In retrospect at least, 1979, 1983 and 1987 appeared to be very simple elections to win. The choice was clear: "efficient but cruel" Tories versus "caring but incompetent" Labour. The difficulty for the Conservatives in 1991 was that the recession had killed the "efficient" tag—leaving only the "cruel." While the Tory party had successfully blunted the "cruel" image by replacing Margaret Thatcher with someone seen as more "caring," Maurice did not believe that John Major should fight the election on soft "caring" issues.[12]

In the subsequent period the Conservatives were seen as even less efficient and even more cruel. The shackling of women prisoners during labor, and its defense by Ann Widdecombe, the Home Office minister, was the most outrageous example of this, but the campaign to legitimize child beating was perhaps more shocking because it was so widespread. The sexuality of Conservatism is certainly very strange. While there are always a few straightforward libertines among prominent Tories, and Thatcher apparently tolerated homosexuals when it suited her, repression and S&M haunt the Conservatives in a way that cannot be put down simply to the influence of the public schools. Like repression, deregulation inflicts pain and suffering. Unemployment, increased inequality, low wages, and longer working hours all lead to depression, ill health, and shorter life expectancy. In May 1996 Maurice Saatchi launched another preelection campaign with the slogan, "Yes it hurt. Yes it worked."

This gothic notion evokes Burke's famous claim in his *Philosophical Enquiry:* "Whatever is fitted in any sort to excite the ideas of pain, and danger, that is to say, whatever is in any sort terrible . . . is a source of the *sublime.*"[13] Alistair, Lord McAlpine of West Green, the Thatcher confidant who was party treasurer during her leadership, lived for most of these years as a tenant of the National Trust at West Green House in Hampshire. The house, which was badly damaged by fire during McAlpine's tenancy and was bombed by the IRA after he had left, was built for General Henry "Hangman" Hawley, who commanded the cavalry at Culloden; and over the door in the facade facing the garden is the inscription *Fay ce que vouldras* (Do as you will), the quotation from Rabelais that was the motto of the Hell Fire Club.[14]

It takes a long time for a political and economic regime to change the character of a landscape. As I write in the last months of 1996, the regime is changing: in May 1996 Stephen S. Roach, chief economist at Morgan Stanley and former chief forecaster for the U.S. Federal Reserve, announced that the doctrine of cost-cutting and real wage compression ("downsizing") of which he had been the most influential proponent for more than a decade, was wrong.[15] Companies would now have to hire more workers, pay them better, and treat them better. In the United Kingdom, whether or not Labour wins the forthcoming election, the attitudes of most leading U.K. companies toward European social legislation and the single currency seem certain to eclipse the Tory Right. The first services through the Channel Tunnel after the fire in November 1996 were international freight trains, the second of which was carrying car components from one Ford plant in the United Kingdom to another in Spain. The United Kingdom really is now (almost) a part of mainland Europe.

With the Conservatives and their obsessions removed, the new industrial landscape of the United Kingdom begins to resemble the computerized, automated, leisured future predicted in the 1960s. Instead of leisure, we have unemployment, a lot of low-paid service-sector jobs, and a large number of people who are "economically inactive," including "voluntary" caregivers and people who have been *downsized* into a more or less comfortable early retirement, many of whom once worked for privatized utilities. The enormous irony of the Tory twilight is that their protestations that the United Kingdom is a prosperous country are largely true. There are even a few signs of a revival in the manufacture of indigenously financed high-technology consumer goods. The United Kingdom is a rich country in which live a large number of poor people and a similar number of reasonably well-off people who *say* they are willing to pay for renewal of the public realm. There *seems* to be no reason why the United Kingdom cannot afford a minimum wage, increased expenditure on welfare and education, incentives for industrial investment, environmental improvements, reempowered local government, and other attributes of a progressive industrial democracy.

Notes

1 *London,* 35mm color, 85 min., BFI Films, London, 1994.

2 *Robinson in Space,* 35mm color, 82 min., BBC Films, London, 1997.

3 "Nations for Sale" a study of Britain's overseas image, was written by Anneke Elwes in 1994 for the international advertising network DDB Needham. Patrick Wright reports ("Wrapped in Tatters of the Flag," *Guardian,* 31 December 1994) that she found Britain "a dated concept" difficult "to reconcile with reality."

4 The statement is part of Lord Henry Wotton's monologue to Dorian on their first meeting; see Oscar Wilde, *The Picture of Dorian Gray,* in *Complete Works,* general ed. J. B. Foreman (London: Collins, 1948), p. 32.

5 The words quoted are from chapter 23 of Raoul Vaneigem's *Traité de savoir-faire à l'usage des jeunes générations,* known in English as *The Revolution of Everyday Life.* This translation is from *Leaving the Twentieth Century,* translated and edited by Christopher Gray (London: Free Fall Publications, 1974), p. 138, in which chapter 23 appears as "Self-Realisation, Communication, and Participation."

6 Rimbaud's letter is quoted in Enid Starkie, *Arthur Rimbaud* (London: Faber and Faber, 1961), p. 359.

7 *Port Statistics* (London: HMSO) is compiled annually by the Department of Transport. Most of the figures I cite are from the 1995 edition.

8 The United Kingdom's total port traffic in 1994 was 538 million tonnes.
    The ten major world ports in 1994 were Rotterdam, 294 million tonnes; Singapore, 224 million freight tons; Shanghai, 166 million tonnes; Hong Kong, 111 million tonnes; Nagoya, 120 million freight tons; Antwerp, 110 million tonnes; Yokohama, 103 million freight tons; Marseilles, 91 million tonnes; Long Beach, 88 million tonnes; and Busan, 82 million tonnes.
    Among major ports in the EU in 1994 were Rotterdam, Antwerp, Marseilles; Hamburg, 68 million tonnes; Le Havre, 54 million tonnes; London, 52 million tonnes; Amsterdam, 48 million tonnes; Genoa, 43 million tonnes; Dunkirk, 37 million tonnes; Zeebrugge, 33 million tonnes; and Bremen, 31 million tonnes.

9 Tony Lane, conversation with author, April 1996.

10 As reported in the *Independent,* 21 January 1996.

11 The Scott inquiry investigated U.K. arms sales to Iraq during the Iran-Iraq war and thereafter. Its public hearings, between May 1993 and June 1994, were a continuing source of revelations about the conduct of ministers and officials of the Thatcher government. Its report was published in February 1996.

12 Sarah Hogg and Jonathan Hill, *Too Close to Call: Power and Politics, John Major in No. 10* (London: Little, Brown, 1995), p. 125.

13 Edmund Burke, *A Philosophical Enquiry into the Origin of Our Ideas of the Sublime and Beautiful* (1757), ed. Adam Phillips (Oxford: Oxford University Press, 1990), p. 36.

14 See Arthur Oswald, "Country Homes and Gardens Old and New: West Green House, Hartley Wintney, Hampshire, the Seat of Evelyn, Duchess of Wellington," *Country Life,* 21 November 1936, pp. 540–545.

15 See, e.g., *Independent,* 12 May 1996.

Doreen Massey

28 Living in Wythenshawe

IMMATERIAL ARCHITECTURE

Places are spaces of social relations. Take this corner of a council estate: on the southern outskirts of Manchester, across the Mersey from the city. It is like many others, an ordinary place.

My parents lived here for nearly fifty years and have known this spot for even longer. Their lives have taken it in, and made it, for over half a century. Both they and it, and their relationship to one another ("place" and "people"), have changed, adjusted, readjusted, over time. Right now, as I write, my mother's infirmities enclose her in a nursing home that stands on "the exact spot" where once my sister and I went to school.

My parents used to come "here" before the estate was built. Venturing on a weekend across the river and up across the rolling farmland. For Manchester's working class what was to become Wythenshawe was then a healthy walk, a cheerful day out south of the Mersey. Young lives were then quite spatially confined: bus rides into town, a week's holiday on the coast, were the farthest you usually went. So a weekend walk in country air was a real expansion of the spatiality of life.

Years later, with two grown daughters now, and living on the estate laid out across that farmland (but the trees were still there, their maturity both contrasting with the rawness of new houses and providing a reminder of when this place had been another place) they made this very same spot in latitude and longitude home base for spatially much more extended lives. From here, my parents made sorties to London, occasional trips abroad, visits to daughters who had moved away. This was where we gathered, at weekends, for Christmas.

Old age brought a closing-in again—a drawing-in of physical spatiality. The body imposes some limits. Infirmity and frailty can close down the spaces of older people's lives. My mother restricted to a wheelchair, her eyesight failing badly. Only once has she in recent years left the nursing home for more than an afternoon walk or ride. "You can see the Pennines from here," we always used to say. You could turn your eyes to them and dream. But my mother's eyes no longer reach that far. My father too, no longer able to drive a car, finding walking difficult, wanting to stay each day near Mum, felt the spatiality of his later life draw in, settle down into yet another new, this time again more local, pattern. It is as though their lives breathed out and in again. And the place of this place in those lives was molded accordingly.

And yet, of course, their lives—all our lives—are lived in spaces (time-spaces) that are far more complex than you would ever divine from maps of physical mobility. Even now, the spaces of old age are stretched by memories of holidays and travel, opened out by visits from family and

28.1

friends, made more expansive by newspapers and TV bringing tales of other lives. And the times of this space are multiple, too: conjoining memories, overlayering images, sneaking in hopes for the weekend ahead.

—

That shifting, complex, microspatiality of individual yet interconnected lives is, moreover, set within a broader social history. Which is also the history of the making and remaking of social spaces. In less than a hundred years "this place" has passed from aristocratic landownership, through municipal socialism, toward attempts at neoliberal privatization. The breathing out and in of individual lives has been set in counterpoint with programs of social reconstruction that have made and remade this place on a wider social canvas.

 The fields to which the working class of Manchester escaped were in their social form an inheritance of feudalism. Much of the area was still in the hands of landowners whose acreages extended over the north of Cheshire, who could trace their landed lineage back to the eleventh century, and whose preeminence is still witnessed in place-names and associations. (The Saturday matinee cinema I used to go to—the Tatton—takes its name from a family whose power in these parts began at least nine hundred years ago.) When Wythenshawe was built, the physicality of the place was changed beyond recognition. A huge council estate (100,000 people, the largest in the world) spread over what had once been scattered farmsteads, small hamlets, and open country. But the transformation in the social relations that constructed this space was if anything even greater. Relations of deference and of knowing one's place in fixed social hierarchies were engulfed by a municipal building project whose whole dynamic sprang from an assertion of rights: the rights of working-class people to healthy, quality housing. The very physical construction of the new estate asserted the social principles for which it stood. It was the birth of a new social place: a municipal garden city (indeed, Wythenshawe is said to have been the first ever). The new architecture of quality cottage housing for the working class was also a new architecture of social relations.

In recent years, the estate has once again begun to be transformed by wider social projects. The national shift to privatization has largely been resisted here. But it has weakened the hold of municipal socialism, the commitments to planning, and guaranteed levels of social provision. This time the adjustment between built form and social relations has been more nuanced, more varied. There has been no sweeping rebuilding, but the shift in social climate has reworked both physical detail and social import. The scattered sales of houses have changed both the physical face and the social meaning and feel of the place. The same houses have signs now of their private ownership—add-on porches, fancy brickwork, different front doors. A slight physical modification bears witness to a little social revolution: a new

28.2

ability to express personal pride and individual imagination, and also the breakup of the old coherent vision—of "the working class," "the public."

The assumptions of security in which my welfare-state generation grew up (and for which our parents' generation fought) have been fractured by a nervousness that it is hard to put your finger on but you can feel, palpably, in the streets. Every now and then a dreadful rumor brings the terror that the rest of the estate might be sold off into private hands, or is it to a housing association? A previous solid security, for which once the very buildings seemed to stand, now feels threatened, one's hold on things much more precarious. The physical estate is still there, but its meaning has—ever so slightly—shifted. And there are new buildings too, which are carriers of the change: the nursing home where my mother is does indeed stand on exactly the same spot where once my sister and I went to school. But the school on that corner (the corner that was once a feudal field) was a state school; the nursing home is owned by a commercial company. In such various ways, changes in physical architecture and in the immaterial architecture of social relations continually intersect with each other.

—

The crisscrossing of social relations, of broad historical shifts and the continually altering spatialities of the daily lives of individuals, make up something of what a place means, of how it is constructed *as* a place. (Such a picture could be endlessly elaborated, and more and more complexities drawn out.) But a few things in particular seem important to stress. To begin with, there is the open complexity of the spatiotemporality of any place. As my parents' lives close in, the estate's new generation regularly saves to go off abroad; a second runway is mooted for the airport up the road. All day long, planes seem barely to skim the rooftops, their flight paths taking them over "Localine" bus stops for wheelchair users. Senior citizens pass day after day within four walls, and not many miles to the south the telescopes of Jodrell Bank look out to the stars. There's a multiplicity of times and temporalities, as well. This "spot," this "location," is a palimpsest of times and spaces. The apparent securities of longitude and latitude pin down a mobility and multiplicity that totally belie their certainties of space and time.

So too with the apparent solidity of buildings, the givenness of "the built environment." That "givenness" is just one moment in the constant process of the mutual construction of the identities of people and the identities of place. Buildings, therefore, as precipitates of social relations, which go on being changed by them and having a life within them. The "architecture" of the city is also the frame of social relations through which we live our lives, which we constantly adapt to, construct, and reconstruct—which is our spatiotemporality. The spaces of social relations *are constructed,* just as buildings are constructed; they can be adapted, as buildings can be adapted; they are *not* "material" as buildings are material, but they can be as hard to walk through as a wall.

THE PRACTICED PLACE

This is an immaterial architecture: the architecture of social relations. And yet, social relations are practiced, and practices are embodied, material.[1] Places are the product of material practices.

It is easiest to imagine this by means other than through the distancing eye. Spatialities are constructed as well by sound, touch, and smell—by senses other than vision alone. On a wheelchair walk around the grounds of the nursing home, smells can signal where you are (you're just passing the kitchens maybe, or the room given over to hairdressing); a sudden whiff of something caught on the air (the beds of lavender in the garden perhaps) can carry your thoughts away, to other times and other places. The changing texture of the path reverberates through the wheelchair into your body; the movement from ruckly gravel to the smooth passage of asphalt brings relief. Sounds and noises can close spaces down, can intrude or threaten, or can give shape or direction to spaces. Henri Lefebvre has written that "Silence itself . . . has its music. In cloister or cathedral, space is measured by the ear."[2] There are local landscapes of senses other than vision. Try imagining—try designing—a city of sound and touch, a city that plays to all the senses.

—

The birth of the estate, indeed, had much to do with the body. Manchester was bursting at the seams. Reports spoke of 15,000 people living in cellars—the city's so-called cave-dwellers.[3] Slum conditions were appalling, life was often short, disease was endemic. This was still, in parts, Engels's Manchester.

South of the Mersey it was a different world. William Jackson, "the father of Wythenshawe," had been moved to Manchester at the age of sixteen, and later remembered how he had been "horrified to see the slums of Gorton, Openshaw and Ardwick."[4] The attention he drew to the slums bothered the city's conscience,[5] and, as a member of its Health Committee, he discovered the fresh air of Wythenshawe. "Fresh air" was then a crucial component in debates about the city and the body, and the earlier establishment of Bagguley Sanatorium (for the treatment of tuberculosis) was a testament to "the healthy, non-polluted air" south of the Mersey.[6] From the very beginning of plans for the estate, smoke control was insisted on, as was low-density housing and preserving trees and ponds from the area's previous incarnation. The vision was both social and physical. Alf Morris, long-serving Labour MP for Wythenshawe, recalled his first visit, in 1936, when building had begun: "Even now I can still vividly recall the striking contrast between the old Manchester and the new. After what seemed a marathon journey, I was amazed by what I saw. It was summer and sunlit. This new Manchester was green and pleasant, spacious and memorable."[7]

Wythenshawe is green and spacious still; the clarity of the air, the freshness of the (constant) breeze still strike me each time I arrive.

—

But other embodied social practices today make of this place something rather different. Practices more daily and more micro level in their encounter. The place goes on being made. That open spaciousness of the fresh air can be closed down in a myriad of daily ways. Because of public-sector cutbacks, paving stones are broken, or tip at angles that crisscross each other. It makes for a bumpy wheelchair ride, hard on frail and aching bones. It's a mini version of the Alps if you're not steady on your feet. And it restricts your field of spatiality. You (my father, say) have to keep your eyes down as you walk. The spatiality of the very ordinary practice of walking to the shops is utterly transformed. And with it, your construction of this place. Your knowledge of it shifts. You don't look up to see the trees, or walk briskly through the bracing air: you're having to concentrate on your feet. Your spatiality is closed down. Place is experienced, known, and thus made by embodied practices such as these.

But "one place" can be known in numerous ways. There are daily battles over the physical appropriation of space and place: sometimes hostile, sometimes just mutual maneuverings to find an acceptable compromise. Children on bikes and skateboards claim the freedom of the streets and pavements—and make going out a hazardous adventure. My father devised a spatial tactic, never walking in the middle of the pavement but always to one side (the inside edge was best)—that way you know which side of you the bikes will go. Skateboards may embody "countercultural practices," but they can also enable acts of spatial appropriation from others. Differentiated demands on space come into conflict; differential spatial powers confront each other on the streets. And sometimes that confrontation is more clearly hostile: public seats are vandalized, in despair the bowling

28.3

28.4

green is closed (it would need a twenty-four-hour guard to keep it open), across our kitchen window a metal grill is supposed to put off burglars— but you feel its presence while you do the washing up, it makes you feel hemmed in (it also spoils the view), violence may stop you going out at night. The utterly material spaces of the city are thereby reworked from the planners' dreams. The place that is this corner of the estate is also the product of a continual—weekly, daily—negotiation between differentiated, practiced spatialities.

SPACE/POWER

Continual negotiation means, in turn, that space/place is a product of and imbued with social power. The spatiality of my parents' lives is negotiated within a lattice of differentially powerful spatialized social relations.

Some of their confinement we regularly put down to "Them": to "capitalism" or "the Tories."[8] The meagerness of state pensions, the low level of social services, and the difficulties of public transport (think what "high tech" could do for the mobility of the old, the frail, the infirm, if only it were differently directed), the broken paving stones. All these things entrench a rigid framework of constraint: they restrict your movement, literally close down your space, hem in that less tangible sense of spatial freedom and ease. Their weight is undeniable.

But things are also more complicated than that. The very creation of this estate was the result of a battle. Moreover, it was a battle in which were ranged against each other a powerful local state (the city of Manchester) and the local people of rural north Cheshire. Planners against the people. The state against private citizens. The classic terms of so much current debate slide easily into place: domination versus resistance, strategy versus tactics,[9] the system versus local people.

That romanticized classification/identification would here be quite misplaced. The state, the planners, the system were here a collection of socialists and progressives battling to win more, and healthier, space for the city's working class. The "locals" combined a relatively small number of villagers, a high proportion of people who commuted into Manchester to work, and a group of large landowners. The commuters depended on Manchester for their livelihood but wanted nothing to do with the consequences of their large incomes—the higher taxes of the city, the necessity of living among the poor. A poll taken in three of the parishes central to "the local struggle" showed that 82 percent of the parishioners wanted to resist Manchester's advances; yet nearly half of them worked there.[10] The landowners had extensive, spreading acres, could often trace a lineage back through several centuries, and lived still at the apex of a set of (spatialized) social relations that had even now more than a touch about them of feudal settledness and an expectation of deference. There is a tendency in recent literature to glorify "resistance," to assume it is always ranged against "domination," to accept without further consideration that it is on the resisters' behalf that we should organize our rhetoric. Maybe this is because today we feel ourselves so relatively power*less*.[11] In any case, it is an assumption that allows us to avoid thinking about the responsibilities of power. It is a way of thinking that reads "power" as necessarily negative. And it is an assumption that can lead to the misreading of many a situation.[12]

Here in north Cheshire, the resisters against the state, clad in the mantle of "local people," were defenders of a local way of life that included property and privilege. There are few, if any, abstract or universal "spatial rules." Local people are not always the bearers of the most progressive values, "resisters" though they may be. Battles over space and place—that set of sometimes conflicting embedded sociospatial practices—are always battles (usually complex) over spatialized social power.[13] Personally, I'm glad this lot of locals lost, and that the Wythenshawe estate was built.

In part, the battle lines were drawn—in public debate if not in actual motivations—precisely over the meaning of this place. Two different, grounded knowledges confronted each other. The progressive planners, it has to be said, on occasions evinced an attitude redolent of that of English colonizers in Canada or Australia. They simply didn't *see* the existing inhabitants. Here was open space, ripe for development. The Abercrombie Report on the suitability of Wythenshawe for Manchester housing noted that here "there is virgin land, capable of being moulded to take whatever shape may be decreed, with hardly a village or large group of houses to interfere with or direct the line of development."[14] But, of course, no land is really virgin land; and these locals were powerful, and they resisted. Yet the spatial terms of their resistance were hardly more convincing, and certainly imbued with less laudable intentions, than Manchester's interpretation of the place. The battle cry "Cheshire should be kept as Cheshire"[15] is precisely that appeal to conservation-as-stasis which indicates only a lack of argument. (Yet how often we hear that refrain, from all parts of the political spectrum and all kinds of "local people".)[16]

And so the estate was begun, a project fueled by idealism, by an idea of what the public sector might be at its best.

—

Negotiations continue to this day over the meaning of this place, over how it might be known, over the rights to particular spaces, and over whose writ rules where. The residents themselves take over the making of the estate, this time in the finely textured, quotidian negotiation of spatialized social relations of differential degrees of power. There is active aggression: vandalism and violence, not necessarily against you yourself but visibly, intimately present—the shattered bus shelter, the massacred sapling (there goes an-

28.5 |

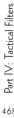

28.6

28.7

other council policy); it is a presence whose meaning closes down your spatiality in a million ways. And there is the entirely nonantagonistic, but still power-filled, attempt to live together by a group of people who—as anywhere—have highly differentiated demands on space: skateboarders and unsteady older folk; babies in prams pushed through City vs. United on the street. The "public" for whom this estate was built turns out to be multiple and differentiated: to have varying demands on space, to give it different meanings, to want to *make* different, and sometimes conflicting, places. "Public space" turns out to be a tricky concept. And binary notions of "domination" and "resistance" fall apart in this intersection of a multiplicity of spatialities.

SPACE/IDENTITY

In this intersection, identities are molded. Your spatiality can "place" you. Places are part of what tells you who you are.

But there are ways and ways of constructing this relation—between personal and place identity. There is, for instance, place as continuity, and there is place as eternal home. Both present difficulties.

If you like, I could tell such a tale of this place, woven around long historical continuities and that kind of notion of "home." In *On Living in an Old Country*, Patrick Wright evokes the standard parish-history format: start from the Domesday book (after brief speculation re earlier occupants) and proceed in gentle linear fashion through the ages to today.[17]

You know the kind of thing. Osbert Lancaster parodies the genre in *Drayne-flete Revealed*:

> Few towns in England can boast so long a continuous history as
> Drayneflete. From the earliest times human habitations of one sort
> or another have clustered along the north bank of the River Drayne
> at the highest point where this shallow but treacherous stream is
> easily fordable. Or perhaps even earlier, for it is conceivable, though
> admittedly there is little to suggest it, that primitive man dwelt
> here before even there was a river at all, at a time when France and
> England were joined by a land-bridge and vast mammoths and
> sabre-toothed tigers prowled through the tropical undergrowth
> where now stands Marks and Spencers.[18]

The Domesday entry for northern Cheshire could make my heart
leap with connections and continuity. In the post-1066 redistribution of
land, one of the benefiting Norman landowners was none other than a certain Hamon de Massey. There's a place called Dunham Massey up the road.
Indeed, the Tattons only seem to have acquired Wythenshawe through the
marriage, in 1370, of their Robert to Alicia de Massey.[19] Had it not been for
patrilinearity, as a moviegoing child I might've gone not to the Tatton but
to the Massey.

In fact—I know this now—there are few continuities here, and no
bloodline connection. The construction of "home" can rarely be accomplished by following back continuous temporal threads in the confines of
one place. One's affection for a place—even a sense of "belonging"—does
not have to be constructed on a romanticism of roots and unbroken, space-
specific lines of descent.

Rather, it is in other ways that places instruct you as to your identity. Those paving stones remind you of your frailty. They actively, materially, dis-able you. Changes in the material environment may tell you that
your time is passing. The blank impenetrability of the security blind on a
once-well-used but now closed shop. As the built space shifts to respond to
other, newer, desires, the consequent exclusions are part of what tells you
who you are. You'd not even know how to enter that shop with all the hi-fis
and computers. The very exclusion is identity-forming. Without hostility,
but simply with the exuberance of the new, a place constructed by and for
your generation (which itself offended the one before) gets taken over by another, which you don't fully understand.

Lefebvre has famously written that

> Monumental space offered each member of a society an image of
> that membership, an image of his or her social visage. It thus con-

stituted a collective mirror more faithful than any personal one. Such a "recognition effect" has far greater import than the "mirror effect" of the psychoanalyst.

The monument thus effected a "consensus," and this in the strongest sense of the term, rendering it practical and concrete.[20]

There are debates about how effective grand monuments can really be. But here on this estate the insight can be turned around. For one thing, these spaces are distinctly nonmonumental. For another, most of them selectively both welcome and reject. To walk along the parade of shops is to feel oneself on occasions drawn in, at other moments repulsed, at yet others most clearly excluded. And the sequence would be different for each of us. Here, in the spaces and places of daily life, are "mirrors" that alternately embrace and deny. Unlike monuments, whose purpose is to gather together in the consensus of a common belonging, a shared identity, all those who walk by, the multiplicities of ordinary spaces reflect the fact of differentiation and fracture—places that you'd go and places that you wouldn't. Monumental spaces strive to tell you (to teach you) of your common membership. The nonmonumental spaces within and through which we more habitually live tell you more precisely of where you belong. (Indeed, monumental spaces may well be needed precisely *because* other spaces so selectively welcome and reject.) These things add to your understanding of who you are, of just how you figure in this society, in the wider scheme of things. It is thus that spatialities can literally place you. They can tell you where you fit in, let you know your relative power.

—

For people like my parents—in their eighties, "working class"—I think what many cities say is that you are living on the edge of what is *really* going on (on the margins of society), picking your way through a world now increasingly in the hands of others. The mirror held up by the spaces of the postmodern metropolis reflects to many elderly people an image in which they don't appear. Like one of those Chinese photographs from which Lin Biao has been airbrushed away.

But that would also be too negative, would be to oversimplify—yet again—the patterns of power and space. Lefebvre also writes that

There can be no question but that social space is the locus of prohibition, for it is shot through with both prohibitions and their counterparts, prescriptions. This fact, however, can most definitely not be made into the basis of an overall definition, for space is not only

28.8

the space of "no," it is also the space of the body, and hence the space of "yes," of the affirmation of life.[21]

And indeed my parents are not passive either. In the middle of it all they, and people like them, continue to carve out highly viable space. They continue to make places: the local spaces of a wheelchair ride, or a picnic on the field. In the evening as we talk, the spaces open out of the memory of longer journeys, of those occasional visits abroad. Most of all, and still, there is that space which is hardest of all to picture, to pin down: the space of social relations. The people on the corner watch out for each other. The neighbors make sure my father's curtains are drawn to every night and drawn back in the morning. They check to see the milk's been taken in.

RETROSPECT

The tenses in this piece are inconsistent. My father, then my mother, both died while I was writing it. The house has suffered subsidence, was boarded up. The garage was vandalized, the front gate stolen, there were graffiti on the boards over the front door. Layers of memory are embedded into built space. The dereliction of the house seemed for a moment to threaten the very medium of memory. All in a few months.

But we go back to see the neighbors. People come out to say hello when my sister and I arrive. There is still laughter and local gossip. Being there again you feel the power of materiality to prompt recall: the feel of the rough brick, the prickle as you run your hand along the privet hedge; the breeze still blows. And now the house has been mended and new people have moved in. "Two daughters again," we are told, and we smile. The making of this estate goes on.

Notes

1   See Nigel Thrift, *Spatial Formations* (London: Sage, 1996).

2   Henri Lefebvre, *The Production of Space,* trans. Donald Nicholson-Smith (Oxford: Blackwell, 1991), p. 225.

3   "Towards a New Wythenshawe: Dreamers and Schemers, Plotters and Planners," in *Wythenshawe: The Story of a Garden City,* ed. Derick Deakin (Chichester: Phillimore, 1989), p. 25.

4   William Jackson, quoted in ibid.

5   "Towards a New Wythenshawe," p. 25.

6   Abercrombie Report, quoted in ibid., p. 28.

7   Alfred Morris, M. P., preface to Deakin, *Wythenshawe,* p. x.

8   This essay was written when the Tory variety of "Them" was still in government. At this moment we still wait to see if New Labour will be understood by those on the estate as "Us" or just another "Them."

9   See Michel de Certeau, *The Practice of Everyday Life,* trans. Steven F. Rendall (Berkeley: University of California Press, 1984).

10   "The Five Year War: 1926–31—From Parkland to Parkerland," in Deakin, *Wythenshawe,* p. 44.

11   It would be interesting to compare this present combination of a language of resistance and a real powerlessness of the Left with the situation in the sixties and seventies, and even the early eighties, when "the Left" in various guises held power (in the form of the state) and had to face up to the responsibilities and decisions which that brings. I'm thinking here of some countries of the South (Mozambique, Cuba, Angola, Nicaragua . . .) as well as the Left in power in various local states in a number of European countries.

12   The second runway that is to be built at Manchester Airport has brought together yet another complex alliance against the city's plans. The Bollin Valley had become the new edge of the urban, where Mancunians *now* walk (Wythenshawe having been built) of a Sunday afternoon.

13   Doreen Massey, "Making Spaces: Or, Geography Is Political too," *Soundings* 1 (1995): 193–208.

14   Abercrombie Report, quoted in "Towards a New Wythenshawe," pp. 27–28.

15   "The Five Year War," p. 48.

16   There were two notable exceptions to the social story. Ernest and Sheena (later Lord and Lady) Simon were relatively recent landowners—they themselves bought Wythenshawe Hall and 250 acres. Both of them tireless and effective campaigners for social reform, they presented both the hall and the estate to the city. To this day, constraints still operate on the use of this land, which was expressly presented "to the people." Lord and Lady Simon of Wythenshawe are still talked of with admiration by those on the estate who know of its history.

17   Patrick Wright, *On Living in an Old Country: The National Past in Contemporary Britain* (London: Verso, 1985).

18   Osbert Lancaster, *Draynflete Revealed* (London: Murray, 1949), p. 1.

19   "Chronicle of Notable Events," in Deakin, *Wythenshawe,* p. xii.

20   Lefebvre, *Production of Space,* p. 220.

21   Ibid., p. 201.

Patrick Wright

29

The Last Days of London

a conversation with Joe Kerr

Joe Kerr:

This discussion is accompanying a chapter from your book *A Journey Through Ruins*,[1] because its distinct evocation of the city has had a strong influence on our own practice. So could I ask you to explain something of the way you researched and wrote the book?

Patrick Wright:

A Journey Through Ruins is an episodic book in the sense that it accumulates through bits of history, territory, and events. That's the polite way of putting it. It was written at the end of the 1980s, a time when the whole city was being shaken by a triumphalist Thatcherism, and when the London of the post-war settlement really was in its last days. I didn't want to do a historical overview of fifty years of social policy in the East End of London and I wanted place to be fundamental and not just as a setting, picturesque or otherwise. I was living around the corner from Dalston Lane, a hard-pressed street that was often choked with cars. I walked along it thousands of times before realizing that this road, which normally one would see only in the perspective of urban deprivation, was actually very interesting and serviceable too. It has never been a grand street—its nineteenth-century buildings are undistinguished as well as fallen—but I realized that I could use a three- or four-hundred-yard stretch of it as a general metaphor. I was impressed by the extent to which, within a couple of miles of the City of London, you could have a place as battered and contrary as Dalston Lane, a street that defied belief by its mere survival.

The 1980s was a decade of "design," when retailing was going to be the answer to all social problems, while urban planning gave way to the market and the Docklands-style enterprise zone. The characteristic symbol of municipal intervention was undergoing miniaturization—from the tower block of the early seventies to the litter bin, street-cleansing machine, or heritage bollard. And the urban texture was diminished too: stripped of memory and rendered comparatively uniform by a pseudo-ecological form of "concrete managerialism" which, as we were finding out, can turn any place into its own kind of "non-place." And in the midst of that you had this stretch of Dalston Lane that was chaotically resistant, a curiously posthumous street that had been scheduled for demolition for nearly fifty years, and which had certainly never been visited by "design." Only a shortage of funds had stopped the Greater London Council (GLC) putting roads through several decades previously, and when I started writing the government was busy planning to bulldoze it again. So here was this disheveled street where the raw ends were exposed: it was the underside of all the transformation that was going on. I was trying to show another form of urban texture, the stuff

29.1

29.2

29.3

that underlies the plan, but I also wanted to use that street as a yardstick for getting the measure of the wider political culture. I wasn't there only as a local recorder, as a witness, and I've had some arguments about this. Raphael Samuel, for example, asked where the celebration of local accents was, but that sounded too dutiful to me; I reckon there is quite a lot to be said for not always celebrating cockney accents in a mixed and diverse city like London.

JK: Although you are always very sympathetic to the characters who populate your narrative, aren't you?
PW: Well, I don't think there's much point simply lifting people into your pages in order to punch them down, or merely using them to illustrate your own preconceived ideas. For instance, in *A Journey Through Ruins* there is a vicar who had become a *Guardian* joke. There was a journalist who lived in the area very briefly (just down from Cambridge, and already heading for the *Daily Mail*), who would pick up the Rev. Pateman's parish magazine on the way to work, and put smirking jokes in the *Guardian* diary about the idiocies of it. Pateman was pretty wild—he once offered to provide a child-beating service for parents who couldn't bring themselves to do it for themselves. A reprehensible idea, to be sure, but when you realize that there are many pious West Indians in the congregation of this hanging and flogging vicar who seemed to deplore the whole postwar period as one long slide into degeneracy, you might still reckon that it demands a more nuanced response. I think that if one is depicting ideas, one should also try to understand what their ra-

Patrick Wright

tionality might be, however weird, and one of the things you have to think about really carefully when writing about a place like East London is the habitual condescension of the better-placed onlooker.

I found out more about this when I started writing for the *Guardian* myself after the book was published. I would be asked for an article whenever anything ghoulish or disastrous had happened in Hackney—the place could only achieve national interest under the rubric of monstrosity. I wasn't aiming to minimize the horrors that do indeed occur in the inner city, but if you're looking for a place where tolerance and reciprocal humanity are to be found at their best, you would probably do better in Hackney than in Tunbridge Wells. Yet the national culture seems unwilling to bring these inner-city areas into focus except as sinks of depravity. This is also a problem for writers or filmmakers who would use the state of the inner city to attack bad or neglectful governments. I wrote about this with reference to Mike Leigh's television films and also Paul Harrison's book *Inside the Inner City*,[2] which was written partly in order to establish that "third world" levels of poverty were to be found in Thatcher's Britain. You could see what he was doing. He was trying to shock mainstream, affluent, Tory-voting Britain into some sense of remorse and shame. Maybe he had some effect somewhere out there. But what you actually got in Hackney was an application of deprivation theory to every aspect of urban life—right down to the street markets like Ridley Road, a diverse and sometimes exuberant place where Harrison saw nothing but grinding poverty. There's a risk of "place abuse" here. It is

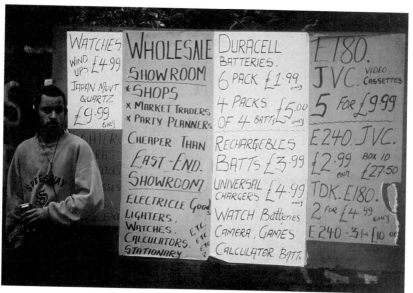

29.4

certainly better to run the poverty scenario in order to get more resources for the city, but as a strategy it doesn't differ that much from the right-wing version which presents the inner city as violent and degenerate in order to suggest that council housing produces brain-damaged children.

JK: Although, if you become too self-conscious about appropriating the city as your subject matter, you give up in the end, don't you?

PW: Yes, and to write about a place is inevitably to abuse it in one way or another. I tried to find a way through this by combining historical research, description, and political polemic with quite explicitly autobiographical material, which at least revealed something of where I myself was coming from. If you're going to write about a world that is so patently, so obviously not just yours . . . I mean, if you are a rural grandee you might imagine that the world you see through the window is yours, and perhaps in some technical sense it is, but in the city you have to realize that your perception is only one among others, and that from many points of view the way you see this place may very well be utterly mad, utterly mistaken. You have to allow for that, so I tried to place myself in the picture, not obtrusively or egotistically I hope, but enough at least to reveal that I don't have all the answers either.

JK: I imagine the parallel concern is whether you find multicultural environments threatening or rather actually celebratory, so that welcoming other voices becomes important.

PW: This is the crux of the matter. People have asked me where that multicultural world is in *A Journey Through Ruins*, to which I'm inclined to reply that even if there are no pages given over to the celebration of local color, diversity should be implicit throughout the book. I was trying to demonstrate how negatively mainstream ideas of national identity, and even ecology, have weighed on the modern, postwar city, which is obviously mixed and diverse and poor, but also industrious, energetic, and full of future possibility. But what I really couldn't do was to speak for other people. I didn't feel it was my role to sit in people's front rooms and say, "Here is X from Bengal and here's this nice person three doors down from Montserrat." Perhaps I was too nervous of that, but I don't think so.

JK: One of the obvious devices employed here is to take a discrete object or environment as a starting point to develop very quickly into a very catholic discussion of the entirety of postwar British culture, and you've described Dalston Lane as "a prism through which to view Thatcher's Britain." To what extent do you think that this "method"—if you're happy to have it called that—is one that has the potential for general application, or is it something more precisely specific to yourself, or to this particular location?

PW: I wouldn't call it a method, in the way that philosophers or social theorists would talk about "scientific" method. I was trying to work out a way of engaging with an urban reality that was undergoing very rapid transformation, and I was doing it as someone who, having failed to get into academic life some years earlier, had discovered certain advantages to being free from the usual curricular attachments. One has to remember that during those years, the whole postwar settlement was just falling to pieces. It was being attacked by the government, but it was also dying of its own inertia and incompetence. So everyday appearances were shaken out of their ordinary routines; they really did seem to be "strangely familiar," and I wanted to capture some of that. I also felt growing reservations about the institutionalized route that academic cultural studies had taken in the eighties. Some theorists just headed into stratospheric abstraction. Others seemed content merely to rush after the changes, affirming that they had indeed taken place, and that they were probably "popular" and "pleasurable" too. I wanted to stay close to concrete reality, and to do so critically. I was interested in engaging with wider political developments like the privatizations of the eighties, but I didn't want to leave the everyday behind. It's in everyday life that people do their thinking, and where ideas are brought into expression. So I was interested in picking up everyday events that seemed to reveal bigger patterns. That's the sort of exposition I admire in thinkers like Walter Benjamin—of finding causality beneath the surface of small events, partly Talmudic and partly political.

Beyond that, I should mention a certain feeling of defeat. In the eighties anyone who didn't like what was going on had a problem, because there wasn't any unproblematic alternative to espouse. Hackney may have been able to muster a mariachi band and a whole spectrum of community organizations thanks to Ken Livingstone's GLC, but beyond those gestures we were completely trounced by what was going on, and, if we were among the new homeowners in East London, additionally humiliated by the fact that Thatcher kept putting the value of our properties up! One couldn't defend the public sector in a total way, or the local state, least of all in Hackney, where the whole story of local government can seem little better than one farce after another. So, rather than falling back into moral disapproval, it was much more interesting to find some event or presence that was obviously intriguing and alive and alert—an episode, or some fragment of news—and follow it through. Sometimes I felt like a demented hobbyist, but I was amazed how many of my interests at that time could be addressed through the apparently incidental details of one small location.

JK: Of course by doing this, you transform the understanding of the object itself, don't you? For instance your discussion of the red telephone box in a later chapter quickly becomes a discussion at the level of national politics, which then in turn transforms how we understand the telephone box.

PW: Until they were politically activated in the eighties, I knew nothing about phone boxes, and would have laughed at the idea that they were significant icons of the time. But with privatization, those kiosks were defined as a national issue, not by me but by the political circumstances of the time. With privatization, the red telephone box was suddenly on the front line of a conflict that developed within Conservatism, between the patrician and overseas image of Britain as a land of red telephone boxes and a government devoted to an asset stripping of the public sector, which had led to them being sold off. So you dig around a little, and find within this apparently trivial argument, a perfect demonstration of the truth of that time. Basically, the book was my response to that thing called Thatcherism. It is focused through a street rather than a curriculum called cultural studies, and is trying to get into the everyday nature of things. If one can do that in a manner which reveals the vitality of a fairly nondescript area of East London, then so much the better.

JK: The chapter in question is one which provides an apparently "authentic" description of just one street. But from what you have told me certain details of this apparently meticulous survey are deliberately invented. Given this, what do you imagine a reader's attitude to this text as a highly place-specific account might be?

PW: It is quite true that I combined objective description with occasional disappearances into rhetoric and even fiction. I never faked the archive, but I did sometimes allow my perceptions to override reality or to twist it a bit. I would justify that on several grounds. To begin with, it is a way of saying that this street, in this incarnation, doesn't exist except as I put it there. In a sense, I'm taking my distance from those grand urbanists who think they've mastered a street because they've written it into some sort of macro plan: it's fixed, they've got it. Obviously, you can't fix a street. The minute you've finished it is gone, although actually it is you that's gone, not it.

But there is something else here, connected to the climate on the Left at the time. There was a curiously silencing concern with "ideological soundness" on the Left in the early eighties—one that preceded the importation of the notion of "political correctness" from North America. I knew this from the conference circuit, and I also saw it in many of the London community and voluntary organizations I worked with at that time. Collective endeavor was good, and individual expression dubious at best. There was a lot of biopolitical assumption around, taking politics back into the body in one way or another. If you were a white man you'd have difficulty speaking at all, and should probably confine your utterances to programmatic statements of support for more authentically oppressed constituencies. I'm exaggerating here, but there were real problems that stood in the way of writing. Merely to describe another person, a café, or a market stall was to abuse them. And to fictionalize anyone else's experience—well, that could seem like a crime against humanity. I couldn't write about the city without breaking through all that, and a certain amount of querulousness and score settling was part of making that visible.

Then there's the opening chapter of the book—a scene which I fictionalized with the help of two leading right-wing political figures, Sir Alfred Sherman and Lord Keith Joseph. They were both inclined to peddle fervid pictures of urban degeneration to justify Tory policy for the inner cities, and one of them at least liked to use Hackney as a reservoir of vile and rhetorically convenient images. I wanted to close the gap between the onlooking rhetoric and the urban reality it exploits. So I took these two figures—Joseph and Sherman—and brought them into Dalston Junction, where I stuck them on soapboxes and had them giving speeches to an imaginary crowd. The speeches did exist. They were articles that Sherman and Joseph had written, so I wasn't putting words into their mouths. Now some readers found this confusing. There were one or two very irritated geographers, if I remember correctly, and some thought the scene, which I was actually careful to describe as a reverie, had really happened! But the main issue here for me is that cities are partly made of stories and fables, and a place like East London especially so. I wanted to keep that narrative quality in view, and to make my own use of it. Once you accept that the city is made of stories, of memories, myths, and traditions as well as concrete and roads and planning dispensations, then you have to accept that narrative and fiction are part of the urban texture—and you can use them without necessarily being untruthful.

JK: To return to the question of method: while your immediate object of study—whether it be street, housing estate, or telephone box—is prominently positioned in the foreground of your discussion, clearly this discussion is informed by a profound acquaintance with cultural theory. Does the fact that you don't wish to create a detailed apparatus of academic references, and that the subject is so grounded, imply a criticism of the normal usages of those ideas?

PW: One of the advantages of not being employed in the university system is that you don't have to encumber yourself with a wheelbarrow full of peer-reviewed footnotes. I've read a lot of cultural theory, and I still keep an eye on the journals. But I'm also trying to write in direct engagement with what time-warped deconstructionists somewhere may still be inclined to dismiss as "the so-called real world." I think a lot of theoretical writing about culture has become very detached, partly due to its retreat into a beleaguered academy and partly to do with a loss of moral and political purpose which, at my least charitable moments, I think has been replaced by a machine-minding mentality with a more or less adequate career structure attached. Twenty years ago, cultural studies was a nonconformist and partly piratical venture interested in extending critical value to new forms and constituencies. It had a strong outward orientation and, while people were always jostling for scarce jobs, its conferences and publications were motivated by something greater than the search for points on the Research Assessment Exercise. I wrote *A Journey Through Ruins* at a time when the distance between academic thought and the broader public domain seemed to be increasing, and it was an attempt to pull things in the other direction. I also wanted to write a book that could be entered by people who hadn't necessarily bought into the current curriculum, and got three degrees to prove it.

Over the years in which Thatcher was shaking up the country, cultural theory seemed to disappear into self-referring isolation, developing its own utterly conventional star system and pursuing themes and preoccupations that often seemed to me unnecessarily marginal, even if they weren't entirely disconnected from reality. Partly, I think this was the result of a growing internationalization of cultural studies. The development of the conference/employment circuit that reaches into North America and elsewhere has introduced a curious "placelessness" into its theorizing—one that is too easily dressed up as "postmodernism" and the rest. I would like to see a younger generation coming forward to transform and reenergize this way of thinking—but I have seen too little sign of that over the last fifteen years. Maybe nowadays your time is up before you have even got to the end of the obligatory reading list. So, yes, I have found myself increasingly at odds with the way this whole area of inquiry has become institutionalized within the higher education system and, as someone with nothing to lose in this regard, I'm happy not to contribute to peer-reviewed journals.

JK: Presumably one way forward, apart from the radical transformation of theory, is on a more modest level, simply the application of those ideas to intelligent subjects.

PW: To start with, we shouldn't assume that all intellectual activity is of the academic theoretical kind. Immigrants are often natural philosophers, for example: their situation obliges them to think things out for themselves. I can't claim to have filled my book with encounters with "organic intellectuals"—nothing so orderly was turning up in East London by the late eighties. However, it does include a lot of wild urban thinkers: anti-fluoridationists, nutty politicians, metal detectorists, fundamentalist vicars, frustrated tenants, a blimpish and idealistic prince, and other exemplars of the ways of thinking, utopian or morbid, that flourished around the expiring edges of the welfare state. As for *The Village That Died for England*,[3] the rural sequel to *A Journey Through Ruins*, that is in some ways modeled on the imagination of the metal detectorists—hunt for metal in the shires of deep England, and you'll start uncovering tanks as well as used cars. But I think you are right. One should use whatever theoretical tools help to elucidate the situation at hand, and to keep a sense of interest and possibility alive.

JK: This is obviously very difficult, but in writing about the city there has to be some sense that you actually feel what you are doing might be useful to the city, don't you think?

PW: Cities are built of arguments as well as bricks and mortar, so I hope it is always useful to elucidate those, draw them out, give them new settings, and make them available for discussion. That's another argument for staying close to the street. But the motivation for this kind of work needs constant reinvention, and I am not sure that anything like that has been happening in the universities recently.

JK: But you must remember that for those of us teaching in the university, our new intake of students were only just born when Thatcher came to power. They certainly aren't children of the welfare state.

PW: That confirms the importance of being explicit about your own formation and about the extent to which you are talking about the experience of your own generation. I can't claim ever to have been inspired by the welfare state when I was a child, perhaps because I was never in urgent need of its provisions. I was raised in a middle-class world that had a certain austerity about it. There was no conspicuous consumption, but no dependency on welfare institutions either. I recall the dentistry, orange juice, and cod-liver oil, but by 1970, when I went to university, that whole world seemed pretty uninspiring—hard to invest your passions in its defense. I remember the Marxists of that time being especially unimpressed by the unrevolutionary limitations of "welfstate man." By the eighties, however, there was good reason to think *that* history through much more carefully. One had to define what all that institutional endeavor had meant if only in order to have a better than sentimental sense of what you were trying to defend. But I accept that students nowadays live in a different world, and there is no reason they should come to the same conclusions. However, if as teachers we are trying to help them develop genuine critical skills, then we'd better not be tying them up in a language and methodology that is abstracted rather than theoretically useful.

JK: In relation to high-mindedness and the apparent superiority of "high" cultural theory, you use narrative as a key organizing device in *A Journey Through Ruins*—both real stories and myths, but narratives of one kind or another. How do you respond to the current, common use of the term "anecdotal," when intended as a damning criticism?

PW: Narrative is what is in people's heads, it's how we make sense of the world. So why not use it to reveal the extent to which we are governed by narratives, bad ones as well as good ones? This was demonstrated with overwhelming force by the privatizations of the eighties: narrative is the stuff of our confusions and of our hopes and political possibilities and, as a social allegorist, I wanted to make my book out of that material. Now there are indeed thinkers who believe true history or policy should stand above all this, and who exhibit a very haughty disdain for "anecdotalism." The anecdote is the small thing, and the implication is that in using it you are trivial, quite incapable of grasping the big sweep. But if your commanding perspective is disconnected from the street, so to speak, from the place where people actually make sense of events, then there is something seriously wrong with the big sweep, no matter how many state papers you've got bundled up in your footnotes. So, while the professors press on through their archives, I was more inclined to pick up small events that are pregnant with latent meaning. I wanted an anecdote with epic ramifications, because in it one sees a future for this critical process beyond academic machine-minding. Then somewhere along the line, one has to demonstrate that it still works.

JK: These ideas are so important for us: the subtitle of our first book was "Narratives of Architecture in the City." Now, while it is part of the conventional rhetoric of cultural theory to promote interdisciplinary thought, would it be fair to say that your ability to range across an extraordinary number of academic disciplines has actually caused problems for your books?

PW: Oh yes. These books fail to thrive and nobody makes a living off them. They're not easy for the booksellers or the publishers. They fall between categories, and have a persistent tendency to go out of print. Obviously, I didn't set out to achieve this result. I'm trying to write books that in their form are appropriate to the late-twentieth-century reality they describe. If I've used small stretches of minor road in both *A Journey Through Ruins* and *The Village That Died for England*, this is because by working with a particular territory I am able to get beyond preconception, beyond the impasses of what I already know, and also what I take to be the limitations of those big sweep historians who think they've got this whole twentieth century of ours pretty well cut and dried already. It is a way of not painting by numbers, and of demonstrating, I hope, that some of the most telling cultural responses to modernity within England have been of a kind that many conventional historians would dismiss as eccentric.

It never occurred to me, although I suppose I could have guessed, that booksellers and publishers would be inclined to think of this as just another name for "local history." But there has been quite a lot of that. You can be a serious and proper historian of the welfare state or of the postwar city without ever feeling the need to read a book like *A Journey Through Ruins*, which is surely only about a small patch of East London. In their method, these books also fall short of the expectations of cultural studies, so it is true to say that they fall between stools, and that is a pity because I think they have a coherence—even if I'm not trying to suggest that everybody should write this way. But in the end I can't think of a category they belong in either, perhaps because I was trying to find a kind of analytical prose, one that moves in and out of history, and that seeks to define the cultural fixes of twentieth-century English life. So the truth is that these books exist in the publishing equivalent of a "non-place"—although I'm glad to think that many of the people who do read them don't find that to be such a problem.

JK: Did you find the fact that *A Journey Through Ruins* was centered on London to be a problem?

PW: That book came out at a time when the whole of Britain seemed to loathe London. Thatcherism was seen as a kind of war on the North because of the destruction of heavy industry and the general exacerbation of the north-south divide. Certainly, the book was anything but overwhelmed by interest in places like Newcastle and Edinburgh. So I think one has to conclude that the book was pretty heavily defeated by reality—certainly, nothing for Bill Bryson to worry about.

JK: When we talked earlier about people getting confused by the books, I was imagining that you take a certain, almost malicious pleasure in confusing them.

PW: I think there is a case for books that work like little mental mines, detonating preconceptions as you go. And in one sense I did want to engender a sense of confusion with *A Journey Through Ruins*. I wanted to portray how we think about the inner city in just that sort of way: the concrete reality of people's lives being all wrapped up in myths, fantasies, and fictions of the onlooking kind. There isn't a single totalizing overview that can clarify all that without in some sense also denying it.

JK: But the totalizing city story doesn't exist anyway, does it?

PW: Well, I've never come across one that works—unless one sees the city as a novel. But the unique thing about the city, which I hope is there at least in the method if not in the explicit text, has to do with the way urban perception operates at its best. If you think about the rural areas of England as they have been defined by prevailing cultural expression, these are places that exist in a single perspective—deeply settled with a common outlook. Well, you can't get far into the inner city on that basis, which is why I called that chapter "Around the World in Three Hundred Yards." Everywhere you go, somebody lives in a different world; every shop is on a different continent. People raised in the rural view of England have long been coming to East London and seeing nothing in this but disorder and degeneration, hybridity as miscegenation. But there is actually this great sophistication in ordinary urban perception. It occurred to me when I was writing *A Journey Through Ruins*, I think I got the idea from Richard Mabey, that this stuff that was happening on the mixed urban street was rather like a recovery of the idea of "common rights." If you were a commoner of old, you had the use of that land, and you used it to gather firewood or graze your animals in the full knowledge that other people would be using that same piece of land in a completely different way, because they too had rights of common. So for me Dalston Lane came to hint at an alternative to homogenizing collectivism, a late-twentieth-century reprise of common rights in which we make our own use of the public domain of the street, but always in the knowledge that others are at the same time using and seeing it differently.

JK: And inevitably that overlapping usage is also about conflict.

PW: Of course there's room for conflict there and that's how conflict breaks out, and that's where racism comes into play with its monocultural insistences. But the best of possibilities lie here too, and we make too little of the fact that people aren't always yelling and snarling at one another. This positive aspect of the city as a place of loosely structured difference, if I can put it that way, still finds too little recognition.

JK: In writing about this strangely familiar piece of London, you marshal much evidence of the past to comment critically on the present, but do you feel able to comment about the future prospects of these utterly ordinary urban environments, given the huge potential changes in the political and economic climate that we are experiencing?

PW: I do think historically; indeed, I reckon that one of the main pleasures of writing lies in pulling forgotten threads of the past through into present visibility. But I am also aware of the saddening fact that the endeavors of previous generations do often seem to disappear into nothing, or leave just an empty street full of cars, which seems to be where we are ending the century. In the 1980s, with all those changes going on, history came to seem weirdly disconnected. The old postwar machinery of "progress" had ground to a halt, and there was a morbid sense of ruin everywhere. I was eager to bring a fuller sense of history into view, to show the causes and effects that were often obscured by this new gothic sensibility, and perhaps to clarify options too. But I wasn't about to prescribe a future in the manner of the old thinkers of the Left who behaved as if history was some sort of magic carpet ride.

I once received a note from the dramatist David Hare. He told me that I seemed to have an appetite for mixing up the jump leads, that having read *A Journey Through Ruins*, he didn't know what to think and, if I remember correctly, that his head hurt. My response was to say that when it comes to Left and Right, the jump leads are confused, but that it was history, rather than just me, that had muddled them up. The confusion is the reality that we're in, and we had better come to terms with it.

I'm not good at divination, but a future of sorts is now engulfing Dalston Lane, and I'm not so sure that I'm entirely innocent. My book came out in 1991, and was soon being cited in the background of Hackney Council's successful application for City Challenge funding—as further evidence of deprivation, I'm afraid. And now Dalston City Challenge is remaking the place. The old Town Guide Cabinet—a timewarped guide to the borough next to which I put Sir Alfred Sherman and Lord Joseph—has been removed and replaced by tasteful York stone. And I gather that the vast old music hall, a building that houses the New Four Aces Club and also the Club Labyrinth, and which David Widgery once described as a dub cathedral, is due to be demolished and replaced by yet another new shopping mall.

Notes

This conversation between Patrick Wright and Joe Kerr took place at the Whitechapel Art Gallery in March 1997.

1   Patrick Wright, *A Journey Through Ruins: The Last Days of London* (London: Radius, 1991); enlarged edition published as *A Journey Through Ruins: A Keyhole Portrait of Post-War British Life and Culture* (London: Flamingo, 1993).

2   Paul Harrison, *Inside the Inner City: Life under the Cutting Edge* (London: Penguin, 1983).

3   Patrick Wright, *The Village That Died for England: The Strange Story of Tyneham* (London: Vintage, 1996).

Patrick Wright

30

Around the World in Three Hundred Yards

What is to be done about Dalston Junction? Successive governments have pondered this question. Their advisers take one look and quickly propose a road-widening scheme or, better still, a really ambitious new motorway that will obliterate the whole area. Ministers pretend to be surprised when carping residents come out against these generously offered "improvements," and the blight settles a little deeper. In the most recent case it was Peter Bottomley, then Conservative Minister for Roads, who provided local campaigners with their best quotation. When questioned in the House of Commons on 10 February 1989 about the environmental damage that would be caused if the roads suggested in Ove Arup & Partners' East London Assessment Study were built, he replied for the government by saying: "We want to improve the environment. If we look at the main spine road through the assessment study, it goes through the most run-down part of the area."

Dalston Junction was under that spine, and a carefully placed rib also reached out to obliterate the short stretch of road that runs through the heart of this book. Dalston Lane extends east from Dalston Junction, and we need only follow it a few hundred yards up to the traffic lights at the next busy junction—a tangle of dishonoured roads still sometimes called Lebon's Corner in memory of a trader who has long since disappeared. This miraculously surviving fragment of old England consists of a constant and often choked stream of traffic edged by stretches of pavement that would not be out of place in the Lake District. The stones jut up like small cliffs, and then crash down as soon as the intrepid inner-city fell-walker mounts them, sometimes issuing a great gush of filthy water as they land.

The south side of Dalston Lane starts with an elegant stretch of ornamented Victorian brickwork, which is all that remains of the recently demolished Dalston Junction railway station. It then passes a tawdry amusement arcade, a few shops, and the New Four Aces Club (the site of occasional shootings and subject of intense Press speculation about the fabled West Indian Yardies). After a derelict site and an ailing public library, the street consists of two continuous blocks of run-down Victorian shops, some in use, others boarded up and abandoned. The first block is owned by Hackney Council, bought up in preparation for the demolition that appears to have been imminent for at least half a century; the second belonged to the now-abolished Greater London Council.

The north side of this unusually dishevelled street is slightly more varied. There are some shops with offices above them and an old pub, once known as the Railway Tavern but now a dingy betting shop with a satellite dish at the back. There is the notorious Dalston police station, a large red-brick building with an ominously windowless and fortress-like annex that has stood boarded up and empty since early in 1990 when the police withdrew to their new "supernick" up in Stoke Newington, where Chief Superintendent Twist offers visitors guided tours of his new "cell-suites," stressing the ameliorating effects of a modern architecture that brings light into recesses where horrible acts of brutality might once have taken place. Then comes a terrace of stuccoed Victorian houses, set back a few yards and shielded from the road by a little strip of corralled dirt where heroic shrubs struggle up through the litter and four plane trees rise up to lend an unexpected touch of nobility to the area. Beyond this residential terrace, there's a nondescript factory, a large and surprising Georgian house used as workshop space by the Free Form Arts Trust, and, finally, a second Victorian ruin to match the shattered railway station with which this atmospheric stretch of English street opens. The old vicarage of St. Bartholomew's may be derelict, but it can still be said to command the north side of Lebon's Corner. It stands like a hollow-eyed skull just across the road from the Unity Club where local Labour MP, Brian Sedgemore, goes to try his luck as a stand-up comic.[1] Saplings sprout from the vicarage's brickwork, and so too do the shattered marbled columns and ornately sculpted capitals left over from the church that was once adjoined to it. New settlers in the area often mistake the ruin for a bomb-site left over from the forties, but it is actually the much more recent work of the Church Commissioners who, finding themselves lumbered with too many churches in this apparently God-forsaken place, called in the demolition men and never bothered to tidy up after them. The vicarage was listed, but due to the "ecclesiastical exemption" that removes churches from the protection of the law, nothing could be done to protect the church from its fate. So this Gothic hulk stands there: a huge pigeon roost, a poster stand, a terrible warning of the destiny that awaits listed buildings in Hackney.

I've come to know this stretch of Dalston Lane well in recent years. I walk along it most days of the week and I'm familiar with its vicious side: I've seen the squalor and the many signs of grinding poverty; and like many other people round here, I've studied the psychotic antics of the man who spends a lot of his time on the traffic island at Lebon's Corner, reading the cracks in the asphalt and cleaning them out with a stick. I've walked into the aftermath of a mugging that could have been scripted by Sir Alfred Sherman: an elderly and blind white man had come out of the sub-post office at Lebon's Corner, having just collected his pension. Seeing his opportunity, a black youth had leapt off a passing bus, hit the man at full tilt, leaving him in a battered and terrified heap on the pavement, and made off with his pension. By the time I arrived on the scene the victim was lying in the stationary bus, surrounded by a great efflorescence of helpless concern:

a shopkeeper had produced a cup of tea, the ambulance was coming, a white stick had been retrieved from the middle of the road, and a collection was under way to ensure that the victim was compensated for at least some of his losses. A few weeks earlier, I had caught the end of another desperate episode. This one was featured in the *Hackney Gazette* under the heading "Devil dog mauls policewoman"; it concerned a ravenous pit bull terrier ("Hackney has become London's centre for pit bulls"), which emerged snarling from under a boarded-up shop front, chased a twenty-year-old policewoman into a nearby bakery, and "ripped her heel off."[2] As a Cypriot witness told me in mitigation, the already exterminated beast had given the terrified WPC fair warning but, not being of local provenance, she hadn't been able to read the signs.

Blight has its hideous aspect but, as I try to convince unbelieving visitors, it can also resemble a condition of grace. Dalston Lane is a jumble of residential, commercial, and industrial activities, but zoning is not the only kind of development on which this street, if not its surrounding area, has missed out. In the fifties it escaped the kind of standardization Ian Nairn described as subtopia ("Subtopia is the annihilation of the site, the steam-rollering of all individuality of place to one uniform and mediocre pattern").[3] While it has certainly suffered daily agonies through the eighties, it was at least spared the kind of theming that has turned genuinely historical streets in more prosperous parts of the country into simulacra, gutting them in the name of taste. No "lifestyle designer" has ever come to divide the "targeted" denizens of Dalston Lane from the non-targeted, or to kill off the old street, with its confusion of nationalities, classes, and styles, and redefine it in marketing terms.[4] We may be sure that Sir Rodney Fitch, design mogul of the eighties, has never worked here.

On Dalston Lane time itself seems to lie around in broken fragments: you can drop in on previous decades with no more effort than it takes to open a shop door. Pizzey's High Class Florist is still trading out of the fifties, and the Star Bakery (a little further down the road) offers immediate access to the decade before that. Until a year or so ago there was even a time-warped estate agency, advertising houses at twenty-year-old prices. People would pause there and marvel at the opportunities they had missed.

This has a human aspect, to be sure. The people of Dalston Lane have their own ways of being in the world. They walk about in a distinctly unsuburban manner, and without necessarily following what planners would recognize as a proper "line of pedestrian desire." They saunter and dawdle and fail to wait for the green light before crossing the road. They hang about without apparent purpose. They do things remarkably slowly, if at all. They indulge in habits that are being extirpated from the national culture. Anthropologists will soon be coming here to study the vanishing culture and society of the cigarette. It's not just that people still smoke on Dalston Lane. They stand around in huddles and offer each other cigarettes with a reckless generosity that is no longer to be found in more stable society. Some of this behaviour comes to Dalston Lane direct from the West Indies or the hills of Kurdistan, but there are more indigenous people round here who still find the health warning provided by HM Government less convincing than the caution that emerged from the trenches of the Great War, and stressed the dangers of the third light.

A broad-minded art historian could wander down this street and find residual traces of the "unsophisticated arts" that Barbara Jones cherished against the industrial and technocratic bias of the Festival of Britain in 1951.[5] As she wrote, "popular arts have certain constant characteristics. They are complex, unsubtle, often impermanent; they lean to disquiet, the baroque and sometimes terror." Dalston Lane has its unnecessary and slightly excessive touches of ornamentation—exemplified, perhaps, by the fake and, like everything else round here, unexpectedly permanent ornamental urns that stand over some of the shop fronts on the south side of Lebon's Corner; most of them are full of weeds, but their teasing tribute to the superior versions that embellish grand Georgian buildings elsewhere is unmistakable. The best example, however, is provided by the undertaking firm of E. M. Kendall ("We are renowned throughout London for our complete inexpensive funeral service . . .") that, despite half-hearted attempts at modernization, fits Jones's description perfectly. The ancient glass sign over the door still promises "Funeral Feathermen and Carriage Masters," and the ornate promise of "Courtesy" and "Reverence" creeps round the side in gilded copperplate letters. At night, the two main windows are deep-black squares with the words "Funerals" and "Cremations" lit up in dull purple and suspended, like souls in the void, at the centre of each. The pall-bearers may look like ghoulish extras left over from the comparatively recent days of Hammer horror films, but they too are the unrefurbished inheritors of the Victorian tradition that Jones celebrated as "a nice rich debased baroque." Dalston Lane still bears out Barbara Jones's assertion that "the colours of death" in England are "black and grey and purple."

The whole area is alive with commercial and industrial activity. Just north of Dalston Lane there are Victorian factories, which resound with the hissing, snipping, and clacking of the textile trade, and the small workshops, some of them in a converted mews, of antique restorers, violin makers, and furniture makers. Dalston Lane itself has its shops and small businesses as well as its boarded-up voids: indigenous north-east London enterprise mixed up with a whole array of brave multicultural endeavour. Most of these traders are unsung heroes who fight on against unbelievable odds: their situation is epitomized by the lady in the Chinese takeaway who treats her customers with the care appropriate to an endangered species, asking repeatedly if they've been away on holiday.

Further down the road from Kendall's the undertaker is the shop of Nichols of London, declared by his own pocket label to be "London's finest bespoke tailor." The real name is Nicholas Economou, a Cypriot who knows better than to sell himself short. He makes high-quality clothes for one of the larger outfitters in the City, but he also maintains his own clients on Dalston Lane. The window shows Mr. Economou with one of his more famous customers, Frank Bruno, the boxer who was a regular here until the sponsorship deals took over. But there are other stylish figures who have a regard for Mr. Economou's needle. Use him for a bit, and the special offers will start coming through at knock-down prices: a richly patterned jacket made of a sumptuous blend of mink, chinchilla, cashmere, and lambswool; trousers in Prince of Wales check or the best white Irish linen; a sparkling suit made of grey silk with a prominent diamond pattern. One of Mr. Economou's more ostentatious customers, a gentleman from Canning Town to be precise, had ordered a load of clothes in preparation for a prolonged sojourn in Spain, but he was arrested on charges of armed robbery a few days before departure and "he'll be an old man" before he can come back to collect them.

A few doors up at No. 58, there's a restaurant called Pamela's. Not long ago, this was just another derelict poster site, but remarkable things started to happen early one recent winter. New hoardings went up, and an unmistakable designer logo appeared shortly afterwards: it showed a waiter in tails holding up a tray with a saxophone suspended above it. Serious money was being spent: a gallery went in, along with a lot of very stylish ironwork and an elegant parquet floor. By Christmas, a rather Utopian-looking establishment called Pamela's had opened for business. Squeezed in between Jon's scooters and a boarded-up shop front, it tempted the apprehensive denizens of Dalston Lane with new pleasures: "a taste of the Caribbean, a hint of French cuisine" and, may Sir Alfred Sherman take note, the first "business lunches" to be offered on Dalston Lane. Pamela Hurley is a fastidious young Anglo-Barbadian who trained as a chef in New York, and the success of her establishment will depend partly on her ability to create a new cultural settlement on Dalston Lane. On one side, as she explains, she has to convince Afro-Caribbean customers that her food is actually worth coming out for, and not just more of what mother does so well at home. On the other side, she is going to have to persuade some of the more affluent whites in the neighbourhood to get over some curious reservations of their own. These people live in the area in quite large numbers, but while they are not necessarily averse to signing away a small fortune at a restaurant table in Islington or Soho, they are less inclined to be seen indulging in conspicuous consumption right on their own doorsteps. Pamela is in a risky business, especially during a gathering recession, but the vision is grand. Come the spring, she wants to throw open her folding doors, and see her customers all mixed up together on the pavement: Montmartre will meet Montserrat on dingy Dalston Lane; the plane trees will burgeon and the traffic will thunder by regardless.

One trader on Dalston Lane has recently found a novel way of achieving corporate growth. If he was in a "managed workspace," of the sort that sprung up in refurbished factories throughout London during the eighties, he would be able to expand by pushing out the partitions a little, but he would also have to pay more rent for the privilege. On Dalston Lane those extra square feet can be had for free. The gentleman in question simply broke through the walls with a pickaxe and moved into the boarded-up shops on either side: his thriving emporium is now one-third legitimate, two-thirds squat. But while occasional success stories emerge from the strivings of Dalston Lane's entrepreneurs, the idea that a wider social redemption might be achieved through enterprise has never really made its way down this street. Most of the traders on Dalston Lane are too busy making ends meet to consider raising up the whole area as well, and they have sharp things to say about the Thatcher government, which banged on about supporting private enterprise and then turned round and hit them all with punishing interest rates and, with poll tax, the uniform business rate. A more dynamic economy would doubtless pull this dishevelled street together in no time, but it would also wipe out most of its traders at a stroke.

Other hints of improvement can be traced along this undemolished stretch of Dalston Lane. The public library is named after Trinidad's revolutionary historian C. L. R. James, and its windows are plastered with yellowing obituaries to C. L. R. and a whole host of signs blazing with promised emancipation over three continents. The rhetoric is ambitious but the activity on the ground is sadly restricted: indeed, the library is closed most of the time due, as another notice explains, to funding and staff shortages.

The public sector flounders, but many of the derelict shops have been taken over and turned into the offices of voluntary organizations, which try to do rather better. The same pattern of refurbishment recurs from one organization to the next: the windows are boarded up from the inside so one can't see in from the street, and then covered with messages announcing events or asserting this cause or that. Each one is, after its own manner, a wayside pulpit lost among the advertising hoardings. There is a whole archaeology of voluntary endeavour on Dalston Lane. To begin with, the British Red Cross Society has its Hackney Centre up at Lebon's Corner—a large Victorian house with a flag-pole over the porch and a prominent red cross superimposed on a white circle painted on the side wall. This institution dates back to 1917, but its spirit belongs to the forties. Indeed, it goes back to the "improvised staffing" Richard Titmuss saw emerge in the early weeks of the blitz before the official relief effort was organized: the British Red Cross Society was there with its volunteer ambulances, first aid, and "light relief," and other more anonymous figures also stepped out of the crowd—people like "Mrs. B.," the Islington beetroot seller who, as the raids started, "left the first aid post where she was a part-time volunteer, walked into Ritchie Street rest centre and took charge."[6]

That red cross on the corner of Dalston Lane speaks of the blitz, but it is also a more general memorial to the spirit of "Voluntary Action," as Lord Beveridge conceived it during the founding years of the Welfare State: Voluntary Action as a trail-blazer for the emerging State ("It is needed to pioneer ahead of the State and make experiments") but also—and Beveridge didn't need a latter-day think-tanker to tell him this—as the self-willed and self-managed activity that defines the proper limits of the State and serves as the "distinguishing mark" of a free society.[7] I sometimes look up at that recently repainted red cross and think of the remarkable, if now sadly disappointed, vision with which Beveridge signed off after the war against Hitler: "So at last human society may become a friendly society—an Affiliated Order of branches, some large and many small, each with its own life in freedom, each linked to all the rest by common purpose and by bonds to serve that purpose. So the night's insane dream of power over other men without limit and without mercy shall fade."[8] That was long before any alley cat dreamt up the idea of Britain's *perestroika*.

Like so much else, the dwindling spirit of "Voluntary Action" has to struggle for life on Dalston Lane (following the example of the C. L. R. James library, the British Red Cross Society's charity shop is frequently closed due to a shortage of volunteers), and there is little sign of relief from Douglas Hurd's more recently enlisted "active citizen"—that implausible hero of the think-tanks who, far from blazing trails for the expanding State as Beveridge imagined, sets out, wearing an inner-city Barbour jacket and a grin as wide as Richard Branson's, to compensate for a few of the more visible failings of a contracting and mismanaged one.

What comes after Voluntary Action on Dalston Lane is really still Ken Livingstone's GLC, and the efflorescence of community organizations that thrived under its wing—even when not directly supported by it. Hackney Cooperative Developments is based here, proudly advertising the alternative shopping centre it has made of a battered Victorian row of shops in nearby Bradbury Street ("A stone's throw from the High Street but miles ahead in style"). Then, in sharp contrast to the unachieved and often corrupted universality of conventional State provision, come the differentiated organizations of the rainbow coalition: the Asian Centre; Africa House with its special Advice and Community Centre and, Sir Alfred please take note, a Supplementary School; Hackney Women's Centre; Hackney Heatsavers; Hackney Pensioners. . . .

A passing think-tanker would be inclined to dismiss this collection of organizations as so many "QUALGOs" ('Quasi-Autonomous Local Government Organizations'), political fronts accountable to no one and serving only to gouge the salaries of their well-connected and far-from-voluntary workers out of left-wing local councils.[9] There were certainly problems with the way the GLC and other Labour councils funded voluntary organizations in the early eighties. Money went into agencies that simply couldn't cope with it, and staff numbers were built up in a way that could hardly have been better designed if it was intended to kill off the old spirit of "Voluntary Action." Voluntary committee members found themselves faced with an ever-increasing complexity of work and, in some cases, with a highly articulate and educated staff who were full of talk about their own collective rights as employed workers. Some organizations disappeared into themselves spending years fighting out the problems of the world internally, while others proved incapable of achieving in practice anything like what they promised in words.[10] When these organizations failed there was just another body of articulate professionals widening the gap between the State and the citizenry it was meant to serve; but when they worked, groups that had been stuck at the margins without effective representation within the Welfare State were suddenly enfranchised and a whole agenda of new concerns, whether cultural, political, or ecological, was brought into focus. The rowdy exuberance that followed was quite something.

Some of this energy continues to produce results in Dalston. The Women's Design Service has recently issued a well-received critical handbook on the design of public lavatories for women. The authors insist that "women do not conform to standard sizes or requirements," comment on the "implications of the loss of the GLC for the state of London's public toilets," and disclose that "the building of women's public toilets was linked to the growth of feminism in the late nineteenth century, since it was largely the increased visibility of women working in the capital that persuaded the authorities to make provision for them." This admirable manual found quite a lot to praise in the underground lavatories left over from the Victorian era (although, as it points out, working conditions for the attendants could certainly have been better). It also provided a key date for future historians of the monetarist experiment: it was on 5 May 1982 that the first coin-operated automatic public convenience to be fitted in Britain was installed by Westminster Council in Leicester Square.[11]

Nor should we overlook the Free Form Arts Trust, one of the organizations that founded the "Community Arts" movement in the sixties and has been based on Dalston Lane since 1973, when it gained a short-life lease on a building earmarked for demolition. The Free Form Arts Trust helped to pioneer the ideas taken up later by the big community-architecture practices. They offer design and "technical aid" services to schools, community groups, and developers, always seeking to work with people in a "participative" manner. The founder, Martin Goodrich, has watched the political framework shift around his practice: in the late sixties his ideas and activities were considered radical to the left, but in the eighties they seemed to find favour with the radical right. The Free Form Arts Trust has survived schisms, break-away movements, and the criticisms of those who want to be "storming the citadels" rather than decorating the hoardings around capitalist building sites or joining "the kindly folk who do good without ever causing trouble."[12] Martin Goodrich is full of enterprising ideas for 'projects' and, in his time, he has had plenty for the miraculously enduring street he calls "Dusty Dalston Lane." There was a brave attempt to form a Dalston Traders Group: Goodrich remembers putting up Christmas lights at Dalston Junction while people passing below cursed and moaned at the folly of it all. There was a project that aimed to turn the derelict vicarage of St. Bartholomew's into a workspace for community organizations, and another that hoped to landscape and put a few seats on the derelict site behind the bus stop up by Dalston Junction. But though Dalston Lane has proved intransigent, Free Form has been more successful up in North Shields at the mouth of the Tyne, a near-derelict fishing port, where a vestigial regatta has been transformed into an amazingly successful Fish Quay Festival, now attended by over a million people each year, which is being used to "catalyse change and community development." That's not "storming the citadels" either, but it's one of Dalston Lane's better stories nevertheless.

Patrick Wright

Notes

1   See *Hackney Gazette*, 23 March 1990.

2   *Hackney Gazette*, 12 January 1990.

3   Ian Nairn, *Outrage*, a special number of the *Architectural Review*, Vol. 117, no. 702, June 1955.

4   On theming see John Thackara's "Unthemely behaviour," *The Guardian*, 8 January 1987. As Thackara concludes: "'Lifestyle design' disenfranchises the 'non-targeted', and kills off the old-style street with its volatile mixture of nationalities and classes. The marketeers claim that theming replaces outmoded class barriers; but control of space planning and the imagery therein remains in the hands of those, such as brewers, who have a close resemblance to old-style bosses." This is an important point, well made, and I'm glad to say that the majority of the people on Dalston Lane have no reason to understand a word of it.

5   Barbara Jones, *The Unsophisticated Arts*, Architectural Press, 1951.

6   Richard M. Titmuss, *Problems of Social Policy*, HMSO, 1950, p. 263.

7   Lord Beveridge, *Voluntary Action: A Report on Methods of Social Advance*, Allen & Unwin, 1948, p. 301. As Beveridge writes, "In a Totalitarian society all action outside the citizen's home, and it may be much that goes on there is directed or controlled by the State. By contrast, vigour and abundance of Voluntary Action outside one's home, individually and in association with other citizens, for bettering one's own life and that of one's fellows, are the distinguishing marks of a free society" (p. 10).

8   Ibid., p. 324.

9   As an influential report claimed, the "Political sympathies of those who staff QUALGOs are almost invariably left-wing. The middle-class Tory lady, once so dedicated a worker for charity, has been elbowed out by ridicule, snubbing and such unacceptable demands upon her time as obligatory attendance at training class." See Teresa Gorman *et al.*, *Qualgos Just Grow: Political Bodies in Voluntary Clothing*, Centre for Policy Studies, 1985, p. 9.

10   See, for example, Ali Mantle, *Popular Planning Not in Practice: Confessions of a Community Worker*, Greenwich Employment Resource Unit, 1985.

11   Sue Cavanagh and Vron Ware, *At Women's Convenience: A Handbook on the Design of Women's Public Toilets*, Women's Design Service, 1990.

12   Owen Kelly, *Community Art and the State: Storming the Citadels*, Comedia, 1984, p. 1.

Sources of Illustrations

Bernard Tschumi Architects: 22.1, 22.2

Bernard Tschumi Architects/PeterMauss/ESTO: 22.3, 22.4

Iain Borden: 1.1, 1.2, 1.3, 1.4, 7.1, 7.2, 7.5, 10.5, 16.1, 16.2, 16.3, 24.2

Building News 56 (10 May 1889): 17.1

Calcutta (London: Longmans, Green, 1945): 8.3

Calcutta Past and Present (Calcutta: Thacker, 1905): 8.1, 8.2

Iain Chambers: 24.1

Sarah Chaplin: 3.4

Branson Coates: 18.6, 18.7, 18.9, 18.10

Nigel Coates: 18.1, 18.3, 18.4, 18.8

Cornford & Cross: 19.1, 19.2, 19.3, 19.4, 19.5, 19.6, 19.7, 19.8, 19.9

Corporate Visual Imaging Ltd.: 15.2

Barry Curtis: 3.2, 3.3, 3.5, 3.6

Sue Evans: 13.1, 13.2, 13.3, 13.5

Fat: 20.1, 20.2, 20.3, 20.4, 20.5, 20.6, 20.7, 20.8, 20.9, 20.10, 20.11, 20.12, 20.13

Gianelli Viscardi Collection: 3.1

Tom Gretton: 12.1, 12.2, 12.3, 12.4

Eddie Valentine Hames: 18.5

N. P. Harou-Romain, *Projet de pénitencier* (1840): 7.3

Dolores Hayden: 21.1, 21.2, 21.3, 21.4, 21.5

Andrew Holmes: 29.1, 29.2, 29.3, 29.4

Hongkong Bank Archives: 9.1, 9.2

Andy Horsley/*Sidewalk Surfer:* 10.1, 10.3, 10.4

Imperial War Museum, London: 4.4, 4.5

International Center of Photography, New York: 7.7

Thomas Jackson: 7.4, 7.6

Joe Kerr: 2.1, 2.2, 2.3, 2.4, 2.7, 4.2, 4.6, 4.7, 4.8, 4.9

Patrick Keiller/BFI Films: 27.1, 27.2, 27.3, 27.4, 27.5

Sasha Lubetkin: 4.1

Doreen Massey: 28.1, 28.2, 28.3, 28.4, 28.5, 28.6, 28.7, 28.8

William Menking: 5.1, 5.2, 5.3, 5.4

Erie Oesterland: 18.11

Mark Prizeman: 18.2

Queen 94 (23 December 1893): 17.2

Royal Festival Hall: The Official Record (London: Max Parrish in association with the London
    City Council, 1951): 11.1

Solo Syndication: 4.3

South Bank Centre: 11.2, 11.3, 11.4, 11.5, 11.6

Robert A. M. Stern: 2.6

Strangely Familiar /Studio Myerscough: 1.5

Terry Farrell & Company Ltd.: 15.1

Helen Thomas: 8.4

Richard Wentworth: 23.1, 23.2, 23.3, 23.4, 23.5, 23.6, 23.7, 23.8, 23.9, 23.10, 23.11,
    23.12, 23.13, 23.14, 23.15

Shirley Wong: 9.3, 9.4

Wig Worland/*Sidewalk Surfer:* 10.2

Clare Zine/No M11 Campaign, *The End of the Beginning* (Leeds: Clare Zine, n.d.): 13.4

Unidentified: 2.5

Index

Index

Index